Psycho in the Shower

Psycho in the Shower

The History of Cinema's Most Famous Scene

PHILIP J. SKERRY

NEW YORK • LONDON

2009

The Continuum International Publishing Group Inc.
80 Maiden Lane, New York, NY 10038

The Continuum International Publishing Group Ltd.
The Tower Building, 11 York Road, London SE1 7NX

www.continuumbooks.com

Printed in the United States of America.

Library of Congress Cataloging-in-Publication Data

Skerry, Philip J.

Psycho in the shower : the history of cinema's most famous scene / Philip J. Skerry.
p. cm.
Includes bibliographical references and index.
ISBN-13: 978-0-8264-2769-4 (pbk. : alk. paper)
ISBN-10: 0-8264-2769-3 (pbk. : alk. paper) 1. Psycho (Motion picture : 1960) I. Title.
PN1997.P79S54 200
791.43'72—dc22

2008046008

For my parents, Angelina and Philip Skerry

Contents

	Foreword by Dan Auiler	ix
	Preface	xi
	Acknowledgments	xiii
	Introduction	xv
Chapter 1	My Research Trip	1
Chapter 2	Janet Leigh	16
Chapter 3	The Trip Continued Two Intersecting Paths to *Psycho*	30
Chapter 4	Joseph Stefano	51
Chapter 5	Constructing Suspense Mise-en-scene	73
Chapter 6	Hilton Green	123
Chapter 7	Montage Creating Terror	138
Chapter 8	Danny Greene	179
Chapter 9	The Evolution of the Shower Scene	188
Chapter 10	Terry Williams	210
Chapter 11	The Culmination of Suspense and Terror The Shower Scene	219
Chapter 12	Homage	261
Chapter 13	The First Time	270
	Works Cited	302
	Index	307

Foreword

This is a remarkable book on a remarkably brief scene in a movie that continues to have a remarkably enormous cultural impact. The shower scene in *Psycho* is probably the most famous scene in film history, so it seems long overdue that a book-length examination of the moment. Understanding *Psycho* requires the right mixture of scholarship, cultural aptitude and personal reaction.

Psycho occupies a unique place in our cultural history and in the work of Alfred Hitchcock. As important as *Psycho* is to understanding Hitchcock's art, it is safe to say that this little black and white film, practically orphaned by Paramount Studios, and filmed with the speed and efficiency of the director's television crew housed at Universal Studios, stands easily alone for the spectator who has no interest in Hitchcock's labyrinthine anxieties that are detailed in rich list of films. It is hard now to divorce any film from the Hitchcock body of work. Skerry reminds us just how stunning it was to be in the audience—when no one sitting in the theater expected, anticipated or even would dread (as we do now) what would happen to Marion Crane in the shower of room #1.

This event—an earthquake on the cultural scene, has an importance which is difficult to match in cinema history. Is there any other moment in film that has the same mnemonic charge? As Skerry's book demonstrates, witnesses of the moment remember very clearly when, where and how they felt as Marion Crane showered at Bates Motel.

Hitchcock is an artist like Shakespeare in that he is a world into which we are encouraged to wander and find something new every day. Professor Skerry has provided more map than narrative, and for true film lovers, the open road with a well-planned map is preferable to the tour guide.

And this shape for the text is an apt one for *Psycho*. *Psycho* remains one of the central film events of the 20th century and one of the principle touchstones for our culture. Explore. Check in. Relax—we all go a little mad sometimes.

Dan Auiler
Long Beach, CA 2009

Preface

I've written this book so that readers can "sample" its contents if they choose, rather than read the text straight through. In keeping with the multiplicity of voices that make up the text, I've organized the chapters around these voices. My voice dominates the first and third chapters, so I suggest they be read as a unit. The temporal structure of these chapters goes from the present-tense narrative of my research trip in chapter 1 to the achronological, "cubist" structure of chapter 3, which ranges in time from 1920 through 2002, with separate time lines for Hitchcock's career as a director and for my own as a film viewer and film teacher and scholar.

The interview chapters—2, 4, 6, 8, 10—can be read either separately or as a group. I believe there is "something for everyone" in these interviews. I talked to Janet Leigh (probably the last significant interview before her death), an actress whose career spanned the transition from the old Hollywood to the new. Her image from the shower scene, mouth agape in agony, has become the iconic image in all of cinema. I interviewed Joseph Stefano, the scriptwriter of *Psycho*, and Hilton Green, the assistant director of *Psycho*, as well as the producer of *Psycho II*, *III*, and *IV*. I also went "below-the-line" to talk to Terry Williams and Danny Greene. Their contributions to the film were significant, but their names do not appear in the credits. They represent a huge cadre of creative people who never received screen credit for their work. Today, if you drive a catering truck, you get credit in the film! Their inclusion in the book, I hope, goes a small way in recognizing those creative folks who didn't have the political clout to get recognized. This recognition is extremely important as these *Psycho* "pioneers" age and die off. In fact, two key *Psycho* participants—Janet Leigh and Joe Stefano—died while I was working on the original manuscript and the revised version.

The interviews reflect the voices of the creators of *Psycho*. But the audience creates a film as much as the filmmakers. This idea of meaning created by the audience is a keystone of postmodernism. Chapter 13 features the voices of audience members who saw *Psycho* for the first time. I asked for memories from a wide variety of viewers, from "ordinary" film fans to extraordinarily creative people, in order to show the power and longevity of *Psycho*.

For those interested in the critical and scholarly approach to the shower scene, I suggest reading chapters 5, 7, 9, and 11. This last, my keystone chapter, is a close reading of the shower scene. For these four chapters, I am indebted to all those scholars and critics who came before me. I've tried to give credit for critical opinions that influenced mine, but it is sometimes impossible to tell if critical insight is "original" or if the seed was planted in an earlier reading. In order to facilitate reading the text, I've used the Modern Language Association (MLA) documentation style and have eschewed explanatory notes, preferring instead to incorporate relevant information in the text. In analyzing the shower scene, I turned to the film itself, to the photographic images and their structures—in effect, to Hitchcock's "pure cinema." The approach of the book grew out of a recursive interpretation of the films leading up to the shower scene. In short, I started with the shower scene and worked my way backward, viewing the films that preceded *Psycho* as evolutionary steps along the way to the shower scene, which heralds a new species of film, as it were. I also trace the evolution of my own creation, a book about Hitchcock's shower scene.

If I could create the ideal scenario for reading chapters 5, 7, 9, and 11, I would set my reader down in front of a monitor, a DVD player, and a stack of the films that I discuss, with *Psycho* on the top. Watch and read. Read and watch.

Acknowledgments

As I was writing this book, I sometimes felt that I was a producer rather than an author. Film is a collaborative medium, and so—as it turns out—was this book. The credits of a film are usually divided into above-the-line personnel—those whose roles are primary and whose names appear at the beginning of a film—and below-the-line, those whose roles are supportive or technical and whose names appear at the end of the film.

My above-the-line collaborators play primary roles. Most important are the five people whose long interviews appear in the book, interspersed among the chapters I have written: Janet Leigh, Joseph Stefano, Hilton Green, Danny Greene, and Terry Williams. These talented people took time out of their busy lives to sit down with me and talk about their experiences working on *Psycho*. Without them, I wouldn't have a book. Other above-the-line people are the contributors of personal reminiscences of viewing the shower scene. The contributors come from all walks of life; some of them are film directors and authors; others are film scholars and critics; still others are lawyers, teachers, social workers—all of them willing to share a piece of their lives with me. A special thanks to Fred Simon, a documentary filmmaker, who gave me this idea.

Films are usually financed through loans or through studios, the logos of which appear in the credits, so I must acknowledge the generous financial backing of Lakeland Community College, specifically its Board of Trustees, who approved my sabbatical leave to research this book; the Professional Development Committee, for travel grants; and the Lakeland Foundation's Faculty Challenge Grants program, for its very generous research support.

Every producer has an assistant, a right-hand man or woman, whose help is crucial in accomplishing the task of making a film—or a book. I was lucky to have two major assistants for the projects. One was a former student, Jim Dunn, who became my research assistant and who traveled to Hollywood with me. His assistance was invaluable in conducting the interviews. The other was Dee Bassett, my "Girl Friday," who undertook the prodigious task of translating my chicken-scratch handwriting into logical, readable text, and she did this wondrous task *always* with a smile on her face and with a zeal for a challenge. Other above-the-line people on my support team include my advisor, Steven Schneider, whose encouragement and support from the very beginning of the project kept me going; my scholar-readers, Con Verevis, Tom Hemmeter, and Ken Mogg, the last of whom made suggestions for this revised edition: and my friend and colleague John Covolo, who edited the original and revised manuscript and made invaluable suggestions; and the renowned Hitchcock scholar Dan Auiler, who agreed to write the foreword for this edition.

My below-the-line collaborators are numerous. I received support from Lakeland's Word Processing Center and its coordinator, Debbie Selan, who spent many hours transcribing the final interviews and then typing the edited copies. Jim Dailey, my faculty colleague, proofread the text, and Frank Prpic, Lakeland's Photo Lab Supervisor, helped me prepare photos. Moral and intellectual support came from my friends Dan Miller and Rich Moran. Dan, my mentor since college, suggested I read Feinstein's *The Punch*, and he also read a few of my chapters in draft form and gave me encouragement in my approach. Rich sent me inspirational postcards as I was researching and writing. These nuggets of authorial wisdom helped to keep me going. I am also indebted to the many students who have taken my film classes over the years. From them, I have learned to see films, especially the Hitchcock ones, through fresh eyes and new perspectives. A special thanks to my former students Nancy McKim, who researched the shower scene links on Google, and Michael McDonald, who created a DVD of the shower scene. My special thanks to the Hitchcock scholars, critics, and fans who welcomed me to the "Hitchcock Club" and who provided ideas, suggestions, and information: Patrick McGilligan, Richard Franklin, John Baxter, David Freeman, Alain Kerzoncuf, Nandor Bokor, and Eric Carlson. Ken Mogg, editor of *The MacGuffin*, is worthy of additional thanks. He aided me in my research by posting my request for "first-time" reminiscences and by tracking down in record time the source of several Hitchcock quotations. I couldn't have completed this book without the prodigious Hitchcock holdings at the Margaret Herrick Library in Los Angeles. Barbara Hall and Faye Thompson and their staff were always eager to help me find what I needed. My research trips to Los Angeles were always made elegant by Eileen Curtis and her crew at the Luxe Summit Bel Air Hotel, where I always felt I was staying in style. Many thanks also to Howard Mandelbaum and Photofest for making my search for relevant stills a successful and enjoyable task. Finally, I owe a special debt of gratitude to David Barker, my editor at Continuum, who helped shepherd my original manuscript into its paperback version.

Introduction

Two books influenced my approach to the shower scene in *Psycho*. The irony is that neither book is about film. The more significant of the two for my topic is John Feinstein's *The Punch: One Night, Two Lives, and the Fight That Changed Basketball Forever* (2002), which is the analysis of the impact of a single moment on sports history. That moment was the punch that Kermit Washington landed on Rudy Tomjanovich during a basketball game on December 9, 1977. Feinstein analyzes the significance of that punch in the lives of the two participants in the altercation, as well as in the world of sports in general. In his introduction, Feinstein calls the punch "a watershed moment" (4).

The second book is Malcolm Gladwell's *The Tipping Point: How Little Things Can Make a Big Difference* (2000), which deals with how diseases, ideas, social changes, or artistic or business trends evolve through crossing a seemingly insignificant threshold and then spreading dramatically. Gladwell describes three characteristics of the "tipping point":

> These three characteristics—one, contagiousness; two, the fact that little causes can have big effects; and three, that change happens not gradually but at one dramatic moment—are the same three principles that define how measles moves through a grade-school classroom or the flu attacks every winter. Of the three, the third trait—the idea that epidemics can rise or fall in one dramatic moment—is the most important, because it is the principle that makes sense of the first two and that permits the greatest insight into why modern change happens the way it does. The name given to that one dramatic moment in an epidemic when everything can change all at once is the Tipping Point. (9)

When I read these books, I realized that the "cinematic moment" of the shower scene in *Psycho* was both "watershed" and "dramatic." It helped to tip cinema, culture, and society in a decidedly violent and sexual direction in the last half of the twentieth century. Was the shower scene the cinema moment that began the "epidemic"—to use Gladwell's term—of explicit violence and sexuality that we witness in today's media and popular culture? I would answer a qualified yes to that question, but I would also caution that the shower scene is an effect, albeit the most memorably and powerfully presented, of social and cultural undercurrents that were coursing through American society in the 1950s.

The choice of these two "noncinema" books was part of my larger strategy to write a nontraditional book about *Psycho*, the shower scene, and Hitchcock, one that would weave multiple perspectives and voices into the fabric of the text. One perspective—and voice—is my own. Like Hitchcock, I make a cameo appearance in this book; in fact, I make several appearances, the most significant of which takes place in 1960, when I saw *Psycho* and became traumatized (and, I later realized, galvanized) by the shower scene. I decided to add other voices to my own. The book contains five interviews with film people, all of whom worked on the original *Psycho*. These interviews address the topic of the shower scene, but they also range far and wide over many areas only tangentially connected to that famous scene. In editing these interviews, I decided to err on the side of inclusiveness, for I believe they are not only a veritable oral history of Hitchcock's cinematic practices but also a valuable record of the lives and careers of the interviewees. The reminiscences of those who provide first-hand accounts of their initial viewing of the shower scene contain another set of voices. Some of these "eye-witnesses" are from my generation and thus saw the film when it was first released; others saw the film on VHS or DVD, in rerelease, or on television. Their voices attest to the film's power to transcend age and cultural barriers. Yet another set of voices belongs to the critical and scholarly community, whose observations and opinions have helped elevate Hitchcock to the pantheon of great directors. And last, of course, there is the voice of the Master himself, almost always evasive about his personal life, but loquacious and revealing about his films and techniques.

In her incisive analysis of *Psycho*, Linda Williams argues that the film should be considered "quintessentially postmodern" (165). In the same way, I should like to argue that my book about *Psycho* is also "quintessentially post modern." John McGowan says, "At the very least, post modernism highlights the multiplication of voices, questions, and conflicts that has shattered what once seemed to be (although it never really was) the placid unanimity of the great tradition and of the West that gloried in it" ("Post-modernism"). In this book, I have tried to capture that "multiplication of voices" as they relate to a film scene that has done much to shatter the great traditions of classical cinema. In fact, many critics—Paul Monaco being the most influential—make a strong case for *Psycho*'s shower scene as the dividing line between classical and modernist and postmodern films.

In devising the scheme for the book, I had my students in mind as part of my target audience. Having taught at Lakeland Community College for more than thirty-five years, I have worked with students from a wide variety of ages, backgrounds, educational levels, and cultural experiences. In the last few years, I have had in my Hitchcock class high school students taking college classes in lieu of Advance Placement courses; retired professionals; foreign students; returning women, with young children; downsized engineers, and an assortment of 18-to-30-year-old traditional and nontraditional students, a few of them with GEDs rather than high school diplomas. Figuring out how to organize and implement my course in the face of such diversity provided invaluable background for writing this book. I hope, however, that I have not lost sight of my colleagues in the field of Hitchcock scholarship, because I have written this book also for them, as a way of adding my voice to the critical discourse about Alfred Hitchcock and his films.

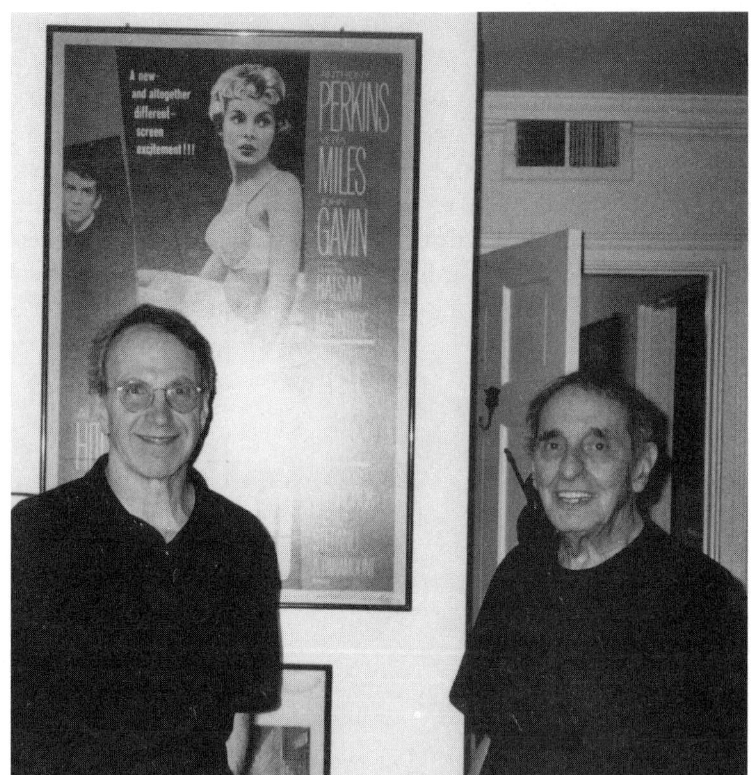

personal collection of the author

Joseph Stefano, scriptwriter of *Psycho*, with the author

CHAPTER 1

My Research Trip

Ozzy Osbourne walks by our table at the Polo Lounge in the Beverly Hills Hotel. He leans forward as he walks, with his arms by his side and his legs stiff, as if imitating a zombie. I'm sitting with Joseph Stefano, the screenwriter of *Psycho*, and with my research assistant, Jim Dunn. We're in Los Angeles doing research for a book on the shower scene in *Psycho*. We look at Ozzy as he shuffles by and takes a seat right behind us, and then we look at each other. Joe asks, "Does he have some kind of disability?" Jim and I look at each other and smile. I think to myself that it is somewhat coincidental that Ozzy should be here today because he, in a somewhat circuitous way, is in a line of descent from the scene that is the subject of my book.

I return my attention to Joe Stefano. He is about eighty years old, but he looks much younger. He's a smallish man, but wiry looking, and elegantly, not gauntly, thin. He wears his clothes well, this day donned in a black sports jacket, with only the top button fastened, over a gray silk jersey accompanied by tan slacks. His hair is in the Roman fashion, with curly bangs. He has coal-black, sparkling eyes and a grin that opens wide when he laughs and that triangulates his face, Joker style. A little more than six months ago, Joe agreed to an interview for my book, and we spent four hours in his Italian-style villa in the hills surrounding Benedict Canyon Drive, about two miles from where we sit now in the Polo Lounge. His house sits on a hilltop and has a breathtaking view of the surrounding hills. The living room where we sat was filled with Southern California light from the large windows that opened out on a flower-filled patio with Italian marble tiles. I have invited him to this lunch to repay his kindness for devoting so much of his day to our interview. I am pleased that our work together has made us friends.

Joe is an articulate, precise talker—I can picture him making very effective pitches for his script ideas—and his interview was a delight, with digressions that contained juicy information about his psychoanalysis at the time of writing *Psycho*, in 1959. According to Joe, Hitch loved hearing about Joe's therapy sessions. Of course, Hitchcock always remained enigmatic, guarded, and Buddha-like in his comments about his own personal life. His private life and thoughts usually stayed within him. Joe remembers, Hitch could tell us what kind of session Joe had had: Hitch would say, "Good session!" or "Bad session!" Hitchcock's therapy was, of course, contained in his films.

Today, as we sit in the Polo Lounge, Joe is talking about his latest project, a film script he has almost finished writing and that he hopes to direct. Entitled *Within Screaming Distance*, it is based on a personal experience that occurred one August night in 1969, when the Manson gang butchered Sharon Tate and her friends. The killings occurred only a short distance from Joe's villa. He describes his script idea—a Hollywood party that takes place on a brutally hot August night and that metaphorically parallels the horrors taking place just across the hills. Joe talks about how he and his friends, during a "real" party that night, heard the echoes of screams and barking dogs but thought that these were only the ambient sounds of the party revelers that were frequently heard in the hills above Benedict Canyon. Joe plans to raise the money for the movie himself. He hopes that finally he will be able to translate his words to the screen with his vision intact, a process that rarely occurs in Hollywood filmmaking. Joe knows this painful process well, having suffered under the eccentric helm of James Foley, who in 1995 directed Joe's original screenplay, entitled *Two Bits*, a largely autobiographical coming-of-age saga. For Joe, the experience of working with Foley was not a good one. Joe believed that Foley disregarded his suggestions and deviated too much from the script. As he talks more about his new screenplay, I realize with a jolt that those horrible killings in Beverly Hills are also tied to the topic of my book.

As Joe is talking, I glance over at the next table and I see Janet Leigh and several of her friends. I had also invited her to join us for lunch, but coincidentally she had made reservations at the exact time and place. However, she had promised to stop by at our table to say hi. I send over a note because Janet's back is to us, but all she does is turn to look at us quizzically and to give us a cursory wave with a polite smile. "Pushy tourists" or "star gazers," she probably thinks to herself. I feel hurt and a bit slighted that she does not keep her promise to visit us, especially because her old friend Joe Stefano is at our table. During my earlier trip to interview Joe, I had also spoken with Janet Leigh, who lives just across the Canyon from Joe, at the very top of Beverly Hills. My research assistant, Jim, and I had sat in her very elegant den and talked with her about her role in the film, especially her recollection of the famous shower scene. Janet's interview was very different from Joe's—more formal, less digressive, and a bit tense.

At age seventy-three, Janet Leigh is feisty and outspoken. A writer herself, she has coauthored a book on *Psycho* and has written two novels about Hollywood, one of which, *The Dream Factory*, I had brought to our interview for her to sign. Even though she is a writer herself, Janet is a bit suspicious of the critical industry that has grown up around *Psycho*. During our interview, I told her that *Psycho* is the most written-about film of all time. She responded, "Only one thing that confuses me . . . but there have been so many books on *Psycho*. I find it so odd, not odd, exactly, but what are they thinking?" I've encountered her attitude before, from industry professionals, who are mystified by the jargon and themes of academic film discourse. In fact, she answered one of my questions about the symbolic significance of the shower scene with one word: "Bullshit!" I was astonished and amused and a bit defensive because I was sure that she had lumped me within the critical industry that she didn't understand. I realized that she was in a way right about my book. I vowed to myself that my book would be different—less jargony and abstruse. It would be about the shower scene, of course, but it would also be about me.

My journey to the Polo Lounge had actually begun many years ago. It was September 1960, and I was sixteen years old. I had made plans with my friend Ralph Spinelli to go to the Olympia Theater in Chelsea, a blue-collar city right outside of Boston. Of the two movie theaters, the Olympia and the Strand (there used to be four, but the changing patterns of leisure time, combined with the impact of television, had cut that number in half), the Olympia was definitely the classier of the two, the one that showed first-run movies in double bills. I had been going to the Olympia—and also to the Strand—since I could remember, sometimes attending two or three shows a week, many times after school. Back then, movie houses opened in the late morning and ran continuous shows all day. It was common for moviegoers to walk into a film halfway through and to stay—through the cartoons, coming attractions, and second feature—to see the half that they had missed. I believe I became an astute movie viewer because of this practice. I could enter the theater halfway through a film, and within minutes, I could make a pretty good guess about how it had started. It was easy for me to verify my guess by staying to watch that part I had missed. On that September evening, however, there was no double feature at the Olympia.

Only one film was showing, *Psycho*. One week earlier, on September 18, the *Chelsea Record*, my hometown newspaper, had carried advertisements for the upcoming *Psycho* in its September 18, 1960, edition. The film had an odd starting time of 8:43 p.m. for the evening showing. No other film advertised, including the ones currently screening on September 18, the double feature of *Portrait in Black* and *The Cossacks*, contained screening times. Clearly, expecting customers to show up for a film when it actually started was something novel. In addition, showing only one film, not two, was a radically different exhibition practice.

The movie that Ralph and I went to see on that September night in 1960—*Psycho*—would help change almost all of these standard exhibition practices and viewing habits. In order to view *Psycho*, we had to arrive at the theater *before* the movie began; absolutely no one was allowed to enter once the movie had started. This unprecedented and extraordinary requirement helped to build tremendous word-of-mouth marketing for the movie. Of course, this marketing was why Ralph and I were waiting in line to see this movie. In July 1960, Hitchcock had recorded a special message to a showmanship meeting for movie exhibitors. In this message Hitchcock claims that he had devised this idea himself:

> You are here at the invitation of the excellent showmanship team from Paramount Pictures—to learn how you can best carry out the theatre presentation policy for PSYCHO. The idea of insisting on this policy that no one—but no one—be admitted to a theatre playing PSYCHO after the start of each performance came to me one busy afternoon in the cutting room, when I startled my fellow workers with a noisy vow that my labors on PSYCHO would not be in vain—that everyone else in the world would have to see the picture from beginning to end. This was the way that PSYCHO was conceived, and this was how it had to be seen, by everyone.
>
> Our opening engagements have proved, beyond a shadow of any showman's doubt, the phenomenal success of our required policy—in all types of theatres, big and small, drive-ins, hardtops and new economy size.
>
> If the word "required" startles you, please try to think of a box office besieged by patrons anxious to purchase tickets. Feel better? Yes, my friends, while nothing in this world is fully guaranteed, you will most probably be happily startled on the way to the bank. (Special Collections)

Hitchcock's publicity campaign had obviously worked; he had helped create an audience for the film. The film theorist William Pechter also saw the movie when it first opened. He says of this experience, "The atmosphere surrounding *Psycho* was deeply charged with apprehension. Something awful is always about to happen. One could sense that the audience was constantly aware of this; indeed, it had the solidarity of a convention assembled in the common understanding of some unspoken *entente terrible*; it was in the fullest sense an audience, not merely a random gathering of discrete individuals attendant at most plays and movies" (Rebello 162).

The experience that Ralph and I had that night would have a profound impact not only on us but on all audiences as well as the film world in general. Forty-two years later, Ralph still remembers the shower scene in the movie: "Regarding my recollection of that night," he writes, "I can only remember the shower scene. Things like that are called 'significant emotional events.' Other examples are JFK's assassination; the loss of seven NASA astronauts; the loss of a loved one; 9-11, etc." (Spinelli). This astonishing linkage of a brief scene in a movie forty-plus years ago with earth-shattering events is typical of the seismic effect of *Psycho* on its audience. As for the type of audience itself, Robert Kapsis points out in his study of the growth of Hitchcock's reputation that the experience of watching *Psycho* would help to create a new audience, a youth audience, who experienced the film as a social event (62). This youth audience, myself included, had been watching Alfred Hitchcock on television since the premiere of *Alfred Hitchcock Presents* on October 2, 1955. This extraordinary series would help lay the foundation for the movie *Psycho*, not only in its look, especially the black-and-white cinematography, but also in its characters, themes, and structure, particularly the ambiguous ending scene. Above all, though, it was the *tone* of the series that was the most significant, a tone that had been developed in the 190 or so episodes that had been aired by 1960 (Sloan 550)—bitterly ironic, darkly humorous, subversively and perversely sexy, incipiently violent, and provocatively immoral. This tone would help generate the skepticism, rebelliousness, and irreverence of the generation that would come to age, power, and influence in the 1960s.

Nothing about the television shows, however, could prepare the audience for the shock and terror it would feel at the most famous scene in *Psycho*—the shower scene. I can remember vividly the anxiety I felt that evening watching Janet Leigh as the character Marion Crane preparing herself for the shower. There was something else I felt, however, in addition to anxiety: sexual stimulation. I can remember Ralph nudging me with his elbow and saying "Jeez!" as we both watched Janet Leigh cinematically undressed by Hitchcock in the Peeping Tom scene, during which Tony Perkins, as Norman Bates, watches Marion undress for the shower, and earlier still, when the film opens with Marion and her lover Sam rolling half-naked on a hotel bed on a bright, sunny day in Phoenix. Seeing the buxom Janet Leigh in her bra and slip was certainly part of the "event" of the film! Feeling stimulation and anxiety, Ralph and I knew that something was about to happen, but we were unprepared for just what that something might be.

We were not alone in our "innocence." For more than twenty-five years, the Production Code had presided over the content of films. Ever since the movies had begun, there were attempts to censor them, but the cries for censorship became clamorous during the licentious Jazz Age of the 1920s, especially after the Fatty Arbuckle scandal. To these demands of censorship, Hollywood responded by creating the Motion Picture Producers and Distributors Association (the MPPDA), which in 1922 hired Will Hays, former Republican National Committee Chairman and later Postmaster General, to head up the new organization. Under the moral guidance of Will Hays, the MPPDA created the Production Code in 1930. In 1934, the Code was tightened with the hiring of Joseph Breen, the new director of the Production Code. A Catholic layman, Breen oversaw the strict application of the Code, which forbid, as the film historian Robert Sklar states, ". . . a vast range of human expression and experience: homosexuality, which it describes as 'sex perversion,' interracial sex, abortion, incest, drugs, most forms of profanity, and scores of words defined as vulgar, including s-e-x itself" (174). As for violence and crime, the Code states, "Methods of Crime shall not be explicitly presented" (Doherty 362). Most important, crime should never pay. In short, the Code ruled.

In effect what Ralph and I had been seeing for the ten or so years we had been viewing films had been controlled by—ruled by—the economic forces that ran Hollywood: the studios, with their control of production and distribution; and the theater chains, with their iron lock on exhibition. The Code's seal of approval was necessary for films to get distributed and shown. Ever since its creation, the MPPDA and the Code had been in a kind of cultural war with the creative forces in Hollywood: the people who wrote, directed, and acted in films. As Joe Stefano pointed out in his interview, the Code people had always been after Hitchcock because of the subversive nature of the themes and topics of his films: rape, murder, adultery, espionage, and madness. As a result, successful Hollywood directors who wanted to deal with topics forbidden by the Code—Hitchcock, Wilder, Preminger, and their colleagues—had developed an elaborate system of visual and thematic tropes to present their visions of violence on the screen. For example, Hitchcock began the 1950s, his most mature and productive decade, with *Strangers on a Train*, which contains a brutal murder by strangulation. Hitchcock, however, shoots the scene indirectly, by replacing the space of the screen with the dark, myopic, distorted mirror of the murdered woman's glasses, which had been knocked off when the psychopath Bruno began to throttle her. We see the scene reflected in the wide-angle distortion created by the victim's thick glasses, which now fill the screen and serve as a symbol of Bruno's twisted mind. In effect, we see a brutal murder, but we see it "through a glass darkly." Hence, Hitchcock is able to present a murder on screen, in essence flouting the Code's strictness about excessive violence, but also able to mute the murder, so to speak, through the art of film.

Hitchcock does this in a different way in his next film, *I Confess* (1953), which begins with a murder already committed. The opening shots of Quebec City contain directional traffic arrows that ominously point us toward the scene of the crime. As in so many Hitchcock films—*Psycho* included—the camera peers voyeuristically into a window and then enters the space of the crime, where we briefly see a body sprawled on the floor, the victim's bloody head, and a blunt murder weapon next to it. The camera then tilts up to reveal beaded curtains still moving as if the murderer had just left. We then pan outside to a dark street with a shadowy figure in the garb of a priest walking away from the camera.

This kind of scene construction and editing had evolved over the years, and directors had utilized these techniques to circumvent the Code by suggesting violence and by transferring the action to the mind of the spectator. Eisenstein had perfected this technique in his theory and practice of montage: shot A + shot B (both on the screen) = shot C (in the mind of the audience). Hitchcock was tremendously influenced by Eisenstein's montage and by the theories and films of the other filmmakers in the Soviet Socialist Realist movement. And of course, the Soviets had been profoundly influenced by the father of modern film technique, D.W. Griffith, who played a major role in developing the lexicon of film language.

This film language was refined and streamlined by the Hollywood studio system into what has become known as "the classical Hollywood style." John Belton calls this style the driving force of the "narrative machine." He explains, "Classical Hollywood cinema possesses a style which is largely invisible and difficult for the average spectator to see. Its invisibility is, in large part, the product of American Cinema's proficiencies as a narrative machine. Like the industry-based, assembly-line process innovated by Henry Ford and his peers in the business world to make the production of automobiles and other consumer goods as streamlined and economical as possible, American movies rapidly evolved during the 1910s and 1920s into a highly efficient mode of telling stories. Every aspect of the production gears itself up to facilitate the smoothest possible flow of the narrative process" (22).

Thus the films that Ralph and I and the rest of the American audience had been watching over the years—the films that we had been "conditioned" by—were tightly controlled and censored through the economic force of the studio system. Moreover, these films were just as tightly controlled in structure, with story and character paramount. Undergirding this narrative system was the star system, the studio's way of guaranteeing audience identification with the characters in the film via the actors and actresses who played these characters, the stars. As Belton says, "The star provided the studio with a tangible attraction, with an image that could be advertised and marketed, offsetting the less tangible qualities of the story, direction, acting, art direction, costume design, and overall studio style" (85).

In the late 1950s, Janet Leigh was a rising star, and many of those sitting in the Olympia Theater on that September night were there to see Janet Leigh and her costar Tony Perkins. The audience got to see more of Janet Leigh than they had expected, however. The Peeping Tom scene mentioned above, in which Janet Leigh undresses, titillated Ralph and me, but this titillation had been inextricably mixed with a feeling of tension and anxiety because we were watching her undress through the POV of Norman Bates as he peers through the hole in his parlor wall. This subtle shift in emphasis from seeing things through Marion's eyes—as we had in the first forty minutes of the film—to seeing things through Norman's eyes was one of the film's most subversive techniques. In his interview, Joe Stefano talked about how he had made the decision when he was adapting his screenplay from the Robert Bloch novel *Psycho* that the emphasis in the film must shift from Marion to Norman because Marion dies almost halfway through the film. Stefano states, "The movie is over unless we get the audience to care about Norman."

A hallmark of the studio style that Hitchcock had absorbed in his forty years of filmmaking experience was its invisibility. That is, the style was subordinated to the story and to the characters. The mise-en-scene and montage were designed to advance the story and to create identification with characters. Of all the cinematic elements of this classical style, none was more important than montage, or "cutting," as Hitchcock sometimes called it, the actual splicing together of shots to create scenes and sequences. The classical style was predicated upon "invisible" cutting; that is, one shot should flow smoothly and unobtrusively to another shot to create a scene that is seamless, as if the action were continuous.

Hitchcock had become known as the Master of Suspense because he utilized the invisible style to help the audience identify with a character and he thus created a psychological bond between the audience and that character in order to heighten suspense. Hitchcock describes this technique as a method of transference of the feeling of the character to the mind of the audience through the POV of the camera. Hitchcock calls this "suspense by forewarning," the process by which the audience shares the knowledge of the character by seeing the world through his or her eyes. In this way Hitchcock is able to utilize what he called his "special field": creating fear in his audience. Hitchcock says of this technique, "My suspense work comes out of creating nightmares for the audience. And I play with an audience. I make them gasp and surprise them and shock them . . ." (Gottlieb, *Hitchcock on Hitchcock* 324).

In having the camera assume the gaze of the character, Hitchcock uses the subtlety of classical editing to shift the action to the mind of the spectator. For example, in the scene during which Marion Crane is driving through the darkness and rain to reach Fairvale and her lover Sam, Hitchcock uses the invisible editing of the Hollywood style to shift Marion's anxiety to the mind of the audience. We see a close-up of Marion staring straight ahead and then squinting and blinking as the headlights of oncoming cars temporarily blind her. The next shot shows us, the audience, what Marion is seeing. We, too, can barely make out the road because of the darkness and the rain on the windshield. In that one cut, Hitchcock has put the audience in the driver's seat with Marion. Her view takes up the whole screen; we no longer see the character looking out at us from the screen. We become the character and share her anxiety.

Later, then, in the first important shift in POV in the film, in the Peeping Tom scene, the audience briefly sees the action through Norman's eyes. This shift helps to create the anxiety that the audience feels, for the audience is now engaged in an act of voyeurism and so becomes a Peeping Tom along with Norman. The psychology behind this shift to Norman's POV is one of Hitchcock's and Stefano's strokes of genius in this film. The audience that had identified with Marion is now engaged in a "forbidden" view of her, not through the neutral camera that had gazed on Norman as a character, but rather through the camera as Norman. Hitchcock has now positioned the audience for the most startling scene in his career, and for the most important scene in film history.

By the time that the shower scene began, Hitchcock had his audience in the Olympia Theater exactly where he wanted them: in a complex state of arousal and anxiety. In many different interviews, Hitchcock emphasized the importance of knowing his audience and the concomitant requirement of manipulating them. "I play them like an organ," he claimed. "I know exactly when to stop, to relieve them at the right moment" (Gottlieb, *Hitchcock on Hitchcock* 15). In an interview with Penelope Houston, Hitchcock answered the interviewer's question—"What is the deepest logic of your films?"—with this statement: "To put the audience through it" (Rebello 174). Hitchcock claimed that he had discovered the importance of the audience when he came to America in 1939 to make films for David O. Selznick. In a television interview, Hitchcock admitted that it was only after the move in 1939 from London to Hollywood that he "really became conscious of the audience" (*The Illustrated Hitchcock*).

With the Olympia audience firmly under his control, Hitchcock prepared us to go "through it." The buildup to the shocking stabbing in the shower is accomplished through the classical style, as we see Marion Crane sitting at her desk writing down the amount she has spent from the stolen $40,000. The camera is unobtrusive; the angles are eye level; the editing is seamless. Plot and character are clearly in the foreground, as the audience assumes the film is still about a young woman who has stolen some money and now appears ready to return it. In an interview, Hitchcock describes his strategy in setting up the audience. He had designed *Psycho* up to this point ". . . to lead an audience completely up the garden path. They thought the story was about a girl who stole $40,000. This was deliberate, and suddenly, out of the blue she is stabbed to death" (Gottlieb, *Hitchcock on Hitchcock* 293). What comes "out of the blue" is a sudden, savage, and totally unexpected "lightning bolt." As the shadowy and ominous figure pulls back the shower curtain, the audience sees through its nebulous translucence, and the sound track explodes into high pitched, piercing, screeching sounds. A dark figure looms over Marion. As the actual stabbing begins, Hitchcock shifts suddenly from the classical, invisible editing style to something much more expressionistic. There is a sudden, jarring cut to an extreme close-up of Marion's screaming mouth, gaping in terror.

A series of jump cuts then follows, edited staccato fashion, during which the shots shift erratically from low to high angle, with alternating shots of the inexorable, driving butcher knife slamming down and into the naked, defenseless Marion. A shot of blood flooding the bathtub floor fills the screen.

Audience members at the Olympia Theater let out involuntary screams when this scene began, and Ralph grabbed my arm with such force that I had black and blue marks for a week. He held on for the forty or so seconds that the stabbing lasts. It was as if we were suspended in time for those forty seconds, mesmerized by the rapid cutting of the editing style, horrified by the screams of Marion, traumatized by the screeching strings of the music track, and mortified by the slicing and stabbing sounds of the knife as it entered Marion's flesh. Of course, many of these psychological effects come about through the editing process itself, during which Eisenstein's A + B = C is working to its full effect. Hitchcock prided himself on not actually showing the knife stabbing Marion. He claims that the violence occurs inside the viewer's mind (shot C, in the Eisensteinian sense). He also claims that the nudity is equally suggestive, never explicitly shown. However, despite Hitchcock's claims, there is something new added to these forty or so seconds and to the shots immediately preceding: the graphic depiction of nudity and violence. There is a single shot during which the knife enters the flesh of Marion, and viewers can see an out-of-focus breast and nipple. These, added to a taboo shot of a flushing toilet bowl before the shower scene begins, multiply the shock of the scene. In addition, these outrageous violations of the Production Code—an institution that had "protected" audiences for years—were presented in a totally disorienting manner that subverted the traditional cinematic language of the classical style. In one bold and brilliant stroke, Hitchcock had presented a scene so revolutionary in its subject and style that it forever changed the way films were created and viewed. In fact, the critic Paul Monaco compares the power and impact of this scene to the premiere of Stravinsky's *Rite of Spring* in 1913. He claims, "Although there were no riots outside the cinemas of 1960, as there had been in 1913 outside the theater in Paris, where *The Rite of Spring* premiered, *Psycho* nonetheless marked the arrival of what was to become the dominant motion-picture aesthetic of the late twentieth century" (190).

Of course, Ralph and I had no understanding of what had happened as we came out of the forty-second fugue we had been plunged into. I could hear people saying, "Oh, my God," and I heard one woman near us whimpering, "Oh, oh, oh." Ralph released his grip on my arm, and I let out a sound that was something close to a gasp but that sounded almost like a laugh, or a snort. The emotional effect rippled through the audience as we watched in wide-eyed horror as Marion slides down the shower wall, reaches for the shower curtain, pulls it off the rod, and slumps, with a sickening thud, across the bathtub wall. The puddles of blood are shown going down the drain, counterclockwise, and the shot of this drain surprisingly dissolves into Marion's eye, which starts to rotate in the opposite direction, this rotation a perfect embodiment of the audience's sense of vertigo and imbalance. The rotating dissolve into the eye of Marion presents the audience with the stare of death itself. It was as chilling a scene as any audience had ever witnessed. What made this scene even more shocking was that this victim of unspeakable horror was the star of the film itself. "She can't be dead," I thought, but my eyes told me a different story. In a little more than a minute of screen time—an eternity of emotional time—the Olympia audience had been launched into a new cinematic universe.

Joe Stefano looks up from his dessert as Janet Leigh and her friends walk by our table. Janet glances at me and then at Joe; she walks by our table and then stops. She turns around, walks up to the edge of our table, and says to me, "Oh, gosh, I'm cognizant. I'm now cognizant!" She reaches out to shake my hand, and then she turns toward Joe, walks over to him, and reaches down to hug him as he simultaneously stands to greet her. She says to Joe, "Oh, I'm so glad to see you," and he says, "Janet, how are you?" She looks back over at me and reaches out to take my hand again, this time warmly holding it with both of hers. "I'm so sorry I didn't recognize you. My husband Bob has been very ill, and I've been terribly distracted. I'm just not myself." I express my sympathy to her and watch as she and Joe talk briefly about her husband.

I experience one of those moments when past and present fuse for one mystifying instant. My sixteen-year-old self and my fifty-eight-year-old self now seem one, as I look at Janet Leigh and Joe Stefano and momentarily see them as they were in 1960, both in the prime of their careers, both collaborating on one of the most important and influential films of all time, a film that had shaken Ralph and me and had catapulted us into the maelstrom of the 1960s. I look at Janet and Joe, and I am amazed at how all three of our lives have intersected at this particular and serendipitous moment. I remember that Alfred Hitchcock came to the Polo Lounge frequently, and I specifically recall reading about how John Michael Hayes first met Hitchcock at this same restaurant to discuss working with him on the script of *Rear Window*. I sense the presence of the Master of Suspense and wonder what he would have thought of my project.

Janet Leigh takes her leave of us and wishes me well on my book. As we prepare to leave, Joe hands me a copy of our interview, which I had sent to him for his final approval. At the same moment, Ozzy and his entourage are also leaving, and I watch him shuffle by our table. He, too, is part of the *Psycho* story because the film—with its seminal shower scene—helped to usher in a cultural paradigm shift from the bland decade of the 1950s, with its emphasis on togetherness and family values, to the 1960s, that cataclysmic decade of political assassinations, student protests, free-speech conflicts, race riots, Vietnam protests, and, above all, violence—in our streets, in our political institutions, in our culture, and most vividly in our media, especially in our films, and in our music. About ten years after *Psycho* opened, and about the same time that the Manson gang went on its murderous rampage, Ozzy Osborne helped to form Black Sabbath, a heavy metal band that revolutionized rock music and that earned Ozzy the epithets of psychopath and Satanist (that is, before he became the darling of reality TV!).

Whether *Psycho* helped to create the paradigm shift (and I think it did) or whether it just reflected the seismic change, there's no question that it played a major role in transforming our culture. The youth audience that this film helped to create and define would be the same audience that embraced a music that was antisocial in its themes and styles and licentious in its performance and spectatorship. The film censorship barriers that the film had crashed were also the same barriers erected in front of our music and our other cultural products.

As we leave the posh surroundings of the Polo Lounge and walk through the elegantly decorated lobby of the Beverly Hills Hotel, Jim, my research assistant, wishes Joe well on his new script. Joe thanks him, and the three of us leave the hotel and walk into the brilliant sunshine of a Southern California afternoon. Waiting for our cars to be brought up by the valets, I look around at the palm trees and the palatial green and pink buildings of the Beverly Hills Hotel. More than thirty years ago, nine years after *Psycho* premiered, the Manson family butchered Sharon Tate and her friends in this very same area of Beverly Hills, the chilling and horrifying echoes of which were heard by this small, dapper man standing next to me. This horror percolated in his mind until thirty years later he decided to dramatize it. In 1959, he also dramatized another murder that would chill a nation—and the world—and I can't help but think that the wicked knife slayings perpetrated by the Manson gang were in a line of descent from the demented figure in a wig who stabbed Marion Crane (a thirty-two-year-old Janet Leigh, now a seventy-five-year-old grandmother worrying about an ailing husband) to death.

The valets bring our cars up, and I give Joe a hug. I wonder if I'll see him again or if he will get to direct his script. Jim and I get in our car, and I wave to Joe and drive out onto Sunset Boulevard.

given to author by Janet Leigh

Head shot of Janet Leigh, given to the author at the time of their interview

CHAPTER 2

Janet Leigh

Janet Leigh was born Jeannette Helen Morrison *in 1927. She was "discovered" at age nineteen by the silent film star Norma Shearer, who saw her photograph. After a screen test, she began working for MGM where she was put under contract. Ms. Leigh starred in two other classics,* Touch of Evil *(1958) and* The Manchurian Candidate *(1962). In addition to being an actress, Ms. Leigh was also a writer. She wrote two novels about Hollywood and a book about* Psycho. *She died at age seventy-seven, on October 3, 2004.*

P: You said in your book about *Psycho*, when you read the Bloch novel you were excited about being in the film and I thought, when you read the novel, did you have any idea of what would be done about the shower scene?

J: I had no idea about anything. There was not a script. I just read the novel Mr. Hitchcock sent me, and he said that obviously we were not going to concentrate on all of the heinous acts, that they were just going to concentrate on the girl and Arbogast. And that's all.

P: In the Bloch novel, Mary gets her head cut off, and when you were reading did you say, "How are we going to do that?"

J: Well no, because I had read Mr. Hitchcock's letter, and he said really to not think about the novel because it's just an idea. It's not going to be the same. Because the way it was, it would be nothing more than a terrible slasher serial, and he had no intention of doing that. Nothing entered my head other than I was going to work with Mr. Hitchcock. That's the only thing!

P: And that was, I'm sure, exciting for you.

J: Very exciting. Absolutely.

P: When did you see the film for the first time, complete, in a theater with participants?

J: The first time I saw it, was in a screening room at Universal with about forty people. I had not seen dailies, and I had not seen a rough cut. This was the finished product.

P: I know you've written about what your reaction was, but when you came to the shower scene, you knew you had been working on that scene for a long time. When you came to it, were you surprised it was so short, and so powerful? Did it just bowl you over?

J: I was on the set; I had seen the storyboards, each shot, each angle. I was still bowled over.

P: So Hitchcock actually had those Saul Bass storyboards there and followed them pretty much?

J: Saul Bass was the instrument, and Mr. Hitchcock was the one who said, "Give this to me in every kind of direction, in every kind of situation, whether the camera is high, low, upside down, whatever. Draw it so that I can see what it looks like, what the camera would tell me it looks like." And Mr. Bass did it. How Mr. Hitchcock arrived at the choices he made I have no idea. He didn't shoot everything that Saul Bass drew.

P: That's what I was asking. He didn't shoot all of the various drawings?

J: No, he chose which ones. His eye was so perfect. I mean, he chose from all the renditions that Mr. Bass offered, and they were all good.

P: These were just Bass's ideas. He said, "We can do it this way," and Hitchcock . . .

J: No, these were not just Bass's ideas. Mr. Hitchcock said, "Give me every possibility," and so what Mr. Hitchcock did with his untouchable eye and knowledge and timing, instinctive built-in timing, he chose the angles to actually use. Then they built the scaffolding or whatever it was so those exact shots would be made, so I knew what shots were being done. I knew vaguely the order, but that means diddly, you know; I'm not technically oriented and I never wanted to be. It's never mattered to me where the camera is or something like that. I really just don't go into that. I have all I can do with my one little cell up there to try to do what I do and trust that the other people are doing what they do, and so in shooting it there's a whole different feeling. Yes, of course, the moment of the actual "roll camera," "action," of course it's terrifying and electrifying; it's shocking; it's all of the things you would expect. But that's for maybe ten seconds, and then the camera stops, and you do it maybe twenty times or maybe you do it two times, but then you move to the next shot, which may take two hours to set up, so you can't maintain that level of hysterics or you'd be in a booby hatch. I was as shocked, as stunned, startled, and terrified as any audience seeing it for the first time. Maybe even more so because my feelings are very close to my skin, so I react usually stronger than most people.

P: Seeing yourself get killed on the screen must be scary.

J: Well, sometimes you forget it's yourself as well. I mean, you know, if you're into a movie, it's whoever's getting killed. Marion was getting killed, and Marion had become very real to me.

P: Had your character ever been killed in a movie before or since?

J: I don't know. I have to think. I can't think off hand.

P: And to be killed so brutally and at that particular moment and so early into the picture . . .

J: If anybody died at that time, one of your leading players died at the end.

P: Yeah. I was so shocked. I saw it when I was sixteen years old with my friend in the theater. He grabbed my arm and it was so visceral; it was so powerful, but it happened so fast it was like, "What did we just see?" And of course you didn't have a videotape to go back and look at it again. And on the big screen it just made such an impact. And I wondered, did the other forty people gasp or . . . ?

J: It was collective, but you know, some are more audible. Some are going "Oh, no!" You could feel the reaction. Only one thing that confuses me, not confuses me, but there have been so many books on *Psycho*. I find it so odd, not odd, exactly, but what are they thinking? It's just interesting to me that these people are going to come up with something that was in this brilliant man's mind. But what I'm interested in is how your publisher would think that you're going to find out something new about the shower scene.

P: Well, I hope I will. Hitchcock studies have become more and more focused. There's Rebello's book about the making of *Psycho*, and then there is your book from the participant's point of view and your work with Hitchcock, and then there is a new book put out by the British Film Institute, which is, the author calls it a "note." It's about one hundred pages just on the film, and there's another book on *Psycho* coming out. I'd like to get back to the shower scene. I have a theory that the shower scene doesn't begin with you getting into the shower. My belief is that the shower scene begins with you sitting at the desk.

J: Oh, that's the whole sequence.

P: I think that's where the scene begins, because Hitchcock builds up the sense of suspense and identification through you, and then . . .

J: And the culmination comes at the end of the talk in the parlor, and the shower sequence starts as she's figuring out at the desk.

P: And a lot of people will say the shower scene starts in the shower.

J: No, there's much more to the shower scene than that.

P: I think when *Sight and Sound* comes out with its ten greatest films, you know they do that thing every ten years, they do a poll of critics and, this year, filmmakers, and they ask them what do they think the ten greatest films are. The last one was in 2002, and *Vertigo* was second on the list. I would like to see *Psycho* on that list.

J: Oh, it should be. It's already been said that that scene is the most internationally famous scene in all cinematic history.

P: When you were shooting it and the woman was stabbing you, what kind of knife was used? Even though it was a set up and everything was controlled, did you ever feel a sense of danger when it was happening?

J: No, because you never saw the knife in the same shot with me. What people don't seem to understand today was that you could not show a weapon penetrating flesh, so you never saw the knife in the same shot with me. What you saw was the knife go up and the next thing you saw was it coming down, and then you saw a shot of my tummy button. And in your mind, the knife went into the tummy button.

P: There were some high angles of you, you kind of putting up your arms or trying to block her hand.

J: Yeah, but there was never anything. First of all it was not a real knife. You wouldn't even fool around with that. And in the shots of him, of the figure . . .

P: That was a real knife.

J: Of course. But once it moves down and you went to the body, the knife never came into that shot. And if there was a struggle . . . I can't tell you every moment of the shots but, you know, I don't look at it every day all day. Marion never struggled. She didn't have a chance to struggle. If anything, she was trying to wield off the barrage and, believe me, there was no real knife, and so the idea was enough.

P: It certainly is enough. One of the points that I try to make in the study of this scene is when you move from the suspense of watching you figure out how much money you spent and then getting in the shower to try to cleanse yourself . . .

J: Cleanse yourself, yes, but you're really cleansing your soul as well as the travel dirt.

P: What happens is that when Hitchcock starts to cut and edit that scene, it's like you're thrust into this very confined space and it becomes sort of an abstract space with all this terror happening, and Hitchcock had a fear of heights and enclosed spaces, and I wonder whether as you watch it as a viewer, the fact that she's trapped in that space with this person with nowhere to go adds to that feeling of terror.

J: Well, I think that's very deliberate because if you think of the dialogue in the parlor and she says, "We all have our own private traps," and she's realizing she's gotten herself into a trap by doing what she did. As she sees this young man, obviously in his own trap, she sees that there's only one way out. So the density of the closeness, the walls coming in reflect what in her mind she almost let herself in for. That's why the shower is so important. The shower, when she gets in, is really so much more than taking a shower. I mean she's realized she's let herself have her moment of rashness, but she's saying, "I don't have to be in this trap; I can get out of this trap." And it's kind of like swimming for freedom in a way. And the whole idea of when she's doing this with the water, it's not just feeling fresh water on her face. She's feeling almost like breathing it in.

P: Is that how you were playing it?

J: Exactly, because this was her cleansing. This was her chance to get out of the trap because she could see how this poor young man was never going to get out of the trap. And this was a very brave decision on her part, but she felt good about it, that this was her chance to get away from the walls closing in. It was like she was breaking free; the water was washing away the sin.

P: And then, bingo!

J: Yeah, that's what the shock is, and that's why it is such a shock.

P: It's brilliantly conceived. Hitchcock talks about this boyhood jailing thing so much and no one knows if it really happened to him or not, or if this was just a convenient way for him to talk about what he was afraid of. I'm wondering if when he conceived that scene and he thought about it and thought about the character that this was a way of reflecting the terror that he felt when that jail door slammed.

J: You know, he and I never talked about Marion very much.

P: That was one of my questions.

J: I don't know what he thought about Marion. I don't know whether he thought about an enclosed room. It was all there. I mean the situation was there to take advantage of and to use, but we never talked about it.

P: Did he ever talk about characters?

J: No. What he said to me was, "I hired you because I think you're a good actress. I will let you do with Marion what you think you can to bring the most out of the character and add to the picture. The only time I will really interfere is if you're not doing enough, if you're not coming up to what I need from Marion. I have to have certain things from Marion. If you're not giving me the basic needs, we will discuss." He could discuss. It's not that he couldn't. He liked people to bring themselves into it. It makes it so much fuller because if it's just his idea, it's not as rich. As long as his idea is met, and his need is met, and then the person brings something added, it's so much better. He said, "So I won't really bother you about that unless I feel that you're not coming up to it, or if you're doing too much to her. Because you know, Marion has a place. You can make her rich or poor, all the things you want to make her, but she does have a place and she can't exceed that. So either if I have to do this or if I have to do that will be the time that I would then confer with you about your interpretation. Otherwise, the only requirement I need is that you be where I need you to be for my camera."

P: Was he true to what he said? He didn't really direct you very much?

J: Absolutely! Because he saw where I was going and obviously agreed with that.

P: You do build that picture. You do build this, in an amazingly short amount of time, this dimension of this character so that when you get killed off the audience has worked its way into identifying with you, being sort of on your side, saying, "Here's somebody who made this one mistake and is now going to go back and try to make it right."

J: Well, hopefully there's great understanding of this woman and feeling for her and the desperation in her life. The fact is that she did a wrong thing; she's grasping for happiness. How many of us have done that? And she's seeing her life slip away. And in my story, in my approach to Marion, I figured that her parents were killed in an automobile accident and she had to forego college to support her younger sister. I think that she also probably did not pursue a romance that she had because he wasn't settled and didn't have enough to take care of the sister. She had to work, and all these things are what I'm thinking Marion is. Now the sister has grown up, but Marion still takes care of her, but her life is passing her by, and she finds a man that she is attracted to and does love. But he's divorced and doesn't have the money to get married, and for her to have an illicit affair is not true to her. She's not a hooker. She's not comfortable in this role. Obviously, she's a terrible thief, but hopefully you see this temptation, the desperation to have a life. And you see it take over, but you don't not like her for it.

P: Oh no, she's one of the most likeable characters.

J: But that's what you have to draw a line with. She's doing something bad, but it was not meant really to hurt anybody; it was to try to find a life. But she's just not capable of bringing that to fruition, and she realizes in time. She thinks, "Thank God. By a chance meeting I've been given the opportunity to set things right . . . to go back!" And so that's what has been done; the audience has been so manipulated: one, they think it's the story of Marion, first with her lover—I mean just in a very superficial stage—and then this young guy at the motel, and they're just like, "Well, will she go back to the other guy?" You know it's all these underlying innuendos that are going on really in her mind and of course then in his mind, and of course then in the audience's. It's like a puppet; Mr. Hitchcock is pulling the strings. So the audience thinks, "Wow, she's going to go back, but I wonder if she'll really still come back and see this guy Norman, or maybe she and Sam can make it after all, but she's going to do the right thing."

P: This film was so different from standard Hollywood, happy-ending stuff. I think it's so significant that things don't work out. I know the Production Code was lessening and was weakened by this time. I think this was the end of the Production Code in a lot of ways.

J: But it held on *Psycho*.

P: But I think the shower scene is significant because it just marked a new kind of film, a new way of moving away from what the audience expected. Rather than having this attractive main character get what she wants and get what she seemed to deserve, all of a sudden this scene comes in and takes away all of that in such a short time, and we're launched into a whole different story. To me, that is a very different kind of film.

J: I don't think they knew it before, but they did after. The phenomenon of *Psycho* took the industry, took the world, by storm.

P: Do you think Hitchcock, because of his television work, maybe had a sense of a different kind of audience, a younger audience, that would go along with this kind of movie.

J: I don't think so.

P: What did you think of the Gus Van Sant version of *Psycho*?

J: I didn't see it.

P: Why do you think he made that film?

J: I don't know. I have no idea. The only possible explanation might be because he thought, or the studio thought, that young people won't see black-and-white movies anymore, so they had to do it in color, which of course is ridiculous. They did a remake of *Dial M for Murder*, Hitchcock's movie. They called it *The Perfect Murder*, with Michael Douglas and Gwyneth Paltrow. I thought it was changed from the original and made its own mark. It didn't make a better picture out of it, but it made a different picture, which is what you do if you're doing a remake. To do a remake of a classic, and do it with the same shots, is the stupidest thing I ever heard of.

P: He added a couple of shots to the shower scene.

J: Well, because you can show nudity now.

P: That's right. And he added a little more blood. You see Anne Heche—and I have to say, Anne Heche is no Janet Leigh, but anyway—he shows Anne Heche as she's dying. She has a vision, and you see this shot of clouds. He does that twice, and then he shows that bird's-eye view of her slumped across the bathtub, which I guess Hitchcock wanted to do but couldn't because it showed too much.

J: Well, because you could show something Van Sant had to put something in that could not be shown when the original was made.

P: Do you think that the shower scene opened up the floodgates, in a sense, to more explicit treatment of sex and violence?

J: Not necessarily. You didn't see anything. *Psycho* was the perfect example of how imagination works miracles. Once an audience is given a fingernail of a real hand, instead of imagining the hand, they only see a hand. And that's what's happened. They've taken away the imagination. An audience doesn't have to think anymore, isn't given the privilege of imagining anymore. I think they've taken away the most wonderful thing in our consciousness, which is imagination. A perfect example; I did a picture called *Angels in the Outfield*, a long time ago, with Paul Douglas and Keenan Wynn. It was a story about this little girl, an orphan, who saw angels in the outfield playing for this very bad team and gruff manager. Obviously, the angels talked, but you never saw them. They did a remake of *Angels in the Outfield*, and they showed me the angel, and I was revolted. I wanted to throw up because he no more looked like my angel, no more looked like an angel I wanted to even think about, that it just took away everything. And that's a perfect example of what they do today. They don't allow the audience to have a dream; they don't allow the audience to have an imagination. Let me imagine my angel. It's not going to be the same angel as you have, but it's mine. I think it's disgusting that the audience has been robbed of their own dream.

P: Maybe the Production Code, as restrictive as it was, forced the filmmaker to deal with things indirectly. I'm thinking of sex and violence in the shower scene. So you deal with things indirectly. You don't have to show everything. And I think having the Code disappear is not such a good thing. How do you feel about that?

J: I think it's terrible. I think it's terrible. And I think you have to have some rules. You know society can't live without rules, or you're having riots; you're having anarchy. And we need to have guidelines, and it's also a question of so much product needed now that people don't take the time. A writer doesn't have to write so that the audience is led up to this point where they take over and use their imagination. They don't even have to do that. All they have to do is say, "The girl takes her clothes off." That's enough. And you don't have to be clever. Since I do write, I know it's much more difficult to write something that involves the audience to get to their own point of taking the dive off the diving board. Today some scripts do take the time; some can afford to take the time, but for the most part, they don't have the time, and why bother? It's like they used to plan scripts. They used to really write every script, not just your big blockbusters, but every script. Every script I got, whether it was your biggest picture ever made or a B picture, I got it three or four months ahead of time. They worked on it. They did wardrobe on it. They thought about it. Today you get a script, and it started yesterday. How can you develop a character? There are some of course, Spielberg, and there are many thinking and careful directors. I'm not saying they don't exist, but it's certainly not the norm and it used to be the norm. And I think it's a shame, but the makeup of the business itself is a cookie monster. There's not enough product, even if it's crap, to fill five hundred stations. So what does that do? It just takes away a little bit from each one.

P: Hence, we get this Gus Van Sant remake of *Psycho*.

J: Everybody says I was jealous. I wasn't anything. They said, "Well, why didn't you see it?" I said, "I didn't see it because if I saw it, I would have to have an opinion. And whatever the opinion would be, it would be wrong. If I liked it, that would be wrong and if I didn't like it, that would be wrong." So I didn't see it. I don't want to see it. I don't want to have an opinion about it. *Psycho*, to me, is something that I was very fortunate to be a part of, and it has a special place in my life, and I believe in cinematic history, and I'm not going to let anybody destroy that by cheap tricks.

P: Did appearing in *Psycho* change your career?

J: No, it did not. Unfortunately, it did [change] Tony Perkins'. The thing it did was that I had maybe 150 scripts a week along the lines of *Psycho*, but I never did any, so it didn't matter. Had I done any, of course, then it would have, but no, I had no intention of doing them. Because I was killed off in *Psycho*, it didn't affect me. Tony wasn't, so they never let Norman Bates die. This is not news, but I'll still tell it to you. It's in my book. In writing the book, I interviewed Osgood, Tony Perkins' son, and he told me something so interesting. He at one point went to his dad and said, "When they came to you and asked you to do *Psycho*, and you could see forty years hence what it did to your career and you knew the future when they brought you the script, would you do it?" And evidently Tony didn't answer right away. He came back in a couple of days, and he said something so profound. He said, "Yes, I would've done it, and my reason is that we are in a business to create images. That's our business. That's our job. That's what I do as an actor. If I was able to give *such* an impression, create *such* a character, that the audience wouldn't let me be anything else, then I, indeed, did my job. And yes, I would do it." Even though it ruined his career. And people ask me constantly, "You've done over fifty features and forty TV movies and whatever. Aren't you sick of talking about *Psycho*?" And the best answer I can give you is exactly what Tony Perkins said. And it's true. If we were privileged enough to be in something representing our industry and doing it in a way that was memorable, then we succeeded. That's our job. And he said it so beautifully and simply.

P: Were you ever asked to be an any of the sequels, like *Psycho II*, *III*, *IV* to play cameos or anything like that?

J: Oh my god, no!

P: No one has ever said to you, "Would you like to be in a sequel?" And you would've said?

J: Oh, please. "Get out. Oh, get out! How could Marion come back?"

P: Have you seen *Psycho II*?

J: I did see *Psycho II*. It wasn't as good to me. Not because of Tony but because they did what by that time you could do. It didn't have any suspense for me. There was no imagination. It was just the same old crap. The one picture I did like was *IV* because it was a prequel. I liked that because it gave me, even though we all made up our own thoughts about it, it did show how Norman got to be Norman. And I found that very interesting. I did like that.

P: What was the difference between working with Welles and Hitchcock? In *Touch of Evil* you didn't have the same kind of scene in the motel, but you had that horrible scene in which he kills the Akim Tamiroff character. How different was Welles in the way he approached a scene than Hitchcock?

J: Welles worked in a much different way. He used his camera brilliantly, just as Hitchcock obviously did, and he could be structured, but he was much more improvisational, and as I said, it wasn't that he couldn't sort of plan out a shot, because Hitchcock planned everything to the last second. Welles could do that as evidenced by the opening shot in *Touch of Evil*, which I think is one of the longest in cinematic history. And it's the first time I had ever worked on a feature with—I think they called it an Eyemo—a handheld camera. Handheld cameras were used in newsreels, but not in features, and that's the first time I had ever worked in a feature film using an Eyemo camera, so that he could get the odd, grotesque angles.

P: I think in a lot of ways, that scene, the way it's edited and the shock value, is a lot like the shower scene. It doesn't happen as fast but it's jagged, with all those weird angles, and it has the same effect: the culmination with Tamiroff's bloated face.

J: It really is.

P: Going back to that shower scene, I've always heard that to get more shock out of you, they used cold water.

J: That's not true.

P: In your book you said that wasn't true.

J: That's the spiel they do on the Universal tour. When they go along and they see the *Psycho* house and they say, "He turned on the cold water!" I was on the tour one day with my children, and I yelled out, "Not true!"

P: Oh, that would be terrific.

J: I did.

P: And nowadays they videotape the guy giving tours, and it would be great to see you say, "That's not true."

J: It's contrary. You read my book, so you know. Exactly the opposite happened. Mr. Hitchcock was so careful about the water being comfortable that the steam melted the adhesive on the moleskin.

P: Can I ask you a silly question? What the heck is moleskin?

J: Moleskin is soft, almost felt-like on the outside, nude colored, and adhesive on the inside.

P: So it doesn't show any of your body.

J: No, since it's nude here and adhesive here. And the steam was kind of pulling it away, and all the guys on the scaffold were getting an eyeful. That's true. So Hitchcock did not use cold water. I am an actress, and I don't need that.

P: A lot of feminist critics have taken Hitchcock to task. They say he's a misogynist and his female characters are always the objects of the male gaze. I mean you've seen probably all of Hitchcock's films, but do you think he's preoccupied with making women victims.

J: No, I think the percentages of male victims and female victims probably end up the same. I wish the feminists—I don't know why it has to be a classification—but I wish they would take time to think about right and wrong in every circumstance, instead of picking out just what they think is against women. It drives me crazy. I have no patience with that.

P: What about the symbolic undertones to the scene? One could see the shower scene as an inversion of the birth process with water, blood, nakedness, and a knife. But in this birth, the mother is destroying life rather than giving it.

J: I think that's bullshit. Excuse me. I think that's complete bullshit.

P: OK. Lastly, how did Hitchcock get this film by the Production Code? Because I have a letter here from the Production Code office that I got from the Hitchcock collection at the Margaret Herrick Library files, and it says they had to reject the film under the Code. And they said the opening sequence, the lovemaking in the bed, is "entirely too passionate" and then they said that there was a line to which they objected at script level and I think that's when Hitchcock took out: "The only playground that beats Las Vegas." They said the shower sequence opens with the Peeping Tom scene in which the murderer's watching her undress, but that is completely unacceptable. You can't do this. They pointed out that the shower scene has a number of shots, some completely realistic, of the nude girl's body and that all of these shots were in violation of the Code, which prohibited nudity "in fact or in silhouette." So I wondered, how did Hitchcock get away with this scene since they objected to so much of it?

J: What did he get away with? He got away with some things. But he didn't show nudity.

P: But they said "in fact or in silhouette." But there's a scene where behind the shower curtain . . .

J: But you don't see anything.

P: But I still think he pulled a fast one.

J: Well, I know exactly what he did. He put in such rash things that he knew they would take out and then, it was like levels. He would put in level C and A, hoping that would compromise it, so he would get B. I know that he deliberately put in that line about Vegas and there were a couple of other lines. I don't remember what they are now. But the point was, he was trying to get B, so he put in the C lines, hoping that the A lines would balance some of those. He'd say, "Well, you're going to take away that? Then you have to give me this." That's what he did. He had to have the piece of paper in the toilet. At that point, you'd never seen a toilet. You'd never seen a toilet in the bathroom. You'd never seen a toilet flush.

P: That was a real shocker.

J: And you had to. He had to. It was the only way, you know. So he put in a scene that sent them running with their hands in the air, screaming. And he said, "Jesus, you're trying to ruin my picture. If you take that, then you have to give me that toilet. That is necessary to my picture." And he would do this. He did another thing which I was not privy to, but this is what he told me and I think it was Hilton Green or somebody, Joe Stefano, I'm not sure who was the other person, so I heard it from two sources, so I have to assume it's true because they're both legitimate people. He had finished the film; he'd shown it to the Code people. This was after all the bargaining, taking away C so he can have B, and he showed them the finished picture. Half of the group said, "We saw nudity." The other half said, "Well, I don't think we did." The other half said, "We did." Hitchcock said, "I'll fix it. I'll take it out." A couple weeks later, he showed it to them again, but he hadn't done anything. The half that had seen nudity said, "Yep, see, you fixed it," but then the other half now saw it. And it's just all up here in your head.

P: Yeah. A + B = C. You show a knife coming down, you show this, and all of a sudden C happens up here.

J: It goes like that.

P: Yeah. It's the imagination. It's the imagination that was in *Psycho* that isn't in those other movies. Because in your mind, your mind sees that knife cutting flesh, but your eyes don't see it. And it was a nice touch to show the toilet because everybody knows there are toilets in bathrooms. Now you've got to show people sitting on them. That just offends me so much.

J: Not only that, you see them actually urinating.

P: *Psycho* defined my generation because I had seen *Alfred Hitchcock Presents* on television and we all knew who he was and it seemed to speak to me because of the way it was put together, the subject matter. And also its relative explicitness seemed to herald things to come. And I think that's why in the history of film, it's important.

J: I hate to put things to come on *Psycho* because *Psycho* never said not to use your imagination and to show everything. It said just the opposite. So I don't know why *Psycho* should get the blame for something that happened. I don't know which film it was, but they showed breasts. Well, then they showed nipples. Then they showed everything! And it wasn't *Psycho*. It was not. So I don't think *Psycho* should get the blame for that. If anything, *Psycho* is the perfect example of what not to show. I'll leave you with this thought. In *Gone with the Wind* when Rhett Butler sweeps Scarlett O'Hara up in his arms and they walk up that big flight of stairs. You see them walk up that flight of stairs. The next shot is her in bed in the morning. My imagination of what happened in that bedroom is so wild no one can ever take that from me. What happened in that bedroom happened to me. It was a wonderful night of my life. Today, they would show you what happened in that bedroom, and it would mean nothing. It would mean nothing. So frankly, *Psycho* is the one that said, "Don't show. Use your imagination."

CHAPTER 3

The Trip Continued

Two Intersecting Paths to *Psycho*

> Success and stability in the director's life had a way of driving him toward darkness and depth in his films.
>
> —PATRICK MCGILLIGAN

In 1959, at age sixty, Hitchcock was at the pinnacle of his art and of his career. He had entered the film industry in England in 1920, landing a job designing titles for the American film company, Famous Players-Lasky (later to be called Paramount Pictures, Inc.). To learn film making during the three years the studio stayed in England, Hitchcock took on as many responsibilities as he could and learned the whole process of creating movies, American style. He had spent formative years in Germany in 1924 designing sets for *The Blackguard* and in 1925 directing his first two feature films, *The Pleasure Garden* and *The Mountain Eagle*, in the process absorbing the style of the German Expressionistic cinema of Universum Film Aktiengesellschaft (Ufa) studios and of the great German directors F.W. Murnau and Fritz Lang. He had become a member of the Film Society of London and had seen and been influenced by the cinema of Soviet Socialist Realism and by the huge output of American silent film that was creating the Hollywood, or classical, style of cinema. He had directed the first sound film of the British cinema, *Blackmail*, in 1929, utilizing the new technique of sound creatively. He had become during the 1930s the greatest director in England, making a series of six films that became the classic formulation of the thriller genre. He had come to America in 1939 with a multipicture contract with David O. Selznick, under whose tyrannical control Hitchcock suffered for years. He persevered under Selznick, however, and during the process, mastered the artistic, financial, and technical intricacies of the studio system. He had also absorbed the essentials of the American landscape and character, directing in 1943 *Shadow of a Doubt*, his first American masterpiece. He had then proceeded to direct, and later produce and direct, films that experimented with subjective camera (*Notorious*); mise-en-scene, long takes, and color (*Rope*); 3-D (*Dial M for Murder*); black comedy (*The Trouble with Harry*); documentary-like realism (*The Wrong Man*); single-set filming (*Lifeboat*); psychoanalysis and surrealism (*Spellbound* and *Marnie*); and wide-screen composition (the VistaVision films at Paramount). He had also mastered the new medium of television, tailoring his stories and style to the stringent demands of the half-hour format and of commercial sponsorship. He had learned the art and craft of marketing, allowing himself to be promoted as the Master of Suspense and making cameo appearances in his films, thus guaranteeing that audiences saw the director as the prime creative force in cinema. He had become the subject of "serious" film criticism in the late 1950s, assuming the honorary title of "auteur" bestowed on him by the French critics associated with the influential film publication *Cahiers du Cinema*. Finally, as a result of all of the above, he had become, in Patrick McGilligan's words, "the most interviewed, most profiled, and most written about and analyzed Hollywood director of all time" (205).

In 1959 Hitchcock was ready for *Psycho* and the shower scene. Patrick McGilligan claims, "It is no exaggeration to say that Hitchcock had been waiting for *Psycho*—working up to it—all his life" (579). The movie would become the culmination of his career and the most influential film he had ever directed. It would help to provide the *coup de grace* to the already vitiated Production Code, which had been weakened during the decade of the 1950s by the influx of foreign films, by the retirement in 1954 of the Production Code's Czar, Joseph Breen, and by the challenge of domestic films released without the imprimatur of the Code's seal of approval. *Psycho* would introduce to the screen a much more frank representation of formerly taboo subjects and depictions, such as nudity, bathroom paraphernalia, including the infamous toilet bowl, illicit sexuality, and, by implication, incest and necrophilia. It would help to change distribution and exhibition practices by making the single film a movie "event," thereby altering the film program of double features, sandwiched by short subjects, cartoons, and newsreels. It would help to position the director as superstar, the prime creative force in cinema. Finally *Psycho* would change forever the nature of American films by subverting the classical Hollywood style and introducing what the critic Paul Monaco calls "the cinema of sensation" (190), creating a new kind of film: violent, ironic, psychoanalytical, iconoclastic, elliptical, youth oriented.

Psycho would have this seminal position mainly because of a single scene within the film, a scene that would come to epitomize the power of Hitchcock's combination of suspense and terror to shock and to frighten; that would define a new cinema aesthetic; that would both liberate the cinema from the strictures of the Production Code and shackle it to sex and violence: the shower scene. Perhaps no other film is as defined by a single scene as *Psycho*. The only other candidate is the Odessa Steps sequence in Eisenstein's *The Battleship Potemkin* (1925), but the Odessa Steps, for all its brilliant montage devices, is not a seminal scene. Donald Spoto says of the shower scene that it "changed the course of Hollywood history" (413), and ". . . has evoked more study, elicited more comment and generated more shot-for-shot analysis from a technical viewpoint than any other in the history of cinema" (419). It would become the apotheosis of Hitchcock's idea of "pure cinema," what Paul Monaco calls the heralding of a "powerful new visual aesthetic" (190), and it would make *Psycho* what Robin Wood names as "One of the key works of our age" (*Hitchcock's Films Revisited* 113).

If it's true that Hitchcock was able to revolutionize cinema because he was ready for *Psycho*, it's also true that *Psycho* was ready for him. A concatenation of events had made it a propitious time for Hitchcock and *Psycho* to come together. Hitchcock's life and career paralleled the growth and development of cinema. Born in 1899, four years after first film showing in 1895 by the Lumière Brothers in France, Hitchcock grew up with the film industry. As a young spectator, he was able to choose from the more than four hundred movie theaters and movie screenings in London in 1913 (Spoto 35). As his biographer Donald Spoto says of Hitchcock, "He was a devoted film buff from the age of fifteen, attending first screenings of the early French and German pictures. The work of Griffith—*Birth of a Nation* and *Intolerance* especially—made a great impression on him, as did the films of Keaton, Fairbanks, and Pickford" (38). When he entered the industry in 1920, Hitchcock was like a sponge, absorbing the technical and artistic aspects of film production. Throughout his career, Hitchcock would be an innovator and an experimentalist, a fact overlooked by some of his earlier critics who saw him merely as a genre director. He responded to technical innovations such as sound, color, and wide-screen with boldness and imagination. For example, after having shot *Blackmail* as a silent picture in 1929, Hitchcock decided to reshoot scenes with the new medium of sound and to release the film as a sound film—the first British talkie. Even with such a novel medium, Hitchcock used sound ingeniously, experimenting with subjective perception of sound (the famous "knife" scene) and with sound effects, just as he would do with long takes in *Rope* in 1948 and with the wide-screen format of VistaVision in the Paramount films of the 1950s. As Dan Auiler points out in his book on *Vertigo*, "Hitchcock's roots were in the art-film movement of the twenties, a movement concerned with experimentation and with the use of boldly symbolic imagery" (18). A devotee of what he called "pure cinema," Hitchcock would frequently subordinate plot elements to the cinematic demands and challenges of mise-en-scene and montage. His championing of form over content ["Who cares if the apples an artist paints are sweet or sour?" Hitchcock asks in one interview (*Inside Hitchcock*)] put him squarely in the camp of classical directors with a formalist or expressionistic bent. In fact, Tony Williams points out Hitchcock's "self-reflexive" techniques that are usually associated with experimental cinema. Williams claims, "Although Hitchcock later became identified with the Hollywood studio system, he was also influenced by the 'underground' films of his day which were first screened at the London Film Society from 1925 onwards" (53).

When I say that *Psycho* was ready for Hitchcock, I mean exactly that. It would take a veteran filmmaker—a director whose career had paralleled the development of cinema—to navigate the treacherous waters that the shower scene of *Psycho* represented. In a sense, this material could only be handled by someone like Hitchcock, whose earlier work would allow the radically new focus that *Psycho* required. As my colleague professor John Covolo has claimed about great innovations in the arts, "The man and the moment came together." Ever since his arrival in America in 1939, Hitchcock had been struggling with the economic and artistic limitations of the studio system. His ultimate goal was to secure the creative freedom to make the kinds of films he wanted to make. His struggles with David O. Selznick for creative control had taught him to be flexible and pragmatic in his filmmaking. In fact, Hitchcock states in an article he wrote for a film journal in 1948, ". . . I try to make my first rule of direction—flexibility" (Gottlieb, *Hitchcock on Hitchcock* 205). He took advantage of the limited freedom the system granted him, and he was able to use the tools of "pure cinema"—montage and mise-en-scene—to create films with extraordinary visual power. It is sometimes difficult for critics to see this visual power because they become preoccupied with Hitchcock's plot lines and plot elements. They fail to see the trees because of the forest. Hitchcock relied on genre—the comic thriller, for example, or film noir—and on the Master of Suspense label because they paradoxically gave him freedom to experiment.

Take, for instance, the extraordinary stalking scene from *Strangers on a Train*, during which Bruno follows Miriam and her two boyfriends to Leeland Lake Amusement Park. In this ten-minute, largely dialogue-less sequence, Hitchcock masterfully and slyly puts the viewers in the shoes of Bruno as he flirtatiously stalks the coquettish Miriam through the park, on the boat through the tunnel of love, and finally to the Magic Isle, where he strangles her to death. Hitchcock uses the classical style, mainly invisible editing, to shift the point of view of Bruno to the mind of the audience. Earlier in the film, we had seen Miriam attempt to blackmail Guy, so we have identified her as an antagonist. Hitchcock's triumph in this sequence is to meld Bruno with the audience in such a manner that the process of transference is hardly noticeable. Hitchcock accomplishes the transference early in the scene with a bit of wicked humor. As Bruno is following Miriam, a little boy in a cowboy hat carrying a balloon in one hand and a toy pistol in the other confronts him. Hitchcock uses a high angle to show the little boy from Bruno's point of view as the boy points his pistol at Bruno and says, "Stick 'em up! Bang, bang!" The next shot shows Bruno with a disgusted look on his face; he takes his cigarette and pops the boy's balloon. The startled look on the boy's face is a wonderful, cynical comeuppance enjoyed by Bruno and the audience. In Hitchcock's world, there are no angelic, innocent children. With a look of triumphant satisfaction on his face, Bruno walks away from the little urchin. And of course, the audience delights right along with him.

Donald Spoto analyzes Hitchcock's employment of the double theme in *Strangers on a Train* in his biography of Hitchcock. The double is Hitchcock's signature motif for suggesting the duality of human nature. Spoto says, "All this doubling . . . is the key element in the film's structure. [Bruno] is [Guy's] 'shadow,' activating what [Guy] wants, bringing out the dark underside of [Guy's] potentially murderous desires" (328). What Guy wants, of course, is to get rid of Miriam. In an earlier scene, Guy, in a fit of murderous rage, says of Miriam, "I could strangle her!" Through Bruno, Guy gets his wish, and through the medium of film, we get to murder Miriam as well. When he finally is able to get Miriam alone on the Magic Isle, Bruno kills her. In this stunning scene, Hitchcock bathes the shot in darkness as Miriam approaches the camera and comes to a stop in a full-face close-up. It is as if she were standing in front of us. Out of the right side of the frame comes a lighter, which when lit by Bruno, startlingly illuminates Miriam's face. An off-screen voice asks, "Is your name Miriam?" and as Miriam begins her answer—"Why, yes, how did you know . . . ?"

—a dark form steps into the frame, with his back toward us, and begins to strangle Miriam, cutting off her words and knocking off her glasses. The hunter has caught his prey. Bruno has become our surrogate murderer. Visually, he becomes our stand-in; his position in the frame matches our position as viewers. In this daring film, Hitchcock subtly uses the methods of the classical Hollywood style to create an experiment in point of view by perversely and subversively conjoining Bruno and the audience in a murderous quest, slyly set in the bright lights of an amusement park.

Strangers on a Train initiated what McGilligan calls "Hitchcock's most cohesive decade" (485). Nine years after this film, Hitchcock would create another pursuit and murder sequence, but in *Psycho* the setting is transformed from the neon lights and glittery fantasy of the Magic Isle of *Strangers on a Train* to the grim, deteriorating, and claustrophobic claustrophic atmosphere of the Bates Motel. Bruno has been morphed into Norman, Miriam into Marion. The double theme personified by two people—Bruno and Guy—has been collapsed into the single figure of Norman, who contains two warring characters and personalities. Norman was Hitchcock's and screenwriter Joseph Stefano's unique cinematic creation—a single figure housing two distinct personalities, a female and a male, a smothering mother and her oedipally fixated son, a virtual killing machine, a serial killer. For Hitchcock, Norman represents a departure from the cinematic characters he had created in his earlier films, characters developed within the dualistic tradition of his Catholic upbringing. In *Shadow of a Doubt*, Uncle Charlie represents the dark shadow of his niece, little Charlie. The two figures are separate but connected. The dark figure taints the morally purer one. In *Shadow*, for example, Charlie houses and ultimately protects her uncle, who is on the run from the police. But ultimately, light overpowers darkness. Little Charlie kills her uncle in self-defense and is a sadder but wiser character. The same is true in the conclusion of *Strangers on a Train*, in which Bruno and Guy struggle on the seemingly innocent merry-go-round in Leeland Lake, with Guy ultimately prevailing over the unrepentant Bruno, who refuses to admit his wrong doings but who dies with the evidence in his hand, which falls open as he dies and clears Guy of Miriam's murder. In *The Wrong Man*, the innocent Manny Balestrero is mistaken for the robber who is his physical double. Uncle Charlie and little Charlie, Bruno and Guy, the "real" robber and Manny Balestrero—these character pairs are essential parts of a Western moral tradition that polarized antagonistic characters into emblems of the eternal war between good and evil. Mrs.

Bates and Norman Bates are different, however; they are more like Robert Louis Stevenson's Dr. Jekyll and Mr. Hyde, but with a Hitchcockian twist. Instead of two characters who are opposite sides of one personality, Norma and Norman Bates are two *separate* characters housed in one person. In creating the cinematic version of Bloch's character, Hitchcock creates a monstrous perversion of nature, a son who gives birth to his own mother, whom he has earlier killed because she would no longer accept him as her lover ("A son is a poor substitute for a lover"). Norman is created in the same perverse imaginative mold as Mary Maloney in "Lamb to the Slaughter," from the 1958 episode of *Alfred Hitchcock Presents*—a pregnant mother who kills her authoritarian, police chief husband (read "father figure") in order to keep him from leaving her for another woman, just as Norman did to prevent his mother from leaving him. One could imagine the homicidal mother in "Lamb to the Slaughter" giving birth to an innocent male child, smothering him with a frustrated love and inflaming his oedipal desires. Thus do the Normans of the world get sacrificed and slaughtered by their monster-mothers.

The events that made *Psycho* ready for Hitchcock were a mix of cinematic, social, and cultural forces that sometimes collided but that mostly reinforced one another. The advent of television in the 1950s transformed popular culture and entertainment. In addition, the weakening of the Production Code coincided with the youth and adolescence of the baby boomer generation—the same generation that would rebel against the values of their parents and create a youth culture of rock music, rebellion, and sexual expression. The studio system, which had been undermined by the Paramount Decrees, began to crumble in the 1950s as television and other leisure-time activities competed for the traditional film audience. With the devolution of the studio system came the evolution of the director, in particular, the producer-director, who would gain the artistic freedom that had been denied to him by the strictures of the producer-dominated studio system. Increasingly, the beleaguered studios, having jettisoned the ironclad contracts that had chained talent to particular studios, began to develop deals with independent production companies. Lew Wasserman, Hitchcock's agent since 1946 and one of the most wily and astute figures in the history of Hollywood, negotiated production deals for Hitchcock with Paramount Studios. Ken Mogg states of this deal, "Before *Rear Window* entered production, Hitchcock signed an extraordinary contract with the studio, giving him complete creative control. It was also agreed that ownership of the films his production company made would be returned to

Hitchcock after eight years" (116). Patrick McGilligan says of Wasserman's negotiations, "But Wasserman's real coup passed almost unnoticed in 1954: a pioneering reversion clause that gave Hitchcock *ownership* of the five pictures he produced and directed, eight years after their initial release. The future implications of this clause would be astronomical" (479).

All of the above forces conspired to bring Alfred Hitchcock and *Psycho* together in 1959. The baby boomers provided the audience; television had educated them; youth culture had primed them. Hitchcock had become a fixture of television popular culture; his profile, his rotund figure and expressionless face, his careful and deliberately paced locutions, his droll and subversive commentaries—all of these had made him as famous as his films. This popularity had given Hitchcock the creative power that he had for so long craved. In his five-picture contract with Paramount, Hitchcock owed the studio one more film. He had bought the rights to Robert Bloch's novel *Psycho*, published in 1959 by Simon & Schuster, and had planned it as his next film after the very successful and popular *North by Northwest*. After reading the coverage of *Psycho* by the Paramount story department, studio President Barney Balaban and Vice President George Weltner decided that they did not want to make such a risky and controversial film. McGilligan claims, "Balaban was anxious to shift the studio's focus toward family musicals," so when Hitchcock's agent, the always resourceful Lew Wasserman, suggested a compromise, the Paramount executives jumped for it. Wasserman proposed that Hitchcock would defer his salary for a share of the film's ownership and that the film would be produced at Universal (McGilligan 580–581). Hitchcock seized the opportunity to finance the film himself, with Paramount acting as distributor. Stephen Rebello states about the deal, "As the sole producer, Hitchcock deferred his director's fee of $250,000 in exchange for 60 percent ownership of the negative. Such an offer Paramount could not—and did not—refuse" (29). *Psycho* was an enormous hit; Hitchcock had made one of the most profitable and successful films of all time.

When the idea for this book first took hold of my imagination, it was as if I were ready for *Psycho*, just as Hitchcock had been. I embarked on the research and writing at just about the same age that Hitchcock had been when he first thought about a film based on the Robert Bloch novel. My youthful film-going career had begun when Hitchcock had embarked on his Great Decade. In 1950, I was six years old and was just beginning my own "career" in film as an avid filmgoer. In the early 1950s, families were able to go to the movies together because films were produced with a moral purpose "guaranteed" by the Production Code. In the General Principles laid out in the first section of the Code, the authors—Father Daniel Lord, a Jesuit, and Martin Quigley, a Roman Catholic layman—state:

> The motion pictures which are the most popular of modern arts for the masses, have their moral quality from the minds which produce them and from their effects on the moral lives and reactions of their audiences. This gives them a most important morality.
>
> 1. They *reproduce* the morality of the men who use the pictures as a medium for the expression of their ideas and ideals.
> 2. They *affect* the moral standards of those who thru [*sic*] the screen take in these ideas and ideals. (Doherty 379)

Whether I went with my older sisters Elaine and Alice to the Saturday matinees at the Strand Theater or with my whole family to the Friday night movies at the Olympia or the Broadway, the double features I watched were strictly controlled not only in content, by the MPPDA's Production Code, but also in production, distribution, and exhibition, by the oligopoly of the studio system.

In 1950 when I was six years old, Hitchcock began work on *Strangers on a Train*, a film that would initiate his Great Decade, during which he produced an astonishing number of important films, also including: *I Confess* (1953), *Dial M for Murder* (1954), *Rear Window* (1954), *To Catch a Thief* (1955), *The Trouble with Harry* (1955), *The Man Who Knew Too Much* (1956), *The Wrong Man* (1956), *Vertigo* (1958), *North by Northwest* (1959), and *Psycho* (1960). Several of these films I remember seeing with my family. My parents enjoyed *I Confess*, in particular, because its "innocent man wrongly accused"—Hitchcock's characteristic protagonist—was a Catholic priest, and this hero was important to my blue-collar, Catholic family. *Rear Window*, too, became a family favorite because of its stars—Jimmy Stewart and Grace Kelly—and because of its unusual plot and setting. Both of these films "hid" their subversive themes and motifs within the classical style and thus not only "protected" young, impressionable viewers from the possible harmful effects of such material, but also older viewers who needed their morals confirmed and shored up. For example, *I Confess* presents its story of temptation, murder, betrayal, and extramarital affairs in an indirect, circumspect manner. *Rear Window* goes even further into forbidden territory in its dramatization of voyeurism, dismemberment, suicide, and sexuality, but it does so through Hitchcock's careful control of point of view so that audience members see things only at a distance and then only through the disjointed and limited point of view of the main character, L.B. Jeffreys.

Throughout most of Hitchcock's Great Decade, he was able to utilize the resources of the Hollywood classical style to treat his "adult" themes in metaphoric and indirect ways. For example, in *I Confess*, Hitchcock suggests an adulterous liaison between Ruth Grandfort and Michael Logan. Logan has just returned from the war, and Ruth, his former girlfriend, greets him at the port of Quebec. The war has estranged them, and Michael has returned with a strong calling to the priesthood. Not knowing that Ruth, rebounding from Michael's breaking off of their relationship, has married, Michael agrees to spend an afternoon with her on a sparsely inhabited island. A late-afternoon rain storm prevents them from catching the return ferry, and they spend the night in a gazebo. Employing the subtlety of classical editing, Hitch shows paired close-ups of the former lovers gazing into each other's eyes. A brief dissolve to a shot of Ruth awakening at dawn with a satisfied smile communicates to the adults in the audience that the two former lovers have spent the night together in the gazebo.

In *Rear Window*, even though Hitchcock conceals his violent and sexual themes within the style of the film, he presents some daring scenes. There is a shot of Miss Torso naked from the waist up but shown from the back in a long shot from the point of view of L.B. Jeffreys as he sits in his wheelchair. From this limited point of view, in a long shot, we see Miss Torso put on her bra when she bends over, in a dance move, to get something out of the refrigerator. She is wearing extremely short shorts, and as she bends over, we are given a distant view of the cheeks of her buttocks straining against her short shorts. Later, we (and L.B. Jeffreys) see Miss Torso in the shower, but we see her only from the shoulders up. The rest of her body is left up to our and L.B. Jeffreys' imagination. The Miss Torso episode in the film prefigures the shower scene in *Psycho*, but with the Code's restrictions still largely in operation. The murder of Thorwald's wife occurs in the apartment next to Miss Torso's. We suspect, but we are not told or shown directly, that Lars Thorwald has killed his wife and dismembered her in the bathtub. When we see Miss Torso's shoulder shot in the shower earlier in the film, we are given a symbolic foreshadowing of the dismemberment. Miss Torso's head is, in effect, separated from her body by the small window in her shower, just as Mrs. Thorwald's head is supposedly contained in the box that was previously buried under Thorwald's flower garden but is housed in his closet at the film's conclusion. The connection to the source of Hitchcock's *Psycho*, the Robert Bloch novel *Psycho*, is clear. Bloch's heroine, Mary Crane, the prototype for Marion Crane, is murdered in the shower, but she is not stabbed; rather, her head is cut off. This shocking scene is reworked by Stefano and Hitchcock in the famous shower scene, but Hitchcock's fascination with decapitation—metaphorically dramatized by him into the more "morally acceptable" act of strangulation—is vividly demonstrated in his reason for purchasing Bloch's novel. As Stefano points out in our interview, Hitchcock chose the novel "because of the murder in the shower."

In *Rear Window*, Hitchcock and his screenwriter, John Michael Hayes, could present these scenes of mayhem on the screen because they had kept their dramatizations within the bounds of the Code's restrictions, although these restrictions were becoming increasingly weaker as the decade wore on. The adults in the audience were able to understand the various plot lines in the film—Miss Lonely Heart's sexual and romantic fantasies; the newly married wife's insatiable sexual hunger in her honeymoon apartment; Lars Thorwald's butchering of his wife; Lisa Fremont's campaign of seduction of L.B. Jeffreys—but the younger members of the audience were "protected" by the oblique presentation of the potentially harmful material.

However, American cinema in general, and Hitchcock's films in particular, would begin to change because of the shock waves that were being generated by the transformations taking place in mid-century America. Much of the energy for those shock waves came from within the film industry itself. In 1948, the antitrust case against the studio system resulted in the Paramount Anti-trust Decrees, which eventually divested the studios of their lucrative theater chains. This case signaled the end of the oligopoly of the studio system and the resultant weakening of the hegemony of the classical style. Other sources of shock waves, though, came from outside the industry and from within society. What the critic Douglas Gomery calls "the social transformation of the United States" (21) began in the late 1940s and early 1950s, with the growth of suburbs and the emergence of the baby boomer generation.

Having been born in 1944, I was a pre-baby boomer, but I shared in that generations's impact on culture and society. Gomery claims that the shock wave that has been assigned the most powerful role—the evolution of television—was not *in itself* the major reason for the decline of the studio system and the reformation of the entertainment industry; the changes that were taking place were part of a larger change in the zeitgeist of the 1950s, of which television was just a part (23). In many ways, I consider myself a product of those forces that were reshaping the industry and that would culminate in the film that capped the decade of the 1950s—*Psycho*. I spent much of my youth watching films that were made within the studio system and that were therefore characterized by the Production Code and the classical Hollywood style. The key aesthetic experience of my adolescence had taken place in the Olympia Theater that September night in 1960, when Hitchcock revolutionized cinema and in the process set me off on a journey that would culminate in a book written partly about that fateful night. At the same time, though, I was also a member of the generation that shared a youth and adolescence with the medium of television. My family got its first television in 1950, just about the time that I began going to the movies. The television helped to transform our family—and the nation—from a movie and radio popular culture to a movie and television popular culture, and eventually to a largely television popular culture. Much of my earlier adolescent years had been spent witnessing television mold and transform American popular culture. From age eleven through age sixteen, I had seen most of the episodes of *Alfred Hitchcock Presents*, absorbing much of the subversive "message" the series carried as its subtext: that the American family—the paragon of virtue in postwar America—harbored within the walls of its urban and suburban homes destructive forces of sexuality and violence. The American family was both imploding and exploding: Norman Bates, the boyish psychopath, would be its symbol and poster boy.

My sister Alice remembers the dramatic alteration of social spaces and of family relationships that occurred in our flat when the television—an eight-inch Crosley—arrived. Before the television, the social space in our flat was the kitchen, where the radio had its honored place. I remember sitting at the kitchen table and listening to *Our Gal Sunday* while eating my mother Angie's delicious chicken soup. The modest parlor in the back of our flat was reserved for company and was largely unused. Its couch, complete with decorative doilies, was still in relatively new shape. When the television arrived, however, the social space became the parlor, and the couch was where the family sat to watch the small screen. As my sister Alice says in her inimitable way, "In a year, the couch was wrecked and the doilies had disappeared!" In that relatively small shift in space from the kitchen to the parlor—no more than twelve feet in our small, cold-water flat—lay a much larger shift in the culture of the American family. By the time that *Alfred Hitchcock Presents* premiered in 1955, many families in America spent their evenings glued to tiny television screens and were enslaved to rabbit-ear antennas that required a surgeon's delicacy of touch to get a semblance of a clear picture. The TV dinner, which revolutionized America's culinary habits, was invented to take advantage of this cultural shift.

When *Alfred Hitchcock Presents* premiered in 1955, I was eleven years old. The changes that would transform American culture in the 1960s had already started to manifest themselves. The first rock-and-roll concert had taken place in 1952 in Cleveland. Called the "Moondog Coronation Ball," it launched a revolution in popular culture that would create a youth culture with its own music and dress. Deriving its identity through rebelling against the togetherness and conformity of the parents who reared it, this generation identified itself with the violence and eroticism of rock lyrics and music, and of movie star rebels. In films, the teenage rebel became a popular film protagonist. Marlon Brando in the *The Wild One* (1954) and later James Dean in *Rebel Without a Cause* (1954) set the standard for the attractive but nihilistic or misunderstood antihero. At the same time, the quintessential American genre of the Western was turning inside out with the onset of the adult Western. When *Alfred Hitchcock Presents* premiered, Hitchcock himself directed the first episode, entitled "Revenge," and he included within its twenty-five minutes or so of this first episode the topics of rape, madness, and murder.

This first episode is emblematic of the cracks that began to appear in the culture of the 1950s. Vera Miles plays Elsa Spann, a newlywed who has moved to California with her engineer husband, Carl Spann (Ralph Meeker), to recover from a "nervous breakdown" caused by the stresses of her dancing career. The newlyweds settle in a trailer park on the California coast, and the episode begins with Carl going off to work and leaving Elsa to relax. Choosing to sunbathe outside her trailer while she waits for a cake to finish baking, Elsa dons a daring two-piece bathing suit, and Hitchcock's camera, assuming the point of view of Mrs. Ferguson, a disapproving next-door neighbor, pans the full figure of Elsa, revealing her halter top, bare midriff, and long, shapely legs. We then cut to a long shot of the husband driving to the trailer later in the day. Opening the trailer door, he sees smoke from the burned cake and discovers his wife has been "badly beaten" (read: raped). Her destroyed innocence is symbolized by the crushed carnation she holds in her hands, and her description of the attack ("He killed me") is sufficiently elliptical to protect the younger viewers such as me. The attack has caused the young wife to descend into a psychotic state, the depths of which are not fully realized by the husband, who, following the advice of the doctor, decides to get Elsa away from the trailer and the scene of the crime and to go for a ride before checking into a hotel. Sitting in the passenger seat, and gazing vacantly, Elsa notices a man wearing a gray suit and fitting the description the police had given the husband of a stranger spotted near the trailer park. The wife says, "There he is. That's him." The enraged husband pulls the car to the curb, follows the man into his hotel room, and beats him to death with a wrench, the violence suggested by shadows on the wall rather than shown graphically. The husband hides the murder weapon in his sleeve, hurriedly returns to the car, and begins driving. After a moment or two, Elsa sees another man matching the description and says, "There he is. That's him. That's him." The episode concludes on a close-up of Carl's face as he realizes that his wife is psychotic and that he has probably killed an innocent man.

"Revenge" was an auspicious debut for Hitchcock's show. It would anticipate *Psycho* in its mad stare, its revenge killing, and its ironic ending. The erotic image of Elsa sunbathing would foreshadow the view of Marion lying half-naked in the bed at the beginning of *Psycho*. The major difference between "Revenge" and *Psycho* is, of course, the explicitness of the violence and sexuality. Although we see Elsa in a two-piece bathing suit, we do not see her get attacked, nor do we see her husband actually beat the would-be assailant with the wrench. The five years between "Revenge" and *Psycho* would seem like five light years when *Psycho* premiered. Given the differences between television and movie censorship (with network television always more conservative), it's amazing that in 1955 *Alfred Hitchcock Presents* could dramatize such material on television. In many ways, the series laid the groundwork for *Psycho*. In fact, James Naremore claims, "*Alfred Hitchcock Presents* led directly to *Psycho*, Hitchcock's most brilliant and frightening exercise in black humor" (22).

When the studio oligopoly was destroyed by the Paramount decrees, the monopoly of the Hollywood style started to come undone. Moreover, as Richard Randall claims, ". . . the authority of the Production Code had also been undercut as a result of an antitrust decree in 1948 requiring production companies to divest themselves of interest in theaters. Previously, five majors had controlled 70 percent of the first-run theaters in major cities and about 45 percent of all film rentals in the country. With such concentration, they possessed tremendous economic leverage on all other elements in the industry. In unhinging their power and forcing decentralization upon the industry, the decree indirectly cut the power of their creature, the Production Code" (512). In addition, the Production Code was seriously weakened by the retirement in 1954 of Joseph Breen, the head of the Code, and by a series of challenges to the Code's authority by films that were released without the Code's all-important seal of approval. One of these films was *The Moon Is Blue* (1953). In one of my after-school forays to the Olympia Theater—this time with my girlfriend, Kathleen Sullivan (our "romance" consisted of holding hands in the Olympia)—Kathleen and I were turned away at the box office because the film was "adults only." Disappointed, we walked to my flat, where my incredulous mother vowed to return to the theater with us to secure our admission. Thanks to my mother, my girlfriend and I ended up seeing *The Moon Is Blue*, but the "adult" content—the words "virgin" and "seduce" and some subtle references to seduction and sex—went over our heads. The real significance of *The Moon Is Blue* was not its content but its release and distribution without the Production Code's Seal of Approval. The first cracks in the Code were starting to reveal themselves. As Leonard Leff and Jerold L. Simmons claim about the film, "It seemed to demonstrate that the mighty Production Code Administration and Legion of Decency had withered, that courageous filmmakers could now afford to probe once-taboo subjects without concession to Breen and the Catholic fathers" (208).

Other assaults on the monolithic power of the Code came from outside of Hollywood. Some European films without the Code's seal penetrated the film market of large American cities, and these franker, more daring movies symbolized the revolution in taste and morality transforming American culture. On Saturdays, I and my friends Tommy Zizza and Joe Donarumo took the subway to Boylston Street in Boston to see these movies. It was 1958, and I was thirteen years old. After we got off the subway and walked up to street level, we went to Joe and Nemos for a snack—three hotdogs for fifty cents and three hamburgers for the same amount. Since there were no tables, we ate standing up. Then we walked down Boylston Street to the State Theater to see the latest foreign films to hit town. In 1957, we saw *And God Created Woman* and in 1956, a revival of the steamy 1949 Italian classic *Bitter Rice*. These films were adult in tone and theme, and Tommy, Joe, and I particularly enjoyed seeing Silvana Mangano with her skirt hiked up and Brigitte Bardot nearly naked.

The 1960s would witness Hitchcock's filmmaking career start to decline as, paradoxically, his critical reputation started to grow. My own student and teaching career parallels the ascent of Alfred Hitchcock. When I went to college in 1962, just as *The Birds* premiered, the University of Massachusetts offered no film classes. It wasn't until 1965–1966, during my senior year, that the college offered its first course in film. To fill this gap, my friend Dan Miller and I formed the American Film Classics series in 1964 in order to bring great films to campus. It's hard to realize in this digital age of DVDs, cable, and Blockbusters, that it was almost impossible to view the masterpieces of cinema. Except for large cities like Boston, New York, and Los Angeles, most cities and towns lacked repertoire theaters to see classic films. Some college campuses had a film series, and it was these isolated pockets that kept international films and American film classics alive. However, there were no Hitchcock films on Dan's and my list of American Film Classics. Hitchcock had not really made it into the pantheon of great filmmakers. But things were beginning to change.

During the 1970s, as film courses proliferated in colleges, Hitchcock entered the academy and became the subject of serious academic study. For the next twenty years, the reputation of Hitchcock and of his films experienced a meteoric rise, mainly due to the influence of the French critics and of the auteur theory on American film criticism and scholarship. The groundwork for this rise had been laid twenty years earlier in France. A few years before Hitchcock began work on *Psycho*, a slim volume of Hitchcock criticism was published in France that would dramatically change critical opinions not only of Hitchcock's films but of Hitchcock himself. Entitled *Hitchcock* (1957), this first book-length, critical study of Hitchcock by Claude Chabrol and Eric Rohmer, French film critics associated with the fledgling but influential film journal *Cahiers du Cinema* and, later, filmmakers themselves, made the startling claim that Hitchcock was not just a suspense genre director but that he was a creative genius who drew upon the great moral traditions of Christianity and Catholicism for his films: sin, guilt, retribution, punishment. As Patrick McGilligan claims, "The critics of *Cahiers* and *Positif*—an equally serious rival French journal—began to redefine Hitchcock as an artist in such a persuasive, assertive fashion that the rest of the world was ultimately forced to take notice" (514). The editors of *Cahiers* actually devoted a whole issue to Hitchcock in 1956 (514). The publication of the English version of Truffaut's *Hitchcock* in 1967 also helped to put to rest the stereotype of Hitchcock as a genre director. In his introduction, Truffaut claims that, among the Hollywood greats, Hitchcock ". . . is the most complete film-maker of all" (18). In that same year, Jean Douchet published his *Alfred Hitchcock*, in which he claims that Hitchcock's films run the gamut, "from pure sensation to pure intelligence" (Sloan 393). As a result, the film critical establishment began to accept Hitchcock as something more than the Master of Suspense. As Jane Sloan points out in her comprehensive *Alfred Hitchcock: A Filmography and Bibliography* (1995), "Until 1965 . . . Hitchcock had been the object of deliberate study mostly in languages other than English" (15). This sluggish Anglophone appreciation of Hitchcock was ameliorated somewhat by the publication in 1965 of Robin Wood's *Hitchcock's Films*, the first line of which asks the provocative question, "Why should we take Hitchcock seriously?" (7). This question was answered by a slew of publications over the next twenty-five years, including the structural criticism of Raymond Bellour and William Rothman, the political studies by John Smith, the psychoanalytical approaches of Bellour and Bill Nichols, the feminist criticism by Laura Mulvey and Tania Modleski, and the film history approach of Tom Ryall. In 1963, the Museum of Modern Art presented the first serious retrospective of Hitchcock's work, coordinated by Peter Bogdanovich. The publication that accompanied this retrospective—*The Cinema of Alfred Hitchcock*—contains excerpts from a long interview that Bogdanovich undertook with Hitchcock over three days at Hitchcock's office at Universal. The booklet also contains analyses of Hitchcock's films and television programs. It is perhaps startling to a contemporary Hitchcock scholar to read Bogdanovich's claim about Hitchcock's films in the second paragraph: "The sort of movies he makes—thrillers, mysteries, macabre comedies, suspense films—are considered by American critics as lowbrow and not art" (3). In that same year, Hitchcock's *The Birds* was chosen to open the Cannes Film Festival, and in 1968 the Academy of Motion Picture Arts and Sciences awarded the Irving Thalberg Award to Hitchcock. The University of Southern California offered the first university retrospective of his work in 1968. The embrace of Hitchcock by the intellectual establishment culminated in 1972, when he was awarded an honorary doctorate by Columbia University.

I taught my first college film class in 1971. Called "History of Cinema," the class reflected the growing acceptance of film as an academic pursuit. For the next twenty years, I added film classes to the curriculum in such areas as the Western, film noir, and screwball comedy. In 1991, I taught my first class specifically devoted to the films of Alfred Hitchcock. During this twenty-year period, 1971–1991, Hitchcock scholarship had grown geometrically. After Hitchcock's death in 1980, the process of reappraisal accelerated rapidly. Donald Spoto's 1983 biography, *The Dark*

Side of Genius, aided the reappraisal effort by subverting the image of the humorous eccentric and Master of Suspense. To Spoto, Hitchcock's dark side was reflected in both his personal and professional life. In addition, Kapsis points out that Hitchcock's own publicity machine deliberately sought to paint Hitchcock as a serious artist, and the systematic rerelease of five of Hitchcock's films in 1983 aided this effort.

In the last decade or so, Hitchcock scholarship has outpaced that of almost all other directors, a phenomenal growth evidenced by the holdings in the OhioLINK system. The first of its kind in the country, this online system links the holdings of eighty-four Ohio public and private colleges and makes available the vast intellectual resources of scholarly books and articles to college students around the state. Under the subject heading of Hitchcock, there are 243 entries, 102 of which are books and videos about Hitchcock, including biographies, encyclopedias, interviews, bibliographies, filmographies, and art exhibit catalogues. Under the specific heading of "Criticism and Interpretation," there are sixty-four books listed, fifty-two of which were published in the last fifteen years. On *Psycho*, alone, nine books are listed, all but two of which have been published since 1990, including Robert Kolker's *Alfred Hitchcock's Psycho: A Casebook* (2004). And the 2003 publication of Patrick McGilligan's biography—*Alfred Hitchcock: A Life in Darkness and Light*—will no doubt generate other works. Scholarly periodicals have arisen solely devoted to the work of the Master of Suspense: *The Hitchcock Annual* and *The MacGuffin*, this last edited by Ken Mogg and featuring a very extensive website. The scholarship and criticism—including this book—continue unabated. Hitchcock, dead since 1980, has become what the baseball scouts call a "phenom."

Finally, the direction, thrust, and effect of Hitchcock scholarship are most vividly and convincingly seen in a poll published in the British Film Institute's publication *Sight and Sound*. Begun in 1952 and taken every ten years, the poll surveys international critics (and directors for the last two polls) on the ten greatest films ever made. In 1952, over half the films in the list were silent films, and half foreign films. No Hitchcock films were listed. Ten years later, *Citizen Kane* had rocketed to first place, reflecting a new orientation to American cinema effected by the French critics of an auteurist slant and by the burgeoning of film classes in the academy. In the 1982 poll, the first Hitchcock film appeared—*Vertigo*, rated in seventh place—reflecting the increased stature of Hitchcock among the critical establishment. In the 1992 poll, *Vertigo* had moved into fourth place, and it had tied for sixth place in the newly conceived Director's

Poll. Not surprisingly, *Vertigo* was ranked second in the 2002 poll, slowly creeping up on the venerable *Citizen Kane*. I predict that *Vertigo* will supplant *Citizen Kane* in the 2012 poll and that *Psycho* will be on the list. Hitchcock's critical star is still on the rise. During the 1970s and even into the 1980s, Welles was considered the genius of American cinema, even though his total output of films was extremely low. Of the fifteen or so films that Welles directed, only one, *Citizen Kane*, was complete, in the sense that the finished product represented Welles' vision (he had final cut, an extraordinary power in the studio-dominated 1940s). In the 1970s, Welles' reputation was at its high point with the publication of Pauline Kael's *The Citizen Kane Book: Raising Kane* (1971). But after *Citizen Kane*, Welles became an anathema to the studios; his politics and his flamboyant personality, coupled with his undisciplined approach to production and postproduction, made him a pariah. In all, it appears that Hitchcock's star is on the rise as Welles' is dimming.

If it's true that I was ready for *Psycho*, then it is certainly true that *Psycho* was ready for me, but it was ready in a very specific way: through the shower scene. In 2000, when I decided to apply for a sabbatical to work on a Hitchcock book, I had no idea that I would settle upon a single scene for my topic. I had begun with the idea of focusing on Hitchcock's use of narration and knowledge in building suspense in the films of his Great Decade. After I was awarded a sabbatical and a research grant from Lakeland Community College, I traveled to Los Angeles to visit the Margaret Herrick Library, which is part of the Fairbanks Center for Motion Picture Study of the Academy of Motion Picture Arts and Sciences. The Herrick Library contains the largest collection of Hitchcock materials as part of their special collections holdings. As I began my research, I was drawn more and more by the siren call of a single film—*Psycho*—and by a single scene in the film.

The actual idea of writing a book on the scene grew out of the increasing specialization of Hitchcock scholarship, which has evolved from general studies of Hitchcock's films to book-length analyses of individual films themselves. The idea came to me in a most serendipitous way and venue: the shower. Just as once before I had conceived of my dissertation topic in the shower at the house of my in-laws, Doris and Todd Simon, in Shaker Heights, Ohio, I now received a similar flash of inspiration in the shower of the Luxe Summit Bel Air Hotel in Los Angeles, California. Perhaps it was because I was in the actual city where the scene had been shot, or because two days before I had spent almost three hours interviewing

Janet Leigh, who lives only a few miles from the hotel, about her recollection of the shower scene, or because the day before I had spent an entire afternoon at Joseph Stefano's house talking about how he had worked with Hitchcock and how they had conceived the shower scene, or because forty years ago I had been part of the audience that Janet Leigh and Joe Stefano and Alfred Hitchcock had conspired to terrify—whatever the reason, I, unlike Marion Crane, emerged safely from the shower with my idea buzzing around in my head. The first place I headed to was my laptop, where I searched online on Google. I typed in "Psycho+shower scene," and to my astonishment I got 18,000 hits. I knew my topic had found me!

given to author by Joseph Stefano

Joseph Stefano with Hitchcock during the writing of *Psycho*

CHAPTER 4

Joseph Stefano

Joseph Stefano worked as a writer *in both film and television. His most famous film work is* Psycho, *but he also did the autobiographical screenplay for* Two Bits. *His television series* The Outer Limits, *which he produced, was groundbreaking. Joe did the screenplay for* Psycho IV *and wrote a play about working with Hitchcock on* Psycho. *Joseph Stefano died on August 25, 2006.*

P: How did you become associated with Hitchcock?

J: An agent at MCA, the biggest and best agency in the business, had been subtly romancing me. When I realized that the smaller agency I was with didn't quite know what the hell to do with me, I moved to MCA—but, with the proviso that they get me a film with one of ten directors I felt could teach me what I needed to know about making movies. Hitchcock's name was at the top of my list. And he was about to embark on a highly secret project. He politely refused to so much as meet with me. They had shown him my first film, *The Black Orchid*, and he thought it "too kitchen-sink." My award-winning *Playhouse 90*, "Made in Japan," he found "important but not my cup of tea." Of course, I knew none of this at the time. The first I heard about it was when MCA agents on both coasts had hounded him into a meeting and I received from Hitchcock's office a copy of a book by Robert Bloch named *Psycho*. As I read it, I thought, "This is exciting, very oedipal. This guy and his mother, and she's going to kill any girl he looks at." And then at the end of the book I found out the mother was dead. I felt it impossible to put that on the screen. So during our first meeting, I said to Mr. Hitchcock, "Here's how I would fix this. The movie's about Marion, not about Norman." Most of the pitch I made up driving from my analyst's office in Beverly Hills to Hitch's office at Paramount. The rest of it I made up as I was looking at his face. And he was just sitting there, with his hands on his stomach. He didn't say a word. He just kept on looking at me. And when I was finished, Hitchcock leaned forward and said, "We could get a star."

P: His mind was working as he was listening to you.

J: Right. As I worked with Hitchcock, I came to realize that you must deal with him on a photographic level. He must know what's going to be on the screen. The dialogue is your business. The backstory is your business. The characterizations, the reasons why people do what they do are all your business. In effect, Hitch would say, "Don't bother me with that. You come up with it."

P: He needs to see it in his head.

J: Yes. So I just would describe every scene exactly as you saw it on the screen except for some changes that he made. But he made no changes in dialogue, except some cuts that I had bracketed for that purpose. I said, "If you need to cut anything, cut these." And I was on the set all the time. He was just an unbelievable person. I had no idea about filmmaking because I was so new. And Hitch just told me anything I wanted to know and drew sketches for me of how cameras get that feeling that they're talking to you.

P: I don't know if maybe this is too personal a question, but you said you were in analysis before you wrote this script. Do you think you got interested in the Bloch book because of your interest in psychology through your analysis?

J: Psychoanalysis was my religion at that time. My life is in layers. My very first analysis made it possible for me to get rid of the neuroses that were stopping me from being able to get married and have children and have real love with somebody. So I achieved that, and I got married. I met Marilyn, and we got married. And then she got pregnant, which we decided would happen, and then we moved out here, and my whole career changed. All of a sudden, I was a Hollywood writer. And I felt that I didn't know if I could deal with this. This was a lot, you know. So I went into analysis again. That analysis was the one that I was in while I was doing *Psycho*.

P: Was it Freudian?

J: Yes, yes.

P: So do you think that, when you got this Bloch book, you were drawn to the psychoanalytical angle of it?

J: Yes, I think that there had always been a very dark side to me, and although my first movie was *The Black Orchid*, a tender love story between two widows, I took to *Psycho* like I had been waiting for it.

And I feel that I got kind of typecast as a result of it and lost a lot of jobs that I would love to have had, but at the same time, as a result of it, I produced and co-created *The Outer Limits*, a big series on television for over a year. Nothing but good has come from writing the *Psycho* screenplay. A lot of trouble came from it, however, while I was writing it because of the analysis, having a session in the morning and then getting in my car and driving to Paramount and being with Hitch all day. He was very interested in my analysis. I don't think he ever met a person who had openly announced that he was in analysis. In those days it wasn't so well accepted. Remember, there was a politician sometime in the '60s who had to drop out of the race.

P: Yes, he was depressed and he had electric shock treatment; he was from Missouri: Eagleton. It was a big scandal.

J: Yes, he had had psychiatric treatment. So I just felt, well if I act like I'm not supposed to talk about it, that's just going to make it worse. So I told Hitch very early on. As a matter of fact, he wanted to meet at 9:00 every morning, and I said to my agent—when he said, "You got it; you got the job, Joe. Great!—"Yeah, but I can't take it now." I told him why, and he said, "So drop out of analysis for a while till you finish the picture." And I said, "No, my life and my wife and my son depend on my getting through this analysis." So he went back in, and he told Hitch I couldn't make it till 10:30, and Hitchcock said it was fine. But then Hitch wanted to know about it. He used to ask me very funny questions like, "Do you have as much fun here as you do in your sessions?" And one time he said, "What do you talk about?" And I gave him a brief rundown of what was going on at that moment. And he said, "Do you talk about other people?" And I said, "Well, I talk about my wife, and my son and you." And he had this wonderful look on his face, like, "Thank God," you know. If I hadn't said that, he would've felt hurt.

P: Yeah, right, like "How come you're not talking about me?"

J: You're working with Alfred Hitchcock and you're not talking about it!

P: Now there's a man who would have been a fascinating subject. Can you imagine an analyst, a skillful analyst, getting into Alfred Hitchcock's mind, his past and his relationship with his mother and with his distant father?

J: You know, I always had the feeling, not from anything that he told me but from things that he said, that he had slightly exaggerated that whole thing with his mother, and it happened right around the time that he was making *Psycho*, and I told him one day that I had found out in my analysis that there was a time when I was tempted to kill my mother, and that's why I understood Norman. I said sometimes they just do things you've got to kill them for.

P: There's no other way!

J: You know you can't go to the police and say, "My mom's trying to castrate me," and expect them to say, "All right, we'll hang her."

P: No, they'll say, "Go home."

J: And so I felt like he exaggerated a little bit about his mother, and the reason I feel this way is two years ago, it was his centennial, Nicole and Ted Haimes did a very, very good documentary called *Dial H for Hitchcock* and it's full of home movies of him and Alma and Pat when Pat was a little girl, and he's doing the wildest things. He gets inside Pat's little playpen and grabs the bars and does a caged ape. And I thought, "He's having way too much fun." Well, he, in person, in private, was very funny and very, very sexually interested. He'd do everything but ask you, "Who are you fucking?" And I think one of the things that he was initially worried about regarding working with me was that I was a kid from South Philadelphia who hadn't even graduated high school and went to New York and became a chorus boy. But *that* turned out to be the very thing he most enjoyed, the street kid. So it was a gorgeous relationship. I've never had a professional relationship like that with anybody in my career since.

P: And that's so different from John Michael Hayes, who said Hitchcock was ungenerous to him. They had that struggle with the screenplay credit, and then Hitchcock just cut him off. And then there's Donald Spoto's book, in which he paints Hitchcock as an ungenerous, unpleasant man.

J: That may be a side to him, but it's not one that I ever saw. It really isn't. I never saw it in relation to anybody else, either. We were like old, old friends. It finally got to the point where he could tell what kind of session I'd had. When I walked in, he'd say, "Good session" or "Bad session."

P: How long did you work with him on the screenplay for *Psycho*?

J: Well, we never really did any writing through this first period. We just pictured it, and now and then I would make a note. After we had laid out how *Psycho* was going to look, he said, "Now you go home and write it." And I wrote it in three weeks and gave it to him, and he said, "I'll see you here tomorrow because I want you to be involved in the preproduction and all of the hard work and everything." And the next morning I walked in and he said, "Alma loved it." I realized that if Alma loved it, no changes were going to be made.

P: I am interested in how you pictured the shower scene. In the book the female character gets decapitated; it's gruesome, but very short. When you read the book, did that stand out to you as a challenge or something you were going to do something with?

J: Well, Hitchcock said, "We've got to talk about that murder scene." And I said to him, "You're not going to cut her head off, are you?" And he said, "Oh my, no. We can't cut Janet Leigh's head off." That's how he told me that Janet Leigh had the part.

P: Oh, OK. You didn't know this up until that point?

J: No. Right after that news, I gave him my reasoning about the murder scene. After the shower scene, we've lost the person we were with, that we identified with, that we cared about. Remember, we didn't want that cop to arrest her. We wanted her to get away with the money. We're all such felons at heart. Then suddenly she's dead. She's buried in a swamp, and you cannot doubt that she's dead. And so I said to Hitch, "At that time, the movie is over unless we get the audience to care about Norman." And he said, "How would *you* get the audience to do that?" And I said, "Well, first of all we give Norman a long, drawn out cleaning-up sequence. It's like the time my mother made me clean up my father's vomit when he came home drunk and got ill. I hated him for it; I hated her for it; I hated the job I had to do; I felt humiliated. It was only because I was the youngest child that I had to do this. We can get that kind of emotion from the audience. We want them to feel, 'Oh this poor guy; he has to clean up after his homicidal mother.'" I said *that* should be a long, drawn-out scene. And he was a little worried about that. He said, "I don't know whether the audience will want to watch that." And I said, "Force them to! Make them sit there and watch this nice, young man, who, by the way, is not a nice young man in the book." Anthony Perkins was a dream because he was just the kind of guy who would *be* in that situation.

P: Yes, looking in the bathroom and wanting to throw up because of the bloody violence.

J: Exactly. But he can't report her; he can't let anybody put his mother away: "I know you're crazy, mother and I know you kill people, but I love you." And that's mom. It's very much the way we're raised, to feel that way. So I said that I felt that the murder scene—we didn't call it the shower scene then, we called it the murder scene—should be over almost before it begins. And then he said that he didn't want to see the knife touching the body, and I asked him, "How will you get that across? The knife goes like this, and then we cut to a fake wound?" And he said, "Oh no, no. We don't need any of that. This is a murder that is taking place in the audience's mind, and it should be just a flash." Then he talked about Saul Bass doing some drawings for it.

P: Whose idea was it? Did Saul Bass approach him?

J: Mr. Bass was doing the titles.

P: I wonder who came up with the idea, whether Hitchcock asked Bass or Bass asked him because, you know, there is all that controversy about who really directed that scene.

J: Oh, I think Saul was out of his mind to say he'd directed it. The set was loaded with people. A lot of us are still alive. He should have waited till we had all died before he said that he directed it. Hitchcock said to me, "I want you to put the shower in the movie. She gets in the shower. The door opens; somebody comes in." And then he said, "Make something up," and I said something about "the knife flashing."

P: Yes, because that's what it says in the script.

J: Yes. He said, "Don't tell them it's going to be this series of fast shots in which we will see parts of her body and her face and blood." He wasn't interested in blood on the body, as a shock. You never see any blood on the body. The blood is only in the water. He didn't want to put blood on her. He just felt that he didn't want her feeling uncomfortable, so they made a very skillful bra for her.

P: Janet talked about it in our interview. I didn't understand what moleskin was, so I asked her to tell me, and she gave me a pretty good explanation of what she was wearing.

J: And Hitchcock said he wanted her to be comfortable, and he kept down the number of people on the set. And he also wanted to hire a nude model. Janet says he didn't. She said that the nude model was not true. But it was true. And I hate to contradict Janet because I adore her.

P: She insists that there was no shot of the knife going into the belly. I didn't want to contradict her and say, "I've got the shot, and I'll show it to you." But the knife does go into the stomach for one brief instant, and I guess they must have made some kind of a device there, but she insisted it didn't happen, so I didn't want to argue with her.

J: Well, she got very upset with me because I said there was a nude model there. But Hitch said to me, "If I hire someone whose job it is to be naked, they're going to be very relaxed and they're going to do what I tell them to do. If I ask Janet to be naked, she's not going to like it." And in those days you didn't have naked stars on the set.

P: No wonder it was a closed set. I don't know if you said this in one of your interviews, but John Gavin came on the set when they were shooting a scene he wasn't in, and he looked and there was a naked woman running around. He said, "What the hell's going on?"

J: She definitely was a very, very well-built model. I mean look at that belly scene!

P: I told Janet Leigh that I was sixteen years old when I saw *Psycho*. I was sitting with my friend Ralph Spinelli and we were like you guys from South Philly. I was a street kid from Chelsea, Massachusetts, no-nonsense. Ralph was my good buddy. We sat there, and he grabbed my arm. It was the most potent, sexual, violent scene; my head was spinning afterward, and it scared the hell out of me. I got turned on and turned off at the same moment.

J: Well, I think a lot of people were bothered by it because it turned them on. And the violence didn't prevent that. And so you know, I said to people that told me that, "Well, you did know that you were at the movie, and this was faux violence. That girl did not really get killed." But the truth is, there's something about the total helplessness of this woman. The thing that used to break my heart about it was a final shot that Hitchcock couldn't put in the movie, because he knew the censors would not allow it. It's a high overhead shot of Marion, lying over the tub, and that shot prevented any sexual thought. All I could think was, "All that youth, all that beauty. All down the drain." It made me think of all the girls I ever liked and how easy it is for men to kill women.

P: I asked Janet Leigh this question, and I want to ask you, too: Do you think *Psycho* opened the floodgates, in a way, for more explicit violence and sexuality? Janet said no. She didn't want the film to bear that guilt, I think she said. She said that really, when you look at it, the violence happens only in the imagination. I sort of half agree with her, and I half disagree.

J: Well, *Psycho* made a lot of money. Hence, filmmakers felt they *had* to do more murder movies. Thus, it became six people having to die, not two. And then, "Let's get the whole graduation class!" And then there's a train and there are teens on it, and of course, you gotta kill teens. But I think there is nothing gross about the shower scene. It had its own dreadful, dreadful, funeral music going for it, underneath. What's happening on the screen is a terrible feeling. First of all, the thing that got me is that if I were going to be attacked and murdered, the shower's about the last place I would want that happening because I would be naked and trapped in a compartment. How do you defend yourself?

P: You're going to slip and fall and you're sliding around, too. You can't even get your balance.

J: And you know, you just start thinking about your body, what's happening. I think before I would think that I was dying or I was going to be killed, I would think about how scarred I was going to be. Because you don't immediately think, "I'm going to be killed; I'm going to die!"

P: Especially when you know there's this big, sharp knife coming down on you.

J: Marion couldn't even think about defending herself because this was the last thing in the world that she thought would happen to her.

P: Especially after having decided she can get back and make amends.

J: The shower was to be a purifying act. She was washing her sins away.

P: Gus Van Sant used that overhead scene you mentioned, the scene that was cut from the original *Psycho*. It is a really unpleasant scene because Anne Heche is not as buxom as Janet Leigh. She looks like she could be thirteen years old. She's so young, and she looks so pathetic there. She's no Janet Leigh. I said that to Janet Leigh, and I'm sure everybody else said that, too.

J: They wanted Janet to see the Van Sant picture, and she kept saying no. And I said, "Janet, you above all should see this. You won't believe it." I saw it in a theater. I wanted to see it in a theater the way I did with the first one.

P: Did you see the final cut of the original *Psycho* with Janet Leigh? She said there were about forty people who saw it before it was released. Did you see it in a theater with an audience the first time?

J: Yes, had to.

P: But I mean were you with a regular theater audience or were you with the cast and crew?

J: He didn't have a cast and crew screening. He may have shown it to Janet and maybe to Tony Perkins, but he would have no screenings. He did show me the assemblage that the editor had done. I can't tell you how sick I felt. It was just that every moment was in the movie and every shot that Hitch had done. And he reached over and said, "It's just a rough cut, Joseph." Later, when I was doing *The Outer Limits*,

I used to see the rough cuts that the directors would give me, and I'd console myself by thinking, "It's just a rough cut, Joseph."

P: He knew what it would look like ultimately.

J: Then he called me when it was in its final cut with Bernard Herrmann and it was almost what was released. I could hardly believe the greatness of that score. Heartbreaking music. So heartbreaking.

P: When you saw *Psycho* with an audience, what was their reaction? Did people gasp or make noises?

J: Oh, they were yelling. Because Hitch wouldn't have any screenings to which you could invite your friends, my wife, Marilyn, and I invited all our friends over here to the house the night it opened in the theater, and we had some hors d'oeuvres and drinks, and then we all went to the theater and got in fast enough so that we could all get in the same rows. And there was a young man amongst us who was sitting next to Marilyn, and after the movie, Marilyn told me, "Joe, from the minute that door started to open in the shower scene, his hand was squeezing my arm!"

P: I'll bet a lot of people had black and blue marks the next day. I know I did!

J: Well, when we arrived, it was weird because people coming out looked like they had been on a rollercoaster ride. And they were all nervously laughing at themselves. And when we and our guests got back to the house, there was the strangest thing: they didn't know whether they should come near me.

P: Well, you created this monster. Had you given anyone the screenplay to look at?

J: No. Nobody was allowed to know anything.

P: It's probably the greatest cover-up, not cover-up, but public relations policy for any film.

J: Well, that's why Hitchcock didn't want me to indicate in the script what the murder scene was going to look like. He said, "Fake it."

P: Because somebody might get some pages out.

J: Oh, somebody did.

P: Now scripts pages are on the Internet.

J: Even in those days, people would steal pages. Some who worked on the set also took things as mementos.

P: I don't think any film has ever had that kind of reaction because it was the first time that people weren't allowed to come in after the movie had started. I remember when I was a kid, we'd go to see double features. I'd go after school, and I'd come in the middle of a movie and I'd watch the next movie and then I'd watch the beginning of the first movie. Of course, I became a good movie viewer because I'd try to figure out how the movie might have begun. And then here's a movie you couldn't do that with.

J: This was Hitch's idea. This was not Paramount's idea. He said, "If you see the end of this movie, you're not going to want to see it again. You'll know the mother's dead." Imagine sitting there, knowing that the mother's dead? What could you do? You couldn't enjoy it at all. But, people, when they see it again, they hear all the hints and secrets that I put in it. I said to Hitch, "You know in that scene in the parlor they don't have much of anything to talk about, so I'm going to really lay out the truth. If you read the scene by itself, you hear the story." And he loved that. He just thought that was "cunning."

P: That whole scene in the parlor is so wonderfully written, and it's so beautifully paced. It's not bing, bing, bing, bing, bing, bing, cut, cut, cut. The audience has to sit and listen. It's a long scene, and all these changes are happening underneath the surface to her and to him. It's an amazing scene. And to me, it sets up the shower scene.

J: Oh absolutely. Actually when Gus did his version, I was in the cutting room one day and the editor said, "Oh, this scene."

P: You mean in the parlor?

J: For the parlor scene, the editor said, "I just want to cut and cut, but he won't let me cut anything." And I thought, "Well, in this case, I'm glad that he's not letting her change anything." But she couldn't stand the tempo of it, and I said, "Just give yourself to it," which is how I go to the movie. It's amazing because, in those days, there were some pretty long scenes in movies. But everyone still thinks of that scene in *Psycho* as being one of the longest scenes, and this whole fucking movie business today, they're so afraid of three pages of dialogue.

P: Did you and Hitchcock anticipate censoring, I mean the censors' response to the film?

J: You know what he told me when I said to him, "Can we show a toilet on the screen? I'm always seeing bathrooms but no toilets." He said, "Well, that's your problem, Joseph, you'll be talking to the Production Code."

P: Is that true . . . the script writer talks to the Production Code people?

J: No. That's Hitchcock. It may be true only with Hitchcock, but because he wouldn't go. So he said, "It's your script. Go fight for it." I got upset.

I said, "I don't want to go talk to them." And he said, "Well, it's your script; you wrote it. You wrote all those lines. You put the toilet in. Why should I have to fight for it?" But he looked like he was saying, "Don't come back without permission to do that. Find a way!" I went there and there was the Production Code: five men in suits sitting at a table. So I began by asking them, "Do you find anything wrong in this script?" And they all kind of reeled back because that's why I was there. But I used the word "wrong" in a different sense. And I said, "No, I mean wrong in a moral sense. Murder is wrong and that's what I'm trying to show you." I went on like I was pitching a movie to them. And I said, "You know, what bothers me is that when someone is murdered, it's the killer who gets all the publicity, and I want this movie to be about the victim. This beautiful, young, woman who gets killed in such a heinous fashion." And I just went on, and I think they began to get frightened that they wouldn't get a word in. And then they said, "Why do you have her throw that stuff in the toilet?" And I said, "Because she doesn't want anyone to see it. It's proof that she stole the money, and she's only just decided to go back and make amends for what she did." And I said, "If she threw it in the wastebasket, somebody might find it." And it just went back and forth. They asked, "Do you have to say, 'Oh God!'" and I would say, "Well, I guess I could change that."

P: Things that you really didn't mind changing.

J: Well, I put them in there to offer them as trades. So it was fun. "You let me leave the toilet in, I'll take out 'God.' "It gave them a way to let me do what I wanted to do with it. And oddly enough, only one of the men objected to her flushing the toilet. And I said, "Well, suppose you had torn up something that you didn't want anyone to see. Would you flush the toilet?" And there really was no argument. What could they say? The problem was that the whole movie just disturbed the shit out of them. But they didn't know how to change it. And I think toward the end of the meeting they just kind of threw up their proverbial hands. And I just put everything in. And now the Production Code is dead.

P: I think *Psycho* helped to kill it. I think the movie showed that the Code really didn't have anything to say to people anymore.

J: That it really didn't have the power that it once had. Because *Psycho* was not a Paramount picture; it was released by Paramount, but it was an Alfred Hitchcock picture. They weren't dealing with a studio that they had any clout with. And they'd been bugging Hitchcock ever since he started making movies. All his movies were objectionable to everybody in that gang. And I could see why he didn't want to go and sit there or have them come into his office and sit around. I don't know whether he would know how to argue for something, you know. Well, it was his kingdom. Nobody ever said no to him.

P: Like Spielberg, now probably. I think Hitchock's private attitude was that he was somehow impervious, untouchable, unassailable. And with the way he spoke, the things he said, with his cultured accent, he seemed to be a person from a different universe.

J: And certainly a different time. You felt that he was a Victorian gentleman. Hitch would ask me to drive him home sometimes, and especially if Alma wasn't coming to pick him up.

P: Didn't he say he refused to drive and perhaps get a ticket because he was afraid of the police?

J: It was true. Well, his father once had him put in a jail cell.

P: I can't help thinking that one thing Hitchcock felt when he was thinking of the shower scene was putting Marion in the same room that he was in when he was a kid, evoking that feeling of total terror. And all of a sudden the audience has no one to identify with anymore. They're as victimized as the character. And I can't help thinking this must have been a way of working out this boyhood experience. But did he ever say that the jailing incident had actually happened?

J: Yes, he did.

P: It did happen. I always thought it happened.

J: I used to ask him about the legends.

P: Oh, you did?

J: And if it was untrue, he would just smile. If it was true, he would nod his head.

P: So he nodded his head for that one?

J: Yes.

P: It seems that Hitchcock changes his method of shooting and composing when he gets to the shower scene. He's employed many of the methods of classical cinema to get us to identify with Marion: point-of-view shots and eye-line match shots. But then when she gets into the shower, Hitchcock launches us into a different world, a different sense of space. Through his use of rapid cutting montage, he creates what I call an abstract space of terror.

J: Your analysis of those scenes is tremendous because that's exactly the way the movie had to be. And you know it also explains why he gave me so much leeway. Because he told me one day that he only bought the book because a girl gets murdered in the shower. I don't know whether he's ever said that to anybody else. But that's what he told me. And so, in a way, when Hitch said let's make her the star, it increased his interest.

P: That was the ingredient that was needed to be able to make the audience identify with her.

J: Well, you can't bring a character in and have her have a scene with somebody and we know nothing about her and then she gets murdered. Who's going to care? So I wanted you to like her, and then I wanted you to like Norman instead. I loved it when the audience gasped in the theater when that car's sinking in the swamp and Norman's standing there eating his things, and then the car stops, before it's totally concealed, and the audience is going, "Oh, no!"

P: They've identified with Norman.

J: Well, I looked at my wife, Marilyn, and I smiled. "You know, I got them! They love Norman now. They don't care if he buries her in a swamp." The audience is so fickle.

P: The thing with Janet Leigh is, she's so perfectly cast. She's so vulnerable and attractive. You really want her to get away with it, and you want her to get to this guy she's going to. And you really want her to succeed if she's going to go back. And then to have her killed is a real shock.

J: I thought that was so. And sometimes, when I'm talking to a group of people, I ask, "What did you think was going to happen to her when she got in the motel and had that nice talk with the guy and then he peeked at her?" And everyone thought, "He's going to rape her."

P: That's what the scene seems to be leading up to. You know I never thought what the audience thinks just before she gets into the shower, what they think is going to happen. Because when I show my class the film, and we stop it occasionally and talk about it, there's that scene when he comes down and offers her food. They're standing in front of her room and she asks him into her room. And he takes a step, but he stops. The "mother" in Norman says, "This woman's a sexual threat—she's got to die." And I think that's when the mother inside him decides she's going to kill Marion.

J: Well, the audience felt that his shyness and sweetness and everything was the other side of a rapist. And of course, I knew what they didn't know. They didn't know about the mother. So as far as I'm concerned all that happened is that he was being very nice to this woman, and he peeps in the hole at her and gets turned on, and he sure would like to have sex with her. But he's too late. She gets killed. He's got to wrap her up and get rid of her. It was strange because some people, to this day, think he was homosexual, and I can't attach that to anything but the fact that some people believed that Anthony Perkins was homosexual.

P: That's when the personality of the actor takes over the character. My students say that too. When we talk about the film, they say "This guy's gay." Because these students are used to having gay characters. They think this would be no big deal. But I don't think it's obvious at all.

J: No, and certainly not at the time. The kinds of questions that I get now are not at all like they were in the '70s and '80s. They've changed.

P: In what way?

J: Initially, no one ever asked me if Norman was gay. Because how could you think he was gay? I mean he's hot for this girl. He peeps in at her. I would not write a gay character using that peephole for a woman. If a stud were in Room 1, that would tell me he was gay. But this tells me that he's not allowed to be hot for any woman because his mother's jealous. And so she stops it.

P: Gus Van Sant has Norman masturbate as he's watching. Why would Van Sant do that?

J: To me Gus's Norman discharges the anxiety and the tension. I mean if you masturbate and have an orgasm, it's over. You're not going to screw anybody *or* kill anybody!

P: That's so true. I never thought of it that way. Of course, you would not do that. You don't have to add that orgasm. What was it like working with Van Sant?

J: When I was on the set one day, Julianne Moore came over to me and asked, "What exactly is my character doing in that motel room?" And I said, "Well, she's looking for some sign that her sister was there." And she said, "By opening drawers and shutting them real fast? I don't know what that's supposed to mean. I spoke to Gus and he won't change it." Gus wouldn't change a mark; it had to be from the original. I said to him one day at lunch, "God, I wish Gus Van Sant was directing this."

P: Did he laugh?

J: Yes.

P: I'm sure other people must have warned him off this thing.

J: Everybody. He said, "I'm able to do this only because I got nominated for an Academy Award."

P: Right, because it gave him a lot of clout.

J: He said to me, "But until now, anytime any studio called me and said, 'What would you like to do?' I would say, 'A total, word-by-word, scene-by-scene remake of *Psycho*.'" And he said that you could just feel the meeting go down the drain.

P: Did he feel some affinity with Hitchcock or that film, or is that just something he took as a challenge?

J: He said he had been wanting to do that way back when he started out. He wanted to just remake that movie, and he wouldn't let me change lines, and I said to him, "This girl would not steal and ruin her life and her romance for $40,000." I said, "Who'd do that today? $40,000 is not a lot of money." TV writers get paid more than that. And I said, "Plus, and this is really what got to him, the man who leaves the $40,000 there says he's going to buy his daughter a wedding present of a house." And I said, "Where is he going to buy this house?" And he said, "Well, what would you make it?" And I said, "Well, let's make it like two million." And he said, "How about $400,000?" It was like he was dealing with me. And I thought, "Well, maybe a girl would go a little berserk over $400,000." It's that hundred in there that helps, you know. But I had some ideas for scenes that I had thought about through the years and that came from some criticism on *Psycho*. And most of it I ignored because it sounded like they didn't like Hitchcock or me or Janet Leigh. But there was some criticism that I thought was very valid. So I said to Gus, "What if we played a scene where the psychiatrist talks to the mother in the room, and then he doesn't have to really do the next-to-last scene that's in the original film." And Gus said, "And Vince Vaughn would be talking in the mother's voice?" I said, "Yes, make it a scene where Norman's sitting there and he thinks he's his mother."

P: That would've been great.

J: It would have been fantastic. So he said, "Gee, I don't know." So I wrote the scene, giving all the same facts that Simon Oakland gave, but through the mother's point of view.

P: I'd love to see that scene. You ought to get somebody to shoot it. I mean here was Van Sant's opportunity to get people to sit up and take notice.

J: Well, you know what he came back to me with? Universal was worried about the reaction to Vince Vaughn speaking in a motherly voice. I said, "Vince Vaughn is an actor. He'll play whatever you tell him to play. And the audience will understand now what's going on." Even though Gus didn't shoot that scene, I thought Vince gave a very good performance.

When I agreed to work with Van Sant on it, I considered my work as a protection. I just wanted to be the one person from the original.

P: You were the only one?

J: Yeah, who was there—Janet wouldn't have anything to do with it. And I was always after Gus. He hardly ever said "cut," and then walked away without me getting hold of him. He said, "This is how I want to do it." When I talked to him about Julianne's scene, I said maybe there's a better way for her to look for something to indicate that her sister was there. And he said, "Yeah, but we're doing it the way Hitchcock did it."

P: Even Hitchcock, if he had redone it, wouldn't have done it in the same way.

J: Look what he did with *The Man Who Knew Too Much*. He made it a big, splashy, Technicolor thriller. I would loved to have sat down with Hitchcock and said, "Okay, what shall we do with this remake of *Psycho*?"

P: That would've been something.

J: It never occurred to me.

P: It would've been great to have the Master and the screenwriter go back and say, "Let's tweak it."

J: He would have flipped over the idea of Norman, I mean of the psychiatrist talking to the mother that's inside Norman. He would have just flipped over that.

P: That scene is so creepy, with him sitting there on that chair, isolated, by himself, with that look on his face and that voice-over. I think of William Friedkin, who did *The Exorcist*, having Linda Blair talk with the voice of the devil. Friedkin must have been thinking of that weird reaction of the audience to another person's voice coming out, a creepy sounding voice.

J: I suggested that, too. I said to Van Sant that it doesn't have to be Vince himself doing it. Hitch used doubles and everything whenever there was anything the least bit questionable about the characters. So they could've had somebody dub it. He could have read the lines in his own voice, taken it in the AD, and put this creepy mother's voice in there.

P: I agree. Getting back to the original *Psycho*, did you ever see the Saul Bass storyboards?

J: Yes, I saw some of them.

P: Were they rough-sketched out?

J: They were like whatever that shot was at the moment, that's the way it was. And Hitch followed a lot of that. Hitch, himself, and his family were very aware of the legacy of Alfred Hitchcock; there isn't anything that they didn't save, even small notes that he wrote. There was, in the same year as the centennial at the Museum of Modern Art, in New York, a showing of all kinds of memorabilia, including letters and notes. I also noticed that, except in one case when he drew something for me, he would tear the note up and throw it in a wastebasket, or else he would put it in a drawer. But in one case he gave me what he had drawn, just little stick figures. And I felt that he was very well aware that all this stuff was going to be valuable. He was a legend at that time. He asked me to drive him home one night. It was rather early. And we drove along Melrose. And at Melrose and Fairfax there's a high school, and we got there just as school was letting out. So the lights meant nothing because people were crossing. And people were passing right in front of the car, and we were sitting there and a young man looked in, and then he looked again, and then he came around to the other side, the passenger side, and he said to Hitch, "Good evening," in Hitch's unmistakable vocal style.

P: He must've got a big kick out of that.

J: Hitch just nodded, but as we drove along he said, "Did you hear that?" and I thought, "He loves every minute of it." He really was like the king whom everybody loved except a certain section of the population that hated him.

P: Not many though.

J: Well, you know his reviews were never . . .

P: Hitchcock never won the Academy Award.

J: Well, that's insane.

P: Your script should have won the Academy Award. That's the most ridiculous thing. It's probably the most read and commented on script. It's an amazing script. And no one I talk to, no one, gets the "I am Norma Bates," when Norman says that; I watched the Universal DVD, and it's really hard to hear it, but Norman says it. He says, "I am Norma Bates," when he runs into the fruit cellar, with a dress on and knife upraised. And I don't know if anybody has ever realized it.

J: Well, that's where the music really hit real loud, and the first time I saw the movie I thought they'd cut that line.

P: When I read your script at the Academy, I said, "Wait a minute; this is an important line. I don't ever remember it being discussed." When that wig comes off, it's so creepy, because you're still thinking that the character is a woman. I think that this idea of a woman with a knife being a menacing figure was even scarier to the audience than a guy with a knife. Also, how outrageous, all the hints of necrophilia with the dead body and the indentation in the bed. This was 1960; even now these things would be controversial.

J: They were then. And a lot of that stuff that was in there had never been on the screen before, as you probably know—the toilet and the flushing of the toilet.

P: Was that your idea?

J: Yeah. I said, "I just kind of want to unseat people," and Hitchcock loved that. I won the argument because I said "unseat." And then when we got to this psychiatrist scene, I told him why I wanted the psychiatrist scene. I said, "I feel that people will leave that theater not understanding what it meant that Norman had a wig on. Was he trying to protect his mother? What was this dead thing over here?" So I said, "You need somebody to explain it all." So I outlined how I would do that scene, and he said, "I'm afraid it might be a hat-grabber," which I had never heard before.

P: "A hat-grabber"? It's not something you hear every day.

J: Yeah, you grab your hat and walk out.

P: Oh, a hat-grabber, interesting. It must be a British term.

J: People need, after that intense scene—you brought them up to this point—they need to be brought down. They need a little discussion so that they can kind of settle their minds. You can't follow that scene with anything that would be too dramatic. I think it works fine, and I even like Simon Oakland's kind of bombastic character. I recommended Simon Oakland for the part of the psychiatrist.

P: I happen to like that scene with Oakland in the original *Psycho*. People say, "Oh, it's too talky and it's not dramatic enough." But I think that's a mesmerizing scene. You know, this is an unsophisticated audience in 1960, which doesn't know much about psychology.

J: My complaint about Simon, whom I knew personally and liked very much, was that he just orated, and Hitch let him get away with a lot of stuff. He should have been more psychiatric, tense, tight. Well, you know what's interesting? All through that whole experience with Hitch, and again when we worked on *Marnie*, he kept saying to me—I don't even know if he knew how often he repeated it—"What do you want the audience to think? What do you want the audience to feel?" Audience, audience, audience. And I thought, "This is the whole key to Hitchcock's work: he does it for us. He doesn't do it for the studio bosses; he doesn't do it for friends; he does it for the people who pay at the box office. And audiences have always loved his pictures." After lunch he sometimes looked a little sleepy, so I'd say, "How about if I go see a movie?" Meaning one of his. And he'd say, "Fine, set it up." Or he'd call Peggy Robertson and say, "Joseph wants to see a movie." And I'd say, "I'd like to see a lot of the early ones before I knew I'd ever be in the business." One day I said, "I'd like to see *Vertigo* again." And he had this look on his face, and I thought, "Oh my, have I made some type of *faux pas*? He said, "Oh very well, if you want to see it." Then he said, "Have you seen it before?" And I said, "Yes, once, when it first came out." And he said, "What did you think of it?" He had never asked me that. And I said, "Well, it was like a symphony. And I was with it every step of the way. And what I wanted to ask you was why you chose that particular moment to tell the audience that this was the same girl?" And he said, "Well, I figured the audience might be getting a little bored by then, and if I let them in on the main clue, they would be very grateful and they'd stay."

P: What a great decision on his part to do that.

J: He thought they'd be bored. He said, "You cannot go too long keeping your audience in suspense."

P: It's a long movie, and he's got a lot of scenes in which Stewart is following Novak in the car, with no dialogue. And I always tell my students when I show that film that you really have to just go with those scenes. They're mesmerizing; there's a real purpose for those scenes. Later, you'll understand this guy's fixation, and how he was tricked into—kept getting drawn into—this thing.

J: It was my favorite Hitchcock movie, except *Rebecca*. One day he asked me what was my favorite movie, and I said, *Rebecca*. He said, "Now, come on." And I said, "No, that's always been my favorite movie." And he wanted to know why, and I began to tell him about how Max DeWinter does something odd and takes this young girl back to his house where everybody's against her and him, and I said, "It just made me feel like, if you really love somebody, nothing else in the world matters." That's what I took home from *Rebecca*.

P: Did you ever feel that, when people talk about *Psycho*, they talk a lot about Hitchcock? Do you think that somehow your contribution isn't appreciated enough when people talk about it, because it is the script that creates the thing? I mean he visualized it, but it is the script, and you can read commentary on the brilliance of this movie without reading anything about the script or the writer. Does it get you frustrated sometime?

J: I was very frustrated when I began to see that *Psycho* was not going to go away. And somebody had written a book, and they mentioned my name, but they spelled it wrong. They spelled it "Stephano" instead of "Stefano." And there's a real kind of ambivalence that I feel about being ignored. I think a lot of it springs from the French and their attitude about the director as God. And also Hitchcock never mentioned writers in any of his interviews. It was always *his* picture. And so I felt that for what I had got out of it, I could do without the praise and the credit. But it was my own kind of victory. I had one of the most amazing pictures of all time, and I had written it.

P: When you did *Psycho IV*, did you and Tony Perkins talk about the original *Psycho*?

J: Hardly ever at all. With the other versions, the producers would call me each time, and I would say "No, I don't want to do a sequel to it." And when *IV* came up, I said, "I really don't want to do a sequel to *III* or anything, but how would you feel about a prequel?" And they said fine. So I went in the next day and pitched the story that *Psycho IV* is, except I put into the script a kind of *Oprah* show; I was even hoping that we could use Oprah's show, but we did a radio talk show instead, which was okay; it was a budgetary thing. There was a kind of analysis going on at the time, a very quick therapy, which might not cure you, but it prevented you from carrying out the same psychological problems that you had before, and I did a lot of reading on that, and I thought, "Well, Norman went into that, and as a result he was able to get married. Originally his wife had a child from a former marriage and there was a lovely relationship between the boy and Norman." And in it I had all the scenes that were in my head when I wrote *Psycho*: the mother teasing him on the bed and then getting furious at him because he gets an erection. I used to talk to Hitch about these things, about how seductive she was with him and how he thought he had a right to be her only lover, although she made it clear to him that he was never to do that to her. So she locked him in a closet and told him he was a girl and all the shit that had come out in my analysis. I thought *Psycho IV* was done rather interestingly, but that Olivia Hussey was not right for the part, because this should have been a woman who could be seducing you one minute and cutting your balls off the next. And I don't think Olivia had quite the insight that a better actress would have had. But I thought Henry Thomas from *ET* was wonderful as the young Norman.

P: The idea of a prequel I think was an unusual idea. It answers the questions you would ask as you were watching the original *Psycho*: "How did Norman get where he is at the beginning of *Psycho*? What did this woman do to him? What did he do to her?" He wanted to kill her but keep her. "I want you dead, but I can't stand you dead so I'll keep you alive; I'll stuff you."

J: "And I'll *become* you."

P: We're all products of our parents whether we like it or not. Even if the father isn't there, he's there, and also the mother. I mean we all take our identity from these people.

J: I felt that working on *Psycho* helped my analysis, and being in analysis helped my writing on *Psycho*. Without analysis, I'd be dead, but aside from being dead, I wouldn't be the writer that I have become. You learn a lot of rules of life from analysis. There are rules, and I don't know where else you learn them. I really one day knew in my soul that you must not try to change people. You can make all the suggestions you want and give them all the help they need but don't try to change them. If they want to change, they'll change. And I learned it because it applied to me. I changed on my own volition, and I think my analyst had gotten me to that point. So after the analysis I was undergoing while *Psycho* was going on, I went into analysis again about fifteen years later. My son had left home, and I was having the empty nest syndrome, and of course I'd always worked at home, and I went into analysis again because I felt "This is for *me*; this is not so that I could get married; this is not so that I could be a good father, or a good writer or anything. Let's go see why you're still feeling this or having these dreams." I think the analyst I was with must have said maybe ten things to me in the course of the years I was with her. Ten. Never more than a sentence. While I was in analysis and while I was doing *The Outer Limits*, working my ass off, twenty-four hours a day to get a series pilot ready and everything, my father died, and I'd been very alienated from him most of my life, but in the few years prior to his death we sort of became friends. I visited him in Atlantic City, and he wrote me letters, and he'd write and say, "The line is now all around the block on *Psycho*." He'd go and check the theater. And when he died, I told my analyst, "I don't know if I can go to the funeral. I'm right in the heat of getting ready to open in September. The series is going on the air in September." And she said, "I think you'll regret it if you don't go." And when I think of what happened as a result of my going to that funeral, I feel like she knew when to say something.

P: It was the right thing to say.

J: I feel like, first of all, I just so enjoyed raising a son, and part of that was because I had hardly known my father. He and my mother separated when I was about eight, I guess. And then he came back two years later, and as far as I was concerned, that dead man had come back to the house, and I was not interested in him. I don't talk to dead people. And it was awful. We hardly ever spoke to each other. But thanks to analysis, I had gone to London, and then on the way back, I stopped in New York and flew down to Atlantic City and went and visited him. And that changed our relationship. Analysis has also helped me to look inside of myself for my characters. I've done a lot of movies that have villains in them; I always look for that villain in me. Not just that I want to identify with him, but I want to know that I'm capable of doing that. I don't want to write a character that I feel superior to. And I think it's absolutely the right thing to do as a writer.

P: I agree. If you look at a lot of the contemporary villains, they have no humanity. They're drawn so superficially. They're so bad that you can't feel that you would do anything like that, and I think when you look at Norman Bates, you can understand what motivates him. You can see his fury, his anger, something you can tap into in yourself.

J: I think you can only get that out of yourself. But the problem with a lot of young writers today is they don't even go there.

P: Maybe they don't even know how to. Maybe they all ought to get analysis.

J: Well, I've been mentoring a young writer since he got out of USC, and I really feel like he does that now. He goes into himself. He was telling me about a short movie he's working on. And I could feel what analysts feel. Because I thought, "Oh, yeah. This is the big nut, isn't it? And this is what you're going to have to crack. And maybe you won't do it in this script, but you're getting near it." And it was such a good feeling, to know that he was really doing that.

CHAPTER 5

Constructing Suspense

Mise-en-scene

> I'm not interested in logic. I'm interested in effect.
>
> —ALFRED HITCHCOCK

Throughout his long career, Hitchcock was always aware of the aesthetic power of the cinema. Among his favorite terms for describing this power was "pure cinema." For Hitchcock, a key element of pure cinema was the way the director exerted creative power through the construction of the film's mise-en-scene. This term, borrowed from the French, was originally a theatrical term that translates literally as "to put on stage." John Gibbs has written an excellent study of the term in his book *Mise-En-Scene: Film Style and Interpretation*:

> For the student of film, a useful definition might be: 'the contents of the frame and the way that they are organised'. Both halves of this formulation are significant—the contents and their organisation.
>
> What are the contents of the frame? They include lighting, costume, décor, properties, and the actors themselves. The organisation of the contents of the frame encompasses the relationship of the actors to one other and to the décor, but also their relationship to the camera, and thus the audience's view. So in talking about mise-en-scène one is also talking about framing, camera movement, the particular lens employed and other photographic decisions. Mise-en-scène therefore encompasses both what the audience can see, and the way in which we are invited to see it. It refers to many of the major elements of communication in the cinema, and the combination through which they operate expressively (5).

One important fact about Hitchcock's mise-en-scene is that his directing career actually had begun in Germany, not in England. In fact,

Hitchcock refers to the year spent in Germany, visiting the Universum Film Aktiengesellschaft (Ufa) in Berlin, the country's largest film company, as the most significant influence on his cinematic style. In 1924, a year before he directed his first feature film, Hitchcock was sent to Germany as a crew member of an Anglo-German coproduction, *The Blackguard*. Hitchcock had been working as an assistant director and set designer for the British production company, Gainsborough. During the 1920s, one of the most innovative and distinctive cinematic styles was being created by the German film industry, most notably by the great German directors, F.W. Murnau, Fritz Lang, and G.W. Pabst. Hitchcock observed this cinematic style firsthand.

German Expressionism had exploded on the cinema world in 1919, with Robert Wiene's film, *The Cabinet of Dr. Caligari*, which featured nightmarish scenarios and distorted, surrealistic sets with shadowy, chiaroscuro lighting. Gottlieb says, "Expressionism typically pictures the physical world as a dark, frightening, violent, and unstable place, often a projection of a disturbed person shown through striking set design and lighting effects as well as subjective camera shots" ("Early Hitchcock" 38). In his visit to Germany, Hitchcock absorbed the techniques and style of the German cinema. During production of *The Blackguard*, he visited the set of F.W. Murnau's masterpiece of *Kammerspielfilm*, *The Last Laugh*. He was so struck by this experience that he stated, "My models were forever after the German filmmakers of 1924 and 1925. They were trying very hard to express ideas in purely visual terms" (Spoto 68). This method of cinema narration—"purely visual"—would become Hitchcock's mantra.

Another characteristic of German cinema would also become a primary goal of Hitchcock: the preeminence of the director. In Germany, unlike in England and even the United States, the film director had unprecedented power. As Garncarz states, "In the German film industry the director's freedom was traditionally much greater than in the British industry. German directors had an influence on the script and much freedom in its filmic realization, calculated the film's budget, and were responsible for its editing" (66). Ironically, when Hitchcock returned to Germany in 1925 to direct his first two features, *The Pleasure Garden* and *The Mountain Eagle*, he was given more freedom to direct than he would have been given in England. The lesson he learned there would forever stay in his mind: the director is (or should be) the prime creative force in filmmaking. Hitchcock believed that only in this way would the director be able to tell his story in "purely visual" terms.

The German cinema that had such a profound influence on Hitchcock—and on films in general—is essentially a cinema of mise-en-scene. German directors had the power and influence to shape and control the visual elements of the film frame so that the narrative was contained in the images on the screen. Because they were silent, German films had to tell their story in almost purely visual terms. The best example of the visual power of German films is F.W. Murnau's *The Last Laugh*, the production of which Hitchcock witnessed first hand in 1924, his seminal year in Germany. Murnau's *The Last Laugh* has very few title cards; it's an embodiment of Hitchcock's idea of "pure cinema." In fact, Hitchcock says of Murnau's masterpiece that it was "almost the perfect film . . . [it] had a tremendous influence on me."

For Hitchcock, though, "pure cinema" never becomes an end in itself: there's always a story to tell. Hitchcock learned American methods of film production when he first entered the film industry in 1920 at the Famous Players-Lasky studio at Islington. During his formative years, then, Hitchcock was not only absorbing the visual style of the Germans, but he was also learning the methods and techniques of the Hollywood, or classical, style of filmmaking. When Hitchcock entered the film industry in 1920 and served his "apprenticeship" from 1920 to 1924, he was learning by osmosis what Kuhn calls the "classical codes . . . a distinct set of expressive resources . . ." that were designed to set a story in motion, to create a "credible fictional world," to present individual characters with clear and consistent motivation, and to connect these characters through causal links to a credible plot.

When Hitchcock invokes the concept of pure cinema, then, he is referring partly to mise-en-scene, to the creation on screen of a "credible fictional world," a world that will draw the viewerviewers in, to hold them spellbound. It is, in fact, Hitchcock's mise-en-scene that later endeared him to the *Cahiers du Cinema* critics and that earned him the honorary label "auteur," a master of images. Hitchcock learned from his early films that the best way to draw a viewer into a cinematic world is through suspense. Hitchcock himself says of his evolution as a suspense director, "In my case there was much dabbling about in so-called versatility before I found my niche . . . I began to get more and more interested in developing a suspense technique. By the time I had made *The Secret Agent*, *Sabotage*, and *The 39 Steps*, I had made up my mind to shoot this type of story exclusively" (Knight, 115). Hitchcock spoke and wrote in great detail about suspense and its "operative logic." In "The Enjoyment of Fear" (1949) and

"Let 'Em Play God" (1948), Hitchcock lays out the principles of suspense, the most succinct of which he presents in his article "Film Production," which he wrote for the *Encyclopedia Britannica* in 1965: "The most powerful means of gripping attention is suspense . . . suspense is created by the process of giving the audience information that the character in the scene does not have" (Gottlieb, *Hitchcock on Hitchcock* 212). In "Let 'Em Play God," Hitchcock asserts, "If the audience does know, if they have been told all the secrets that the characters do not know, they'll work like the devil for you because they know what fate is facing the poor actors. That is what is known as 'playing God.' That is suspense" (Gottlieb, *Hitchcock on Hitchcock* 113).

However, as Gottlieb points out, Hitchcock's essays on fear and suspense "set out principles and formulas that Hitchcock's films both elaborate and challenge" (*Hitchcock on Hitchcock* 101). One of these challenges is in the role of knowledge in the narration. Frequently, the characters have knowledge that the audience does not have. Sometimes the audience has false knowledge. Sometimes the audience and the protagonist have knowledge that the other characters do not have. Take, for example, the opening scenes of *I Confess*. Through careful control of mise-en-scene, Hitchcock presents opening shots of the Quebec City skyline at dusk as the credits roll. We then see several low-angle shots of cathedrals and buildings, interspersed with traffic directional arrows, all pointing to the right side of the screen. On the fourth shot of a directional arrow, the camera peers to the right and discovers an open window, through which it tracks to reveal the scene of a murder. This presentation of the camera as a voyeuristic witness outside a window is characteristic of many of Hitchcock's films—*Rope*, *I Confess*, *Shadow of a Doubt*, *Psycho*. The camera position is sometimes playfully reversed—the camera inside Scotty's window in *Rear Window*—but then reasserted as the film progresses—the camera outside the windows of the Thorwalds' suite. In *I Confess*, the peering camera discovers a dead body and tilts up to beaded curtains still moving from the recent departure of the murderer. The camera then tracks back outside the window and pans right to show a priest under the cover of darkness of night walking away from the camera. This shot, beautifully and compactly composed, presents the viewer with the crime and its perpetrator, but there's something wrong with the knowledge the audience possesses; it is half-knowledge. The figure moving away from the camera is indeed the killer, but the figure is not a priest; he is merely dressed as one, as we discover three shots later, when the figure removes his robe to reveal a suit underneath. In four bold shots, Hitchcock uses the techniques of mise-en-scene to present the ambiguities of appearance and reality. In addition, the dark, shadowy photography, combined with unusual angles, shows the strong influence that German Expressionism had on Hitchcock's mise-en-scene. The fourth shot, in particular, is the essence of Expressionism with its low, canted angle, and with its distorted, oversized shadow of Keller thrown on the wall of the narrow street. This shot is typical of Hitchcock's use of mise-en-scene to graphically portray his notion of the "double," or doppelgänger, the divided self, a concept that was, as Spoto claims, "available to Hitchcock from the literary traditions that were familiar to him" (329). Keller/killer's duality is symbolized by his oversized shadow, which looms threateningly on the wall. Keller's dark half has overwhelmed his other self: the killer has replaced Keller. In many ways, these dark opening shots become a distillation of Hitchcock's "cinema," which employs mise-en-scene to advance the narrative. At the end of the decade, Hitchcock would again use a black-and-white palette for his mise-en-scene in presenting his darkest and most terrifying dramatization of the double—*Psycho*.

In the opening scenes of *I Confess*, Hitchcock employs mise-en-scene to create a complex web of suspense. Hitchcock states, "I prefer murder by the babbling brook. . . . All backgrounds must function" (Gottlieb, *Hitchcock on Hitchcock* 313). Hitchcock's camera is what makes all backgrounds function. As Janet Leigh claims about her experience of being directed by Hitchcock, "I had to move when his camera dictated" (IX). This dictating camera is everywhere present in Hitchcock, creating a mise-en-scene carefully composed to parcel out knowledge and thus to create suspense. In the opening scenes of *Rear Window*, for instance, Hitchcock creates a theatrical mise-en-scene by running the credits over a window with the venetian blinds being raised, like a curtain in a theater. This theatrical mise-en-scene, though, is subverted as the credits end and the camera tracks forward through the middle window. The mise-en-scene, then, shifts from the fixed seat of theater spectatorship to the more involved and engaged position of the cinema spectator, who moves as the camera moves. Working within the narrative codes of classical cinema, Hitchcock uses his camera to establish the credibility of the diegesis, the world of the film, by presenting long shots through the rear window of the protagonist's apartment. The camera moves through the window, and the sashes and casements disappear as the viewer enters the world of the diegesis, what Thomas Leitch calls "the world contained within the cinematic discourse" (2). From this point on in the film, the audience and the camera become one, as Hitchcock uses pure cinema to tell his story. The next three shots take up a little more than two minutes of screen time as they pan the courtyard and introduce several of the minor characters. The third shot of this opening sequence is a brilliant pan that begins with a couple waking up from their sleep on the fire escape balcony, pans left to reveal Miss Torso preparing her breakfast, and comes back inside the apartment, pauses briefly on a thermometer registering 94 degrees, and settles on a medium shot of L.B. Jeffreys (James Stewart) sleeping in his wheelchair. The camera pans down the figure of Jeffreys to reveal a large cast on his left leg, with an inscription that reveals the character's name—L.B. Jeffreys. Patrick McGilligan describes Hitchcock's shot as ". . . a sweep of the camera across the walls of Jeff's room adorned with awards and glamorous magazine covers . . . , ending with a shot of a racing car cartwheeling toward the camera—the shot that broke the photographer's leg" (481). In his "purely visual" style, Hitchcock has conveyed the idea of the danger involved in viewing, in watching, in being an observer of forces that can spin wickedly out of control, including human passion, symbolized by the heat inside Jeff's apartment.

In just a little more than two minutes, Hitchcock has created a fictional world, and he has put in that world an immobilized character whose profession is revealed to us in a purely visual way. Hitchcock has not only planted the seeds of suspense in this scene by having the audience deduce L.B. Jeffreys' profession and condition through accumulated visual evidence, but he has also established watching and deducing as the major themes of his film, and he has created a bond between observation and danger that becomes the underlying tension in the film narrative. For the rest of the film, we watch L.B. Jeffreys as *he* watches the characters through his rear window, and we deduce, along with him, that one of his neighbors, Lars Thorwald, has committed a murder. In this film, Hitchcock is stingy with knowledge; he presents it in bits and pieces; he fragments it in windows—some of them tiny—and he presents his characters in enclosed spaces and in long shots. In short, he makes us and the protagonist work hard for our knowledge. At one point in the film, Hitchcock even slyly presents the audience with knowledge that the protagonist doesn't have: Thorwald leaves the apartment with a mysterious woman ("Is it his wife?" we ask ourselves) while L.B. Jeffreys is asleep in his wheelchair. Now *we* know something that the protagonist does not know, but we are not sure what we know. Thus Hitchcock confronts us with the precariousness of knowledge through the mise-en-scene of the film. Furthermore, he creates suspense by suggesting that spectatorship—watching—can be as risky as acting or doing. Jeff exposed himself to danger by trying to photograph a racing car in action. In effect, he tried to contain the chaos of movement within the frame of a picture, but in the process, he was swallowed up and almost destroyed by the chaos itself. In tying the audience's point of view to that of Jeffreys, Hitchcock is suggesting that the act of viewing a film exposes the audience to the same kind of danger, not physical, but rather psychological—the danger of the dark side of the human heart. Throughout the 1950s, Hitchcock would hint at this theme in many of his greatest movies, until he gave it its fullest expression in *Psycho*, the most powerful expression of the dangers of voyeurism and spectatorship. And Hitchcock creates this powerful expression partly through his ingenious use of mise-en-scene techniques to create suspense.

Hitchcock's consummate expression of mise-en-scene techniques occurs in *Psycho*. Beginning with the credits, Hitchcock brilliantly employs mise-en-scene to create suspense. The Bernard Herrmann score explodes with five startling fortissimo minor chords over a gray screen. Two beats later, the Saul Bass-designed credits begin. From the right side of the screen come horizontal lines that carry fragmented parts of the film's title. From the other side come more horizontal lines, with the missing parts of the title. The word "Psycho" appears, but its letters appear fragmented and wavy. The credits continue in this manner. The words literally split apart and disappear at the top and bottom of the screen, jarringly preparing the audience not only for the splintered personality of Norman and Norma but also for the tearing and splitting of Marion Crane's flesh by the butcher knife wielded by the jealous mother. In effect, this sequence utilizes graphic mise-en-scene to hint at the film's themes and motifs.

After the credits, as in so many of Hitchcock's films (*Shadow of a Doubt*, *Rope*, *I Confess*, *Rear Window*), the opening mise-en-scene presents us with an extreme long shot that establishes a specific locale. In documentary-like fashion (he does this earlier in *Notorious*), Hitchcock pinpoints the exact date, time, and location of this world—Phoenix, Arizona, Friday, December 11, 2:43 p.m.—in three separate titles, all three not just appearing on the screen but rather entering from the sides of the frame and then exiting to the sides. In the first two titles, half of the words come from the left and half from the right—"Phoenix" from the left, "Arizona" from the right; "Friday" from the left, "December" from the right. The titles then exit on the left side of the frame. The third title "two forty-three p.m." enters from the left and exits to the right. These titles appear as the camera pans to the right and, in a series of dissolves and a cut, centers upon a specific building, then a single half-opened window, with the blinds drawn three-fourths of the way down, revealing an almost pitch black space with a few points of light gleaming off the furniture. Then, in a startling move, the camera does the seemingly impossible by entering this dark space, perhaps six or seven inches high, in a smooth tracking shot, and then by panning to the right to reveal the characters.

These establishing shots echo the credits in providing subtle, almost subconscious, plot hints through graphic representation. The two halves of the first two titles forming together in the middle of the screen are a visual representation of the doubling, splitting, and reformulating that are the leitmotifs of the film. In *Vertigo*, the swirl in Madeline's hair, prefigured by the lissajous spirals in the Saul Bass-designed credits, is a visual symbol of the spiraling descent of Scotty into madness and *liebestod*. A lissajous spiral is named after the French physicist who discovered its shape. In *Psycho*, Bass presents us with images forming, fragmenting, reforming, and splitting apart—all of these representations of the characters, plot, and themes of *Psycho*. Moreover, the entrances and exits of the words and letters, as well as their temporary centering in the screen, prefigure the significance of the horizontal limits of the frame and of the center of the frame as a beginning point of perspective and depth. Throughout the first half of the film, Hitchcock will use the full dimensions of the frame to advance his narrative. In addition, the bright, glaring sunlight of a Phoenix afternoon is in contrast to the darkness of the space that the camera enters as it peers into the room. This tonal juxtaposition of public and private spaces had intrigued Hitchcock in *Rear Window*, one of the most famous shots of which is the darkened room with the only visible light being the glow from Lars Thorwald's cigarette. It is perhaps the weakening of the Production Code during the 1950s that allowed (or prompted) Hitchcock to show explicitly the violence that occurs in the darkness of private spaces in *Psycho* while only obliquely hinting at it in *Rear Window*. Patrick McGilligan goes so far as to claim a deliberate trend—or motive—in Hitchcock's career, "a career spent pushing the cinema closer to unflinching depictions of violence" (577). In these establishing shots, Hitchcock is drawing upon his formidable skill in formal design (after all, he entered the industry as a letterer and title designer) to create a mise-en-scene that fills the frame with visual information.

As the camera peers into the window of one of the rooms in the opening scene of *Psycho*, Hitchcock indicates that this story is haphazardly discovered, one of many possible stories taking place in the numerous hotel windows that we had seen earlier, almost as if he has streamlined and focused the multiple stories of *Rear Window* into a single incident. The camera voyeuristically enters the dark room, and the scene gradually brightens—almost like lights coming on in a theater—to reveal a startling scene: a man ominously looming (we find out later his last name is Loomis) over a woman lying in bed, who is dressed only in a white slip and bra: the man is naked from the waist up. This opening scene, tame by today's anything-goes bedroom settings, was shocking to 1960 audiences, conditioned by Production Code morality. Even more risqué and unsettling is the next series of shots showing the man, Sam, and the woman, Marion, lying in bed together, and kissing, obviously enjoying a postcoital moment before they each go their separate ways. The ensuing dialogue indicates that this is indeed a tryst, and that the characters have seemingly insurmountable barriers (Sam's alimony payments and his deceased father's unpaid debts) that prevent their marriage. Sam: "I sweat to pay my father's debts, and he's in his grave. I sweat to pay my ex-wife's alimony . . ."

The themes and motifs of *Psycho* are economically presented in the scene: hidden and guilty sex; psychical, emotional, and monetary debts to dead parents; the sins of the parents visited upon the children; unsatisfying and failed marriages; and naked and exposed flesh. To the 1960 audience, the content of the scene was enough to set them on edge; to contemporary audiences, however, not used to black-and-white cinematography but very used to nudity and sex in the cinema, the mise-en-scene has an ominous feel to it, an unsettling tone. The dark, shabby, sterile room, cut off from the bright sun of a Phoenix afternoon by drawn blinds, has a pervasive atmosphere of gloom and foreboding, underscored and emphasized by Bernard Herrmann's eerie strings and further heightened by Jack Russell's flat, gray-toned cinematography.

This first room, one of five spaces that make up the major settings of the first act of the movie, reflects the inner state of the film's characters and foreshadows their fate. Marion will die in a room like this, and Sam will repay the debt of his father by unwittingly aiding in the sacrifice of his girlfriend to the revenge and jealousy of Norman's mother. Sam's inability to commit to marrying Marion helps to launch her into the underworld of crime; she steals money to help Sam repay his father's debts and his wife's alimony, but in the process, Marion steps into the dark world of the Bates Motel.

Norman: "They moved away the highway."

Marion: "Oh, I thought I'd gotten off the main road."

Norman: "I know you must have. Nobody ever stops here anymore unless they've done that."

Marion's journey to the Bates Motel is one we all take, according to Hitchcock's fallen view of the world. None of us is innocent; none of us can escape sin and guilt, but many of us pay for the sins of others. *Psycho*'s twisted, fallen world is best epitomized in the shower of the Bates Motel, where Hitchcock perverts Christ's parable of the sower of seeds—"Many are called, but few are chosen"—into the motto of *Psycho* (and of all his great films): "All sin, but some pay for the sins of others as well as for their own." The scriptwriter, Joseph Stefano, in an exercise in foreshadowing, has Marion say to Sam, "Hotels of this sort aren't interested in you when you are checking in, but when your time is up. . . ." Continuing the motif of debts, Marion later says, "They also pay who meet in hotel rooms."

My analysis of *Psycho*'s mise-en-scene owes a great deal to Raymond Bellour's *The Analysis of Film* (2000), which attempts to create a "textual system," while at the same time recognizing "the problem of the plurality of codes, of their diversity and multiple relations" (8). Also important to my analysis is Larry Crawford's approach in his article "Subsegmenting the Filmic Text: The Bakersfield Car Lot Scene in *Psycho*," which subjects a single scene to an exhaustive analysis of its cinematic infrastructure. I should like to appropriate Bellour's methodology in order to understand how form becomes the shape of content (to borrow Ben Shahn's term) in *Psycho*. For example, Bellour sees three codes that undergird the alternation in the film: "seeing vs. being seen, camera movement vs. stasis and distance vs. proximity" (Allen 129). However, mise-en-scene is not simply alternation. Camera placement—and I'm not speaking simply of angles—for instance, creates a code of its own: its placement within a setting and within the diegesis provides the semblance of reality that makes classical cinema work. Is the camera a fourth wall? Is it a ceiling? Is it a floor? Is it a character? Is it the windshield of a car? In addition, the rectangular limits of a frame—its four-sidedness—provide entrance and exit points for dramatic action. The depth of the frame—its perspective—is also a code. These visual codes are not alternations as much as they are variations on an infinite scale.

The opening scene in the Phoenix hotel, for example, is composed of nineteen shots (not counting the four exterior, establishing long shots), the first of which is a complex moving shot during which the camera starts as an aerial vehicle outside the hotel room and becomes an object inside the room. The camera reveals to us two figures in contrast, a vertical male figure—half dressed—and a horizontal female figure—also half dressed. The camera's low angle provides a truncated perspective: the vertical bars of the bed frame and the dingy wall of the hotel room prevent the viewer's eye from peering deeper into the frame. We are as enclosed in the room as the characters are. The camera's placement accentuates the claustrophobia of the scene, as does the camera lens's distortion of the female figure's prone body. The lens does not see depth as the human eye does. Hitchcock plants a visual clue as to Marion's ultimate fate in this scene. She will again be at the mercy of a dominant figure in the shower of the Bates Motel. She will again descend to the bottom of the frame and will end up in a prone position, this time face down.

As the scene develops, we find out that Marion and Sam are indeed as trapped in their lives as they are trapped in the room. Beginning with shot 3 and continuing to the end, the camera becomes the fourth wall of the room, the interior wall. The camera's placement creates an orientation to the structure of the set. The door to the room is on the right side of the frame; the hotel window is to the left side—where the camera came in at the beginning of the scene. The characters orient themselves to the camera in the quarter turn, traditional to classical cinema (Giannetti 77–78). The camera placement is typical of Hitchcock's mise-en-scene. In providing a consistent camera placement as an interior fourth wall, Hitchcock presents the viewer with a traditionally defined diegesis. One might call this a concrete space; it has substance and viability. The scene is about four minutes long, and its nineteen shots average ten seconds each.

In the five scenes leading up to the shower scene, the average length of each shot is approximately eight seconds. The opening scene contains shots averaging about ten seconds. These relatively lengthy shots provide the audience with a time-space continuum that is characteristic of the classical style. As the scenes follow one another, the average length of the shots decreases, as the film's tempo speeds up somewhat. The third shot of the opening scene begins with a medium shot, and then the camera tilts down as the couple lies on the bed and begin a long, daring kissing scene. Hitchcock tweaks the by now vitiated Production Code—as he did fourteen years earlier in *Notorious*—by having a kissing scene last for a considerably longer time than the Code usually allowed. As a sign of the times, though, both Marion and Sam are half-dressed, and they are together on the bed. Hitchcock places them in the center of the frame.

Like many directors trained in the studio style of classical cinema, Hitchcock prefers central dominance for the construction of his mise-en-scene. However, Hitchcock likes to surprise his audience by frequently having the threatening element appear near the center of his frame, not on the sides, as conventional thriller and horror directors do. Unbeknownst to either Sam or Marion, this will almost be the last time they share such an intimate moment. Two other shots will show Sam and Marion together in the frame. The remaining eleven shots are alternating shots, either close-ups or medium shots—of Sam or Marion. These are not point-of-view (hereafter POV) shots or eye-line match—both of which are features of montage and thus discussed later—but rather isolating shots in the quarter turn. Moreover, in several shots, the characters are placed on the outer edge of the frame—Marion on the left, Sam on the right—emphasizing their distance from one another. When they come together in the center of the frame in shots 7 and 13, they come from their respective sides of the frame and then part and return to their former position. The viewer detects visual echoes of the credits, during which graphic elements come together from either side of the frame, coalesce momentarily, and exit to a side of the frame. Uniting, separating, and reuniting are major patterns in the film.

Bellour claims that *Psycho* "contains two narratives slipping one under the other, one into the other" (240). However, I should like to add two more. *Psycho* contains at least four narratives or stories, and they spiral into one another, like the lines of a spiral—one pushing the other into the center of the spiral. There's Marion's story, an unmarried woman with an unmarried sister, whose parents are deceased and who is involved in a seemingly dead-end relationship with Sam. In her interview with me, Janet Leigh says that she created a fictional autobiography for Marion so that she could construct a rounder character:

> . . . in my story, in my approach to Marion, I figured that her parents were killed in an automobile accident and she had to forego college to support her younger sister. I think that she also probably did not pursue a romance that she had because he wasn't settled and didn't have enough to take care of the sister. She had to work and all these things are what I'm thinking Marion is. Now the sister has grown up, but Marion still takes care of her, but her life is passing her by, and she finds a man that she is attracted to and does love. But he's divorced and doesn't have the money to get married, and for her to have an illicit affair is not true to her. She's not a hooker. She's not comfortable in this role. Obviously,

> she's a terrible thief, but hopefully you see this temptation, the desperation to have a life. And you see it take over, but you don't not like her for it.

Then, of course, there is Sam, with no mother (at least he doesn't mention her) but with a very much present dead father—present in the debt he leaves to Sam—and a very much present divorced wife—present in the alimony she demands and is legally entitled to. Sam is crippled by debts he owes to absent people present in his life. Next is Norman, also fatherless, but also possessed of two mothers, one physically dead but the other very much psychologically alive, living within him, like an alien life force. Like Sam, Norman is in debt to a dead parent, but he has the extra burden of a psychic tax collector, who extracts her debt by possessing his body. This grim accountant is of course Norma Bates, the ultimate mother figure, who—unlike the mother of Freudian psychology—is palpably alive, a sort of economic Siamese twin, whom Norman drags along. As frequently with twins in utero, one will eventually win the struggle for survival by destroying its rival for sustenance.

Finally, there's Norma's story. Widowed when Norman is only five, she takes up with a man who lies to her about the fact that he is already married and who convinces her to use her money to build the Bates Motel. We're not quite sure what happens to Norma—how she died. Norman, of course, claims that she is not dead but rather mentally ill. The sheriff tells Sam and Lila that Norma committed suicide after she poisoned her faithless lover. The psychiatrist claims that Norman's mother, Norma, told him that Norman killed both his mother and her lover in a fit of oedipal rage—"Matricide is probably the most unbearable crime of all." Whatever the case, Norma is very much alive in the film, a character in her own right, a powerful, avenging female who strikes a blow at the sexual and economic infrastructure of family and society. Stefano's script mentions Norma by name in the fruit cellar scene, during which she rushes in, knife raised, to kill Marion's sister Lila, who, like Marion, has come to the Bates Motel and house to threaten her son. As she approaches Lila, Stefano has Norma say, "I am Norma Bates!" but the words are hard to hear because of Bernard Herrmann's screeching violin score. Stefano mentions this aural conflict in his interview with me: "Well, that's where the music is real loud, and the first time I saw the movie I thought they'd cut that line."

These four narrative strands eventually intertwine in the film and provide its underlying structure. Sam and Marion's stories become pronounced in the first four scenes in the film; Norman's and Norma's stories begin in the motel scenes, when Marion and Norman meet and exchange verbal intimacies in the parlor sequence. Norman and Marion are strange soul mates, both trapped by another character's past: Marion by Sam's, and Norman by Norma's.

Hitchcock claims, "all backgrounds must function," and his mise-en-scene assures that this happens in *Psycho*. Next to *Vertigo*, *Psycho* has perhaps the richest mise-en-scene in Hitchcock's oeuvre. Much has been made of Hitchcock's decision to use his camera crew from *Alfred Hitchcock Presents* to photograph *Psycho*. Jack Russell was a fast, efficient cinematographer, but he was not "just" a television cinematographer: he had a long list of film credits, having shot his first film in 1940. Next to *Psycho*, his most important film was Orson Welles' *Macbeth* (1948). Along with art directors Joseph Hurley and Robert Clatworthy, and set director George Milo, Russell constructs a rich mise-en-scene with numerous "signifying elements." These are graphic elements and actual physical objects that take on thematic or characteristic meaning in the film. They function like imagery in poetry or timbre in music by adding depth and resonance to the story. In their essay on Hitchcock's employment of suspense—"Suspense and Its Master"—Deborah Knight and George McKnight use the term "cataphor," coined by the suspense theorist Hans J. Wulff. A cataphor, according to Wulff's definition, is "an advance reference signaling some event or action that could occur later in the story" (108–109). Knight and McKnight call cataphors "future-directed narrative cues," and their claim is that Hitchcock was a master at creating not only "object cataphors" (Guy's lighter in *Strangers on a Train*, for example) but also "situational" or "thematic" cataphors, which "help to frame our understanding of the dangers that threaten protagonists under conditions of uncertainty" (109). The many "signifying elements" that Hitchcock uses in *Psycho* could therefore be called "cataphors."

In the opening scene, Hitchcock uses a window as a cataphor and as a portal to the narrative. What is it that attracted Hitchcock to windows? As a geometric shape, a window is like an inverted film frame that adds height to a largely horizontal frame. Windows also provide a filter or membrane between the inside and the outside, between macro and micro settings. In addition, blinds, shades, and curtains can vary and alter windows, so they become part of the lighting pattern of the film. They are like doors in that they provide ingress to a setting, but unlike doors, which open and close to admit characters, windows open to admit the camera. Hitchcock is too clever a filmmaker to rely on a door to admit the camera. Even though a camera may become a character in certain montage techniques like POV and eye-line match shots, the camera is the director's domain; it is extra-diegetic and thus given much more authority and freedom than a diegetic character. Hitchcock uses windows most creatively in *Rear Window*, constructing micro films within films. *Psycho* also employs windows inventively. Threats from outside come through windows in *Psycho* (the shower curtain is a kind of window) and imperil a confined "safe place." These threats include the bright sunshine of Phoenix flooding the dark room of Sam and Marion's tryst when Sam angrily raises the blinds in shot 7.

Other cataphors in this first scene include the horizontal and vertical shapes with which Hitchcock constructs the mise-en-scene, especially the lines of the bed frame, the reclining and upright stances of the characters, and the contrast of sash and blinds in the window. Hitchcock told Truffaut about *Psycho*'s design: "Definitely, that's our composition: a vertical block and a horizontal block" (Truffaut 269). The horizontal lines represent stability, just as the vertical represent threats to that stability, whether the threat comes from a butcher's knife plunging downward in the shower, an enraged Norma pursuing Arbogast down the stairs in her house, or Lila going down the stairs to the fruit cellar. Vertical lines also represent the horizontal limits of the frame, which can move when the camera pans. The frame carves out a space within which the diegesis proceeds. What is outside the frame is always potentially present in the classical cinema, which employs the film frame as a window into a larger social, political, or physical milieu. In an aesthetic sense, Hitchcock's frame is its own window, and he's fond of having one window enter another, as he does in so many of his films—*Shadow of a Doubt*, *Rope*, *I Confess*, *To Catch a Thief*, *North by Northwest*. Hitchcock also cleverly places another kind of frame within his diegesis to contrast with windows—mirrors. Unlike windows, mirrors reflect back rather than lead through, unless we are in the world of dreamscapes. Hitchcock places mirrors strategically in both *Vertigo* and *Psycho*. As a visual trope for the doppelgänger theme, they function strikingly. Witness Madeline/Judy reflected in the mirrors throughout *Vertigo*, and Marion Crane/Marie Samuels in the first shots of the Bates Motel scene. There's an optical-philosophical dimension to mirrors as well. As we know, they reflect back things in reverse—as Scotty realizes when he sees in the mirror Judy's necklace transform into Carlotta's necklace in the painting. What mirrors reflect back is distorted shapes—a world in reverse, but a self-contained world. Unlike the window into the world, the mirror has no reality outside of it. When it moves horizontally or vertically, it does not reveal an extension of a world, only the world that's created within or on its mirrored surface. In response to this, one could argue that the lens of the camera has its own distorting quality and that the film image is imprinted negatively; it must be printed positively to seem real. Yet the classical cinema within which Hitchcock worked was a cinema of realism; that is, its goal was to recreate a semblance of the reality that its viewers lived within and through.

The second scene of *Psycho* continues where the first scene ends, but in reverse. The camera is inside the Lowery Real Estate office, looking out. Its position is an interior fourth wall. The entrance to the office is to the right of the screen, and there we see through the window to a physical embodiment of the camera itself, the famous Hitchcock cameo. This shot is very clever; it is an example of what Patrick McGilligan calls "Hitchcockery." Hitchcock is outside the office; we see him through the window. He is in the camera position with which so many of his films begin, outside. But he is not looking within, but rather away, except for a very brief turn-of-the-head acknowledgment of Marion as she walks by. The real purpose of Hitchcock's cameo is to replicate the function of his camera. He is there as a reminder of the extra-diegetic power of the film creator—the artist—to include within the frame whatever he wishes. His appearance is not a signature; that is the function of the credits. It's not a self-portrait because he is *not* the subject of the film. It's not like a theater director making a character appearance in a play; the play will eventually outlive its creator. The cameo is a unique cinematic creation, mainly the province of one director—Hitchcock. Hitchcock's cameos thus serve a dual function: they deconstruct the realism of the film by reminding viewers that the cinema is a construct of reality, yet they also function to emphasize the film's formalism by including the artist into the shape of the text, even so far as to dress him as a figure of the West, as Hitchcock does to his cameo character in *Psycho*, by having him don a cowboy hat.

Earlier, in the hotel scene, Marion exited the room to the right of the frame, leaving Sam stranded in the room, the shot implying Sam's continual entrapment in his past. At the beginning of the real estate office scene, Marion enters from the same side of the screen from which she exited the hotel room—the right. She walks into an office dominated by cataphors: two large paintings—both mirrors, as it were—that provide some symbols and foreshadowing. The large painting on the right is of a river surrounded on both sides by hills or mountains. The eye follows the river into the depths of the painting, and it doesn't take long for the audience to register the notion of an escape into a bucolic, Edenic world—a pastoral, in effect. This pastoral is in direct contrast to the urban setting that began the film, the cityscape planted unnaturally on the desert of Phoenix. The river is a traditional literary symbol of a journey or an escape—the Mississippi of *The Adventures of Huckleberry Finn*—and it has the added dimensions of a watery escape from the desert. Later, Marion will arrive on her own river as the highway disappears in a deluge of rain, and she is figuratively floating down an unknown river toward the Bates Motel. The other painting is an additional pastoral, this time without water. It resembles the place where Marion pulls her car over to catch some sleep on her way to Fairvale—a perfect name for a pastoral retreat. Both paintings, through perspective, draw the reader's eye into the frame and thus stand in vivid contrast to the opening scene, with its dingy walls entrapping the characters.

In many ways, *Psycho* is Hitchcock's great antipastoral. The classical Hollywood cinema that he worked in from the 1920s through the 1950s was essentially a pastoral cinema; its characteristic movie was the Western, with its promise of a trek westward to an Edenic garden. The urban landscape—the dark city—was the province of film noir, essentially an eccentric, European vision (the product of American lost innocence in World War II). When Marion steals the $40,000, she treks west in search of her "private island," as she tells Norman, hoping to get to Fairvale, where she will reunite with Sam in matrimony. Marriage, as many commentators have pointed out, is the great consummation of the narrative journeys of classical American cinema.

In Hitchcock, though, marriage is not always a resolution. The journey that the characters go through to reach their destination usually involves murder, sabotage, deceit—in short, a catalogue of the dark side of the human heart. At the end of *Strangers on a Train*, Guy and Anne have become a couple, but their newfound knowledge makes them suspicious of the friendly overture of the minister who recognizes Guy; they leave the compartment without a word. In *Rear Window*, the movie ends where it begins, with Jeff asleep in his chair. He now has two broken legs, and his fiancée, Lisa, pretends to read a travel book called *Beyond the High Himalayas* but then surreptitiously substitutes *Bazaar*, a fashion magazine instead. In the apartment next door, the newlyweds have begun to bicker, and we wonder if they will end up like the Thorwalds. Deceit and sexual tensions are the elements of which Hitchcockean marriage is composed of.

Essentially, classical American cinema upholds marriage and the family as the foundation of social stability and as the model of social interaction. The *Alfred Hitchcock Presents* episode entitled "Lamb to the Slaughter" (1958) acts as a kind of prelude and prequel to *Psycho* in its presentation of marriage and the family. Mary Maloney's policeman husband, Patrick, informs her at the beginning of the episode that he is leaving her. A huge, hulking man, he delivers his statement wearing his police uniform, a perfect symbol of male authority and power. The facts that Mary is pregnant—she is wearing a maternity smock—and that she is solicitous in her wifely duties make her husband's announcement that much more shocking. After begging her husband not to leave her, Mary retreats to the kitchen and seizes a frozen leg of lamb that she had planned to serve for dinner. Stealthily, she comes from behind her husband and hits him with the lamb-leg club, killing him instantly. In his 1943 *Shadow of a Doubt*, Hitchcock has the ghoulish neighbors Joe and Herbert—both good family men—talk about the crime: "The best way to commit a murder? I know! I know! Hit them in the head with a blunt instrument." Thus do Hitchcock's preoccupations create a string of connections through his films. In "Lamb to the Slaughter," Mary had followed Herbert's direction: she coolly and collectedly constructs the crime scene to make it appear that she had come into their apartment after shopping and had discovered her husband's body—she even puts the leg of lamb in the oven to roast. The police, of course, hungry from a long night of investigating the murder, devour the leg of lamb, and the episode ends with a long shot of Mary sitting in the living room staring directly out at the audience. The camera tracks in slowly to a shoulder shot of Mary as she listens to the police officers describing the mysterious murder weapon while devouring the weapon itself. Mary breaks into a smile and then a laugh. This chilling moment exposes the fundamental violence within the meekest soul and strips bare the veneer of the "happy family."

Roald Dahl's black comedy teleplay and Hitchcock's understated direction work together to create a drama that deconstructs the institution of marriage and family to reveal their patriarchal foundations. Moreover, in attempting to assert power through violence and lawlessness, Mary Maloney prefigures both Marion and Norma, the first desperate to enter the system (marriage) that would legitimize and give meaning to her life; the second, in revolt against a system that has left her abandoned, burdened with a child, and deceived by a conniving lover. Norma's probable incestuous relationship with her son and her murderous rampage—unforgettably presented in the shower scene—are directed against the very essence of marriage and the family—sexuality. When Norman asks "permission" of his mother to invite Marion to dinner, the following interchange takes place:

Norma: No! I tell you no! I won't have you bringing strange, young girls in here for supper . . . by candlelight. I suppose, in the cheap, erotic fashion of young men with cheap, erotic minds! And then what, after supper? Music? Whispers? Touching?

Norman: Mother, she's just a stranger! She's hungry . . . and it's raining out!

Norma: "Mother, she's just a stranger"—as if men don't desire strangers. Ah! I refuse to speak of disgusting things, because they disgust me. Do you understand, boy? Go on! Go tell her she'll not be appeasing her ugly appetite with my food—or my son! Or do *I* have to tell her cause you don't have the guts? You have the guts, boy?

The mother's possessiveness of her son's sexuality is a way of preventing further marriage and family: it is the ultimate feminine revolt against patriarchy in its most basic forms.

It's significant that Hitchcock did not work in the Western genre at all; his one foray into screwball comedy, *Mr. & Mrs. Smith*, is mildly amusing. His real forte, of course, was suspense, but even here, Hitchcock presents a resolution that reunites his characters: Guy gets his upper-class girlfriend, Anne Morton, in *Strangers on a Train*; Father Logan reunites with the church in *I Confess*; L.B. Jeffreys gives his blessing to a union with Lisa in *Rear Window*; Manny and Rose reunite in *The Wrong Man* (though only in a postscript); the McKenna family has a reunion at the end of *The Man Who Knew Too Much*; Roger Thornhill lifts Eve Kendall up to his berth in *North by Northwest*. Only in the two great films that ended his golden period, *Vertigo* and *Psycho*, however, does Hitchcock depart from the narrative closure characteristic of classicism. Both *Vertigo* and *Psycho* are two sides of the same coin—*Vertigo* undermines the romantic vision that is essential for joining a couple in matrimony; *Psycho* undermines the family structure that marriage makes possible. When Norma–Norman kills Marion in the shower, the death reverberates beyond the diegesis of *Psycho* into the cultural landscape of the late 1950s and early 1960s. Marion dies, but so also does the raison d'etre of classical cinema. The shower scene is the death knell of the pastoral.

Psycho's second setting—George Lowery's real estate office—features a camera fixed in the position of an interior fourth wall. Opposite the camera, Marion sits at her desk beneath the two large paintings, while characters enter and exit to and from the sides of the frame. The walls containing the painting prevent the viewer's eye from gaining access to the depth of the frame—except in the perspective of the two large paintings. Like Sam in the hotel room, Marion seems trapped in this setting, her only escape in the imaginative world of the paintings. When the oilman Cassidy enters the frame, he comes from the right side, from the outside world, and he brings with him the passkey that allows him to traverse the door from outside (freedom) to inside—money. Cassidy is the father that Sam does not have. Cassidy's beneficence to his daughter—a $40,000 cash payment for the gift of a house—is in direct contrast to the debt that Sam's father has left him. Cassidy's attempt to buy happiness for his daughter through a dowry is the verbal trigger for Marion's scheme to steal her own happiness via a "borrowed" dowry.

Hitchcock constructs the interior space of Lowery's office through thirty-eight shots with an average length of six seconds. The mise-en-scene is classical scene construction, with an unobtrusive eye-level camera. The lighting is higher-key than the lighting of the hotel room, with the even illumination of an office setting. The camera has free access to the interior space of Lowery's private office at the end of the scene; the office is first seen on the left of the frame at the beginning of the scene, with a dark sliding door cutting it off from the space of the outer office. This interior space is a male-dominated area, where Lowery keeps his "bottle" and where the "big deals" are made, in air-conditioned space. If all backgrounds must function, then Hitchcock uses this small but power-filled space as the first of several privileged areas where only selected characters—and the camera—are allowed. Marion's car is such a place, and so are the restroom of the car dealership, where Marion counts the forbidden money; the briefly glimpsed bathroom of her apartment; Norman's parlor; and of course the bathroom and shower of Cabin 1 at the Bates Motel. The irony is that, unlike Lowery, who has the power of money to travel from outside to inside and vice-versa, Marion, Sam, and Norman never seem to escape their enclosed spaces. Marion and Sam lack the money that would allow them to enter the legitimate world of marriage and property (Sam says to Marion, "Yeah, and live with me in a storeroom behind a hardware store in Fairvale"), while Norman and Norma lack the prerequisite sanity and mental health (they're not "normal") to live anywhere other than "off the main road."

The real estate scene ends as Marion leaves Lowery's office at the left of the frame and moves to the right side of the frame. She pauses briefly to speak to the other secretary, Caroline (played by Hitchcock's daughter). Caroline, inquiring whether Marion has a headache (little does she know!), offers her tranquilizers rather than aspirin, drugs that had been given to her, she claims, by "My mother's doctor . . . [on] the day of my wedding. Teddy was furious when he found out I'd taken tranquilizers." What a sly attack this is on the institution of marriage and the family: a parent tranquilizing her daughter in order to "offer" her in marriage! Hitchcock closes the scene with a long shot of Marion leaving the office and walking outside the right side of the frame, which holds on a long shot of the river painting and then begins a long dissolve into the next scene.

The third scene of the film, in Marion's apartment, is relatively brief—a little under two minutes—but it is significant in terms of camera function and cataphors. Instead of entering the space through a window, or referring to an outside space through a window, the camera begins and ends the scene as an interior fourth wall. When Janet Leigh called Hitchcock's camera "dictating," she was referring to its authoritative positioning vis-à-vis actors. But in an aesthetic sense, Hitchcock's camera "dictates" in both a diegetic and nondiegetic sense. In other words, it can see what characters see, but it can also see what characters cannot see, what only the enunciator, the director surrogate, can see. Or the camera sees better than a character can—closer and more clearly, such as when the camera tracks in to reveal Bruno's tie clip in *Strangers on a Train*. Sometimes the camera is able to "see" the director (the cameo) and thus becomes the essence of the nondiegetic: the camera viewing its own maker. The role of the camera contains the real essence and meaning of Hitchcockean suspense.

Scene three begins with the fourth-wall camera showing a closet door half open. Marion enters the frame from the left side, her shadow preceding her reflection on the wall. This subtle expressionistic device of a projected shadow reinforces the doppelgänger theme. Just as Keller has become "killer" in the opening scene of *I Confess*, symbolized by the oversized shadow thrown on the narrow wall of the darkened street, so also does Marion start to become Marie Samuels (the alias she uses to check in to the Bates Motel) as she contemplates stealing Cassidy's money. In a long shot, we see Marion as she takes clothes from her closet and puts them into a suitcase. Wearing a black bra and half-slip, in contrast to her white underwear in the opening scene, she looks at something on the bed. The moral meaning of this costume change becomes clearer as the camera tilts down to reveal the object of Marion's stare—the envelope of money on the bed. The money is Marion's passkey to the world that has been evading her, but her appropriation of that key lacks the legitimacy of commerce and the law. In the pastoral dimension of classical cinema, money, and those who possess or abuse it, are frequently immoral forces. But in the claustrophobic, antipastoral world of *Psycho*, money is the fulcrum; it's the currency of the fathers who bestow it upon their children, or who leave legacies of indebtedness on their children. Money is the means by which Norma Bates is taken from Norman by the man who persuaded her to build the Bates Motel (Norman: "He talked her into building this motel"). To emphasize the importance of currency to the world of *Psycho*, Hitchcock has his camera track in to a close-up of the money and then pan to the left to reveal an almost fully packed suitcase. This bit of visual storytelling is characteristic of Hitchcock's mise-en-scene. We can see it in the openings of *I Confess* and *Rear Window*. The visual connection between the money and the suitcase, accomplished in a single tracking and pan shot, establishes the idea of money as power. Marion, in effect, co-opts the male power of money by substituting herself for Cassidy's daughter and thus incurs the wrath of the father ("If any of it is missing, I'll replace it with her fine soft flesh," Marion imagines Cassidy saying of the money as she escapes in her car in the next scene).

Hitchcock generously fills the mise-en-scene with cataphors in this short scene. Over Marion's right shoulder, Hitchcock shows, in soft focus, the doorway into her shower. Hitchcock's fascination with bathrooms and toilets is manifested in many of his films. *Psycho* is his most daring exploration of the private space of the bathroom. Like Lowery's office, where males share the camaraderie of money and power, the bathroom has its own power. It is where we touch and expose our most intimate parts. Hitchcock was acutely aware of the taboos associated with bathrooms, and he shared the British fascination with excretory functions and with humor associated with WC's and "loos." Hitchcock's fondness for the "dirty joke" is legendary. The fact that a sexually oriented joke is called "dirty" only goes to underscore Freud's and Yeats's observation about nature's "joke" in putting in such close proximity our sexual and excretory organs. Hitchcock was also well aware of the Production Code's "sensitivity" to certain film settings, such as bedrooms and bathrooms. The fact that *Psycho* opens in a bedroom and features its most famous scene in a bathroom underscores both how far Hitchcock had gone in tweaking the nose of the Code people and how weak the Code had become.

Universal Pictures/Photofest

Figure 1. Hitchcock foreshadows the shower scene in Marion's apartment, putting the shower in soft focus in the background.

As Marion takes things from the closet and begins to get dressed, we see over her left shoulder a picture of a small child in a white dress, most likely a picture of Marion as a child, still "innocent." As Marion comes closer to her suitcase, the camera pans left with her and we see another soft-focus glimpse of the bathroom behind her, Hitchcock guiding the viewer's eye by providing an interior space framed by the vertical lines of the door frame. In the interior space provided by Hitchcock's mise-en-scene, the shower head gleams with a shiny light, revealed by a half-open shower curtain, decorated with a floral pattern. Just as Marion finishes dressing, Hitchcock frames her in a silhouette with the shower to the left of her face and the baby picture to the right. Through this shot, Hitchcock suggests that Marion is turning her back on her childhood innocence and heading toward her final moments in the shower. In shots 6 through 10, Hitchcock follows Marion with the camera as she moves left to finish packing, to check herself in the mirror, to organize her car papers, and finally to put the money in her purse and leave the room to the right of the frame. In these shots Hitchcock again fills the frame with signifying elements. We see on the wall behind Marion a framed photograph of a man and a woman, presumably Marion's parents, who because of the position at the top of the frame, seem to be looking down at her: their profiles face Marion. In shot 6, the large mirror in Marion's apartment dominates the frame as she looks at herself (another visual embodiment of the double). There's anxiety on her face; she is obviously struggling with her decision to steal the money. Of course, there are two Marions in *Psycho*, just as there are two Normans and two Normas. Hitchcock uses his incredibly rich mise-en-scene to tell Marion's story visually. Not only do we see her childhood and her parents, but we also see her taste and economic circumstances laid out in front of us. The small detailed pattern of the wall paper is picked up by the large floral pattern of the window and shower curtain. The small floral pattern is echoed in the living room chair placed under the photograph of her parents. On the bureau that sits underneath the mirror we see family photographs, some bric-a-brac, a portable phonograph, and a small glass lamp with a chintz shade. This modest and drab efficiency apartment is the extent of Marion's world, a stark contrast to the home that the "oil-lease man" Cassidy will buy for his daughter. Marion's desperate plight to buy happiness reminds us of her statement to Sam in the opening scene—"When you're married, you can do lots of things"—and Lowery's statement about his goal in buying a house for his daughter. "You know what I do about unhappiness? I buy it off. . . . I'm buying this house for my baby's wedding present—forty-thousand dollars cash! Now that's not buying happiness. That's just buying off unhappiness."

The scene ends with Marion resolutely taking the money off of the bed and putting it in her purse. Hitchcock will make the association of money, bed, and purse again in *Marnie*. The act of thievery in both movies has a psychological component. Marnie's compulsion to steal is directly related to the trauma in her childhood, when sex, violence, and maleness are inextricably intertwined. The visual association that Hitchcock creates between money (power) and bed (sex) helps explain Marion's plight—and women's in general—of having to use one to get the other. Marnie's mother is a prostitute, and prostitution is the essence of women using sexuality to gain power. Norma takes a lover to gain security and assuage her loneliness. Marion sleeps with Sam to keep him interested in their relationship, and she tolerates Cassidy's sexual innuendoes to appease her boss. Throughout the first half of *Psycho*, Hitchcock deconstructs the institution of marriage and the family to reveal their patriarchal sexual and economic foundations. In the traditional marriage, a daughter is given away by her father to another male, who bonds his bride to himself via sexuality (procreation) and money (property). A man without property but with sexuality (Sam) is as hobbled in this world as a man with property but without sexuality (Norman). A woman with unbridled sexuality but without property/marriage (Marion)—she has no one to give her away and no one to be given away to—becomes a sexual object and scapegoat.

Hitchcock begins the fourth scene—in Marion's car—with a dissolve from the previous scene, during which Marion walks out of her old life, closing her closet door as she leaves. The fourth scene begins with Marion in a full front pose, directly facing the audience as she drives her car out of Phoenix. The camera has now become part of the vehicle (the windshield) or even the vehicle itself. The mise-en-scene has suddenly shifted dimension, and the audience is now face-to-face with the character, sharing intimacies with her via voice-overs, not of her voice, but of absent characters' voices.

This car scene is an extraordinary one. In it, Hitchcock demonstrates that he is indeed the enunciator by shifting the film spectatorship into a different gear (pun intended). By placing the camera in front of a character—receiving the character's stare and providing one of its own—Hitchcock has created an alternate, nondiegetic position for the camera. It's not unusual for Hitchcock's camera to assume the full frontal view and to receive the gaze of a character. In *Rear Window*, for instance, the camera seems to become the character Jeff as he sees Lisa looming over him and coming closer to kiss him. In *Vertigo*, Scotty looks directly into the camera in his dream sequence. What's unusual about the fourth scene of *Psycho*, however, is that Marion is not part of a POV shot or eye-line match, or a dream sequence. She is not being viewed by anyone in the diegesis; she is being viewed by the enunciator—Hitchcock. What's also unusual about the mise-en-scene is that we hear Marion's thoughts, but they are not in her voice and they are not the "actual" words of a character. The words that we and she hear are imagined voices, but they carry the authority of real voices. Hitchcock has moved from the realm of realistic time-space continuum (the province of classical cinema) to the region of psychological space, from an exterior reality to an interior one. The direct stare of Marion draws the viewer into Marion's mind and, by extension, into her dilemma. The gradual darkening of the scene—she experiences two descents into darkness—is actually a metaphorical or symbolic movement into the world of the Bates Motel.

Marion: "I thought I had gotten off the main road."
Norman: "I know you must have. Nobody ever stops here anymore unless they've done that."

Hitchcock's psychopaths live in worlds of darkness. Uncle Charlie's train that deposits him in Santa Rosa belches forth black smoke; Bruno's boat that transports him from the tunnel of love to the island where he kills Miriam is named for Pluto, the god of the underworld. Norman's world is the dark parlor, surrounded by birds of the night—his trap and Marion's. Marion's trip to the Bates Motel is a journey into the heart of darkness, a Conradian trip to the essential violence and brutality of the human soul. This is a dark terrain, indeed, peopled usually by men who kill women, either on a whim or a bargain—Bruno—or for more personal reasons—Uncle Charlie. Speaking to the Newton family at the dinner table, Uncle Charlie says of rich widows: "And what do the wives do, these useless women? You see them in the hotels, the best hotels, every day, by the thousands. Drinking the money, eating the money, losing the money at bridge, playing all day and all night. Smelling of money, proud of their jewelry but of nothing else. Horrible! Faded, fat, greedy women. . . . Are they human, or are they fat, wheezing animals, huh? What happens to animals when they get too fat or too old?"

Hitchcock constructs the car scene—Marion's "escape" to the hoped-for reunion with Sam in Fairvale—around two descents into darkness sandwiched among three discrete mini-scenes. This tripartite "master" scene is fourteen minutes and fifteen seconds long and comprises 151 shots. The first mini-scene is made up of sixty-five shots. As Marion looks directly at the camera—and at us—we hear her imagine the voice of Sam as she surprises him in his hardware store in Fairvale:

> "Marion, what in the world. . . . What are you doing up here? I'm glad to see you, I always am. What is it, Marion?"

What it is, of course, is that Marion has attempted to co-opt the male world of power by using the currency of that world to escape it. The $40,000 has given Marion the freedom that she and Sam lack but so desperately desire. The money will pay off Sam's father's debt and his wife's alimony, and will somehow right the wrong of patriarchal privilege. But, of course, Marion wants to be married. She says to Sam in the hotel room, "I haven't even been married once yet. . . . Sam, let's get married!" To Sam's sarcastic reply to her proposal, "I tell you what. When I send my ex-wife alimony, you can lick the stamps"—Marion debases herself by declaring, "I'll lick the stamps." In shot 4, Marion comes out of her reverie as the camera becomes Marion and as she sees her boss Lowery walk by the front of her car as she is stopped at a light on her way out of town with the $40,000 in her purse. After at first smiling, Lowery pauses and looks puzzled, as the audience—along with Marion—realizes that something is not right: Marion should be home in bed, not driving out of town. Seeing

Lowery snaps Marion back to reality; he is the true recipient of the money, not Marion, and her realization brings on fear and guilt, which are accompanied by the gradual darkening of the scene. Shot 13 plunges Marion into darkness; the shot ends with a fade into blackness and then a fade-in to a long shot of a car in a hilly terrain strikingly similar to the one in the picture above Marion's desk. It's as if we were back in the world of *Rear Window*; one of the window-shaped cataphors has now become a movie of its own. The difference is that we are now the voyeurs, not L.B. Jeffreys. We might call this part of the scene "the hoped-for world of Fairvale." Marion is asleep in this world; it is as if she is in a dream, but a rap on the window of her car rudely awakens her; again, the outside world intrudes on the private space Marion has appropriated for herself—the interior of her car. The window of her car is another portal in the film; standing outside it is the embodiment of male power itself, the policeman, with his threatening demeanor and dark glasses, both of which we and Marion see in shot 20. "This is what we do to naughty boys," the policeman at the local jail tells the young Hitchcock in the oft-repeated story explaining Hitchcock's fear of police and confinement. In *Psycho*, though, Marion is not Hitchcock's classic protagonist—the innocent wrongly accused. This protagonist can exist only in a pastoral world where a kind of innocence is still possible. Marion's world is the world of *Alfred Hitchcock Presents*, the world of "Lamb to the Slaughter" (the title is significant), where the pregnant, mild-mannered Mary Maloney kills her policeman husband and laughs as she gets away with it. During Marion's exchange with the nameless policeman, which covers shots 19 through 46, the camera shifts position from outside of the car (the policeman's position) to inside the car, Marion's position. In shot 40, however, there is an abrupt shift as Hitchcock places his camera next to Marion on the passenger side of the car, so that we can see her trying to conceal the money from the prying eyes of the policeman.

Marion's car, like most of the enclosed spaces in the first half of *Psycho*—the hotel room, her apartment, Lowery's office, Norman' parlor—functions as a cataphor of her predicament, trapped, imprisoned (unfairly—like the five-year-old Hitchcock) by the institutions of the world of *Psycho*. The spaces get increasingly smaller and finally culminate in the shower of Cabin 1, the most terrifying space in all of cinema. By placing his camera in the position of a passenger in Marion's car, Hitchcock almost guarantees our identification with this young, attractive victim. In an interview, Janet Leigh claims, "Hitchcock's camera was absolute"; it could go anywhere

("The Making of *Psycho*"). Hitchcock makes full use of this aesthetic flexibility in his films by surprising the audience either through sudden shifts in the camera placement—the bird's-eye view in *Vertigo* after Scotty leaves the bell tower—or through unexpected camera movements—the famous crane shot in *Notorious*—or the vertiginous camera movement in *Vertigo*. The first part of the car scene ends with Marion's escape from the threatening policeman as he seems to stop following her. The camera alternates positions, inside the car—Marion's POV—and outside the car, with Marion staring straight ahead at the audience and registering both fear and guilt, feelings shared by the audience because of its identification with her in such an intimate space.

In the second third of the car scene, there are forty-three shots taking place in 5:50, giving a rough parity to the three subscenes:

1. First car escape and first descent into darkness: 4:50, sixty-five shots.
2. Bakersfield car lot: 5:50, forty-three shots.
3. Second car escape and second descent into darkness 3:35, forty-three shots.

The Bakersfield subscene is characterized by Marion departing from the seeming safety of her car to the dangers of the outside world, symbolized by the intimidating policeman, who returns to "hunt" Marion, and by California Charlie, a salesman-businessman in the mode of Lowery and Cassidy, who reduces human transaction to barter ("Ah—you always got time to argue money, uh?")

Marion's exchange of cars in the Bakersfield subscene takes on greater meaning in shots 97 through 99, during which Marion has retreated to the women's room to count out the $700 for her used-car purchase. Hitchcock positions his camera at a high angle and paints the tiny room in darkness. The light seems to emanate from Marion herself. The top right third of the screen is dominated by a mirror cataphor; in it we see a truncated reflection of Marion as she retrieves the money from the white envelope. This dark, enclosed space, with Marion and her reversed image, is like Lewis Carroll's rabbit hole down which Alice tumbles. It is a surreal space, cut off from the world of the bright sunlight of a California morning; it is a world in which Marion transforms herself (or is transformed by Hitchcock) from impulsive thief to a real crook and fraud. When Marion decides to spend part of the money that she has stolen, she sinks deeper into the moral hole she has fallen into. The reflected half-image we see in the mirror is

Figure 2. Marion and her double count out the stolen money in one of Hitchcock's enclosed spaces.

Marion's other self—her dark half: Marie Samuels, from Los Angeles, the name she signs in the Bates Motel register.

This brief interlude in the Bakersfield car-lot scene is crucial in understanding Hitchcock's use of mise-en-scene in *Psycho*. By placing Marion in this dark, abstract space—cut off from the outside world—Hitchcock prepares his audience for the key scene in the film, the shower scene, which also takes place in a similar abstract space. The irony of Marion's private places is tellingly conveyed in these three brief shots. Marion seems to escape from the dangers of the world, from the prying eyes of the men who control her (Lowrey, the policeman) or who desire her (Sam, Cassidy) by retreating to "safe," private places: the hotel room, her apartment, her car, the women's room, Cabin 1 at the Bates Motel. Yet, she is never really out of the gaze of the power of men, including the director himself, the enunciator.

The irony, of course, is that there's nothing really safe about these places, nor is there anything really private about them. Norman can look through the peephole of his office at Marion getting undressed, just as Lowery can see Marion in her car as she tries to escape, just as J.B. Jeffreys can peer into the lives of his neighbors with binoculars and long-range lenses, and just as Bruno can follow Miriam and spy on her on her outing to Leeland Lake. It is at the heart of Hitchcock's suspense that the camera not only takes us to places where we really want to go, where we feel safe and perhaps privileged (his famous elegant settings and national monuments), but also *not* want to go (Thorwald's apartment, Manny Balestero's jail cell, Father Logan's confessional, the shower), where we feel unsafe, off-balance, uncomfortable.

Marion is Hitchcock's most complex and "problematic" heroine; she is clearly the character the audience identifies with in the first half of the film. In addition, she is also the sympathetic victim of the men who run the world—the Lowerys and the Cassidys—and of their institutions, particularly marriage. As feminist critics would say, Marion becomes the victim of the male gaze of the classic American cinema, the object of the voyeurism institutionalized in the technology (camera), personnel (patriarchal producers, directors, and studio heads), and audiences (patriarchal American society). Yet, Marion is also a strong character, almost a female Prometheus, who steals the fire of the gods (money) to create a new life for herself. Like Prometheus, she, too, must be punished, confined, chained, as it were, pecked at by the bird-like sounds of the *Psycho* musical score, mutilated, and murdered in the shower. Through thievery, Marion is like Marnie, who is also like Madeline, even like Miriam, also like Mary Maloney—all names beginning with "M," like "Mother." All of these characters defy the patriarchal order of things: Madeline defies the institutions of marriage, as does Miriam; Marnie defies the institution of business and capitalism, as does Marion; Mary Maloney commits homicide/patricide by striking a blow at domineering, philandering males and husbands, as does Norma Bates.

When Marion returns from the women's room and into the bright sunlight of California Charlie's used-car lot, she has actually fallen deeper into the rabbit hole: she is ready to assume a new identity with the new car she purchases. The last shot of the Bakersfield lot subscene shows her symbolically driving off without her luggage and then being stopped by the mechanic, who puts the remains of her old identity in the back seat. As she finally drives away, Hitchcock positions his camera at a low angle, showing only the driver's side of the car to the left of the frame and the three men—the policeman, California Charlie, and the mechanic—to the right side. As the car drives out of the frame, the camera stays focused on the three men, who now fill the frame and stare ominously out into the frame, their position reflecting the domination of men in Marion's life.

The last third of the lengthy car scene begins with a dissolve to Marion, again staring out of the frame straight at the audience. We hear echoey

Universal Pictures/Photofest

Figure 3. Hitchcock subverts the classical style by having Marion stare directly at the audience.

voices as Marion imagines the words spoken by California Charlie and the policeman:

Charlie: She look like a wrong-one to you?
Patrolman: Acted like one.

—and by Lowery and Cassidy as they discover her theft:

Lowery: After all, Cassidy, I told you—all that cash! I'm not taking the responsibility! Oh, for heaven's sake! A girl works for you for ten years, you trust her.
Cassidy: Well, I'm not about to kiss off forty thousand dollars! I'll get it back . . .

As night comes on, Marion experiences her second descent into darkness, and the prophetic words of Cassidy reverberate in the blackness surrounding Marion: "I'll get it back, and if any of it's missing, I'll replace it with her fine, soft flesh. I'll track her, never you doubt it." The first splatters of rain begin in shot 118, and Marion turns on the windshield wipers in shot 122 as the rain now becomes a deluge. The lights of the oncoming traffic blind Marion, and her view of the road is almost totally obscured. One can imagine Rod Serling's voice in the background saying, "Marion has now entered the world of the Twilight Zone." The world of night that Marion now finds herself in is the world of the Bates Motel.

The Bates Motel scene is approximately nineteen minutes long and contains 186 shots. The scene is actually composed of three subscenes. The first takes place in the office, in Cabin 1, and on the exterior walkway of the Bates Motel. This subscene lasts 7½ minutes and comprises sixty-four shots. The scene begins with Marion exiting her car in the pouring rain and waiting for someone to come from the dark house on the hill to check her into the motel. As the scene progresses, Marion—soon to identify herself to Norman as Marie Samuels—goes deeper and deeper into the labyrinth of the motel, into more and more enclosed spaces, until she finds herself in the most confining space of all, the shower of Cabin 1.

Next to *The Wrong Man*, with its largely vertical compositions suggesting the constrictions and entrapment of Manny's life, *Psycho* is Hitchcock's most claustrophobic film. Its dimly lit, enclosing spaces most closely emblemize the nightmare of confinement, whether it be in the much-reminisced-about jail cell of his youth or the many manifestations of that space in his films—ubiquitous handcuffs, train compartments, a lifeboat, a wheelchair, a crazily spinning merry-go-round, a phone booth, a bell tower. Hitchcock is perhaps most indebted to Poe for this artistic rendering of claustrophobia, in both physical and psychological manifestations. Poe's tortured characters are immobilized—tied down or buried alive—and this physical confinement is symbolic of psychological confinement, or madness, as well. Throughout his career, Hitchcock had shown morbid interest in deranged states of mind, from *The Lodger* all the way up to *Frenzy*. It was in the films of the 1950s, though, that Hitchcock explored the tragic etiology and consequences of madness, and he does this without the amelioration of a happy ending—as in *Spellbound*. Beginning with the premier episode of *Alfred Hitchcock Presents*, "Revenge," Hitchcock explores the descent into madness as a consequence of some act of violence, usually inextricably intertwined with sexuality and almost always carried out in a confined space. In "Revenge," Elsa Spann is attacked in her tiny trailer, and her mind snaps because of the assault; she descends into a dark, paranoid world where all men are potential rapists—"There he is. That's him. That's him." In *The Wrong Man*, Manny's wife, Rose, retreats "to the dark side of the moon," as her psychiatrist explains it, the initiating episode of her madness taking place in the dark confines of her bedroom, where she hits Manny with a hairbrush and cracks the mirror (her mind) in the process. In *Vertigo*, Scotty descends into madness as a result of his vertigo attacking him in the narrow confines of the bell tower and of his failure to save the object of his sexual and romantic fixation. Hitchcock's visualization of the feeling of vertigo—a zoom in and a reverse tracking shot—puts the viewer into the very vortex of paranoid fear, a kind of hole that the character is both repulsed by and attracted to.

Psycho is the culmination of Hitchcock's obsessive interest in crime, madness, and claustrophobia. When Marion enters the black hole of the Bates Motel, she is very much a sane young woman who has done an impulsive thing. She is like all of the characters in Hitchcock's fallen world—one step away from catastrophe and death. This is a world in which an innocent gesture—raising your hand in a cocktail lounge to get the attention of a page—can land you into the hands of assassins, or a flirtatious look can get you strangled by a perfect stranger. Hitchcock's world is one in which while you are baking a cake, a stranger can break into your trailer and attack you. And usually, there is nowhere to run, because you're handcuffed, or alone in a boat or in the attic or in a phone booth, or confined to a wheelchair, or hanging by your fingertips or stuck on a runaway merry-go-round—or perhaps trapped in your own body, as is the character in the *Alfred Hitchcock Presents* episode entitled "Breakdown."

I believe there is a physical etiology to Hitchcock's fear of and attraction to confined spaces. Throughout his life, Hitchcock was "trapped" in his own body, a "victim" of obsessive eating and drinking, with the resultant obesity he was plagued by his entire adult life. The compulsions that lead to obsessive eating and drinking and resultant weight gain are a complex mix of self-loathing and self-indulgence, the body both a repository of the pleasurable stimuli of food and drink and at the same time a shameful symbol of gluttony. Hitchcock struggled with his weight all of his life, alternately starving and stuffing himself. In his films, Hitchcock dramatized this neurotic fixation on food by linking the act of eating or dining with violence and death. In *Sabotage* (1936), Mr. Verloc stuffs food in his mouth after he admits responsibility for Mrs. Verloc's brother's death. He is soon after killed by the very knife that Mrs. Verloc uses to prepare his dinner. In *Blackmail*, the artist Crewe is killed by a knife that sits next to a hunk of cheese on the bed table. In *Strangers on a Train* Miriam gorges herself with treats—fattening herself, as it were—for the slaughter by Bruno. In addition, the fear of losing control is usually represented in his films by the fear of heights and of falling—of spiraling out of control. The opposite fear is of *not* being able to move—of being confined, of being trapped in one's body.

In the two great antipastoral films of the late 1950s—*Vertigo* and *Psycho*—Hitchcock explores both falling—losing control—(*Vertigo*) and entrapment

(*Psycho*). And in Norman, Hitchcock creates the great embodiment of his own very personal demons. Norman is trapped. He says to Marion in the extraordinary parlor subscene, "You know what I think? I think that—we're all in our private traps—clamped in them. And none of us can ever get out. We scratch and claw, but—only at the air—only at each other. And for all of it, we never budge an inch." Norman is not only trapped in his predicament—being the caretaker of his mother and the proprietor of a failed motel—but he is also trapped in his own body—with another person. Norman is the most ingenious of all of Hitchcock's doubles, an amalgam of youth and age, male and female, mother and son—a self-contained family, the ultimate oedipal structure. When Hitchcock ate and drank himself into a stupor, it was as if he had surrendered himself to some gluttonous strain of the Id—as if another being was possessing him. *Psycho* is Hitchcock's therapy, his surprising and shocking solution to demonic possession.

To visualize the claustrophobia of the Bates Motel and the duality of his characters, Hitchcock fills the frame with cataphors in the first subscene. In shot 4, as Marion waits for someone to check her into the motel, she sees a light in the window of the house that looms over the motel. Using a low-angle POV shot for this extreme long shot, Hitchcock again presents us with a window cataphor; this window, though, reverses the tonal pattern of the film's opening scene, during which the camera goes from the brilliant sunshine of a Phoenix afternoon into the darkness of the hotel room. The window itself exhibits the narrow, vertical style of Victorian architecture, and its long-length glows brilliantly in the rain-soaked darkness. Hitchcock further extends this contrast with the opening scene by preventing the camera from entering the window and revealing the room's characters. This is clearly a taboo space—a forbidden space—where, as we discover later, a mother and son share the same bed. This is clearly a space that no camera—no enunciator—was allowed to go in the restricted cinematic world of the late 1950s. We are still in the economic and aesthetic infrastructure of *Rear Window*, although this infrastructure is beginning to crumble and will be hastened in its disintegration by *Psycho*. As in *Rear Window*, we see the figure in the window from a distance, but we don't see her only from Marion's POV. Hitchcock presents us with two shots of the figure, the second one closer to the figure than the first. The first shot, from Marion's POV, is shot 4; the second shot, 6, is from the enunciator's POV, from the nondiegetic camera of Hitchcock. This very subtle shift to a closer perspective is Hitchcock's way of asserting the freedom of his camera from the POV of a character. He does this earlier in *Rear Window*, as noted previously, by presenting us with a shot not seen from Jeff's POV.

The brilliantly glowing light from the window silhouettes a female figure in a graceful pose. The glowing whiteness of the light foreshadows the eerie glow of the bathroom in Cabin 1: both are cinematic spaces inhabited and dominated by the maternal figure of Norma Bates. Hitchcock brilliantly uses the shining window framing the female figure as a cataphor for the shower scene. In a world of darkness, we feel safest in the light; in a world of moral ambiguity, we feel safest when we choose to do the right thing; in a world of strangers and of patriarchal authority, we feel most protected by the feminine, the maternal. In *Psycho*, Hitchcock gleefully and perversely reverses the audience's expectations about the moral universe. In some senses, Marion Crane is like a film audience. In the darkness, she looks at a glowing rectangle (ironically reversed in dimensions) to find safety and security, just as the audience watching *her* sits in darkness and hopes to find meaning and affirmation of its own values in the cinema screen.

Perhaps this is what Hitchcock meant when he said, ". . . it's my humor that enabled me to tackle the outrageousness of it" (Bogdanovich, *The Cinema of Alfred Hitchcock* 42). Throughout the first half of *Psycho*, Hitchcock comically toys with the audience's sense of what is right or wrong and what is real or illusory. In essence, suspense depends upon a subverting or questioning of the nature of truth and reality.

As Marion Crane stares at the comforting appearance of the female figure in the glowing window, she and we feel that perhaps in this dark world she's entered there is hope of refuge and safety. Marion's hope is somewhat confirmed in shot 11, where we see a figure come out of the house, and, in subsequent shots, awkwardly offer Marion an umbrella, with these comforting words: "Gee, I'm sorry I didn't hear you in all this rain. Go ahead in, please."

Hitchcock loads the mise-en-scene of the first motel subscene with visual clues and with cataphors. In shot 15, inside the motel office, we see Marion's figure reflected in a mirror, Hitchcock's traditional device for adding depth to a scene and for suggesting the duality of human nature. Shot 21 emphasizes the duality further, as we see from Marion's POV the Bates Motel registry, which Marion signs as Marie Samuels, her thieving self, her dark half. As Marion/Marie is signing in, Hitchcock presents us with shot 25 of Norman from the rear as he selects a key for Marion's room. At first, the viewer may think that this is a shot from Marion's POV, but the next

Figure 4. Norman's glance over his shoulder and his hesitation in choosing a cabin give the audience its first sense of foreboding.

shot clearly shows her still looking down at the registry as she concocts her false identity. Shot 25 is a critical shot in this first subscene, for it provides the viewer with information that Marion/Marie does not have. In shot 25, we see that Norman hesitatingly selects the room key. He begins reaching for key two, then shifts over to key three, but then moves his hand to key one. But just before he chooses this key, he looks over his left shoulder, as if to check whether Marion is watching his indecisiveness. Clearly, Norman is thinking of something other than choosing an appropriate room. There is a reason why he is choosing Cabin 1, but of course we don't yet know what that reason is. However, we get a sense of uneasiness from this shot mainly because we don't see it from Marion/Marie's POV. This shot is the essence of Hitchcockean suspense, which depends upon a blending of technique and plot to parcel out knowledge extra-diegetically. Hitchcock further adds to the suspense by highlighting the cabin number; when Norman takes off the dark circular disk that is attached to the key, he uncovers a lighter disk with the number one on it. This number stands out as Norman hands the key to Marion. This light-dark contrast, coupled with the two number ones, brings together the dark-light tonality of the film and the double theme. Norman's left-handedness adds to the audience's sense of uneasiness and its new found knowledge; his arm movement, from the right side of the screen to the left, is in contrast to the majority of movement in the film, from left to right. And the hand reaching up to take the key is almost an exact reverse image of the shot of Mrs. Bates raising up her hand to begin stabbing Marion in the shower. The ironic twist is that Mrs. Bates is right-handed! Thus does Hitchcock use visual cataphors to work on the audience's subconscious level of perception.

In shot 31, Norman and Marion enter the fateful Cabin 1, Marion's final place of residence—although neither the audience nor Marion realizes this. The camera assumes the position of the fourth wall. From this vantage point, we are able to see the twin taboos of the Production Code and the Hollywood studio system: the bed and the bathroom. In a sly poke at the Production Code, Hitchcock has Norman unable to say either word "bed" or "bathroom":

Norman: Well, the uh—mattress is soft and there's hangers in the closet and stationery with "Bates Motel" printed on it in case you want to make your friends back home feel envious—and the uh [gesturing toward the bathroom]

Marion: The bathroom.

Norman's inability to say the taboo words adds to his charm and boyishness, and Marion seems to be attracted to these two qualities. Norman is in the mold of the charming psychopath, embodied earlier in the character of Uncle Charlie in *Shadow of a Doubt* and of Bruno in *Strangers on a Train*. Hitchcock says of his conception of such a character, "He had to be an attractive man. . . . He had to be charming, attractive. If he weren't, he'd never get near one of his victims" (*Inside Hitchcock*).

In a further bit of irony, Hitchcock positions Norman to the left of the eerily glowing bathroom door with his left arm extended, almost as if he is inviting Marion to enter. Hitchcock composes the mise-en-scene brilliantly in this shot. To the right of the bathroom door, which holds the dominant central portion of the frame, hang two pictures of birds, each facing in a different direction, seemingly mirror images of one another (Norma and Norman). To the left of Norman is the window of the motel, echoing—in its long, rectangular shape—the window in which Marion first saw Mrs. Bates. If one were to reverse directions and place himself outside this window, he would see the figure of Norman in the window. At the bottom of the frame is the top portion of the bed. The shot is crammed full of rectangular shapes, including the towels hanging on the rack. What better way of suggesting entrapment than this predominance of long rectangles? Hitchcock used this technique earlier in the opening scenes of *The Wrong Man*. Restricting vertical shapes dominate the Balestreros' apartment, suggesting the psychic imprisonment of Manny's wife and the

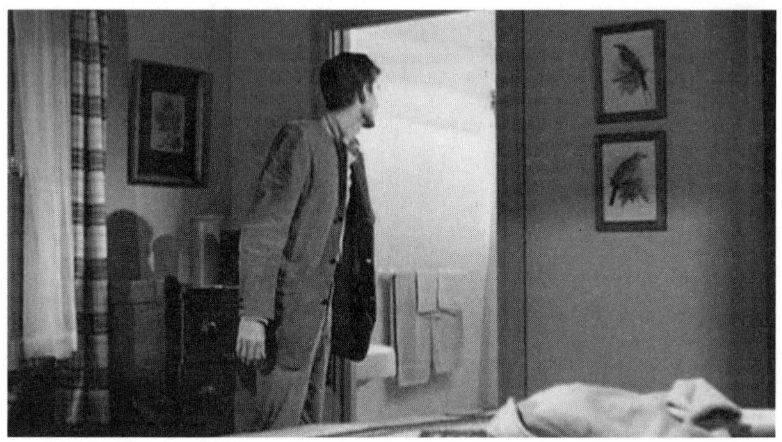

Universal Pictures/Photofest

Figure 5. Norman turns on the light in one of the most terrifying spaces in cinema history.

coming physical incarceration of Manny himself. In the ingenious parlor subscene of *Psycho*, we find out that Norman is trapped in his world, just as the birds are "trapped" in their picture frames. In the parlor subscene, we also see that Norman has surrounded himself with dead, stuffed, predatory birds, the perfect symbol for Norma Bates.

In the next ten shots of this subscene (34 through 43), Hitchcock uses mise-en-scene to reveal character in a purely graphic way. When Hitchcock described himself as a formalist, he was surely referring to this kind of formal representation of the film's content. Shots 34 through 43 are alternating medium-shoulder shots of Marion and Norman in profile, seen from the camera's fourth-wall position. The shots of Marion are composed with her on the left side of the frame, with her image reflected in a standing mirror on the right side of the frame. These two figures—Marion and Marie—are prefigured earlier in the film in shots showing Marion in white underwear in the hotel room with Sam, but in black underwear in her apartment with the money. In the hotel scene, Sam is on the bed with Marion; in her apartment, the stolen money on the bed has replaced Sam. In Hitchcock's world, love alone can never guarantee happiness, nor can it stand up against competing motivations and drives: power, sexual dominance, jealousy, control. The alternating shots of Norman show him on the right side of the frame with the cabin door's number one clearly visible over his shoulder. Unlike Marion's shots, with their balanced mirror images, Norman's shots reveal an empty space; half of the frame is dead air,

Universal Pictures/Photofest

Figure 6. Hitchcock's ubiquitous mirror presents Marion and her double, Marie Samuels.

unoccupied space. This off-center framing is a visualization of Norman's psyche—half of him is not "there." This unbalanced frame throws the audience off slightly, upsets its visual desire for a balanced composition. Jack Russell's flat, shallow cinematography keeps the viewer's eye from entering the frame. There's nothing interesting to look at, no diagonal lines drawing the viewer's eye into the frame, no mirror image, no arresting set design. When Marion is showering, the menacing figure comes from the left side of the frame, as if this part of the frame has been reserved for Norma Bates. Why has left-handedness traditionally been associated with evil? Our word for "sinister" comes from the Latin *sinister*, "on the left, unlucky." The left side of the frame is perhaps directly connected to the primitive brain, where dangers are perceived almost subconsciously. When dangers are in front of us, they can be sized up, evaluated, reacted to. But when dangers come from the side, we feel the most vulnerable. Horror directors use the side of the frame to surprise and terrify audiences. Hitchcock is not this obvious. He realized, from his experience as a graphic designer, that we tend to read an image from left to right, so there's an additional visual weight associated with the right side of the frame. As we scan to the right, we are even more surprised when information comes in from the left.

During this ten-shot segment, Norman invites Marion to his home above the motel to have dinner with him. Is Norman asking Marion for a date? It seems so, and it is part of Hitchcock's black humor that Norman and Marion seem attracted to one another. Neither knows that the other is involved in a romantic-sexual relationship, Marion with Sam, Norman with his mother. Hitchcock continues the complicated interchange of diegetic and extra-diegetic knowledge in the next series of shots, as Norman leaves the cabin to prepare dinner and as Marion searches for a hiding place for the $40,000. After deciding to hide the money in a folded newspaper, Marion hears voices emanating from the house on the hill behind the motel.

Shots 52 through 59 show alternating shots of Marion looking out the window as she overhears the angry exchange between Norman and his mother and of low-angle point-of-view shots of the house itself. What Marion hears puzzles and upsets her. It seems like an argument between Norman and his mother, but the mother's voice is not the one that should be coming from the figure in the graceful repose that Marion sees at the beginning of the scene, framed in welcoming light in the rainy darkness. This is the voice of a harridan, with an aggressive, ugly, cackling tone, like that of a witch from the fairy tales: "Go on! Go tell her she'll not be appeasing her ugly appetite with my food, or my son! Or do I have to tell her 'cause you don't have the guts? Huh, boy? You have the guts, boy?" Both Norman and Marion have secrets that they are keeping from one another. The audience knows Marion's secret, but it does not yet know Norman's. In fact, Norman knows only part of his own secret—that his mother's physical body is in the house and that she is a living presence. The other part—that Norman *is* his mother—he never finds out: only we do, at the end of the film.

Universal Pictures/Photofest

Figure 7. The half empty frame hints at the other half of Norman.

The house itself is the repository of secrets, and the manner in which Hitchcock shoots the house, from a low angle, combined with its Gothic appearance, adds to its mystery. This is a house right out of Poe—it is Roderick Usher's house—and so it has a palpable sense of evil. Just as in Poe, the *Psycho* house is destroyed in the prequel to *Psycho—Psycho IV*. In fact, the house itself seems to be speaking, and in the three separate shots of it from Marion's POV, it has been transformed from the hope of refuge and safety in the opening shots to a place of fear and anger now. At the beginning of this nine-shot segment, Hitchcock shifts his camera's position to the adjacent wall—a shift to the left—to accommodate both Marion's shoulder-shot profile as she hears the argument between Norman and his mother and the camera's rightward panning movement as Marion crosses the room and exits the cabin. This subtle shift exemplifies Hitchcock's genius as an auteur, as an artistic manipulator of the film's mise-en-scene. Shifting the camera to the left "opens" up the scene, allowing us to see Marion's reaction to Mrs. Bates' haranguing of Norman. In addition, the camera's placement allows Marion to cross to the right and exit to the right of the frame, through the door, to meet Norman, whom she has seen leaving the house with a tray of food—all captured in one smooth pan that preserves the film's pattern of rightward frame exits.

The last six shots of this first Bates Motel subscene contain typical Hitchcock mise-en-scene techniques. As Marion leaves the room, we see her from behind as she opens the cabin door, which is positioned to the right of the frame. For the next shot, Hitchcock positions his camera outside of the cabin door, on the walkway of the motel, thus continuing the inside-outside motif of the film. The vertical shape of the door provides a smooth visual transition between the two shots, with the door functioning as a portal between outside and inside. There's also a tonal shift from the relatively bright interior of the door to the darkness outside Cabin 1. Again, Hitchcock is toying with audience expectations that the darkness is dangerous and mysterious and that the light is safe and secure. In the shower scene, Hitchcock will dash those expectations. This relatively lengthy shot—a little over fifty seconds—again shows Hitchcock's bravura technique. As Marion exits the door, she faces the camera, but as she comes out and closes the door, the camera tracks slightly to the right, positioning itself behind her. Jack Russell's lighting is magnificent in this shot. Two small outside lights at the top of the frame divide the frame into two halves. The one above Marion, which is not visible, silhouettes her in a soft romantic light and provides halo lighting for her golden hair. The left half of the frame is bathed in soft light by the visible light fixture as we see over Marion's left shoulder Norman come around the dark corner with the tray of food. He pauses briefly when he sees Marion. It seems like a romantic moment. It certainly is lit that way: the attractive mystery woman at the right side of the frame, bathed in warm light, and the "eligible" attractive suitor at the left side of the frame, providing food and shelter from the dangers of the outside world. Russell creates planes of light that both create a romantic aura but also suggest something else, a sense of entrapment highlighted by the vertical shutters and door in mid-frame, separating Marion and Norman.

As Norman approaches Marion, the camera tracks to the left and fixes the two characters in a medium two shot, from waist up. Both are in profile, and we see the windows of Cabin 1 in the background. Marion is on the right side of the frame, Norman on the left. This positioning is a reversal of the previous shots inside the cabin and suggests a development of their relationship. In Hitchcock, food is a prelude to sex or death, and in using in a sinister way this most civilized ritual of breaking bread together, Hitchcock continues his black comedic subversion of a romantic tryst. We also get echoes of the film's opening scene, during which Sam notices that Marion has hardly touched her food, shown on the bed table. She has been too busy with other things! Hitchcock adds to the comedy by having Norman say, ". . . Mother-Mother, uh—What is the phrase? She isn't quite herself today." At this point in the film, Norman's double meaning isn't clear to the audience. Hitchcock provides an ingenious visual clue to

Universal Pictures/Photofest

Figure 8. Cinematographer Jack Russell lights this scene in a romantic way as Norman offers sustenance to Marion.

this doubling by showing the dim reflection of Norman in the window of Cabin 1. It's almost as if the emanation of Norman is entering the cabin. Such dialogue is in the mold of James Allardyce's droll writing for the television series *Alfred Hitchcock Presents*. Now that *Psycho* has become one of the most enduring staples of popular culture, Norman's statement takes on added meaning as people view the film today and chuckle knowingly.

In the final moments of this lengthy shot, Hitchcock has his camera track back slightly as Marion says the fateful line, "But as long as you've fixed the supper, we may as well eat it." As she speaks, Marion glances into the cabin, smiles invitingly, and leans somewhat seductively against the open cabin door. Again, the audience is reminded of the connection between food and sex in the opening scene. In the middle of the frame, slightly to the bottom, we see the edge of the bed with Marion's open suitcase sitting on it. This "open" invitation to Norman continues the romantic aura of the scene, but adds a hint of sexual temptation. Norman finds himself invited into Marion's bedroom, with the obvious *double entendre* of "we may as well eat it." Marion's motivation is unclear in this scene. She knows that she is sexually attractive to men. The audience has seen how her "sexual scent" was immediately detected by Cassidy in the real estate office. Norman is attracted to Marion and is tempted to enter her room. He takes a step forward and then hesitates. There's a world of meaning in this hesitation. Marion's attractiveness to Norman has triggered a taboo response in Norman. It is at this point, I believe, that Norman's mother half—Norma—has had enough; this attractive young woman possibly threatens her hegemony and must be dealt with. We received a forewarning of Norma's limit of toleration earlier in the scene in her verbal lashing of her son—"Go tell her she'll not be appeasing her ugly appetite with my food, or my son!" Norman turns down Marion's request to enter her room, but Norma has accepted that request, which she will fulfill in the shower scene.

The second subscene is Hitchcock's tour-de-force of mise-en-scene: the parlor scene. This is one of the longest scenes in the film involving a single location: 8 minutes and 45 seconds, with 106 shots. Simply put, the parlor symbolizes Norman's mind and is a cataphor for the shower scene. As Norman enters the room with his food tray, the camera views him in a low angle from the position of the fourth wall. The room is dark and funereal, with heavy, brocade drapes, imposing furniture, Victorian lamps, and silver candlesticks. Placed strategically around the room are stuffed birds of prey—a swooping owl, a crow on a perch. Norman talks of his hobby of taxidermy, and we would swear we are in a funeral parlor for a consultation. Russell lights this scene in somber tones of velvety black, and Hitchcock's low-angled camera adds a sense of claustrophobia and oppressiveness to the atmosphere. This room is the dark mind of Norman—trapped by a domineering mother who watches his every move, just like the birds on the wall—"We're all in our private traps clamped in them." This is the mind of the oedipal victim—"A son is a poor substitute for a lover"—as well as the oedipal perpetrator—"And when he died, too, it was—just too great a shock for her and—and the way he died."

To emphasize and broaden the "trap" motif, Hitchcock keeps Marion and Norman in separate frames, alternating medium shots of them as they speak. Each seems "trapped" in his and her separate cinematic worlds. In addition, Hitchcock isolates each character to the side of the frame: Marion to the left, Norma to the right. The antithesis of the pastoral world is the Darwinian/Freudian deterministic zeitgeist. If we are unable to determine our own futures—if we are trapped—we lack the sine qua non of the pastoral—freedom of will. If our childhoods are the architecture of our adulthoods, how are we to free ourselves of the blueprint that determines our shape? If our gender and patriarchal environment predetermine our lives, how can we act as free agents? Hitchcock brings these two "victims" together in a brilliant analysis of the illusion of freedom and the impossibility of redemption. In its depiction of two victims temporarily reaching out to each other, this scene is the bleakest in the film.

When Marion enters Norman's parlor, she does not realize that she has also entered the lair of the wolf, for Norman is indeed a wolf in sheep's clothing. *Psycho* has a mythic, fairytale quality to its infrastructure—a "good" character who commits a transgression, a journey that results from the transgression, a detour or wrong turn on the journey that leads to danger, an encounter with an evil figure who kidnaps or traps the character. The danger for Marion in this mythic scenario—as well as for the audience—is that she does not realize that there's a wolf inside the sheep, nor does the audience. Yet there are hints of it throughout this scene: the birds, the funereal atmosphere, the dark, ominous lighting. It's true that the victim in Marion reaches out to the victim in Norman, but there's another person inside Norman, the ever-watchful maternal presence. However, there's some ambiguity about the presence of the mother. Is "she" the one who hesitates in choosing the key for Marion's cabin and in entering the room with Marion's food? Or is this Norman, the "harmless" voyeur, who hopes to put Marion in an adjacent room so that he can watch her get undressed?

This is certainly not monstrous behavior. After all, we all have a bit of the voyeur in us, as Hitchcock well understood: "My exertion is all from the neck up. I watch" (Spoto 21). But Norma does peer out every once in a while. She does this tellingly in shot 75, when Marion asks, "Wouldn't it be better—if you put her—someplace?" In the next shot, Hitchcock brings the camera closer to Norman, who—as he incredulously asks the question, "You mean an institution? A madhouse?"—leans threateningly into the left side of the frame, toward Marion. In purely graphic terms, this positioning of Norman in a quarter turn with his sharp featured profile resembles the earlier shot of the crow on its perch, with a large exaggerated shadow cast on the wall. This is Norma appearing. The threatening movement toward the camera "invades" the space of the audience. We feel threatened—just as Marion does.

Joseph Stefano's script is filled with brilliantly placed clues about the presence of Norma: "Why, she's as harmless as one of those stuffed birds," Norman says of his mother to Marion. Norman also says, "She just gets a little mad sometimes. We all go a little mad sometimes. Haven't you?" The irony in these lines reverberates throughout the remainder of this scene and into the shower scene. It turns out that Norman–Norma's angry outburst has somehow convinced Marion that she can free herself from her trap, from her "one time" act of madness. Marion sees in Norman a reflection of her dilemma, but she believes that she is not "born" into hers, as Norman says about his trap: she can extricate herself. A further irony is that Marion's decision to return to Phoenix has triggered her to tell the truth of her identity to Norman, but her truthfulness has also triggered a similar decision in Norma to rid herself of this female threat to her son. When Marion leaves the lair of the wolf, her fate has been sealed.

The last part of the Bates Motel scene is relatively brief—two minutes and twenty seconds—but it features a densely composed mise-en-scene in its sixteen shots. The first three shots reveal that Norman–Norma has detected Marion's initial lie about her identity; shot 2 shows Marion's false identity as Marie Samuels. And shot 3 reveals a slight smile on Norman's face as he realizes Marion's "mistake" in identifying herself as "Miss Crane" to him as she leaves the parlor. Hitchcock positions his camera slightly below eye level as Norman reacts to this information. Have we seen Norma peeking out again? The low-key lighting of this shot is carried over into the next shot, as Norman returns to the parlor, but the expressionistic overtones are heightened as Jack Russell bathes half of Norman's face in darkness. Hitchcock's camera is fluid in this subscene, moving effortlessly and subtly from outside the parlor and then to inside and then outside the motel. The camera placement is below eye level, and this angle, combined with the low-key lighting, gives Norman an ominous, threatening appearance. The camera pans right as Norman approaches the wall of the parlor; he pauses briefly and turns in a full frontal position, facing the audience. He glances to his left, toward the wall separating the parlor from Cabin 1 ("Ah-ha," the audience says to itself. "This is why he hesitated in choosing the cabin key!"); and then he glances to his right, with his head slightly upturned, as if signifying his awareness of the mother residing in the house above the motel. As Norman turns his head again to his left, he pauses ever so briefly and appears to be staring directly at the audience. What a brilliant triangulation! To his left is the temptation of Marion Crane, fleeing from guilt but now attempting to redeem herself: she is the essence of vulnerability, alone and unprotected. To his right is his ever-vigilant mother, wishing to protect her son from the likes of Marion. In the middle of these two sides is the audience, now made accomplices in this choice.

In his interview with me, Joseph Stefano describes how he solved the major dilemma in adopting Robert Bloch's novel: how to shift the audience's interest from Bloch's Mary, who gets decapitated in the first half of the book, to Norman. One way was to get the audience on the side of Norman. Stefano says, "After the shower scene, we've lost the person we were with, that we identified with, that we connected to, that we cared about . . . and so I said to Hitch, 'At that time, the movie is over unless we get the audience to care about Norman.'" This short subscene, which occurs right before the shower scene, is Hitchcock's initial strategy in getting the audience "to care about Norman." Hitchcock accomplishes this shift in a very subtle way, by having Norman make fleeting eye contact with the audience. Lighting is an essential aspect of mise-en-scene, and Hitchcock uses the glowing eyes of Norman as a cataphor in the visual and thematic pattern of the film. As Norman peers out at the audience, we see above his head the spreading wings of the stuffed owl. Another large predatory bird thrusts out from the right side of the frame, as if ready to attack Norman. These birds, one a nocturnal predator with keen eyesight, signal the presence of mother ready to protect her offspring. We are soon to see with our own eyes Norman preparing to spy on the unsuspecting Marion, who cannot "see" him. In order to see Marion, Norman removes a rectangular painting on the wall, depicting Susanna and the Elders. This painting is another window—another portal—this one revealing a taboo and forbidden scene. Behind the painting is a large, circular hole in the plaster of the wall, with a smaller peephole in the center. This is an additional eye, much like the binoculars and telephoto lenses in *Rear Window*. The actual shape resembles an eye that a child might draw (Norma's child Norman eats candy throughout the subscene). Hitchcock shifts the camera's position so that it is next to Norman in a close-up, almost as if we are next in line to take part in the peep show. The light from Cabin 1 glows eerily on the front part of Norman's face.

The voyeur trespasses in forbidden territory, watches taboo scenes, hoping to see the "unseeable" but thrilling in the possibility of detection and punishment. The voyeur can never possess in actuality the object of his gaze. In this sense, L.B. Jeffreys is the consummate voyeur, unable to move, incapable of sexual fulfillment because of his broken leg. Norman is also hobbled, crippled, made impotent by his mother's sexual possessiveness. Thus he can only watch. And the irony of this scene—Hitchcock's supreme irony in *all* of his films—is that Norman can see what *we* cannot see because of the "protection" of the Production Code. Cabin 1 is inaccessible territory even to the enunciator's gaze. Hitchcock "privileges" Norman's gaze by having him witness Marion undressing, but Hitchcock denies this privilege to himself and his audience. We see only part of the striptease. Shot 7, from Norman's POV, shows Marion again in the black underwear as she steps out of her skirt and reaches to unhook her bra. Shot 48 is a brilliantly executed extreme close-up of Norman's eye, seen from the side, with the light from the peephole creating a brilliant point of light on his pupil. Norman has seen Marion naked; he has seen what no audience for a commercial film had seen up through 1960. This extraordinary situation of having a character not only see what an audience cannot in the diegesis of the film, but also see what an audience could not in the extra-diegetic world of cinema in general, is unique in Hitchcock's oeuvre. In this subscene, Norman is the principal viewer, but what he sees cannot be shown to us. This disruption of the point-of-view shot creates a break in the usual pattern of the film and teases the audience into thinking that it is still "safe," that it is still in the protected confines of the Production Code and the studio system. In the shower scene, though, Norman's forbidden knowledge will be transferred directly to the audience in a burst of violence and sexuality that literally "blinds" the audience with this same forbidden knowledge.

The shower scene in *Psycho* is Hitchcock's exploration of the moral irony of knowledge. His Catholic upbringing had introduced him to the guilt associated with knowledge. It is significant that eating of the fruit of the Tree of Knowledge is what thrusts Adam and Eve out of the Garden of Eden. Throughout his career, Hitchcock had been fascinated with the revelatory quality of his camera. He used it to explore taboo areas of sexuality and violence. He had brought it tantalizingly close to the very epicenter of human passion, of the human propensity for sex, power, and violence. But there is a price to pay for such knowledge, and in *Psycho*, Hitchcock has his audience pay that price, along with Marion.

The giant close-up of Norman's eye soaking up the naked form of Marion through his peephole will be transferred graphically in the shower scene into the extraordinary dissolve from the circular drain, disposing of Marion's life blood, to the dying eye of Marion Crane. In between these two scenes, of course, are the audience's eyes, symbolized by the circular hole in the wall, with the tiny peephole/pupil in the center.

Shot 9 of this subscene shows Marion putting on her bathrobe and exiting to the right of the frame, leaving Norman looking at the brightly lit tub and shower, framed by the rectangular doorway, and at the two pictures of the previously seen birds. Norman has now seen Marion naked, and the audience wonders what will happen next. Hitchcock's mise-en-scene has painted a complex, conflicting view of Norman: boyish and charming, but voyeuristic and deceitful. In the next shot, Norman is shown replacing the picture, and then for the next shot, Hitchcock shifts his camera to the left so that Norman again faces us in a full frontal shot very similar to the earlier shot from the same position. Russell's lighting is again ominous, with extreme low-key tones. Norman looks troubled, even angry, as he clenches his jaw and again looks to his right, with his head slightly raised, up at the house on the hill, and then exits to the left of the frame as the camera pans with him. This leftward exiting is in keeping with the pattern of identifying Norman with that side of the frame. Hitchcock positions his fluid camera on the walkway outside the door of the office motel for the next shot. Norman hurriedly walks out of the darkness toward the camera until he is in a close-up shot with the invisible light fixture bathing half of his face in light. At this point in the film, Hitchcock has subtly shifted the focus of the film away from Marion and toward Norman. As Norman stops in front of the camera and looks quickly up and to the left, the camera begins to move left in a stunning tracking shot as Norman finishes turning his head. It is as if the camera has anticipated his movement toward the house on the hill. The camera seems to glide as it tracks to the left of the frame, slightly away from Norman, who then hurriedly moves toward the left side of the frame, across the camera's field, and out of the frame to the left. Shot 13 is a long shot of the house seen from the walkway of the motel. In fact, the shot is very similar to the one that came at the beginning of the Bates Motel scene, during which Marion, trying to find the motel owner, walks out of the office toward the camera and looks up to the left. What she sees is similar to the shot of Norman walking up to the house.

This doubling of the mise-en-scene is typical of Hitchcock's formalistic approach to cinema. We have seen it earlier in the two films that use doubling as a major thematic device: *Shadow of a Doubt* and *Strangers on a Train*. The similarity of the mise-en-scene seems to work on almost an unconscious level on the audience's perception. In fact, this additional long shot of the Bates house on the hill is not seen from a character's POV but rather from the enunciator's, again part of the shifting of emphasis from Marion to Norman.

In the next shot, Hitchcock's camera is positioned inside the Bates family house. This is a surprising placement, because it takes the audience into a seemingly mysterious location, but the placement is subtle, unobtrusive, and has an unsettling effect on the audience. The camera is positioned just inside the foyer of the Bates house, facing the door. We see three curtained windows: one is the top half of the door; the other two are narrow, vertical side windows. These resemble in shape the three windows in *Rear Window*, the bamboo shades of which are rolled up—like theater curtains—to begin the film. This seemingly innocuous shot is a perfect example of Hitchcock's practice of making all backgrounds function. The three white shirred café curtains echo the rectangular shapes that have acted as portals and cataphors in the first half of the film. These windows, however, emit no light; rather, they act as vertically shaped barriers to the outside world, suggesting that entering may be risky or dangerous. This camera placement is repeated later in the film, after the seminal shower scene, when the private investigator Arbogast enters the house and gets murdered and, even later, at the climax of the film, when Marion's sister Lila enters the house looking for Mrs. Bates. Is this the innocuous looking Gate of Hell? Norman enters the door and walks past the camera, which reverses direction in the ensuing shot and shows Norman from the rear as he approaches the center hall staircase, seems to begin ascending the stairs, hesitates, and then walks nonchalantly, hands in pockets, past the staircase and into the kitchen, Hitchcock framing him with pervasive rectangular shapes as he takes his seat in the kitchen.

Hitchcock has now positioned his audience for the shower scene by using one aspect of "pure cinema": mise-en-scene.

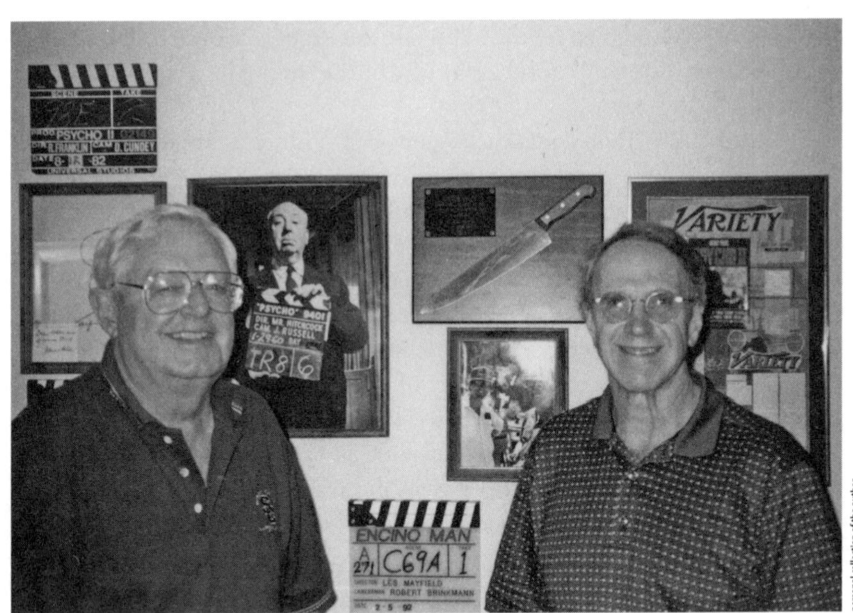

personal collection of the author

Hilton Green, assistant director of *Psycho*, with the author. The *Psycho* knife is on the wall.

CHAPTER 6

Hilton Green

Hilton Green was born into the film industry. *His father was a director and his mother was the silent film star, Vivian Reed. After graduating from USC with a degree in business, he got a job at Disney working on the television show* Davy Crockett *and eventually ended up working as an assistant director on* Alfred Hitchcock Presents. *Hilton was the assistant director of* Psycho *and later the producer of* Psycho II, III, *and* IV. *He was one of Hitchcock's most trusted coworkers. Hilton lives with his wife in Pasadena.*

P: Are you surprised by the amount of controversy and commentary that *Psycho* has provoked since its release in 1960?

H: The critics have analyzed every inch of it, and much of it has been inaccurate, *I* think. The controversy started off with Saul Bass, who did the credits on the movie, and he came out and wrote, or he was quoted and then it was in a story, that he directed the shower scene. Do you remember him saying that?

P: Oh, absolutely.

H: Well, I was there every moment, shot for shot for that thing, and Saul Bass was never on the set. He did lay out the storyboard with Hitchcock, and all that. But I saw Saul years and years later—he's dead now—and I said, "Saul, how can you possibly say you directed that?" And he was very embarrassed.

P: Maybe it was just a little fib that got out of control. Janet Leigh said that Bass had made the storyboards from every conceivable angle and that Hitchcock took the pieces and put them together in his mind and that's what he directed. Did Saul Bass come to Hitchcock and say, "I have some ideas for this sequence"?

H: Hitchcock went to him and said, "This is what I want."

P: I see. And did Hitchcock say, "I want to shoot it staccato"?

H: He wanted a lot of different angles, and he said, "I never want to see the knife penetrate the body."

P: Well, Janet Leigh also said the knife doesn't penetrate the body, but it does. There's one shot where you can see the knife go in below the belly button.

H: We never did a thing like that. And that was before the computer things where you could do things like that. It was way before that. We never did a dummy, or never did anything where it penetrated.

P: But where does that shot come from because it's in the film? I did a shot-by-shot analysis of the film.

H: We never shot it.

P: Where the hell did it come from?

H: Hitchcock was very proud of that restraint. Maybe that was put in later by somebody, after the fact.

P: Janet Leigh claims there was never any other woman on the set. Joe Stefano said there was a nude, and Rebello's book said that there was a nude, whom Hitchcock had hired to be there, to stand in for some of the scenes that they were blocking and so forth. Do you remember that?

H: Oh, yes.

P: So there was another person there. Did that model ever stand in for Janet Leigh for any of the actual scenes that were shot?

H: Oh, we shot her behind the shower curtain, sure. Because Janet wasn't nude.

P: But the person behind the shower curtain is nude.

H: She was nude. Her name was Marny something or other. [Marli Renfro]. She doubled Janet behind the shower. Janet wasn't there, so maybe she didn't know that we had done that.

P: There are so many points of view about this scene, and I think that there is so much discussion about the scene *because* it's so important. People want to get it right. They say, "Here's what exactly happened because this is a scene that people should have the facts about." I mean you don't see anybody arguing about any other scene like that.

H: No one was allowed on the stage while we shot the shower scene. No guests, not anyone was allowed on the set. We had police at the door. And in those days, it was 1959, to shoot a nude was unheard of. Today it's very common, but in those days it was unheard of. It was a big thing. And Hitchcock kept it quiet that he was doing it this way, and only the crew was there. Tony Perkins was in New York.

P: You see the mother coming down with the knife, and you see Marion raising her arms to protect herself. But she was never faced with a knife. It was all done in the imagination. Is that your perception?

H: I think we did have a rubber knife there, but it looked too phoney, so we never shot it.

P: I see that you have the *Psycho* knife on your wall. Do we know where that knife came from?

H: A hardware store or a knife store. A prop man went out and bought it.

P: Just like the car with the famous ANL license thing? Some critics say that the ANL was meant to be part of a sexual pattern.

H: If that was the intent of Hitchcock, we had no orders to go out and make a special license or anything like that.

P: Didn't someone say at a conference that the license plate was intentional, and you said something afterwards about how unintentional the plate was?

H: Yes, I said that. See, that was even before personalized license plates.

P: Did you read the Bloch novel?

H: Yes.

P: The character was named Mary in the novel. In the scene in which Mary's head gets cut off, did you wonder how you were going to shoot that?

H: In those days you didn't shoot that sort of thing. You couldn't. The censor would never allow it. In fact *Psycho* was the first movie that ever showed a toilet. That was a big deal to get permission to get that by.

P: So whose idea was it to do the shower? Was it all Hitchcock's idea? No one suggested to him that we could stage something in the bathroom, in a shower with a knife?

H: No, that was all Hitchcock, or with Joe Stefano, you know. I wasn't in when they sat together and talked story lines. But Hitchcock was always the one who gave the writers what he wanted.

P: Do you remember the first time that you sat together and talked about this scene or other scenes and about how you were going to do them?

H: There were a couple of things on *Psycho* that I had to rig and prepare. The one that we rehearsed way ahead of time was the staircase scene. We didn't have the equipment you have today. We had to manufacture something to make the camera go up the staircase, turn around, and, when mother comes out the door, shoot straight down.

P: That's a great scene.

H: That was rigged. That had to be manufactured from the top of the stage. We had two operators on one camera because our camera man couldn't get around up there because it was so tight. And the grips had to push the dolly to get the camera up to the top.

P: It was a pretty heavy camera, too. Was it a studio Mitchell?

H: Oh yes—it was before today's stuff. I guess for about a week, or a week and a half, we rehearsed that move.

P: It's a brilliant move. And it's done so beautifully, not flashy.

H: Right. Well, if you notice Hitchcock, he loved to do things like that. In every movie he did he had at least one shot that was really experimental for that day and age. Today it wouldn't be that difficult to line that up, but back then there wasn't any of this equipment.

P: And so you've got to have a person pulling focus too, right?

H: Oh, yes. He had one assistant camera man, who was a focus puller, and then two operators on the contraption. Back then we didn't have television replay, so you couldn't look at the monitor down here and know what they were doing. You had to rely on the operator saying, "I got it" or "I didn't get it."

P: What did you think of working with Jack Russell?

H: I worked with him for all the TV stuff. At Revue, we had three crews: we had an A crew, a B crew, and a C crew. We had three cameramen; Jack was on the A crew.

P: What else did he do?

H: Lots of films and television series. I believe he shot Orson Welles' *Macbeth* in 1948. He was in the business for years. It's interesting that from the *Psycho* crew, with a few exceptions—just a couple people—they're all dead. Unbelievable.

P: It's hard to believe that the film was done forty plus years ago.

H: 1959–60.

P: Janet Leigh is one of those survivors. During our interview, I was delighted to find her so feisty and funny. She said, in no uncertain terms, what she thought of this *Psycho* critical industry. I told her, for example, that this scene has so gripped the popular imagination and popular culture, that if you go on your computer and get on Google or any of the search engines, and you type in *Psycho* + shower scene, you can get 18,000 hits.

H: You're kidding!

P: First of all, she didn't know what Google was. Even though she has a computer, she doesn't like the Internet. I don't know why, and she was very suspicious of this and she said, "The hits?" It sounded dangerous to her. I thought it was very funny. She was astounded that the film has produced such a popular and academic outpouring. You didn't think that you were making history with that particular scene, did you?

H: No. I realized that we were doing some amazing shots with the shower scene. These shots were difficult. For example, at the end of the scene, when the shot dollies from the swirling of the water, down the drain, into the eye, and then pulls back from there and then up to the house. Boy, that was a tough shot to get.

P: And this was done without the computer effects that they have now.

H: Yeah, we didn't have those.

P: And no playback to see what you're getting.

H: Right.

P: And you got her lying with her face smashed into the tile with that water dripping down. I know in her book she said that she wanted to blink or itch at it.

H: She did move in it.

P: She did; you can see. I guess that's when they cut away to the shower head. Alma supposedly spotted Janet's movement.

H: Yes, she saw it after the scene was finished shooting. No one else found it or saw it.

P: How did you get into the film industry? Did you go to film school?

H: No, I went to USC, which has a fine film school. But no, I never went to film school. My father was a director, and my mother was a silent film star and that's how I got my break.

P: What was her stage name?

H: Vivian Reed. She quit when they got married. I came along really late in their career. My brothers, who are gone now, were much older than I. My parents were married in 1917, and that's when she stopped.

P: She was in the early silent movies. So what brought you into the industry?

H: I never wanted to go into it, and after I graduated from USC, I went into the army. It was the Korean War. And I came out, got married, and needed a job. I was pulling weeds to make a living. And I went to dad, who was directing television. He went over to television because he saw the handwriting on the wall. So I drove him to work one day, and I said, "I'd like to get in this business." And in those days, if you were a son of a member, you could get into the Director's Guild. So I was the son of a member, so I got in the Director's Guild, and I went to work at Disney on a television series as a second on *Davy Crockett*. And from there, I went to Paramount as a second second on *The Desperate Hours*, with Bogart and William Wyler directing. But Wyler closed down the company; he wanted to go to Sun Valley over Christmas. And I needed a job, so I drove Dad to work again, and we were at Revue, which is now Studio Center. It was Republic Studios in those days, and he introduced me to the head of production, and the guy said, "Do you want a three-day job?" And I said, "I'll take any job." So I did *General Electric Theater* as a second assistant with Henry Fonda and Dorothy Malone. And from those three days I was never out of work for the next twenty, thirty years.

P: Now, how did you hook up with Hitchcock?

H: I was a staff assistant director with Revue, and Hitchcock came and did his show at Revue.

P: *Alfred Hitchcock Presents*: Shamley Productions, right?

H: Right, but I wasn't on his first show. He didn't particularly care for the AD [assistant director] on that one. And so I was assigned to work on the next show. During the shoot, he never said a word to me. It was a three-day shoot, and I thought he hated me because he never talked to me, only to the cameraman, who was Jack Russell.

P: He never said anything to you?

H: Never even acknowledged my existence. I'd roll the camera and get everything ready and do everything that an assistant does but never a word from him. And so I said, "Well, that's the way he works." And so I said to myself it was a great experience and I got some good credit there. So at the end of the show, I said goodbye, and he just nodded. And about three weeks later, he was going to do another show, and I was called into the office and told, "You're going to be the first assistant," and I said, "I don't think so." It turns out that Hitchcock had asked for me. I said, "Asked for me? He never talked to me!" Usually, he'd look at the set the day before we shot to see if everything was just the way he wanted it. So he came in, and I was there. He came over and said, "Hilton, how are you? Glad to see you," as if we were old friends.

P: Were you always the AD on the show?

H: No, no. We had so many shows at Revue, we rotated. We had tons of shows, and we just jumped around. Every day a different episode would be shooting. I just didn't stay on Hitchcock. I went to

General Electric Theater, *Chrysler Theater*, *Leave It to Beaver*, I don't know . . . many different shows.

P: Were all the Hitchcock TV shows done at Revue?

H: Started there. And then MCA bought Universal in 1959, I think it was, and we moved to Universal.

P: And that's where *Psycho* was shot? Do you remember which sound stage it was?

H: Sure, the house was on what they call the Phantom Stage, where they made *Phantom of the Opera*. And then the shower and motel, they broke up. They had regular feature stages, big stages, and they broke two of them up to make four stages for television. I can't think of the number of them now. But we put the motel set, the interiors, on one, and we put the hardware store and other little things on the other. But the house, everything in the house, was on the Phantom Stage.

P: I see. And you said there might be even some part of that left there someplace.

H: You mean the interiors?

P: Yes.

H: No. Well, the thing that was left there was the rig for the camera that went up the stairs. That was hung from the ceiling of the Phantom Stage. I don't know if that's still there or not, but it was there for years afterwards. They didn't bother to take it down. But that was the only thing left. When we did *Psycho II*, the house had been moved three times on the back lot. So we moved it again to put it where we wanted it to make it as close to the original as possible. We couldn't do it where we had the original; that was all changed.

P: What's your favorite of the sequels and the prequel?

H: Of *Psycho II*, *III*, and *IV*?

P: Yes.

H: Well, I liked *II* and I liked *IV*. *III* I hated. Richard Franklin directed *II*.

P: When you did sequels, was the shower scene in your mind when you were making them? Did you think, "Let's do an homage"?

H: Well, if you'll remember in *II*, there is a shower scene, not a shower scene as such, but the nude double for Meg Tilley is behind the shower and the curtain.

P: When you shot it, were people saying, "Let's go back and look at the original to see how it was done?"

H: No. We didn't want a copy of the original. We didn't want to make people think, "Oh, here they go again."

P: So you mustn't think much of Gus Van Sant's remake.

H: No. Gus called me and wanted me to put my name on it just to have part of the original, and I talked to Pat, Hitchcock's daughter, and I said, "What do you think, Pat?" And she said, "Go ahead." I said, "I don't think they ever should do this. I think it's terrible." But I did it, and my name's on there as a technical advisor.

P: So you were on the set when they were doing it?

H: I just went on the set one day when they were shooting it just to talk, and they were shooting the office where she steals the money. Anne Heche was doing that scene. In fact, I had lunch that day with Anne, and Ellen DeGeneres.

P: Van Sant adds a couple of shots to that shower scene. After she gets one of the knife cuts, she envisions something. Joe Stefano thinks it's a cow. I can't remember, but it's like a pastoral something; it happens so fast.

H: It's interesting how directors deify Hitchcock. Directors want to meet Hitchcock. I'm good friends with John Landis; I did a lot of John Landis stuff when he was at Universal. And John said, "You have to introduce me to Hitchcock before he dies. I must meet him." I said, "No, you don't want to meet Hitch." He said, "Yeah." I said, "He doesn't even know who you are, John." He said, "What?" I loved to kid him. Anyhow, I did go to Hitchcock, and I said, "There's a director that would love to meet you and have lunch with you sometime." And he said, "A director?" I said, "Well, he admires your work so much, and he just asked to meet you." "Who is it?" he asked. I said, "John Landis." He said, "Who's that?" He loved to rib that way, too. He knew who he was. Eventually the three of us had lunch in the back room of his office, Hitchcock, Landis, and myself.

P: What did he talk about? Did he talk about his movies?

H: Sure.

P: Did he ever say anything about *Psycho*?

H: He just talked about how he shot certain things. We used to sit in the projection room by the hour, the two of us, running all of his old movies. By the hour.

P: And would you ask him questions about why he did a certain thing?

H: Yes, and he would tell me why he did certain scenes and what the reasons were. It was very interesting. It was an education. He never had a son, and he kind of adopted me as his son.

P: Did you socialize with him at all?

H: One time, he invited Bob Burks and me when we were shooting *Marnie* to his ranch in Santa Cruz. He had a beautiful home that overlooked the bay, and Alma and he were there. Alma cooked the meal. It was just the four of us—Bob Burks, Alma, and Mr. H. and me.

P: Did you always call him Mr. Hitchcock?

H: Oh yes. Everybody else called him "Hitch." I would never call him "Hitch."

P: I know Janet Leigh always called him "Mr. Hitchcock." She even refers to him that way now.

H: I called him "Mr. H."

P: I wonder what he thought of the industry that started to grow around him after the Truffaut interviews, and after the French critics had got hold of him and started to say what a great director he was. I know he wanted to get recognized as a great director.

H: Everybody thought that he was very aloof and very rude. He wasn't that way at all. He was an introvert. He didn't like strangers around. That's why he always shot with the same crew. He didn't like new faces. In fact, if there was somebody different, he would call me over and say, "Who's that standing over there?" He never wanted little kids around. My daughter was about twelve or fourteen and she was with me one day. I was upstairs in production then. But he was shooting; I forget which picture. Well, maybe it was his last one. And she wanted to go over and see the stage, or see him shooting. And I said, "No, you can't go on there. He doesn't like kids around." She said, "Oh, Dad," I'll stay in the back, and he won't even know I'm there." I said, "Okay, I'll bring you on, but you must stand in the dark, over in the corner, and I don't want you to move." So I came in and put her there and went over to talk to him and sat down, and he said, "So how's everything today?" And I said, "Great." And he said, "And who's that young lady?" He knew everything. I said, "That's my daughter." And he said, "Why is she standing over there? Are you ashamed of her?" He said, "Bring her over here." And I said, "Well, I didn't want her to bother you." And he got the prop man to bring a chair right next to him, and she sat next to him, and he started talking to her about all that was happening and the whole thing.

P: Did you ever see him lose his temper on the set, get really angry and have a tantrum?

H: Once, on *Psycho*. We were having difficulty getting the shot he wanted. You know how you get a flare on the camera, and it ruins the shot. But he wanted a flare; it was when Vera Miles comes into the basement, turns mother around and goes, "Ahhhh!" And she hits the light bulb. As it swings back and forth, Hitchcock wanted a flare to come across. It was hard to pull off. The prop man was on his back, and mother was in the chair, and the chair was on the camera wheel, and he worked the thing on his back like that so when she turned, it would turn with the camera. Jack Russell was the director of photography; Alan Davy was the operator. In those days, you didn't know whether you got it or not. You had to rely on the opinion of the camera operator. Well, you don't shoot very many takes with Hitchcock. I mean you better get it in the first couple takes. During shooting, he ran his dailies at lunchtime with Peggy Robertson, but I didn't sit with him and Davy because I was always on the set getting ready for the next thing. And, oh God, he came in. . . . Well, the first day, it wasn't right and he came over to Jack and said it didn't work; the flare wasn't there. "Let's do it again, and let's do it right," he said. So we did it a second time. Russell said, "Well, we got it." Well, they didn't. And the second time he came back, he didn't go to Jack. He came to me, and he yelled, "Hilton!" He chewed me up and down, "You told me you got this," and he was talking to Jack, but he was looking at me. Jack was sitting right there. "Why did you lie to me?" he asked. And I said, "Well, I thought we got it." What was I going to say? But we did it a third time, and we got it.

P: When you were setting up the shots for *Psycho* and for the shower scene, did you think that they were an unusual way to get the scene? I mean did you think that this scene was something special you were doing?

H: Oh, yes. Because I was used to television where it's "wham, bam, get everything and you're out of there." If you look at the script, there aren't many pages, but we spent a week on it.

P: Joe Stefano claims Hitchcock didn't want the scene written down specifically because people took pages and passed them out, and then word would get out about what they were doing.

H: I have one of the original scripts right here. Why don't you read the shower scene, starting with the appearance of mother.

P: "We see the shadow of a woman fall across the shower curtain. Marion's back is turned to the curtain. A low terrible groan begins to rise, a hand comes into the shot. The hand holds an enormous bread knife. Bingo. The flint of the blade shatters the screen to an almost total silver blankness. An impression of the knife slashing as if tearing at the very screen, ripping the film. Over the brief gulps of screaming and silence and then the dreadful thump as Marion's body falls in the tub. The blank whiteness, the gore of the shower water, the hand pulls the shower curtain back."

H: You know, as you read that, you would never dream that the filmed shower scene came from it.

P: Would somebody have held on to the outtakes, because Hitchcock says there were seventy-eight different camera setups? And in the actual shower scene beginning with when she steps into the tub and when the mother leaves, there are about forty shots. Were there a lot of shots that weren't used?

H: No, not a lot. With Hitchcock you never shot extra things. He shot what he wanted.

P: So you think that most of the stuff that was shot, most of the angles, ended up in the scene. So there weren't a lot of outtakes?

H: Shouldn't have been. He shot what he wanted. Other directors, you know, say, " Let's try it this way; now give me a shot over here and over here, and put it together and see how it plays."

P: Well, that makes the scene even more unbelievable. He knew exactly what he wanted.

H: Yes. He had it visualized exactly the way he wanted it. I saw him many times, not only in *Psycho*, but in other films, cut in the middle of a scene where two actors are talking, but the scene isn't over. Right in the middle of a sentence, he says, "Cut." And the actor says, "What did I do?" And he said, "No, no, that's fine, but I don't need that because I'm going to be over here for the rest of the scene. You don't have to do that."

P: Did you ever work with a director like that?

H: No, and in fact, it spoiled me because, you know, directors today, the younger directors shoot it this way, that way.

P: Well, I think they're spoiled. They have too much technology on their hands.

H: Yes, they say, "Let's do it again for protection." And I remember one show, I won't go into which one it was or anything, but there was a very involved and tough shot, and it took a long time to line up and get the marks where it followed a car in and moved in until they got close up. There were a lot of things involved. There was a night shot, which made it go longer and everything, and we rehearsed, and the very first take was perfect, perfect. Now to take two would be a good forty-five minutes, and I didn't know if we could get it, because you had everything backed up, and the director asked the operator, and he said, "Perfect." And the director was watching it on a television screen, and he saw it was perfect but said, "Well, let's do it again for protection." And I said, "Why?" And he said, "Well, it might get ruined in the lab." And I said, "If it's ruined in the lab, probably the whole roll will be ruined in the lab, and then we have to come back and do the whole thing over anyway, and it's going to take another forty-five minutes to an hour to get this shot, and we're going to be in overtime. There's no reason for it." He said, "I don't understand what you're saying." I said, "Look, I've worked with a lot of directors, and they never protected it. There's no reason for it."

P: Yeah, I don't blame you. They have outlandish budgets for films.

H: There's no reason in the world to do it again. And we saw it in dailies, and it was beautiful.

P: You worked with Hitchcock until his last film, *Family Plot.*

H: Yes. I was with him through his last script, the one that was never shot, *The Short Night.* Bob Boyle, a production designer, and I went to Europe and laid out the whole show in Helsinki, London, Toronto. I was upstairs in production, but Hitchcock wanted me to go over and shoot backgrounds and bring them back to him to take a look at.

P: Is that the one with the character named Brandt?

H: Yes. *Short Night.* It was a good story. I read part of the script, and I thought it was damn good. Well, I brought it back later, quite a bit after Hitchcock died, to Frank Price who was in charge of production. Frank and I go back a long ways. In fact, I worked for Frank. I said, "Gee, I've got this script: Universal owns it. Why not do the movie Hitchcock couldn't complete? And we'll get Norman Lloyd, who was Hitchcock's protégé, so to speak, and Norman and I can do this movie and make it Hitchcock!"

P: But they didn't go for it?

H: Well, Frank thought it was a good idea, but then he said, "No, I don't want to do it."

P: What happened? How come Hitchcock didn't do it?

H: He was too weak. In fact, I remember one of the saddest days. I was upstairs in production, feature production, running the feature end of it, and I got a call to come down and Sue, his secretary, said, "Mr. H. wants to see you." In those days, toward the end, we never wore ties anymore. It started getting informal. Well, I always carried a tie in the office when I went to Mr. Hitchcock because I never went to him without a tie on. So I put on my tie and went into his office, and he was behind his desk. He said, "Sit down. I want you to do a favor for me." I said, "Sure, what do you want?" He said, "I want you to go to Lew Wasserman and tell Lew that I'm all through." And I said, "What do you mean you're all through?" He said, "I'll never direct again." I said, "What's wrong with you? Come on! That's ridiculous." He said "Hilton," and there were kind of tears in his eyes, "my legs . . . I can't go out and do locations." And I said, "Yes, you can. We'll get the cameraman, Norman, and myself, and you will be there in the car. You won't even have to get out of the car. You just tell us what you want; we will get it, and you will get this movie. He said, "I know, I know, I know you'll do it, but I don't want to make a movie that way."

P: That's sad.

H: He said, "Will you go up and tell Lew," who was his closest friend, "that I'm all through." I said, "Oh, golly, I can't . . ." He said, "No, please." So I said, "All right." So I got Sue to call up to Wasserman's office, which I hated going to. And the secretary said, "What's it concerning?" And I said, "It's concerning Mr. Hitchcock, and he wants me to see Mr. Wasserman right away." And she said, "One moment." Then she says, "Come right up." So I went up and knocked on the door, and Wasserman said, "Come in." And here he was behind his desk. And I said, "I've got some terrible news." And he said, "What is it?" He used to come on the set everyday when Mr. H. was shooting. In the morning, he would come over to me and ask, "How's Mr. Hitchcock today? Is everything all right? Is he feeling well?" Then he would go over and say good morning to Mr. Hitchcock and then leave. Wasserman never went on sets. But every morning he would come on ours. Anyway, I told him the story, and he had tears in his eyes. And he said, "I knew it was coming." It was really a sad day.

P: He looked so frail at the American Film Institute Life Achievement Award Ceremony.

H: I got a call one day from his secretary Sue, and she said, "You've got to get down here right away and don't bother with your tie—get here!" I ran. He had fallen behind his desk, and they couldn't get him up. He weighed almost three hundred pounds, and he wouldn't let anyone come in but me to help him. I got him up and into his seat. He didn't have strength in his legs. He couldn't get his body up. He was on the floor. And I stayed with him for a couple hours after that. It breaks your heart.

P: Yeah, it's a heartbreaker.

H: That's how close I was to him.

P: You were like his adopted son.

H: Well, I remember that night in Santa Cruz when we had dinner. That was a wonderful dinner. They served us. He would go out and get the dishes and bring them in, and we asked them not to bother, but they insisted on serving us. It was a gourmet dinner. And then the brandy afterwards. It was a great night, one I'll never forget.

P: Well, you were so fortunate. You had a wonderful career with him.

H: And remember, he didn't talk to me on the first show.

P: That's right. Well, what was it he said about the script when he knew it was good?

H: He said, "Alma loved it."

P: That's true. What do you think of Donald Spoto's *The Dark Side of Genius* and the other debunkers of Hitchcock? They're not debunkers, but they want to focus on the ungenerous, the negative.

H: The dark side. Always the dark side, and I don't believe in the dark side. I don't believe you should bring that up. I think if he had a dark side, which I didn't see, but if he had it, let it be. There was too much good about him, too much great about him.

P: I think Spoto was looking for an angle for his biography.

H: Hitchcock always showed me his human side. We were working on *Alfred Hitchcock Presents* with Keenan Wynn. It was aboard ship when there was an auction. Keenan Wynn falls off the stern of the ship. It was a two-day show, and we were in the afternoon of the first day. Well, he didn't come out after lunch. And in television you had to move. And I knew something was wrong, so I went and knocked on his door, and I came in and he was crying. And I said, "What's the matter?" And he said, "Alma just found out she has cancer." And he was completely shaken.

P: This was before there were lots of treatments for cancer, too. It was like a death sentence.

H: Anyway, he said, "I can't shoot today. I'm leaving." I said, "Well, I'll close it down." And he said, "No, no, no, no, we can't close it down. No, no, no. I want you to direct it." I said, "I don't want to direct this movie." He said, "No, you direct it." And he left. So I did it.

P: Did you enjoy it?

H: Yes. And Keenan was great. I told him what had happened, and he was great. But it was a terrible day.

P: Speaking of terrible days, my mother, Angie Skerry, passed away on the centennial of his birth—August 13. I was going to Boston. I knew she had been feeling bad. My sister said that I had better come home. I'd been home four or five times in the past when she was ill, and I'd go up there and expect her to be on her deathbed but she'd be playing poker with the other people at the nursing home. So I thought it would be the same thing. I remember, we drove and drove, and it was pouring rain, and I remember there was a big tribute for Alfred Hitchcock on the radio because it was the centennial of his birth. I had the worst sinking feeling in my stomach that day that something bad was going to happen.

H: And she died on that day?

P: She died on that day. So I will always remember that particular day, and it just kind of made that uneasy connection for me. I remember how sad I felt when Hitchcock died, and earlier when Orson Welles had died. I felt this was the passing of two incredible people. And there's no one who can even touch them.

H: I remember when John Ford died. I went to his funeral, too. It was sad.

P: That generation that had their heyday in the studio system and made the transition to television or made whatever transition they had to make; they were amazing. Hitchcock was amazing. He starts off in silent films, goes into sound, experiments with color, experiments with 3-D, with wide-screen, sound. No one else was like that.

H: Well, right after we put men on the moon for the first time and everybody was talking about it, Hitchcock said, "You know what's going on today with the advancements in science and technology?" And then he said, "Look around you." We were on the set. He said, "Look at that light up there. I've had those same lights since 1933. They haven't changed a bit. There is no creativity in the motion picture business. It's stagnant. I want to see new things. . . ." And just after he died, it popped open with everything.

CHAPTER 7

Montage

Creating Terror

Now this terror is Hitchcock's first, if not entire, objective.

—JEAN DOUCHET

When Hitchcock invoked his "pure cinema" mantra, he was referring not only to mise-en-scene but to montage as well. In interview after interview and in essay after essay, Hitchcock extols the virtue of montage. In his essay "Direction," he points out the uniqueness of the medium of film, especially its montage properties: "The screen ought to speak its own language, freshly coined, and it can't do that unless it treats an acted scene as a piece of raw material which must be broken up, taken to bits, before it can be woven into an expressive visual pattern" (Gottlieb, *Hitchcock on Hitchcock* 256). Hitchcock sums up the importance of montage to his filmmaking by saying, "It's limitless, I would say, the power of cutting and the assembly of the images" (Bogdanovich, *The Cinema of Alfred Hitchcock* 4). Montage would become, with the support of mise-en-scene, the infrastructure of Hitchcock's construction of terror.

When Hitchcock simply wanted to move the action along, to move a character from one place to another, he was utilizing narrative montage, a fairly straightforward, unobtrusive kind of cutting, a staple of the classical continuity of the studio system, which had as its goal the creation of a realistic time-space continuum. Yet Hitchcock's most characteristic cutting involved "expressive montage," a technique that allowed him to meld the rich compositions of his mise-en-scene with complex editing techniques, the end result being the expression of a feeling or an idea. When it came to the creation of terror, however, Hitchcock would employ the montage style developed by the Soviet Socialist Realists, particularly Eisenstein.

This style frequently was in direct contrast to realism by creating a purely cinematic space and time.

In Hitchcock's greatest films, *Psycho* in particular, scenes of terror almost always follow from scenes of suspense. In addition, scenes of suspense are frequently constructed on a mise-en-scene approach, while scenes of terror are almost always based on an Eisensteinian montage style. Hitchcock's formula for equating suspense with mise-en-scene and terror with montage developed over a period of years and culminated in the shower scene of *Psycho*.

In Hitchcock's conception of "pure cinema," both mise-en-scene and montage are the products of the preproduction and production processes, although the actual job of cutting the film takes place in the postproduction process. Until the publication of Bill Krohn's book, *Hitchcock at Work* (2000), the reigning orthodoxy on Hitchcock was that the film was made in his head in the preproduction process—in the same way that an architect would produce a blueprint—and that the production and postproduction phases were simply the "building" of the film from that blueprint. In many interviews, Hitchcock claimed that he wished he didn't have to go through the production or postproduction process because he had already created a mental ideal—a platonic film, so to speak. Bill Krohn, however, challenges the critical orthodoxy about Hitchcock's production methodology. Krohn states, ". . . as I talked to good film-makers through the years in my capacity as Hollywood correspondent for *Cahiers du Cinéma*, I began to question how one of the greatest film-makers who ever lived could be such a thoroughgoing exception to the conditions for creation that other film-makers seemed to respect, because they were inherent in the nature of the artform" (10).

It's true that Hitchcock worked assiduously on script preparation and that he planned his production largely through storyboards. But Krohn makes a strong case for seeing Hitchcock not as an anomaly among filmmakers but as a representative of the best of the filmmaking process. As Richard Franklin, director of *Psycho II*, claims, "Editing becomes a function of mise-en-scene, when montage is predesigned in storyboards. Usually the shots will only go together one way." David O. Selznick's complaint about Hitchcock's editing practice is relevant here. Selznick fumed about Hitchcock's "damned jig-saw cutting," because it denied Selznick his customary role in the postproduction process of shaping the film to *his* (the producer's) end. Seen in this way, Hitchcock's montage became a way of enhancing the power of the director in the producer-controlled environment of the studio system. Hitchcock's montage, then, is the product of both aesthetic and practical choices, some of them made during the production and postproduction processes themselves, as Krohn points out. The ultimate goal is to create a film that would meet the marketing demands of the studios, adhere to the Production Code, and at the same time, enhance the stature and reputation of the director by fulfilling a directorial vision. This elusive goal required a delicate balancing act that Hitchcock performed at various levels of success throughout his long career.

Hitchcock's narrative interests and experiences would contribute to his talent for montage, for moving a narrative through time. From the age of fifteen or sixteen, Hitchcock had begun to read fiction, being particularly struck by the morbid and surrealistic stories of Edgar Allan Poe. Dennis Perry's *Hitchcock and Poe: The Legacy of Delight and Terror* lays out a very convincing argument for the creative synergy between Hitchcock and Poe: "Born in America in 1809, Poe was the child of literary romanticism. Hitchcock was born in England ninety years later and the child of cinematic modernism. Nevertheless, their aesthetic paths crossed and their common artistic goal transcended the gulf of a century: both perfected ways of terrorizing readers and audiences through precise narrative forms born of a set of common obsessions" (xiii). While at Henley's, Hitchcock was also the founding editor and the most prolific contributor to the *Henley Telegraph*, an in-house magazine featuring company reviews, but also original short stories and essays.

It was Hitchcock's German experience that convinced him of the crucial importance of visual storytelling, of using the full range of cinematic possibilities inherent in the film frame. But it was two other countries that contributed to his ingenious use of montage: the United States and Russia. As Hitchcock claimed numerous times, his first job at Famous-Players Lasky meant that he was "American-trained" in the studio, or Hollywood style. In terms of montage, this training meant that the editing of a film would largely be subordinated to the narrative thrust of the film—the reestablishment of the equilibrium of the film, which had been disrupted in the first act. Consequently, characters and their goals became paramount. The montage must always serve the story by being invisible and not disruptive. However, Hitchcock considered himself a stylist above all: "I put first and foremost cinematic style before content" (Gottlieb, *Hitchcock on Hitchcock* 292). It's true that characterization and narrative were always of paramount importance to Hitchcock, particularly in the preproduction process of script development, but it's also true that Hitchcock never lost sight of the expressive power of montage. From the Russians, Hitchcock learned to temper the narrative thrust of his films—his American training—with the montage techniques of the Soviet filmmakers.

The Soviet filmmakers had a profound influence on Hitchcock's conception of montage. Through his membership in the newly organized Film Society of London, founded in 1925, Hitchcock would see the films of Sergei Eisenstein and V.I. Pudovkin, and he would hear about and see in action the film theories of Dziga Vertov, Lev Kuleshov, and Sergei Eisenstein. As Tom Ryall points out in his excellent book on Hitchcock's British films, the cinema of Soviet Socialist Realism had profoundly influenced Hitchcock, with its strong emphasis on montage as the sine qua non of cinematic form. By his experience with "experimental films" through his membership in the Film Society of London in 1925, Hitchcock became aware of an art form that, as Ryall explains it, frees "the film from what were sometimes perceived as the artistically debilitating constraint of narrative" (8). Yet Hitchcock was not essentially an avant-garde filmmaker. As Peter Wollen claims, "Hitchcock's project as a filmmaker . . . was to have his cake and eat it, to achieve massive popular success while, at the same time, experimenting artistically in ways which were carefully camouflaged . . ." (81). Ken Mogg reiterates this idea, calling Hitchcock's oeuvre "a popular mix of avant-garde and conventional storytelling" (10).

As I have pointed out in chapter 5, the classical style relies on mise-en-scene to create a plausible sense of space, a world in which characters can pursue their goals and go through their various "arcs." Characters exist, however, in a story, a narrative structured around conflict and resolution. This dramatic structure requires not only space but time. Classic montage provides the mechanism to produce a space-time continuum in the film. Such montage can extend space into time through the basic editing technique of continuity cutting, during which space becomes elastic, flexible, and continuous. In addition, montage can juxtapose spaces—and therefore actions—in such techniques as parallel editing, or montage, can fragment a single setting into various spatial fragments, in the shot-reverse-shot technique, or the POV and eye-line match shots. These techniques elevate montage from the basic narrative to the more suggestively expressive.

When Hitchcock came to America in 1939 under contract to David O. Selznick, he was no stranger to American methods of film production, nor was he a novice in the studio system, thanks to his early work at Famous Players-Lasky. When he arrived in America, he brought with him the cinematic legacy of his British period. This legacy was a complex mixture of mise-en-scene and montage techniques from a number of sources—literature, theater, film movements—and of practices—art direction, script writing, directing. The films of Hitchcock's fertile and lengthy American period would allow him to utilize all of his considerable talents to create a body of work that ranks as the apotheosis of the American cinema.

This apotheosis reaches its apex in the great films of the 1950s and early 1960s, particularly in *Psycho* and specifically in the shower scene, his most virtuoso montage effort. I should like to demonstrate how Hitchcock arrived at this high point of his career by analyzing his employment of montage to complement mise-en-scene in the creation of suspense and terror in films leading up to *Psycho*.

I begin my analysis with *Rear Window*, a showcase of how montage works with mise-en-scene to create suspense and ultimately terror. In the opening scenes of *Rear Window*, Hitchcock presents a densely composed mise-en-scene to establish the strict confines of L.B. Jeffrey's world and to suggest the danger involved in watching and seeing. Mise-en-scene, however, is only half of the suspense equation in Hitchcock's cinema: the other half is montage. Hitchcock presents many scenes of L.B. Jeffreys looking out of his apartment window. The camera, in effect, becomes a window—a cataphor for the act of seeing—and in some scenes the audience views L.B. Jeffreys from the vantage point of the very same people *he* is observing—a clever piece of extra-diegetic voyeurism on the part of the director himself, but the director as enunciator, not as cameo character. For the director can get closer to the characters of L.B. Jeffrey's world than any diegetic character can. On that note, in his cameo, Hitchcock becomes one of the characters that Jeff observes—an object of Hitchcock's own voyeuristic gaze, a sort of montage "tit for tat." As the camera faces Jeff, his position assumes the quarter turn traditional to classical mise-en-scene. Montage comes into play in creating suspense by showing the audience what the character sees in POV and eye-line match shots, both of these part of Hitchcock's suspense repertoire. Both eye-line match and POV shots are combination mise-en-scene and montage techniques. Ira Konigsberg defines eye-line match in this way: "For example, a character looks in a specific direction with a specific angle of view and the next shot is some object that is placed exactly where we think he or she would be looking" (127). A POV shot is "[a] subjective shot that shows an object exactly the way a character would see it, hence dramatizing his or her perspective and putting us at least for the moment, in the character's shoes" (299). Hitchcock shifts fluidly from one technique to another in *Rear Window*. These techniques are what Hitchcock meant by montage to create ideas. In discussing his montage techniques, Hitchcock talks about two types of cutting: montage "to create ideas" and montage "to create violence and emotions." To illustrate the first type, Hitchcock refers to *Rear Window*:

> I consider one of the most cinematic films I have ever created is *Rear Window* . . . look at the structure. He looks, he sees, he reacts. Purely by this man's reactions you construct a whole murder story.
>
> We take a close-up of the man (Jimmy Stewart) and cut to what he sees, and what do we show, a woman nursing a baby. You cut back to your face reaction and he smiles. Now what is he? He's a benevolent, nice gentleman.
>
> Take away the middle piece of film (the mother and the baby) and substitute a girl in a bikini. Now he's a dirty old man. That's what I mean by the purity of montage and the control of the film." (Gottlieb, *Alfred Hitchcock Interviews* 79).

In this sense, montage links continuous spaces together by eliminating "dead air" and contracting or expanding chronological time. Hitchcock once said that cinema was life with the boring parts left out. True to form, though, Hitchcock presents himself with a unique challenge in *Rear Window* by linking camera position in the B portion of the POV shot to Jeff's immobilized position. Let's say that a POV shot is made up of A and B shots linked by a simple cut. Shot A is the enunciator's shot, with a character looking at some point outside the mise-en-scene, usually to the horizontal limits of the frame but sometimes out toward the enunciator's POV. The dramatic situation that motivates the look of the character in shot A is usually the function of mise-en-scene: something within the mise-en-scene motivates the character to look, and the camera's position supports and facilitates the dramatic situation. Shot B then functions as the object of the character's look, a sort of direct object, if one considers the character as the subject, the cut as the transitive verb, and the object viewed as the direct object. In situations like this, the tradition of classical montage is to contract or even eliminate the distance between viewer and viewed by presenting shot B *not* as a person would normally see it in the physical world, but as a character would see it in the diegetic world of the film. Occasionally, however, Hitchcock would announce the superiority of the enunciator's POV by showing shot B, not as a character would see it but rather as the enunciator would see it, or he would free his camera from any connection to a character as he does in the opening of *Rear Window*, when the camera pans the courtyard and comes to rest on a sleeping L.B. Jeffreys.

Hitchcock was a technical innovator, and *Rear Window* is one of his technical triumphs. Earlier in his career in *Rope*, he had challenged himself to create a film virtually free of montage, replacing it with a fluid and mobile mise-en-scene instead. I believe that Hitchcock learned a lesson in *Rope* about the essential nature of montage in his suspense format. In *Rear Window*, Hitchcock employs montage to create suspense, but he limits his montage's range by preserving much of the "dead air" between shots A and B. In this sense, the space of the courtyard becomes a cataphor in the mise-en-scene of the film by inflecting montage, by deliberately limiting what the camera can see. As a practitioner in the Hollywood studio system, Hitchcock knew well that the freedom of his camera—and by extension the freedoms of his mise-en-scene and montage—were strictly limited by studio policies and by the Production Code. In effect, there were many things that the mise-en-scene could not show or reveal, usually details of the human body or of human bodies in sexual or violent contact. So in *Rear Window*, Hitchcock slyly incorporates the very limitations he had faced in his many years in the studio system into the very fabric of the film itself. Many commentators on *Rear Window* have pointed out that Jeff becomes a surrogate for the director himself, choosing angles of observation, dollying his wheelchair back and forth, and selecting lenses for dramatic effect (binoculars and long-range camera lens). Thus does Hitchcock build self-reflexivity into the visual structure of the film. To the audience, Hitchcock seems to be saying, "Ladies and gentlemen, I am presenting to you a film that demonstrates and symbolizes the constricting and restricting limits placed on directors such as myself, who want to present adult dramas to adult audiences. Mr. Jeffreys, in trying to piece together evidence of a murder, has the same handicaps that all directors face: he (and they) can't see the necessary elements of passion or murder." Thus *Rear Window* presents a brilliant variation of Hitchcock's suspense formula because the film gives the audience only a tiny bit more information than it gives the diegetic character of Jeff. In addition, *Rear Window* further delimits the range of montage by limiting the action of the narrative to Jeff's apartment. Throughout the film, the camera either stays within

Jeff's apartment or it strays slightly by positioning itself right outside Jeff's window. In *Rear Window* Hitchcock further narrows his montage choices by avoiding foregrounding of juxtaposed images. In Hitchcock's "favorite" film, the superb *Shadow of a Doubt*, he opens the film by juxtaposing two scenes linked only by the formal composition of their mise-en-scene. Each exposition contains six shots. The first scene opens on a long shot of an urban setting, with a large bridge spanning a river, with homeless men sitting on its banks. Using pans to the right and dissolves, Hitchcock presents us with a skyline view of the city with gray skies above and with a junkyard at the bottom of the frame. The next shots bring us into a city street with young boys playing baseball, and to the exterior of a cheap boarding house. The last shot of the scene is taken from a left-canted angle and reveals the ubiquitous Hitchcock window, through which we dissolve to a room with a male figure, fully dressed, lying on a bed. The scene ends with the character eluding the police, who have been waiting outside the boarding house.

The second scene opens with a sunny long shot of a town nestled in a valley. In subsequent shots, Hitchcock brings us closer to the town, as we see a friendly policeman directing traffic and a beautiful white house on a corner. The last shot of the scene presents us with a right-canted-angle shot of a window as we dissolve into another room, this one a bedroom, with a young girl, fully dressed, reclining on the bed. In both of these last shots, the camera has assumed the same position as an interior fourth wall.

This is not parallel editing per se because there's no real indication that these two scenes are taking place at the same time. They are therefore elevated from simple classical parallel editing to the kind of montage that Pudovkin and Eisenstein employed—creating an intellectual space, a thematic motif that grows out of the juxtaposition itself. It does not reach the level of quintessential Eisensteinian montage—collision; that will come only with the brilliant eye-to-drain dissolve in the shower scene. But it is certainly what Pudovkin meant by creating "filmic space," because Hitchcock creates, through montage, the idea of the double—that the man lying in the bed, known to the audience at this point as Mr. Spencer, is somehow linked to this young girl lying in a similar position in her bed. Both exist in a thematic space, moreover, because the opening shots of these linked scenes are almost exact duplicates of one another.

The settings are linked, too, but they are connected by the contrasted content of the shots—city versus small town. The two scenes are thus conjunctive—two reclining figures in two beds in two bedrooms—and disjunctive—one bedroom in a cheap boarding house, the other bedroom in a comfortable home. Hitchcock has presented his audience an intriguing and provocative opening sequence that visually establishes the theme of the duality of human nature via linked visual motifs.

In *Rear Window*, though, Hitchcock does not link foregrounded spaces; rather, he links the backgrounded spaces of the courtyard. It is as if the film exists in two different time-space continuums. The first—let's call it the primary one—consists of Jeff's apartment. Hitchcock constructs this space theatrically; it seems very much like the Wendice apartment in *Dial M for Murder*, or Brandon's and Phillip's apartment in *Rope*. The next space, the secondary space, is the world outside Jeff's apartment, which is made up of two additional spatial layers—first, the various apartment windows and balconies; second, the street outside the apartment, where Thorwald goes to dispose of his grisly cargo. Throughout most of the film, Jeff's apartment is a "safe" place, where the cares and concerns of the outside world enter only through various messengers, or emissaries, from the outside world—Stella, the cynical, acerbic nurse; Lisa, Jeff's love interest; Doyle, the skeptical detective. *Rear Window* in this sense resembles Greek tragedy in its offstage violence and its messengers. Yet, to Hitchcock no space is ever really safe, especially domestic spaces. Uncle Charlie tries to kill his niece Charlie in the garage of her home; Margot Wendice is almost strangled to death in her apartment; David Kentley is strangled to death in the apartment of his friends Brandon and Philip in *Rope*. And, of course, Thorwald evidently kills his wife in their apartment. Finally, Thorwald enters Jeff's space to try to silence him. As many commentators have pointed out, in *Rear Window* Hitchcock treats the secondary spaces of the courtyard apartments as mini-films, each with its own "screen," a window or balcony. These cataphors function as symbols of perception itself, of the ambiguity of appearance. As in all of Hitchcock's backgrounds, they have a specific function. They act as metaphors of Jeff's dilemma with Lisa: Should he marry her and live at first like the newlyweds, and then later (horror) like the Thorwalds? Should he continue his life of bachelorhood and end up like Miss Lonely Hearts? In a related metaphor, Hitchcock links Miss Torso with the fate of Thorwald's wife; we see her in truncated shots in her bathroom, from the shoulders up, visually dismembered, as it were, just as we see below Miss Torso's apartment, the sculptured human figure, also truncated, of the female artist, who argues with Thorwald as he works in his flower garden, itself a metaphor for the deceptiveness of appearances: the flower garden is really a miniature graveyard, the burial place—we surmise—of Mrs. Thorwald's head.

In a film made two years before *Rear Window*, Hitchcock also uses montage to complement mise-en-scene. In the opening scene of *Strangers on a Train* (1951), Hitchcock links Bruno and Guy technically before they are linked thematically. This clever piece of technical foreshadowing is accomplished in much the same way as the opening of *Shadow of a Doubt*, both films exploring the notion of the double by presenting dual characters and dual mise-en-scene linked through montage. The difference between the two films is that the spaces that Bruno and Guy inhabit are contiguous spaces, and the time is almost simultaneous. This is Pudovkin's "filmic time," which can be expanded or contracted, depending upon the dramatic situation. The most famous example of filmic time is Eisenstein's Odessa Steps scene, in which editing techniques carve up the action into numerous subactions, and fragment almost infinitely the space of the action (the slaughter on the steps), like *Rear Window*'s secondary spaces, the difference being that there is no primary diegetic foregrounding. Except for the student who views the action from the bottom of the steps, only the director-enunciator views the entire action.

In the opening of *Strangers on a Train*, Hitchcock places his camera at ground level to present characters from the bottom up, a reversal of classical style, which usually presents from the top down. This disconcerting camera position is meant to throw off the audience's perception of character presentation, foreshadowing somewhat the distant and truncated views of Jeff as he peers through his window with his lenses in *Rear Window*. In the opening montage of *Strangers on a Train*, Hitchcock first presents his viewers with a long shot of the exterior of a train station, with a barely noticeable Capitol in the background. This subtle reference to law and order acts as a kind of symbolic template throughout the film. The next shot is a medium low-angle one of a cab pulling up and depositing its occupant at the train station, with just the pants (nattily striped) and shoes (two-toned) visible. The camera pans as the feet walk out of the left side of frame. The next shot reveals a cab coming from the left side of the frame and depositing another character, with only the pants (plain wool) and shoes (monotone) visible. This character has two tennis rackets (part of the doubling and pairing pattern of the film), which we see as he and the porter walk past the camera and out of the frame to the right. The next two shots are contrasting duplicates, the first showing fancy shoes and pants walking to the left of the frame, the camera tracking; the second showing plain pants and shoes walking to right of frame, camera tracking. The next two shots are similar in form and content. The subsequent shot is again from a low angle and shows the characters from the rear as they approach the ticket taker and enter the boarding area. The next shot is a surprising shift from the characters to the railroad tracks, seen from the moving perspective of the locomotive. This is a startling shot, for it doesn't continue the cutting pattern of the opening scene, but it suggests a similar idea in its mise-en-scene. Using the perspective of the camera lens, Hitchcock mounts his camera on the front of the locomotive, with the railroad tracks extending into the frame, on either side. The tracks narrow, through the perspective, and get closer together. At the top-middle section of the frame, switch-over tracks connect the two diagonal lines of the track and make a criss-cross pattern—hence, graphically suggesting the theme of the criss-cross ("You do my murder; I do yours"), and the double-cross. The next two shots continue the pattern of the opening shot, with fancy shoes and pants walking in the railroad car and taking a seat, and then plain shoes and pants walking toward the same table, taking a seat, crossing legs, and then accidentally kicking one of the fancy shoes. Thus does Hitchcock suggest the serious consequences of seemingly inconsequential acts.

In *Shadow of a Doubt*, the montage technique suggests, through its use of conjunction and disjunction, that the theme of the film is somehow connected to the montage itself: the filmic space makes manifest the topic of the double. In *Strangers on a Train*, though, Hitchcock uses contiguous actions taking place in a continuous time to suggest the inevitability of a certain sequence of events. Bruno and Guy were meant to be brought together; they were heading in the same direction—Bruno through his oedipally driven madness and Guy through his marital woes and social climbing. When Hitchcock talked about the director "playing God," he was not kidding. *Strangers on a Train*, through its brilliant use of montage, shows a director inexorably shaping the ends of his characters.

In the three films discussed above—*Shadow of a Doubt*, *Strangers on a Train*, and *Rear Window*—Hitchcock utilizes montage to link settings separated by space, to link spaces separated by time, and to link times separated by space. Hitchcock uses his technical mastery of pure cinema to create suspense and thus to instill fear and foreboding in his audience. In his essay "The Enjoyment of Fear," Hitchcock states, "Fear in the cinema is my special field, and I have perhaps dramatically, but I think with good cause, split cinematic fear into two broad categories—terror and suspense . . . On the screen, terror is induced by surprise; suspense by forewarning" (Gottlieb, *Hitchcock on Hitchcock* 119). It is clear that Hitchcock prefers suspense to terror; he states, "The most powerful means of gripping attention is suspense." He even goes so far as to say that "suspense and terror cannot coexist." However, terror is more complicated than Hitchcock gives it credit for; it depends for its success upon a foundation of suspense, with some degree of knowledge of the character and audience. Then there's a surprise introduction of violence that shocks both character and audience.

Hitchcock's suspense depends upon a hierarchy of knowledge: enunciator, audience, and characters. Hitchcock preferred suspense to mystery because, in the latter, the audience lacks knowledge, but in suspense, the audience sometimes has knowledge that the character in the scene does not have. Hitchcock admitted in a documentary on his films, "It's when I came to America that I became more aware of audiences" (*Inside Hitchcock*). In effect he moved from a director mainly of thrillers to the consummate director of suspense films. Suspense would allow Hitchcock to employ the full range of cinematic techniques he had developed in his career. In suspense, Hitchcock could use the montage techniques of eyeline match and POV, combined with the complex palette of his mise-en-scene, to thrust viewers into a scene. Thus the audience identifies with the characters (Hitchcock calls the process, "transferring . . . to the mind of the audience"), and they become knowledgeable together. During our interview, Joseph Stefano reinforced the idea of the paramount importance of audience to Hitchcock's conception of pure cinema: "All through the whole experience with Hitch, and again when we worked on *Marnie*, he kept saying to me—I don't even know if he knew how often he repeated it—'What do you want the audience to think? What do you want the audience to feel? Audience, audience, audience.' And I thought, 'This is the whole key to Hitchcock's work—he does it for us. He doesn't do it for the studio bosses; he doesn't do it for friends; he does it for the people who pay at the box office.' And audiences have always loved his pictures."

Hitchcock's 1942 film *Saboteur* illustrates an early example of how Hitchcock blends suspense and terror in the same film. The film is ostensibly in the tradition of the thriller, a form Hitchcock had perfected in the thriller sextet, the greatest films of his British period: *The Man Who Knew Too Much* (1934), *The 39 Steps* (1935), *Sabotage* (1936), *The Secret Agent* (1936), *Young and Innocent* (1937), and *The Lady Vanishes* (1938). The thriller was very much in the pastoral tradition, with a somewhat feckless but always resourceful picaresque hero. The hero is frequently an innocent wrongly accused and goes on a journey or quest to redeem himself and to save society from evil. This journey is sometimes in the form of a chase or double chase, involving a dastardly villain and a female co-questor, who is usually initially antagonistic toward the hero but who eventually helps him. The films end with the reunion of hero with his society, symbolized by a romantic union with his female co-questor.

Saboteur, however, although it shares many of the same characteristics as the thriller, evolves into something else: a film that blends suspense and terror. For most of the film, the audience has become allied with Barry Kane, and later with his female helper, Patricia Martin, through Hitchcock's careful control of mise-en-scene and montage, especially in POV and eye-line match shots. The final chase scene, which takes place at one of Hitchcock's characteristic famous locations—the Statue of Liberty—has been set up through the continuity style, using essentially straight cuts to carry the chase along toward its climax in the torch of the Statue of Liberty.

The torch scene is extraordinary in its mise-en-scene and montage. The scene lasts two minutes and fifty-five seconds and is composed of forty-seven shots, with an average length of 3.5 seconds. There is no music in the scene and very little dialogue; the sounds are mainly the wind and an occasional boat whistle. Hitchcock's camera is more fluid than it has ever been, capturing the action of the torch on the Statue of Liberty from myriad angles and views—everything from extreme close-ups of grasping hands and tearing sleeves, to extreme long shots of the head of the statue, with sightseers gazing out at the view, blissfully unaware of the life and death struggle going on above their heads. Through his rapid cutting and extreme angles, Hitchcock fragments the space of the action, creating an abstract space, a place of pure terror, as the audience is thrown into a totally unknown world where they have little control or mise-en-scene anchors. Before this shift in montage, Hitchcock had utilized the architecture of realistic space, created by mise-en-scene and montage techniques, most notably the adherence to the 180 degree rule, which Debbie Elliot describes in this way:

> The 180 Degree Rule is a product of the classical continuity style, which strived to make film "realistic" for the audience. It helps to maintain visual clarity and consistency in editing. It states that the camera must remain along the same plane in front of the characters. In any scene, an imaginary line can be drawn through the centre of the filming area, dividing it into two equal parts. . . . The camera must not extend past 180 degrees or out of its half of the circle. . . . The 180 degree rule maintains continuity by allowing the viewer to absorb a

> sense of space and perspective. The viewer's spacial sense of the mise-en-scene scene will be disrupted if the camera moves all over or cuts to change our perspective. The 180 degree rule provides consistency for the viewer by minimizing the amount of space we see, allowing us to perceive quickly and to concentrate on a specific visual area. The 180 degree rule does not allow the artificial structure of cinematic space to be revealed. (Elliot)

By freeing his camera from the architecture of "realistic" space, Hitchcock thrusts his audience into a space where, literally, anything can happen. In this scene, Hitchcock has shifted his montage from the classical to the nonclassical, to the Eisensteinian, which is the characteristic style of his scenes of terror.

In effect, paradoxically, Hitchcock's control of his audience's response is greatest in the scenes in which they possess the least knowledge of what might occur—*after*, of course, having had knowledge and control via the mise-en-scene and montage. In effect, through nonclassical montage, Hitchcock catapults the audience into a space where the control they once had because of their character identification and knowledge now boomerangs, as they become victimized, along with the characters. This is terror, pure and simple—a feeling of total loss of control. In *Saboteur*, in the famous falling shot—during which the saboteur Frank Fry's sleeve unravels and he falls backward, into space, arms flailing. We have seen Fry from Barry's POV and vice versa, as Fry desperately hangs on to the smooth, circular shape at the base of the torch. Hitchcock speeds up the cutting as Barry desperately hangs on to Fry, blending his altruistic motive of saving someone from death with his survival motive of trying to clear his name and redeem himself. Some of the shots last a second or less in a rapid-cutting technique that anticipates the shower scene. After Fry falls, the audience falls, too. Neil Hurley points out, in his provocative study of Hitchcock's Jesuit influences, *Soul in Suspense*, that Hitchcock's two primal fears are height and space (10). The shower scene shows Hitchcock's space anxiety; the ubiquitous dangling scenes in many of Hitchcock's films clearly reflect his height anxiety, as widely separated in time and storyline as *Young and Innocent*, *Vertigo*, *To Catch a Thief*, *Rear Window*, *The Lodger*, *Saboteur*, *Shadow of a Doubt*, and *North by Northwest*.

In his next film, *Shadow of a Doubt* (1943), Hitchcock again includes a scene of pure terror created by montage. As in *Saboteur*, Hitchcock builds suspense meticulously by creating a masterful mise-en-scene during which

Uncle Charlie's nefarious nature is slowly revealed to his niece Charlie. The penultimate scene takes place in a railroad car as Uncle Charlie has been forced to leave Santa Rosa by his bitterly disillusioned niece. The scene lasts 1:47 minutes and contains twenty-seven shots with an average length of 3.9 seconds each. The first shot is a relatively lengthy one and shows Uncle Charlie walking in the aisle toward his niece Charlie, who has her back turned to the audience. She cannot see what we see, which is that Uncle Charlie has identified his next victim, the wealthy widow, Mrs. Potter. As he walks closer to the camera, he waves smilingly and charmingly, and then in a long shot, we see from Uncle Charlie's POV a stylishly dressed older woman wave back and walk out of the car. As Niece Charlie turns to acknowledge her uncle and to escort the children out of the train, Uncle Charlie, fitting his sociopathic personality, immediately shifts demeanors from charming suitor to contrite sinner. He holds Charlie's hand and admits, "I want you to know I think you were right to make me leave." But in the next two shots we see Uncle Charlie again shift demeanors, this time to a threatening one, holding Niece Charlie's hand tightly in both of his hands and forcing her toward the still open train door. Niece Charlie, realizing what is happening, tries to scream, but Uncle Charlie brutally puts his hand over her mouth and maneuvers her to the open door of the accelerating train. As in the torch scene in *Saboteur*, Hitchcock shifts to nonclassical, Eisensteinian cutting as the shot tempo speeds up in concert with the rapidly accelerating train. We see quick cuts of struggling feet, as Uncle Charlie seems to be leading his niece in a circular, macabre dance of death. We also see close-ups of Niece Charlie's hand trying desperately to hold on to the train door, and then we see a close-up of Niece Charlie's terrified face as she looks down at the train tracks now speeding by. We see three quick shots, less than a second each, of the rail tracks from Niece Charlie's POV, the speeding tracks converging and diverging, just like the relationship of Uncle Charlie and his niece. Just at the crucial moment when Uncle Charlie says "Now!" Niece Charlie manages to get her free hand around the edge of the train door. We then see a long shot of the niece maneuvering her uncle so that she is able to assume the dominant position and push him out of the speeding train. Hitchcock surprises the audience by then positioning his camera outside of the speeding train, as we see Uncle Charlie, arms flailing, fall into the path of an oncoming train. As the trains cross, Hitchcock adds to the startling shift in camera position by superimposing over the violence a scene from the beginning of the film: a low-angle shot of dancers dressed elegantly in nineteenth-century garb and twirling gracefully to the strains of the "Merry Widow Waltz." The juxtaposition of grace and violence is a key to Uncle Charlie's twisted personality and psyche.

Hitchcock was very much aware of Eisenstein's experiments in editing, and it seems that in this scene, just as in the scene in *Saboteur*, Hitchcock utilizes the metric and rhythmic techniques of Eisensteinian montage. In his treatises on editing, Eisenstein writes about five kinds of montage: metric (shot length), rhythmic (pattern of movement within and between shots), tonal (visual patterns of light and dark), and intellectual (juxtaposing seemingly disparate visual metaphors) (Macdonald 123–146). The metric and rhythmic montage in *Shadow of a Doubt* splinters the sense of integral space that Hitchcock's mise-en-scene had worked hard to create. We are again in an abstract space of terror. The characters are dangling (Niece Charlie) and falling (Uncle Charlie). Niece Charlie's safe and secure world of Santa Rosa has been turned into a violent, sinister space, where the rules of civilized behavior have been undermined, a world where uncles try to kill their nieces. This is a preview of the matricidal world of *Psycho*. As Hitchcock says about Niece Charlie's world view, "So we can't say there is somewhere to hide. The sheltered life in the town of Santa Rosa where this young girl lived—may have been her world, but it wasn't *the* world. . . . Unfortunately, you see, today, to a great extent evil has spread. . . . Every little town has had its share of evil" (*Inside Hitchcock*).

The film that initiated Hitchcock's "great decade"—*Strangers on a Train* (1951)—contains a scene that in its employment of montage to create terror prefigures the shower scene. The famous merry-go-round scene in Leeland Lake is a virtual catalogue of Eisensteinian montage techniques. Coming as it does after a brilliant parallel-editing sequence, during which the double chase of Bruno by Guy and of Guy by the police, the merry-go-round scene creates a coda of pure terror through its employment of montage. The scene lasts 3:45 and contains seventy shots, with an average length of 3.2 seconds. The scene begins when Bruno spots Guy after Guy has tracked him down to the boat dock leading to the island where Bruno had killed Marian. It's characteristic of Hitchcock's narrative infrastructure in *Strangers on a Train* to have the climactic moment involve a doubling of locations (he does this again in *Vertigo*, when Madeline/Judy and Scotty return to the bell tower). Earlier in the film, Bruno had stalked Miriam to the very same merry-go-round that he rode as he flirted with her. In addition, the very same song—"The Band Played On"—plays as Guy chases Bruno onto the merry-go-round.

A policeman shooting at the seemingly guilty Guy but hitting instead the merry-go-round operator disrupts the leisurely pace of the scene, emblemized by the gracefully spinning merry-go-round. The ride starts to spin madly as the operator falls and pushes the control level to its farthest position. What better way to dramatize one of Hitchcock's major themes: that the world is a dangerous place! Hitchcock sets the scene in an amusement park, where the cares of the "outside world" are seemingly left behind, but where in reality the forces of chaos are lurking and ready to strike. In this setting, little boys in cowboy outfits point toy guns at adults; hormone-rich adolescents have petting parties on a dark island; law-abiding citizens shoot lethal weapons at targets, and people go on thrilling rides that threaten their safety. When the merry-go-round starts to spin wildly out of control, Hitchcock has found the perfect metaphor for the precariousness of the human condition.

Hitchcock edits the scene so that the unleashed forces seem to be animated by the montage itself. The horses appear to come to life as they spin dizzily. The song also speeds up, and Hitchcock must have relished the fact that, although the organ tune had no lyrics, the audience would have heard them earlier in the film:

Casey would waltz with a strawberry blonde,
And the band played on.
He'd glide cross the floor with the girl he adored,
And the band played on.
But his brain was so loaded it nearly exploded,
The poor girl would shake with alarm.
He'd ne'er leave the girl with the strawberry curls,
And the band played on.

Bruno is certainly the character whose "brain was so loaded it nearly exploded," and the poor revelers caught on the run-away merry-go-round are shaking "with alarm." Hitchcock creates this chaos not only by employing metric montage—speeding up the action by using increasingly shorter shots—but also by artfully employing rhythmic montage. There are at least five different patterns of movement within the shot. When we first see the merry-go-round before it begins its wild ride, we see it from a camera position outside the merry-go-round, which is seen at the left corner of the frame, spinning counter clockwise. When the policeman fires the shot to try to stop Guy from escaping, he hits the ride operator, who falls to the left of the frame, in the opposite direction from the spin of the carousel. The next shot shows the gear mechanism of the ride speeding up, the belts moving in the same direction as the fallen operator. In the next shot, the camera shifts position somewhat to a lower angle, closer to the carousel, which is still spinning counterclockwise, from the left side of the screen to the right. Now a dangerous, out-of-control machine, and no longer a carnival ride, the carousel throws off the policeman trying to follow Guy onto it. In the next shot, Hitchcock has moved his camera into the very whirlwind itself, into the demonic force that has been let loose by Bruno. As an audience, we are now in the center of the cyclone. Hitchcock has put us at risk, just as he would do nine years later in the shower of *Psycho*. Hitchcock fragments the space by shifting the angle and position of his camera to catch the various rhythms and patterns of movement.

With the camera now on the carousel, Hitchcock has chosen a camera angle that shows the merry-go-round now spinning in a clockwise direction. With this movement setting the pattern, Hitchcock adds additional layers of action. Bruno and Guy fight on the merry-go-round, moving horizontally back and forth, sometimes in opposition to the clockwise movement. All the while, the carousel horses are moving vertically, up and down, but then Hitchcock includes a low-angle close-up of one horse, nostrils flaring, seeming to lunge toward the screen, as if it had broken free of its pole. In the background, there's a tonal contrast as the outside world turns into a blur. Hitchcock engages in a bit of "montage relief" by moving the camera to the safe confines of the world outside the carousel as we see a carny mechanic slowly and carefully crawl under the spinning disk of the carousel platform. This is a dramatic illustration of both rhythmic and tonal montage. The light-colored platform is spinning wildly in a counterclockwise direction. Underneath, the ground is static and dark. The carny operator moves into the depth of the frame, entering the dark calm under the vortex. A few shots later, Hitchcock positions his camera underneath the spinning carousel itself, where the audience feels as vulnerable as the carny mechanic who crawls slowly toward the camera, now placed at his level.

The three camera positions—outside the carousel, on the carousel, and under the carousel—form a triangle of camera points of view. It's as if Hitchcock had discovered the geometry of violent action. The three locations of action determine perception itself: the police view the action from the outside, but their view is unreliable because they believe that Guy is the murderer and aggressor; the participants of the action are caught up in the maelstrom of violence, and they have knowledge that the police as observers do not have; underneath all the action itself is the calm figure—an objective, detached observer—who crawls below the swirl above to control the mechanism of movement itself—the machine that controls the carousel. Is this triangle Hitchcock's sly philosophical statement about perception itself and the roles of observers, participants, and director? For is not the calm, determined, carnival figure under the carousel Hitchcock himself? In a 1964 interview, Hitchcock comments about his intentions in *Psycho*: he wanted his audience to scream and yell as if they were on a switchback railway. The interviewer then asks: "You do see yourself as a switchback railway operator?" Hitchcock answers: "I am possibly in some respects the man who says, in constructing it, 'How steep can we make the first dip?'" (Gottlieb, *Alfred Hitchcock Interviews* 69). Hitchcock does make the dip very steep when the tiny man finally reaches the controls. He causes a catastrophic accident by dramatically altering the movement of the carousel rather than gradually slowing it down. Thus, both the carny operator and Hitchcock are responsible for the horrific entropy of the carousel's disintegration in an editing frenzy of quick, fragmented shots.

In the sequence of shots that precedes the carousel's destruction, Guy has become another of Hitchcock's dangling figures. In their fight, Guy and Bruno move horizontally among the various people caught on the runaway merry-go-round, one of whom is a small boy seeming to enjoy the wild ride, oblivious of its danger. This is the second small child who acts as an aggressor (the first was the cowboy who pointed his gun at Bruno): the former begins to emulate the violent adults by hitting at them, especially Bruno, who grabs the child and tries to throw him off the carousel in an action reminiscent of the psychopath Uncle Charlie trying to throw his niece off the moving train. Fitting his role as "hero," Guy rescues the child but makes himself vulnerable to Bruno's ruthlessness. Eventually, Guy is forced to the spinning circumference of the merry-go-round, where he dangles from one of the carousel poles, his body parallel to the ground because of the centrifugal movement of the merry-go-round. Bruno kicks mercilessly at Guy's hands, which become bruised and dirtied by Bruno's shoes.

At this point, Hitchcock is drawing on two visual motifs presented earlier: the feet of Guy and Bruno from the opening montage, and the hands of both Bruno (who uses them to strangle) and Guy (who uses them to play tennis). A lengthy study could be done on Hitchcock's use of hands as symbols of the duality of human nature. Hands, especially the opposable thumb, are perhaps the quintessential instruments of human creativity and accomplishment. Guy uses his hands to control his tennis racket; Manny Balestero uses his hands to play his upright bass; L.B. Jeffreys uses his hands to hold a camera to take pictures; Mary Maloney uses her hands to cook; Barry Kane uses his hands to keep Frank Fry from falling; Norman Bates uses his hands to practice taxidermy. However, humans use their hands to kill and maim, to hold guns, or knives, or explosives, or legs of lamb. In *Shadow of a Doubt*, the newspaper article that Uncle Charlie tries to hide from young Charlie describes the merry widow murderer as "the strong-handed strangler of three wealthy women." In *Strangers on a Train*, Hitchcock uses Bruno's hands to emblemize the destructive, murderous impulses in human beings. We first see Bruno's hands in a close-up as Bruno flexes them to feel their power. In the first Leeland Lake scene, Bruno demonstrates the strength of his hands when he wins the kewpie doll by ringing the bell. Later, when Bruno accosts Miriam in the island, he begins to strangle her, and Hitchcock surprisingly shifts to an expressionistic style by showing the murder reflected in the convex distortion of the lens of Miriam's eyeglasses. As Bruno finishes his grisly task of strangling Miriam, he brings his hands up, and the distortion caused by the lens elongates his hands so that they resemble claws, the same claws we saw earlier in the lobsters on Bruno's tie. Later in the film, Bruno circles his hands around the throat of the unsuspecting Mrs. Cunningham to demonstrate the "perfect murder," almost choking her to death in the process when he sees Barbara Morton, a look-alike for Miriam.

The circular shape of Bruno's hands around Mrs. Cunningham's throat is the first in a pattern of montage motifs in the films of the 1950s. I call this pattern a "vortex of violence," for it involves the symbolic portrayal of violence as a circular figure, sometimes stationary but most often swirling or spinning. This effect is created through an Eisensteinian montage style. In a 1959 interview with critics from *Cahiers du Cinema*, conducted by Douchet and Domarchi, "Hitchcock offered an intriguingly ambiguous self-analysis, to be taken with a circular grain of salt: Everything was round for him. He had a round temperament. He was *O*. Others were *I*" (Vest 197). The vortex usually culminates in a catastrophic fall or descent, precipitated by the dynamics of the circular shape. This pattern makes an early appearance in *Saboteur*, when Barry circles the torch in pursuit of Frank Fry, who then tumbles backwards and falls to the circular base of the torch, and then later falls to his death, spinning, as Barry is unable to save him. Fry's sleeve, unraveling in a circular pattern, causes this fall. The carousel of *Strangers on a Train* becomes a kind of template for Hitchcock's fascination with this circular, spinning vortex. The transformation, via montage, of the carousel from a tranquil, calming, soothing circular motion to a violent, sickening, and dizzying maelstrom is like human nature itself, sometimes Apollonian but in many cases Dionysian—uncontrollable and murderous.

The vortex of violence makes another appearance in *Rear Window*, first suggested by the circular shape of L.B. Jeffrey's binoculars and long-range lens. At first, Jeff's use of these circles of perception leads him along the path to the "truth" of the events in the Thorwalds' apartment. Yet what Jeff views can't really be captured by the technology of perception. In fact, Jeff has seen—but only indirectly—into the very nature of evil itself, which reveals itself to him only indirectly in the person of the hulking, menacing presence of Lars Thorwald. Because of the restrictions of the Production Code and the studio system, the audience was not allowed to view this kind of evil because of its potential damage; they might be turned into pillars of salt! The Production Code states:

> Motion Pictures are very important as *Art*. Though a new art, possibly a combination art, it has the same object as the other arts, the presentation of human thoughts, emotions, and experiences, in terms of an appeal to the soul thru [*sic*] the senses.
>
> Here, as in entertainment: Art *enters intimately* into the lives of human beings. Art can be *morally good*, lifting men to higher levels. This has been done thru [*sic*] good music, great painting, authentic fiction, poetry, drama.
>
> Art can be *morally evil* in its effects. This is the case clearly enough with unclean art, indecent books, suggestive drama. The effect on the lives of men and women is obvious. (Doherty 348).

In the penultimate scene in the film, during which Lars Thorwald enters Jeff's apartment, Jeff realizes the evil power of the forces he's called down upon himself and Lisa by his insistence on looking at evil. Cinematographer Robert Burks lights this scene beautifully, vignetting both Thorwald and Jeff within pools of darkness. Hitchcock positions his camera low and slightly to the left of Jeff's apartment door to catch Thorwald in a shoulder shot. When Thorwald closes the door, he's enveloped in a foreboding darkness with two oval planes of light, one emphasizing his white hair (Hitchcock's ironic deployment of a halo); the other, highlighting the upper part of his face, with his glasses catching a white hot pinpoint of light in each circular frame.

One can't help but think that the shot of Thorwald opening the apartment door and entering Jeff's room is an early graphic representation of the shower scene. The camera angle, the frightening figure with a dark face, and the helplessness of the victim—all are similar to the beginning of the shower murder. Hitchcock's next series of shots is seen from Thorwald's POV, but he can see only a figure in a chair, bathed in a circle of soft light coming through the window. As Thorwald approaches, Hitchcock positions his camera low, near Jeff's POV, looking up at the ominous, towering figure of Thorwald.

Jeff attempts to blind the advancing Lars Thorwald by flashing light bulbs in his face, and the resultant red glare that momentarily halts Thorwald is the color of violence itself. In typical fashion, Hitchcock has the audience share in Thorwald's violent intention by having us see the circular red glare as Thorwald would see it. The red color envelopes the screen and prefigures the employment of the same technique ten years later in *Marnie*. In 1953, Hitchcock could not flood the screen with actual blood itself; he had to work symbolically. He would go a step further in *Psycho* by flooding the screen, not with red blood, but with "black" blood. Three years later, Hitchcock would paint the screen with the crimson blood of the dying sailor in Marnie's cathartic flashbacks.

Jeff flashes the bulbs four times, each flash resulting in a circle of redness that begins in the center of the screen and extends outward until the whole screen is red. Hitchcock is playing with ironic reversals here, having Thorwald now enter Jeff's apartment, as Jeff had "entered" his through his binoculars and long-range lenses. Now, however, Thorwald is a threatening physical presence. As he approaches Jeff, he is momentarily blinded by the light, seen by him as a widening circle of redness, a circle similar in shape to the binocular lens that had provided Jeff's "truth." Through montage, Hitchcock has again created a vortex of violence, and the circular motif is much like the spinning carousel in *Strangers on a Train* or the circular dance of young Charlie and Uncle Charlie as they struggle near the open train door, or like the circular nineteenth-century dancers, twirling gracefully to the strains of the "Merry Widow Waltz" superimposed over Uncle Charlie's fall into the path of the oncoming train.Hitchcock accomplishes all of these effects through a skillful and ingenious combination of mise-en-scene and montage.

Just as in *Saboteur, Shadow of a Doubt,* and *Strangers on a Train,* Hitchcock shifts his editing style in *Rear Window* to depict a scene of violence, in this case, Thorwald's attack of Jeff and his attempt to throw him out of the window. The pattern in each film is remarkably similar, with an Eisensteinian montage style depicting a vortex of violence that leads to a fall. The scene lasts two minutes and forty-nine seconds and contains sixty-three shots, with an average length of 2.4 seconds. However, the editing tempo speeds up as Jeff runs out of light bulbs and Thorwald attacks him, arms outstretched, his menacing movement toward the protagonist seen from Jeff's vulnerable POV. Hitchcock not only speeds up the editing tempo, but he also intensifies the action by having Robert Burks undercrank the camera to speed up the movement. This technique is used in the intercuts of neighbors, who respond to Jeff's cry of "Lisa! Doyle!" as he sees them across the courtyard. What the audience experiences is a swirl of violence—a vortex—that spins out of control. As in *Saboteur,* Hitchcock employs no musical cues, only the ambient sounds of the rooms (chair falling, flash bulb clicking, car horns beeping). But we also hear Jeff grunting as he struggles with the much stronger Thorwald, who is shown in a fragmented series of shots of choking hands and flailing arms and legs. Hitchcock's camera is again fluid, capturing the action as if it were a participant in the violence. In an interview at the American Film Institute, Hitchcock describes his technique: ". . . but the moment the man attacks him, I mean [*sic*] to legs, arms, head, then at that moment, the moment of contact, then you are into your pieces of film. You involve the audience right in the sense of violence" (Gottlieb, *Alfred Hitchcock Interviews* 100). Just as in *Shadow of a Doubt* and *Strangers on a Train,* the villain forces the protagonist toward a precipice—in this case, the very same window that Jeff had been using to "spy" on his neighbors.

This window is pure cataphor in *Rear Window.* We saw it in the opening of the film when the bamboo curtains magically rolled up, theater style, to reveal the setting of the film. The window was Jeff's and the audience's portal to the outside world, but it was also a gateway to danger. Lisa climbs into Thorwald's window to get evidence but is almost murdered. Now Jeff is forced to the ledge of the window and pushed outside. Like Guy and Niece Charlie, he is hanging on for dear life, having "invited" into his life the evil Thorwald by constructing in his mind a grisly murder.

What makes Hitchcock's protagonists complex and multi-layered characters is that they, in some sense, invite evil into their lives. They seem open to it, ready for it. Did Hitchcock's Jesuit education prepare him for this fallen view of human nature? Hitchcock's Christianity seems to be an amalgam of Jesuit and Miltonic. In fact, Stefano's script contains an echo from Milton's Sonnet XIX: "When I Consider . . ." "which contains the line, "They also serve who only stand and wait" (Mogg, *The Alfred Hitchcock Story* 159). In the opening scene of *Psycho*, when Sam complains about his debts to his dead father and divorced wife, Marion says, "I pay too. They also pay who meet in hotel rooms." Man in his fallen state, Milton claims in *Paradise Lost*, is actually morally superior to prelapsarian man because fallen man can choose to be good or bad—hence, Milton's "Felix Culpa," fortunate fall. The encounter with evil is a necessary step in the moral life. In *Rear Window*, when Stella says to L.B. Jeffreys, "I can smell trouble right here in this apartment," Jeff counters, "Right now, I'd welcome trouble!" In *Strangers on a Train*, when Bruno makes his murderous proposition to Guy—"They swap murders. Like, you do my murder; I do yours"—Guy counters, "Sure, Bruno. We talk the same language." In *Shadow of a Doubt*, Niece Charlie feels a lack in her life, a gap, which she fills with the welcoming of Uncle Charlie into her life. Young Charlie says to her mother, "I know a wonderful person who'll come and shake us all up—just the one to save us. All this time there's been one right person to save us. Mother, what's Uncle Charlie's address?"

When these characters bring their evil into the lives of the somehow incomplete protagonists, the evil culminates in a vortex of violence, which precipitates a fall into experience, a "wound," that stays with the character forever more. As Jeff is dangling from the window sill of his apartment, he is literally suspended between two worlds—one characterized by solipsism, isolation, and disengagement; the other characterized by risky entanglements and love. As the police arrive to capture Thorwald, Jeff can no longer hang on: he must fall, just like Guy and Charlie. All three are "fortunate falls."

However, in the two dark films that come at the end of Hitchcock's great decade—*Vertigo* and *Psycho*—the vortex of violence does not precipitate a "fortunate fall." To the contrary, the vortex swallows the protagonists, destroys them. There's no moral growth, no love—only obsession and madness. *Vertigo* prefigures *Psycho* in its explicit foregrounding of the swirling vortex, which appears in the eye of the mysterious woman in the credits. Saul Bass's lissajous spirals become the dominant visual pattern of *Vertigo*, appearing first as an ocular manifestation of galaxy-like, abstract shapes accompanied by Bernard Herrmann's hypnotic, pulsating, revolving motif. The protagonist Scotty is swallowed by this vortex, as he falls in love with the counterfeit Madeline Elster, following her car down the steep, dizzying streets of San Francisco, slowly making turn after turn, going deeper into the labyrinth. Madeline's hair is fashioned into a circular shape at the back, and this shape is echoed in the hairdo of Carlotta in the painting and in the floral bouquet that both Madeline and Carlotta hold. When Scotty first loses Madeline, he climbs up the tower with its spiraling staircase (a reverse of his following her *down* the streets of San Francisco). When he loses Madeline (Judy) the second time, he again mounts the spiral stairs, this time successfully, only to lose her again. Scotty's dream is filled with vortex-like shapes, especially the floral bouquet disintegrating as the petals spin outward and the frightening close-up of Scotty's face seeming to be trapped in the very epicenter of a tornado, this movement a connection to Hitchcock's famous camera visualization of vertigo—a tracking out with a zooming in. When Scotty falls in his dream, he dangles in a white, existentially pure space, with no visible top or bottom. He is suspended in a void, a perfect symbol of madness.

The most vivid montage representation of the vortex of violence is in *Psycho*, Hitchcock's most terrifying film. Part of Hitchcock's strategy in *Psycho* is to foreground the mise-en-scene in the first half of the film, but to background the montage, to employ mainly the "invisible," classical editing that he had been trained in by the American filmmakers at Famous Players-Lasky. By keeping the editing style subtle and unobtrusive, Hitchcock would be able to shock his audience through the suddenness of the violence and through the radical alteration of montage technique. In his essay "The Enjoyment of Fear," Hitchcock says, ". . . terror, to be truly effective, must come all at once, like a bolt of lightning . . ." (Gottlieb, *Hitchcock on Hitchcock* 120). In his book on *Psycho*, Stephen Rebello quotes Hitchcock discussing the montage techniques of the shower scene with his camera operator, Lennie South: "I'm going to shoot and cut it staccato, so that the audience won't know what the hell is going on" (101).

Hitchcock subtly positions his audience in the first five scenes of the film by creating suspense via mise-en-scene and montage. In his interviews with Truffaut, Hitchcock calls suspense ". . . simply the dramatization of a film's narrative material or, if you will, the most intense presentation possible of dramatic situations" (15). Narration is the province of montage, which is not simply the cutting of the film but rather the shaping of the content of the film's narrative thrust. When Hitchcock says to Peter Bogdanovich, "Pure cinema is complementary pieces of film put together"

(4), he is not in any way denigrating mise-en-scene; for montage, in a sense, is the culmination of the film's mise-en-scene structure. This is what Hitchcock means when he says, ". . . a cut is nothing. One cut of film is like a piece of mosaic. To me, pure film, pure cinema, is pieces of film assembled. Any individual piece is nothing. But a combination of them creates an idea" (Gottlieb, *Hitchcock on Hitchcock* 288).

In describing the montage structure of *Psycho*, Hitchcock says, "*Psycho* has a very interesting construction and that game with the audience was fascinating. I was directing the viewers. You might say I was playing them like an organ" (Truffaut 269). Part of Hitchcock's game was to understate the construction, to present a seamless foundation for the film's narrative. In the credit sequence, for example, Saul Bass designs a pattern of vertical and horizontal lines that enter and exit the top, bottom, and sides of the frame, but he runs these lines—and the film's printed credits—against a solid dark background, thus giving the sense of foregrounded movement on a stationary background. The effect is of both stasis and movement, of change and constancy. This idea is reinforced in the opening four shots of the film. These consist of extreme long shots that pan the modest skyline of Phoenix, each shot connected by a dissolve that provides a sense of contiguous and continuous space. This opening is a traditional one in terms of the classical style, for it presents a realistic environment against which the narrative will play out. Hitchcock is fond of this kind of opening; he uses it in almost all of his films in the 1950s. Establishing a time and place for his narrative allows him to condense the preliminary details of plot in order to focus exclusively on character. In one interview in the documentary *Inside Hitchcock*, the director says that he is always "trying to avoid the repetition of the same situations. And the only way to avoid it is through character." This kind of opening is analogous to the dark background of his credits. Time and place are thus somewhat like the painted sets of the theater—something against which characters play out their roles.

Hitchcock's montage style inside the hotel room is again traditional. He strictly observes the 180 degree rule to maintain a logical, architectural space through which the actors move. The fourth-wall placement of the camera facilitates this kind of cutting. The shots are long in duration and convey a realistic sense of time, something Hitchcock emphasizes as the scene progresses: this is stolen time, illicit time. The longest shot in the scene—1:45—is the daring kiss, during which Marion and Sam, both half-naked, lie on the bed, embrace, and kiss in extremely explicit ways for the late 1950s (the film was shot in 1959–1960). A man's naked upper torso was a common sight in the 1950s—not so a buxom woman in a bra, exposing her bare midriff. In one sense, this lengthy shot exploits Marion's body in flagrant violation of the General Principles of the Production Code.

1. The effect of nudity or semi-nudity upon the normal man or woman, and much more upon the young person, has been honestly recognized by all lawmakers and moralists.
2. Hence the fact that the nude or semi-nude body may be *beautiful* does not make its use in the films moral. For in addition to its beauty, the effects of the nude or semi-nude on the normal individual must be taken into consideration.
3. Nudity or semi-nudity used simply to put a "punch" into a picture comes under the head of immoral actions as treated above. It is immoral in its effect upon the average audience. (Doherty 357).

Laura Mulvey's groundbreaking 1975 feminist essay, "Visual Pleasure and Narrative Cinema," claims, according to Tania Modleski, that "women in classical Hollywood cinema are inevitably made into passive objects of male voyeuristic and sadistic impulses" (1–2). In another sense, though, one could argue that Hitchcock's constant pushing against the boundaries of the Code's strictures opened up the geography of the female body for further exploration. The patriarchal system of producers and studios had appropriated the female body in order to "protect" it from the gaze of the audience. In *Psycho*, Hitchcock decides to expose as much of this body as he could, even so far as to have a naked stand-in for Janet Leigh on the set. In this sense, one would have to agree with Tania Modleski when she asserts that "the question which continually—if sometimes implicitly—rages around Hitchcock's work as to whether he is sympathetic toward women or misogynistic is fundamentally unanswerable because he is both" (5). This statement perhaps explains why Hitchcock would present Marion's body in the opening scene in the film as a thing of desire, beauty, and morality (white bra and slip and expressions of traditional morality), but halfway through present her body as a victim of violence and hatred, in a black bra and slip. Hitchcock's montage in this opening scene employs the simple cut to join shots, each one of which preserves the sense of integral space, allowing the audience to view the characters "objectively" in order to get to know them. Occasionally, Hitchcock will show Sam from what appears to be Marion's POV, but actually the camera is placed slightly to the right of Marion.

This cutting pattern is continued in the Lowery real estate office scene, this time with the montage so understated that the scene seems to be one continuous action. Again, the camera assumes its fourth-wall position, and the cutting pattern generally observes the 180 degree rule. One might ask here, just what is the purpose of this kind of continuity cutting? One answer, of course, is that this type of cutting allows for the fullest utilization of mise-en-scene. We know from Hitchcock's experimentation with long, continuous takes that he had a fascination with contiguous space, with the full insertion of time into a spatial arrangement. His youthful fascination with time tables and his meticulous preproduction methodology attest to his sense of orderly and logical arrangements. However, Hitchcock eschews the traditional classical approach to cutting a dialogue sequence. As Hitchcock claims, he was always "avoiding the cliché in my type of material" (*Inside Hitchcock*). Thus, because of the ingenious use of his camera, Hitchcock transcended the hackneyed approach to cutting that makes so many dialogue sequences seem numbingly alike. For example, Hitchcock departs somewhat from classical scene construction to add a bit of variety to the dialogue scene between Marion and Cassidy. During this short segment, which is made up of twenty-three shots, Hitchcock violates the 180 degree rule seven times by positioning the camera low, behind Marion, over her right shoulder as she looks up to the lecherous oil-lease man. In effect, the character position is reversed. In addition, Hitchcock adds variety to the usual over-the-shoulder dialogue sequence by cutting away from the main speakers, Marion and Cassidy, ten times, with seven shots of Lowery and three shots of Caroline, each one relatively brief. If one were to run the scene with the volume off, one would discover that the scene has a musical structure to it, like a theme and variation. Thus does Hitchcock deal with a common dialogue scene in an uncommon way. Hitchcock adds to the "cliché avoiding" by frequently making a cut in the middle of a line or having a line of dialogue run over into the next shot. One would have to examine the scene carefully for these small touches because Hitchcock keeps the technique subtle and unobtrusive.

The third scene of the film—in Marion's apartment—contains the first significant POV shot in the film, a type of shot that is the primal contact point between the aesthetics of mise-en-scene and montage. As I pointed out in my discussion of *Rear Window*, the classic POV shot involves three elements: two individual shots connected by one cut. In the two shots, mise-en-scene is critical, because it provides the motivation for the character to engage in the art of observing or seeing. The dramatic situation that gives rise to the shot, however, may be created earlier in the scene—or in previous scenes—in the presentation of plot elements. Hence, one may say that the POV shot is the end result of narrative and characterological streaming.

In the scene in Marion's apartment, Hitchcock constructs the dramatic situation out of twelve individual shots, linked by eleven cuts. Earlier Hitchcock had presented two scenes to establish the exposition of the first act of the film. In the first scene, Hitchcock had presented two characters, each of whom could have been the main protagonist. The second scene, however, establishes Marion as the protagonist, by focusing exclusively on her and by introducing the film's MacGuffin, the $40,000. The apartment scene, in one sense, then, serves to bring the character and the MacGuffin plot element together to create motivation and to launch the major plot movement. Of the twelve shots constituting this scene, five are POV shots that meld the consciousness of Marion with the collective consciousness of the audience.

The first two shots of the scene are from the enunciator's POV, with the camera assuming the position of the fourth wall. Hitchcock begins the first with a long shot of Marion looking down at something off-camera, and then in a tilt and a dolly, the camera comes to rest on a close-up of the envelope, its torn flap revealing a thick stack of one-hundred dollar bills. The audience realizes that this is indeed the envelope containing Cassidy's money that Marion had nonchalantly stuffed into her purse in order to deposit it in the bank on her way home. She has thus stolen Cassidy's means to "buy off unhappiness" for his daughter. Marion now has on her bed *her* means of buying off the unhappiness that characterizes her and Sam's relationship. The question of whether she will employ this tempting means is answered in the next two shots. The second shot of the scene moves us closer to Marion in a medium shot as she continues to look, with a troubled expression, down on the bed. From the information we had gained in the opening shot, we know that she is looking at the envelope. The third shot of the scene is the key POV shot in the film, because it establishes Marion's temptation in the most potent way possible—by having us, the audience, see the temptation the way she would see it, according to the architecture of the mise-en-scene. The first two shots showed the envelope from the camera's fourth-wall position. In this third shot, though, the camera reverses direction, surreptitiously crossing the 180 degree line, and suddenly, magically entering the mind (or at least the eyes) of the character. Is this not the apex of camera mobility and fluidity? The POV shot establishes that the camera can indeed go anywhere. It can transcend the spatial limitations of the theater by actually entering a character's mind, or inhabiting the space behind the character's eyes. It also transcends the barriers of language by actually eliminating the enunciator-author altogether. The things we are seeing are *not* mediated through the eyes of the enunciator; we are seeing "the thing-in-itself," Kant's "*Das ding an sich*."

The POV shot gives the power of Dr. Spock's mind meld. It's crucial in understanding the aesthetics of mise-en-scene and montage to examine the characteristics and implication of POV. One question we may ask is whether there's a significant difference between an enunciator's shot and a POV shot. For example, in the opening scene of the film, Marion and Sam have a meaningful dialogue that establishes their characters and that plants some important plot points. As I mentioned in my chapter on mise-en-scene, Hitchcock isolates the characters in separate medium shots as they discuss their future together. When Marion is listening to Sam, we see him not from her POV but rather from a displacement angle of vision, as if the enunciator were in the room, standing next to the character. Most dialogue scenes are shot this way in order to preserve the quarter turn of classical mise-en-scene and, more importantly, to facilitate the montage by providing more opportunities for coverage and for cutting the sequence. Strictly identifying a character with the camera this early in the film would preclude shots that might include that character interacting with other characters. It's essential, especially in the classical style, to observe a character interacting with the setting and with other characters. Thus the choice of POV is inextricably intertwined with strategies of exposition. *Psycho* opens with an extreme long shot of the Phoenix skyline and dissolves into a particular building and then into a particular room. The next step—into a particular consciousness or character—must be delayed until we know the characters a little better. This happens in the scene in Marion's apartment, where the willing suspension of disbelief operates to its fullest extent by asking the audience to share momentarily the eyes of a character. In the legitimate theater, the "willing suspension of disbelief" is both easier and more difficult than in the cinema. On the stage, we have living and breathing human beings, while in the cinema we have beings constructed only of light. In cinema, the camera can go to "real" locations, while the theatrical set is not a "real" place, only a construct of a real place. If we wish to see the way a character sees, we must rely on a soliloquy or on a character who breaks the fourth wall. There is a reason why Hitchcock preferred the cinema to the stage, above and beyond his fascination with technology. The reason is the camera, the mechanism behind the aesthetics of mise-en-scene and montage.

In Hitchcock's first significant POV shot of the film, his "absolute" and "dictating" camera captures the significance of the envelope of money in a close-up that shows how the money has loomed in Marion's imagination and perception. We see the envelope of money on the bed from Marion's POV, but we see it in a reversal of the previous shot, which provided a tantalizing peek at the $40,000. From Marion's POV, though, the envelope looks innocent—even inconsequential—with its torn flap and flimsy rubber band. The envelope fills the horizontal limits of the frame, and it stands out from the dark bedspread and the gray wallpaper with Marion's characteristic decoration of small flowers. Hitchcock took great pains in the montage and mise-en-scene of *Psycho* to use close-ups to reveal the psychology and the emotional make-up of his characters. He says about his technique, "I [maintain] the rule of varying the size of the image in relation to its emotional importance within a given episode" (Gottlieb, "Early Hitchcock" 74). In this crucial POV shot, not only does the envelope loom large for Marion, but it also does so for the audience as well. Hitchcock seems to be saying that this is the trivial-looking stuff that dreams are made on.

The fifth shot of the scene is of Marion's suitcase seen from her POV as she packs. The cheap suitcase and the rumpled clothes clearly evidence the drabness of her life, a stark contrast to the gleaming white envelope with *its* contents of newly minted one-hundred dollar bills. Hitchcock's montage is clearly tied to the technique of the Russian filmmaker Pudovkin in this series of shots. Both Marion and the viewer's minds subtly link the contrasting shots of envelope with money and suitcase with clothes. In fact, the linkage goes one step further in connecting the shots, for in the first shot of the scene, we see Marion in a black bra and slip, a vivid contrast to the white bra and slip from the opening scene. By using unobtrusive cuts to link the shots together, Hitchcock has created a worldless micro-narrative filled with visual cues and prompts.

The contrasting underwear color stands out in the audience's mind because of the taboo nature of the costume, clearly a violation of the strictures of the Production Code. Furthermore, the mise-en-scene works in conjunction with the montage in the first shot by showing Marion in a long shot reaching into her closet and turning her back to us, revealing an almost naked back with only a thin black bra strap, this view a foreshadowing of Marion's naked back in the shower scene. The camera then tilts down and tracks in, putting both the envelope and Marion's bare back in the same shot. Thus, when Marion sees the money from her POV, the audience has already been visually cued through the linkage that the black underwear, the suitcase, and the money are the three sides of a plot triangle. In fact, one could trace the triangle through the mise-en-scene and montage. The hypotenuse is the straight vertical line the camera movement follows when it tilts down from Marion and tracks into the money. The two other sides of the triangle are evident in the pan to the left that reveals the open suitcase and then the cut to Marion as she turns from the closet and moves toward the suitcase to continue packing. The POV shot of the suitcase completes the triangular shape.

This kind of mise-en-scene and montage allows Hitchcock to create a three-dimensional architectural space that has a palpable feel to it, exemplifying Truffaut's judgement about Hitchcock's realism. In shot 6 of this scene, Hitchcock augments this three-dimensionality when Marion finishes packing and dressing, and walks to the left, the camera panning to follow her. She stops in front of the mirror to check her appearance, and we see two Marions, one on each side of the frame, in almost perfect symmetry. Such a mirror image allows the director to transcend for a moment the 180 degree rule, but in order to do this, the camera must be positioned next to the character so that the camera is not visible to the audience. A mirror shot such as this has a two-fold function. In the mise-en-scene, the shot allows the director to portray graphically the leitmotif of the double—in this case, the two Marions; in a philosophical sense, our divided nature. On a technical level, though, the mirror allows the director to combine a POV shot with a quarter turn. The audience sees Marion, but Marion sees herself; however, she sees herself from a reflection that allows us to see her seeing herself. And what Marion sees—and what we see—is the struggle of conscience with desire. If this scene were a Disney cartoon, we would see this struggle of desire and conscience vividly—on Marion's right shoulder her good angel urging her to deposit the money, and on her left shoulder, her bad angel—her devil—urging her to take the money and run. In the mirror, the open door that separates the two Marions is a cataphor that foreshadows her decision. We would be rooting for the devil with the pitchfork to win Marion over, and of course, we would not be disappointed, because Marion takes her suitcase and the money—and her fate—out of the door of her apartment. As scriptwriter Stefano said in our interview about Marion and the audience: "We wanted her to get away with the money. We're all such felons at heart." Marion is therefore taking along something else—something extra-diegetic—and that is the audience, who, because of Hitchcock's subtle cutting of POV shots into the texture of the scene, now go on the journey with Marion, as "partners in crime."

Hitchcock claims that the chase is a key element in his suspense: "So long as a plot has either flight or pursuit, it may be considered a form of the chase. In many ways the chase makes up about sixty percent of the construction of all movie plots" (Gottlieb, *Hitchcock on Hitchcock* 126). This certainly holds true for *Psycho*. When Marion decides to leave Phoenix with the money, she has decided to transform herself—to "reinvent" herself, to use a contemporary cliché. Her wardrobe transformation from white to black underwear signals this. We must, of course, keep in mind that the transformation takes place in Phoenix, named after the mythical bird that lives for four hundred or five hundred years in the Arabian Desert, plunges into flames and renews itself, reborn. However, in the antipastoral world of *Psycho*, the journey, or chase, does not lead to renewal but rather to death and destruction. Hitchcock's irony, of course, is that Marion's death occurs not in flames, but in water, that potent symbol of life and rebirth.

In Hitchcock's classic suspense chase, the wrongly accused protagonist chases the real villain, while the police chase the "innocent" protagonist (the double chase). Hitchcock plays a theme and variations on this plot motif by having Marion actually be guilty; she is not chasing the actual criminal but is that criminal herself. Her attempt to escape the confines of her world and travel to Fairvale—the name has almost mythic qualities—is actually a chase after happiness in the person of Sam Loomis, the hardware man, who holds out the possibility of marriage, that symbolic union that is the pot of gold at the end of the pastoral journey. Of the 151 shots that comprise the three-part journey or chase scene, fully one-third of them are POV shots. This extraordinarily high number of subjective shots serves to cement the relationship between protagonist and audience. Hitchcock says, "I'm a believer in the subjective, that is, playing a scene from the POV of an individual" (McGilligan 34). Hitchcock accomplishes this bonding task by making the audience both ally and accomplice in Marion's journey.

The audience goes through the whole gamut of emotions via the fifty-three POV shots in this long scene. In the first third, when Marion is in her car and attempting to leave Phoenix, she is facing the audience in a frank, full frontal position that pleads for identification through eye contact. When the montage presents the world through Marion's eyes via a simple cut, we are magically brought into her mind as she feels anxiety at seeing Lowery walk by her car. The anxiety, apprehension, and guilt reflected on Marion's face are feelings we share as we say to ourselves, "Oh, shit! It's her boss! What will she do now?" Hitchcock has Marion see Lowery in three discrete POV shots separated by two cuts. In between these shots are reaction shots of Marion. The six shots are masterfully orchestrated so that they have two beats to each shot, almost like a heartbeat.

In typical fashion, Hitchcock presents himself a challenge in the montage structure of the car scene. By placing the camera right in front of the character, Hitchcock deliberately limits the range of his montage. Once he has established the pattern of the direct stare of the character, he can't very well shift the camera position so that Marion is in the quarter-turn position, thereby giving himself more options for coverage and cutting. Hitchcock solves this problem in two ways. One is through varying the image size and lighting—bringing the camera closer to Marion as the night comes on; the other is through the internal monologues Marion hears. These "voices"that Marion hears are an unusual use of the dialogue track. We're not sure if they're "actual" words or imagined words; having these words spoken by the actual characters further blurs the issue of their origin. However, it is as if these words were being projected—like images—on Marion's face, which is lit in a flat manner so that it seems like a screen. It is almost as if we're in the world of *Rear Window* again, but this time, we are not looking into someone's apartment but into her mind and soul. We know from many interviews that Hitchcock loved silent films. What he does in the two car scenes is to present us with a "silent" film, in that there is no actual dialogue. The voices are almost like an additional musical track.

When Marion pulls over to take a nap, Hitchcock shifts his camera so that we are no longer facing Marion. When the policeman wakes her up, Hitchcock presents us with a startling POV close-up of the menacing presence with the dark, opaque glasses. There are at least ten of these chilling, tight POV close-ups, and their claustrophobic proximity to Marion's face makes her—and us—feel threatened and frightened. Marion sees the ominous face just as she wakes from her nap, and her startled movement in reaction to this dark figure is a foreshadowing of what is to come in the shower scene, when she is again startled by an ominous presence that violates her personal space—and ours. Through these numerous and compelling POV shots, Hitchcock brings us into intimate relationship with Marion—probably more so than with any other character in his films. It's true that L.B. Jeffrey's POV controls the storyline of *Rear Window*, but until the very end, he never gets close enough to the worlds that he's observing to draw us into them. With Marion, however, the audience confronts the fears exactly as she does, through her eyes.

Other POV shots are utilized by Hitchcock to reinforce the claustrophobia and entrapment that Marion feels. In fact most of the 53 POV shots are associated with enclosed spaces—mainly Marion's car, but also the rest room of California Charlie's used-car lot, where she goes to count out the seven crisp one-hundred-dollar bills to buy her escape vehicle. Associating Marion's POV with an enclosed space helps Hitchcock to prepare the audience for the shower scene. If the formula for *Psycho* is that interior spaces equal metaphors for the mind of the protagonist, then the progressive narrowing of Marion's spaces (hotel room–Lowery's real estate office–car–motel room–parlor–shower) equals the enclosing trap of her predicament. The irony is that these enclosed spaces exist in the vast, expansive landscape of Arizona and California. In the antipastoral world of *Psycho*, Hitchcock subverts the trek westward of the American Western by having Marion not journey to freedom and possibility but rather to constriction and death.

The one genre that Hitchcock avoided was the Western, but it's possible to see echoes of the Western genre in several of his films, particularly in his employment of Western settings and the Western mythos. In *Saboteur*, for example, Barry Kane reverses the usual trek westward in his quest for the rehabilitation of his reputation, traveling west to east. One scene features Kane stealing a horse from the Tobin ranch and being pursued by a gang of men on horseback. (I once showed the clip at a film conference, and not one member of the audience identified the clip as a Hitchcock film.) *North by Northwest* features Roger O. Thornhill making the trek westward in pursuit of the mysterious Mr. Kaplan. There's even a showdown between a renegade crop-duster and Thornhill on a landscape that could be right out of a Western. The dark, cinematic twins appearing at the end of the 1950s—*Vertigo* and *Psycho*—use the West as a place of nightmares, madness, and delusion, rather than as the locus of the American dream. The couples in the films—Scotty and "Madeline," Scotty and Judy, Marion and Sam, Marion and Norman, Norman and Norma—are all deeply flawed people, who prey on the weaknesses of each other. Placing the settings in California is part of Hitchcock's larger strategy of questioning the myth of American innocence and optimism, a task he brilliantly accomplishes with the Santa Rosa setting of *Shadow of a Doubt*.

The last part of the journey or chase scene takes place in Marion's car as she heads toward Fairvale. Hitchcock again places his camera in front of Marion, and the camera changes positions effortlessly, from full frontal close-ups of Marion to POV shots of the increasingly dark and ominous road. The audience's vision is as obstructed as Marion's; the car seems to float on a landscape of darkness—and to make matters worse—rain. The territory that Marion is now in is pure existential space, the same space that Scotty falls into in his mad nightmare in *Vertigo*. The difference is in scale and graphic representation. Scotty's body—a blazing black in color—falls into a pure white space; Marion's face—made almost pure white by the oncoming headlights—floats in a black space. The connection between Marion and Scotty is also made stronger through the full frontal position, used in *Vertigo* to show Scotty seemingly caught in a G-force machine, with the background streaming by him, and used in *Psycho* to show Marion lost in the psychotic world of the Bates Motel, with traffic streaming by her. A moment later, though, the traffic has disappeared, and Marion is alone in the darkness. In this black void, something floats into Marion's and our field of vision. At first, it is a dim light; then the light gets brighter as the Bates Motel neon sign beckons to her and us, like a beacon on a dark ocean, a beacon with a vacancy—twelve vacancies, in fact. As Marion pulls into the parking lot of the motel, the car seems to float, and the soundtrack is filled with two sounds, the rain and the windshield wiper. In Marion's field of view, we see a single lawn chair next to the building. These are aural and visual set-ups, pure and simple; both the rain and the chair have powerful, suggestive dimensions. We will hear the rain again, in the shower scene, as the shower pours down on Marion. But the chair will have to wait until the end of the film, when Mrs. Bates sits in wait for Marion's sister Lila.

Hitchcock's plan for the Bates Motel scene is to shift POV focus from Marion to Norman. Of the 186 shots that make up this scene, only fourteen of them are point of view shots, or about seven percent. Of these fourteen shots, Norman has five, more than one-third. When Hitchcock referred to himself as a formalist, or when he protested that he was not really concerned with content, only form, he was referring to this kind of technical and aesthetic practice. Hitchcock shifts the narrative focus by means of a montage technique. And he does this surreptitiously, using the mise-en-scene—mainly camera placement—to complement the montage. Throughout this long scene, Hitchcock either positions his camera as a fourth wall or places it unobtrusively outside of the motel. He also generally observes the 180 degree rule and utilizes continuity cutting. Frequently, he will carve up a contiguous space to make a narrative point, such as when he presents the dialogue between Marion and Norman in Cabin 1, isolating each in the far corner of separate frames. We don't really know whether Hitchcock covered this scene with a traditional medium two-shot, with both characters contained in the frame. But we do know that the shots that appear in the film are not in the style of narrative continuity but rather of expressive continuity, that is, the mirror double image of Marion and the missing half of Norman's personality.

The key shift in POV occurs when Marion invites Norman to eat in her room. Norman hesitates, and then Hitchcock suddenly shifts to the POV of Norman by sandwiching a POV shot of Marion in between two quarter-turn shoulder shots of Norman. The shift is extremely subtle, accomplished by unobtrusively slipping in the POV shot between almost identical shots of Norman. The transfer of POV thus occurs almost subconsciously. Hitchcock waits until the end of the parlor scene to speed up the transfer of POV to Norman. The long interchange between Marion and Norman serves to provide a back-story for Norman. It's Hitchcock's sly way of making an introduction of the character: "Mr. Bates, would you mind telling the audience a bit about yourself and your family? And, oh yes, would you mind giving us a teeny-weeny glimpse into your twisted psyche?" At the end of the parlor scene, Norman has gained the upper hand on Marion by revealing enough about himself to get her to reveal enough about herself—her real name, place of origin, and her dilemma,

Universal Pictures/Photofest

Figure 9. Hitchcock begins to shift emphasis from Marion to Norman in this point of view shot.

"I stepped into a private trap . . . and I'd like to go back and try to pull myself out of it—" enough to give Mother the edge in the sexual power play for Norman. The second key POV shot shows Norman looking at the forged signature—Marie Samuels—and knowing that Miss Samuels is actually Miss Crane from Phoenix, not Los Angeles. Earlier, when Marion leaves the motel office, the audience has Norman to itself. We see, through Norman's eyes, Marion exiting the motel office. As she turns her back to us and leaves, the shift to Norman's POV becomes more potent.

Norman now dominates the screen, Hitchcock emphasizing this dominance through a low angle that shows Norman's growing narrative power. In effect, Norman has no co-opted Marion's story; he has gained power over her by becoming a confidant, a fellow sufferer in the world of traps and snares. In a sense, Norman has performed his taxidermist's art on Marion. He has caught her. He will now fix her in his stare—capturing her, as it were—and he will later, in the person of his "best" preserved work—his mother—kill her, but not preserve her. That is reserved only for his mother. Norman hates "the look of beasts when they're stuffed." We know from the next series of POV shots that he does like the look of Marion unstuffed, because he spies on her as she is getting undressed for the shower, and Hitchcock kindly allows the audience to spy with him, but this time not from a distant apartment window, but from only a few feet away. Again, Hitchcock's statement about varying the size of the image comes into play. In *Rear Window*, we can see the half-naked Miss Torso only because she occupies such a small part of the screen. If L.B. Jeffreys is the surrogate for the director, who must use the magnifying power of a long-range lens to bring the image closer, but not too close to the audience, then we must conclude that Norman is also a director surrogate. His ability to see a body in an undressed state at such a close range is an extra-diegetic comment by Hitchcock on the unraveling of the Production Code in the fabric of mid-century America, with its burgeoning youth culture, its exploding suburbs, and its increasing violence. L.B Jeffreys' voyeurism exposes violence, but it does not cause violence. Norman's voyeurism, however, becomes part of the etiology of violence. His viewing of the forbidden body of Marion triggers the murderous punishment by the mother. It is a bit of Hitchcockery that the director includes two POV shots of Norman looking at Marion, each one separated by a tight close-up of Norman's glowing eye seen from the side. However, there's a POV shot missing. The first shot shows Marion in a black slip and bra, with the shot ending as Marion reaches to unhook her bra. The second shot shows

Marion wrapping her bathrobe around herself. Where is the middle shot—of Marion naked? We could just not see Marion in such close proximity remove her bra. But we certainly can't see the character Marion naked, let alone the star, Janet Leigh. The Production Code "protected" not only the audience but also the stars themselves. We know from Rebello's book on *Psycho* (104) and from the daily production sheets that Hitchcock used a nude stand-in—Marli Renfro—for the part of the shower scene featuring the naked body of Marion Crane (Special Collections).

There's significance in the narrative shift from Marion to Norman. In terms of the script, Stefano had solved the structural challenge of the Robert Bloch novel, with its focus on Norman from the outset and with its early dispatch of Marion, less than a quarter into the novel. We know from many of Hitchcock's comments about the film that he enjoyed "tricking" the audience into identifying with Marion so that when she dies, we are left hanging, in a sense, dangling like Scotty after he loses his first Madeline. Thus, if we accept the notion of identification, which was first discussed in Aristotle's *Poetics* in the analysis of catharsis, then we can conclude that the killing of Marion creates for the viewer what Ortega y Gassett calls "existential shipwreck": "Instinctively, as do the shipwrecked he will look round for something to which to cling, and that tragic, ruthless glance, absolutely sincere, because it is a question of his salvation, will cause him to bring order into the chaos of his life. These are the only genuine ideas; the ideas of the shipwrecked. All the rest is rhetoric. . . . He who does not really feel himself lost, is lost without remission; that is to say, he never finds himself, never comes up against his own reality" (McFarland 219). The piece of driftwood—or life preserver—that we cling to is thus the seemingly innocent, naive, charming, boyish, and attractive character of Norman. In the cinematic world of the late 1950s, Norman would be the perfect romantic protagonist. He lacks Uncle Charlie's transparently dark nature or Bruno's lugubriousness and unctuousness. He's not the smooth villain like Philip Van Dam, Tony Wendice, or Gavin Elster. It is probably Hitchcock's greatest casting decision to propose Anthony Perkins for Norman. The decision led to cinema history, but the casting was so perfect that Anthony Perkins was forevermore identified with Norman Bates, to the detriment of his acting career.

Yet, there's even greater significance in this POV shift, and this significance had to do with the enunciator's transfer of focus from Marion to Norman. In no other Hitchcock film had the audience and enunciator identification been so exclusively centered upon the antagonist. In the earlier films, Hitchcock had always maintained a balance between protagonist and antagonist, especially in the "double" films: *Shadow of a Doubt, Strangers on a Train, The Wrong Man.* But in the second half of *Psycho,* Norman has the film to himself, and Hitchcock has a field day in letting Norman run the show, even going so far as to let Norman's "Puppet-Master" show herself. Would Freud have loved *Psycho*? There's no question in my mind that he would. Here is the primal oedipal mover finally revealing herself to the audience. Every oedipally fixated adolescent or adult could now face his "mother" in all of her terrible power. What does this exclusive focus say about the director himself, who finally decides to let his dark half become a whole? If we could start with *Psycho* and let Hitchcock's "dark whole" remake his masterpieces, then Bruno would have succeeded in planting the lighter on the island at Leeland Lake, thus sealing Guy's fate; Uncle Charlie would have thrown his niece from the train; Lars Thorwald would have murdered Lisa and L.B. Jeffreys; Scotty would have fallen from the tower with Madeline/Judy; Manny Balestrero's double would never have been caught; Eve Kendall would have slipped from the grasp of Roger Thornhill; and Barry Kane would have died trying to save Frank Frye. We get a clear picture of Hitchcock's dark whole in *Alfred Hitchcock Presents.* That series was the preview of coming attractions for *Psycho* and its shower scene.

Hitchcock has now maneuvered his audience into the perfect position for the frontal assault of the shower scene. By using mise-en-scene and montage in the first five scenes to establish his characters in their world, he will now pull a surprise attack on that world. I am using war metaphors with a purpose here. Hitchcock's shower scene is an attack—on the Production Code, on the studio system, on the star system, on the American family, on the American dream—and finally on the audience itself. In actuality, it would be a sneak attack, coming out of nowhere. It would come in the form of a low-budget, black-and-white film, without "A" actors, without big studio production values, and without Hitchcock's usual repertory group. As any war, it would change the landscape and alter history—the landscape and history of cinema.

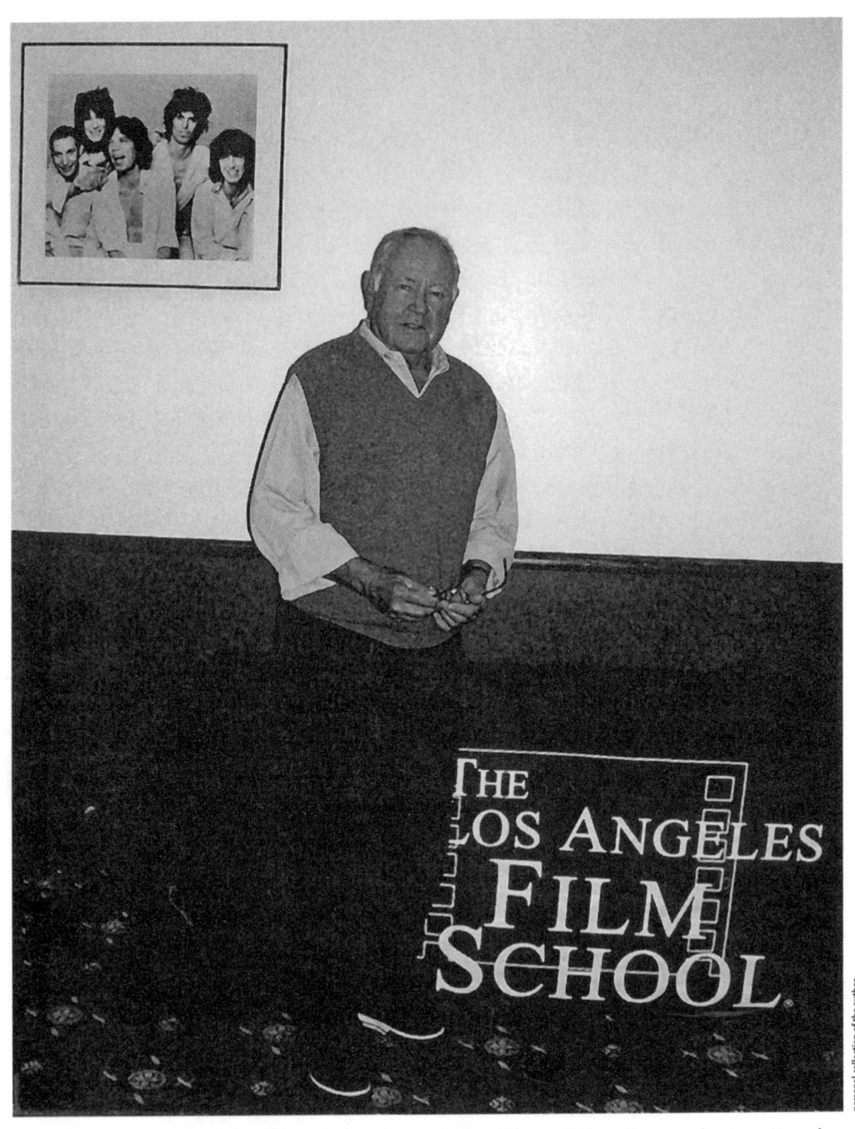

personal collection of the author

Danny Greene, sound designer of *Psycho*, outside of his editing class at the Los Angeles Film School.

CHAPTER 8

Danny Greene

Danny Greene began working in television *as a sound editor when an opportunity arose to work on a feature film. That film was* Psycho. *He has had a long career as a film editor, working on* Blazing Saddles *and* Rocky II, *among many others. Only thirty-three people received screen credit for* Psycho, *including the actors. Danny was not one of them. In contrast, 215 people received credit for the 1998 remake of* Psycho. *Danny lives in Los Angeles and teaches editing at the Los Angeles Film School and the American Film Institute.*

P: Can you give us a little background of your career up to the time you worked on *Psycho*?

D: As you know I was head of the sound effects department at a young age. Television was just mushrooming then.

P: What led you to that part of the industry?

D: It just actually happened. I'll tell you how I got into the business. The year was 1950. My grandmother knew Marvin Schenck, who was a top MGM studio executive at that time. Have you heard of the Schenck family? They were among the motion picture industry pioneers in this country. Anyway, I got an interview while I was going to USC. I was in the Marine Corps. for a couple of years and got out and started at USC three weeks after I was discharged. I got an interview with Schenck and two other producers, George Sidney Jr. and Nicholas Nayfak. They were the top producers at MGM. I put on a tie, and I was nervous; my hands were perspiring as I went into this rather foreboding and grand Irving Thalberg building.

P: How old were you?

D: Twenty-two. Anyway, here I was ushered into this giant office. You know, the elaborate studio kind of office. Two of the gentlemen said that if they had a son, they would put him into editing; the other one said if he had a son he would put him in script supervision, being on the set and various locations and seeing firsthand how movies are shot. I chose editing, and through the back door I got a job in the MGM Film Library. I was just a runner, a can carrier. There was another fellow there doing the same thing, and he was with the labor union. He was paying union dues, and I wasn't, and he couldn't deal with that. So the studio had the agent from the labor union and the agent from the editors' union come in. They classified the job as being under the jurisdiction of the editing union. So I became a member. The job was pretty easy. We had a truck and driver who was on standby all day, driving us to the MGM back lot to the film vaults and getting stock footage negatives for the librarians. We would just sit around and wait for an order to get the needed film negative. Not a pressure job, to say the least. So then things got tight, and I was laid off. Anyway, after I got laid off, I thought, "Oh Jesus! I'm in trouble." I was going with a girl named Suzanne Reinhardt, who later became my wife. Her mother was quite a prominent screenwriter. Her name was Elizabeth (Betty) Reinhardt. She won an Oscar for the screenplay for the movie *Laura*. So she had a lot of friends and mentioned to one that her future son-in-law had fourteen cents in the bank and no job. So her friend got me an interview with the head of postproduction at Revue Productions, which was owned by MCA. I got a job! I started there as an apprentice film editor. I worked for Dick Currier, who was a lovable old chap underneath a tough exterior. As soon as I got the job, I said, "I have to tell you something: I'm getting married in three weeks." And he said, "For Chrissakes, I suppose you want the weekend off!" We were working six days then. I said, "Just Saturday." And he said, "Jesus Christ, okay—but you better have your ass back here Monday at 9 a.m.!" So we went to Palm Springs for two nights, and then I went back to work. About a year later, I was promoted to assistant film editor. To celebrate my promotion and my first anniversary, I wanted to go back to Palm Springs. I said to Currier, "My anniversary is coming up Thursday," but before I could finish asking for a day off, he said, "For Chrissakes, I gave you a day off last year." Honest to God, he really said that! I was naive; I never knew if he was kidding or not. I was shaking in my boots. He said, "Oh, take the day off." I stayed at Revue, and I made some friends in the sound effects department. They were teaching me to cut sound effects. So they brought me into their department to take their place—knowing that they would shortly advance to picture editors.

P: When you were working for this Dick Currier, were you doing mainly picture editing at the time?

D: No, it took a minimum of eight years to even be eligible to become a picture editor. I started out as a splicer, which was an apprentice film editor. We used to hot splice film in those days. The cut picture and the sound track would come to me paper clipped together. My job was to splice it. The editors would physically cut the picture and the track with scissors and then paperclip it and wind it onto a reel and send it off to the splicing room. I had to scrape and glue the film together. Anyway, I did that, and then I was promoted to assistant editor. And it wasn't long before I was in sound effects, and eventually I took over the department. My good friend and mentor Dick Belding advised me that the way to get ahead in this world is to take on more responsibility. He suggested that I take over the looping department, which is now called ADR (Automated Dialogue Replacement) and I did just that. MCA (Revue) bought Universal Studios, and I soon had crews at both studios. Revue rented space from the old Republic Studio, which was located just off of Ventura Boulevard in Studio City.

P: Is that where Hitchcock would work?

D: Hitch had his own division within MCA, and he too moved to Universal. MCA had to divorce themselves from their talent agency because they had moved into the film production business. This was a no-no! Apparently, MCA was in violation of U.S. anti-trust laws. One could not control the talent that was used and owned by the same film production company. So, MCA now was exclusively in the movie making business—hence, the purchase of Universal Studios. As I recall, there was about a six- or seven-month transition to Universal. It was a relief to be under one roof, so to speak, as we had personnel at both studios.

P: What happened next?

D: I was promoted to film editor. I got my first series, which was a summer replacement for *The Jack Benny Show*. It was called *Holiday Lodge*, starring the Canadian comedy team of Wayne and Schuster. Cecil Barker and Seymour Berns from *The Red Skelton Show* produced and directed, respectively. They were very creative, terrific guys. I moved on to editing more shows and more series. Everything happened so fast. If an editor fell behind, due to a variety of reasons, other editors just jumped in and helped get the show finished so we could make the air date. Man, it could get hectic! You *had* to make the air date! It was a wonderful experience and gave me a great background, because I worked on every genre. I don't remember all of them. I did some Hitchcock and some *Wagon Train*, *Kraft Theater*, *Laramie*, and *McHale's Navy* and many pilots.

P: So how did you get to *Psycho* from there?

D: Well, remember that I was still in charge of the sound effects department (now called sound design). They asked me if I had time to do the sound effects for *Psycho*. I jumped at the chance.

P: That was your first work on a feature?

D: Yeah. I don't know why we were asked to do it other than Universal sound effects was too busy. My department was doing TV only, but, I said, "Oh yeah," and I assigned two of my best guys to the show, terrific guys. Jack Jackson and—oh God, I can't remember the other man's name—Dick, Dick something—I'll get his name; that's embarrassing! Anyway, we get down to the shower scene.

P: Oh how exciting! Before you did the sound, did you see a rough cut of the shower scene?

D: No. We didn't see the picture until they were finished and ready to go into mixing sound.

P: But you got directions on what kind of sound they wanted. Is that it?

D: I don't remember. I don't remember anyone saying do this and do that. It was quite obvious what we had to do. I know in the shower scene, with each different angle, there would be a change in the quality of the sound, the shower sound, the water. And so, all of that had to be stripped out, and we put in one or maybe two shower sounds, depending upon the perspective of the shot. When we started to mix the sound, and the whole film, all went very well until we came to the shower scene. Hitchcock didn't like the stabbing sounds, even with the help of the chilling music incredibly composed by Bennie Herrmann. It was now about 6 p.m. We had changed the stabbing sounds three times, but they still didn't work. I know that Hitch was getting upset, so I called for a dinner break. Man, I was upset, too. I dashed to the prop shop for a knife and some petty cash. I was going to go to the closest market, buy a big roast beef, and stab it in front of a microphone. I told the prop shop guy what I was going to do. He said, "Here, you might as well take the same knife we used in the scene. I've got it right here." So, I got this giant chunk of meat, a big roast with gristle on the side. I stabbed it about fifty times, in the gristle and in the meat part. It was just a vicious sound of slicing meat. I guess that's what a stabbing sound is like. I've never stabbed anyone; can you believe it?

My assistants Jack and Dick cut the new stab sounds into the scene, and we started to mix again. I was nervous. The scene started, and the new stab sounds were a hit! Hitch leaned back in his chair and simply said, "Ah, yes—very nice." I took the roast home that night, and my wife, Suzi, made a wonderful pot roast the next night. Isn't that a great story? A true Hollywood story, and I was involved with it!

P: That is the "Lamb to the Slaughter," the *Alfred Hitchcock Presents* episode with Barbara Bel Geddes. She kills her husband with a leg of lamb and then serves it to the police. And Hitchcock loved that weird stuff with food and killing. I mean, there was always a weird connection with sex, food, and death.

D: And they never found the murder weapon. The leg of lamb was devoured by the police at dinner.

P: She has the leg of lamb in the oven. She says to the lieutenant, whose men are investigating the murder, "Ask them all in, why don't you, and give them a nice hot meal. It's good meat. I promise you that." And they all sit around and consume the murder weapon, even the lamb bone, which one cop takes home to his dog. So the murder weapon is gone. As they are eating, the cops talk about the murder weapon, and the lieutenant says, "Well, for all we know it might be under our very noses."

D: That's so clever. By the way, I've heard that in a book written on *Psycho*, the author claimed melons were used for the sound effects.

P: Steven Rebello's book on *Psycho*.

D: Melons were never used in any way to create sound effects for *Psycho*. Perhaps *Psycho II* or *III* or whatever.

P: There are so many contradictory things about the film. I mean Janet Leigh swears that there was no other woman used in the shower scene, and Joe Stefano claims there was. Hilton Green claims the knife never enters the flesh, and it does. Of course, this film was made forty-two years ago.

D: God, I don't know. It was all illusion to me. I didn't hear anything about flesh being penetrated.

P: I'd imagine if Hitchcock had anything to say about what they were using, he would have rather had the meat!

D: Yes, authentic flesh.

P: Yes, because it is meat. In fact, in the Gus Van Sant remake, when the mother sticks the knife into Marion Crane, who is played by Ann Heche, you can hear the knife hitting bone. It goes "cutch-chuck."

Oh it's grotesque! She sees something as she is getting stabbed, some clouds. Then there's a shot of her eyeball with her pupil opening. Those are things that aren't in the original shower scene.

D: Every time we'd run that scene on the mixing stage—you know we ran it I don't know how many times—when that music cue hit, I literally had chills going up and down my spine. I would get ready for it—I would know—but it would get to me every time.

P: Hitchcock was there every time you were mixing the sound on the dubbing stage?

D: Yes.

P: So you were mixing sound effects, music, and dialogue. Did he ever say anything when he was supervising the mixing of that scene?

D: He didn't say much, as I recall. In our first pass of the shower scene, we used everything we had in the library. And he said, "Not quite right, gentlemen. We are getting closer, but not quite right." And that's what prompted me, about the third time he said that, to try something else. That is when I went out to get the meat.

P: And when he saw the scene with these new sounds, he liked them?

D: Oh, yes. He smiled, and he sat there like this in his blue suit, hands clasped on his lap, and said, "Ah, yes—very nice."

P: Do you remember seeing it from beginning to end with your sound effects? What was your reaction?

D: We were very pleased. The sound of the slicing of flesh was vicious!

P: I'm sure that in your library there were not many sounds you could have used. Where in your library would you get that kind of sound? No one had ever done that before. There are always a million gun shots, but a knife sticking into flesh? I mean where the hell would you go to get something like that?

D: Just take a recorder and just go out and stab someone! You would need to gag them so their yells wouldn't be recorded! You would need good, clean stab sounds, you know?

P: Did you work with Hitchcock on some television shows before you did *Psycho*?

D: Yes, but he was never there. Norman Lloyd and Joan Harrison, two very creative and bright people, were the producers of his television shows. As a matter fact, when the Hitchcock television series went to an hour format, I did a couple of those. I remember vividly one of them. I ran a first cut for Lloyd and Harrison, and they said, "Come to the office in fifteen minutes and we will talk about what we need to take out, change, etc." I walked into the office a little later on, and everyone was hysterical and in tears. They informed me that President Kennedy had just been shot in Dallas. I thought that I was in the middle of a Hitchcock movie.

P: Were any other things changed during the time the shower scene was being worked out and Hitchcock was watching it? Do you remember if he said, "Make this louder," or "Make this softer," or "Add this," or "Make this shot shorter"?

D: It used to amaze me that experienced producers and directors would complain that a sound was too loud or too soft the *first time* the mixers viewed the reel! Remember that the mixers were running the reel for the *first time*. They needed to know what they had to work with; they had to rehearse, too! While mixing *Psycho*, viewing a reel for the first time, the mixers played the sounds up loud the first time so everyone knew what they were dealing with. Hitchcock would say to them, "Okay, just have a hint of that, and keep the music up," because the music was the thing that really made the scene. It enhanced it so much. It just put it over the top.

P: Those slicing sounds are underneath. They are layered underneath the music. If I'm not mistaken, in Gus Van Sant's version, those slicing sounds are more pronounced. They are louder. I have a theory that films are getting louder now than they used to be.

D: I completely agree with that.

P: I mean when I go to the theater now, I sometimes have to go to the manager and ask him to turn the sound down. It seems to me that the trailers are even louder than the picture.

D: Many of today's directors and producers think that loud is better.

P: That is exactly right. And the sound effects are so loud. I know sometimes you want to shock the audience with a loud sound. But if you could go back in time, you probably would be amazed at how low the sound levels were even in action pictures. The balance is much more subtle in Hitchcock's *Psycho* than it is in the Van Sant version.

P: When you saw this shower scene for the first time, you know when you were checking the sound levels, what was your reaction to the scene? Did you think it was a revolutionary scene?

D: I didn't think it was revolutionary at the time. I just thought at the time it was one hell of a scary scene. We saw it with just the shower sounds the first time. At that moment, we didn't know what kind of music Hitchcock was going to use. He may have not known at that time either; I don't know. But, it was pretty crazy and pretty frightening with the curtain and that shadowy figure. I do know that over the years, when the subject of Hitchcock and *Psycho* comes up, invariably, every woman I talked to has said that she couldn't take a shower alone for a long time. For example, I had to get a little minor surgery this morning, and I asked the nurse who was bandaging me if I was going to be okay as I had an interview about *Psycho*, and she said, "My god, I couldn't take a shower for about five weeks or so." It affected women very dramatically.

P: It did; it is the most vulnerable you can be—naked in a wet place, where you can't get your balance.

D: And it is so private, so terribly private. It is like taking a crap someplace and . . .

P: You don't want anyone to be there. There was a good reason why the Production Code never allowed toilets or bathrooms. They know these are places where people are by themselves and they are exposing and touching intimate parts of their body and they are doing things that are very private. Joe Stefano said in his interview that the shower scene evoked not only the fear of dying but also of being scarred and disfigured if you did live. You can't imagine any other scene that so many people remember so vividly.

D: Correct.

P: Do you remember when you first saw it in the theater for the first time? Did you go to a screening? Was there a screening for people who worked on the film?

D: Not that I recall. But I saw the picture so many times on the dubbing stage.

P: You don't remember seeing the film whole for the first time?

D: Yes, it was a sound effects—looping, and music spotting—session.

P: Watching the picture over and over again.

D: Yeah, on the mixing stage, reel by reel—probably ten times per reel.

P: Why do you think this scene is so powerful?

D: I think we touched on it a little bit. I think the combination of the voyeurism, the shock of this figure bursting in, a female naked and totally vulnerable, a private situation. You wouldn't dream of anything like that happening. And then the music, it sends chills up your spine and the knife, the blood—the whole terrifying situation.

P: This combination of nudity, of violence and sexuality, had probably never been shown that way.

D: Right. Imagine a woman being naked, so personal, and so guarded, to be exposed in that matter, and with a knife.

P: Well, if you take a good print of the DVD, the Universal DVD is beautifully done, with the commentary and documentary. If you slow it down and go through it frame by frame, you can see glowing eyes. Now, there was actually a woman doing that because Tony Perkins was in New York, and they had a stand-in. So the funny thing is that it was actually a woman, not Tony Perkins, in a wig, even though you are supposed to think it is a woman at first, but at the end you realize it is Norman Bates dressed as mother. What is different about *Psycho* is that in other films, it is almost always a guy killing a woman, but in *Psycho* it is a woman killing a woman; but then of course it isn't a woman killing a woman; it is a man dressed up as a woman killing a woman. But it is really a woman killing a woman, because Tony Perkins was in New York when the scene was being filmed, so they had a stand-in for him—a woman. Makes your head swim!

D: It's like a funhouse mirror. At first, you think it is the mother; later you know it is Tony Perkins dressed like his mother. When you first learn about the production, you find out it was not Tony Perkins playing Norman, but a woman playing Norman. Then you find out that Janet Leigh had a female stand-in.

P: What effect has *Psycho* had on your career?

D: I feel privileged to have worked on *Psycho*. I mentioned that it was the first feature to pass through my department. Needless to say, it being a Hitchcock film, I wanted the sound effects to be perfect. I believe they were. It took a year or more to realize what an impact the sound effects of the shower scene had on the audience, particularly on the women. The stabbing sounds helped. It was not too long after I worked on *Psycho* that I moved on to become a film editor. I was fortunate to have edited so many very good films before I retired. And now a little travel, a little golf, time with my family. I'm a lucky man. I shall always be thankful.

CHAPTER 9

The Evolution of the Shower Scene

I can hear them scream when I'm making the picture.

—ALFRED HITCHCOCK

The shower scene is the culmination of Hitchcock's pure cinema. He poured everything he knew about mise-en-scene and montage into this scene. In addition, he complemented the art of the cinema with a virtual catalogue of his thematic preoccupations. But, in creating the scene, Hitchcock surpassed himself and launched his art into a different stratosphere: the scene becomes seminal and paradigmatic. It marks a boundary between two different worlds of cinema. The Hollywood studio system, the classical style, the star system, and the Production Code dominated the first world. The transformation of the studio system and the Hollywood style, both of which surrender their hegemony to the cinema of sensation, and to the rise of independent productions, with their experimentations in style and narration, characterized the second world—the world of present-day cinema. Both the studio system and the Production Code were victims of this seismic transition.

Whether the scene created by itself the conditions that made film modernism possible or whether it was itself the result of intellectual climatic change is a moot point. It was probably a little of both. The important thing is that the scene does indeed occur, approximately halfway through the film. After its brief and furious appearance, the scene would leave its audience transformed, as if they had been sitting in a time machine rather than in a theater.

When it comes to the etiology of the shower scene in Hitchcock's own work, the antecedents are plentiful. In chapter 4, I discussed the shift from suspenseful mise-en-scene to terrifying montage, creating a vortex of violence, as demonstrated in films as diverse as *Saboteur*, *Shadow of a*

Doubt, *Strangers on a Train*, and *Rear Window*. However, there are other cinematic foreshadowings in five of Hitchcock's films. These films illustrate underlying patterns of narration, character, and visual style that pave the way for the shower scene.

The five films that exhibit these patterns traverse three decades of Hitchcock's output: *Blackmail* (1929), *Sabotage* (1936), *Spellbound* (1945), *Dial M for Murder* (1953), and *The Wrong Man* (1956). Each of these films presents a narrative event that pits a male against a female in a violent, or potentially violent, incident. Two of the films, *Sabotage* and *The Wrong Man*, contain scenes of spousal attack. In *Sabotage*, Mrs. Verloc stabs to death Mr. Verloc, the saboteur, when she realizes that he's responsible for her younger brother's death. In *The Wrong Man*, Rose Balestrero, in a psychotic state, attacks her husband with a hair brush, leaving a cut on his forehead. In contrast, *Blackmail* and *Dial M for Murder* feature scenes in which a woman, who has been attacked and who is defending herself, kills a stranger. *Spellbound* is a special case, because it features a paranoid amnesiac who, in a somnambulist state, poses a threat to his therapist, who is herself pretending to be his wife. I am particularly interested in this latter film because its multiple role playing and psychological layering find correspondences in the shower scene of *Psycho*.

I would like to start by examining the earliest of the films, *Blackmail*, because it plays a pivotal role in Hitchcock's development as a filmmaker. Shot originally as a silent film, *Blackmail* was pulled from distribution and partially reshot as a sound film. The film represents Hitchcock's ambivalent relationship to sound. Two significant cinematic influences were silent film movements: German Expressionism (mise-en-scene) and Soviet Socialist Realism (montage). His many discussions about pure cinema and the power of cinema are almost always couched in visual terms. In an interview at the American Film Institute, Hitchcock answered a question about problems with writers, "Well, I have had problems with writers because I find that I am teaching them cinematics all the time. You have got to remember that with a lot of writers you have to go by the page, what is written on the page. I have no interest in that. I have that square, white rectangle to fill with a succession of images, one following the other. That's what makes a film" (Gottlieb, *Alfred Hitchcock Interviews* 90). Yet Hitchcock broke new ground in *Blackmail* by using sound expressively and creatively, most importantly in the often-cited scene during which Alice's subjective perception of the word "knife" drowns out all the other words.

The key scene in the film is the killing of the artist Crewe by the coquettish Alice White, whose flirtatious and enticing behavior is complicit in an attempted rape. The scene is three minutes and twenty-five seconds long and is composed of five shots. These relatively lengthy shots underscore Hitchcock's mise-en-scene approach to the scene's construction. This approach, with shots averaging more than twenty seconds each, gives the film almost a tableau look, most likely due to the primitive nature of early sound recording, which inhibited camera movement.

Although it would seem at first glance that this scene, with its mise-en-scene approach, would have little bearing on the shower scene in *Psycho*, a closer examination reveals startling similarities. In the scene immediately preceding this one, Hitchcock uses a dressing screen to divide the frame in half. On the left side of the frame is the artist Crewe playing the piano; on the right side is Alice getting undressed in clear view of the audience. The structure of this shot not only prefigures the scene that precedes the shower murder—Norman peering at Marion as she is getting undressed—but also the scene of the murder itself, with the shower curtain divided into left and right halves.

Both scenes contain structural and thematic elements that are similar, even though the cinematic techniques are in contrast—mise-en-scene versus montage. In *Blackmail*, Crewe intends to seduce Alice, but Hitchcock places both characters in the same frame, equalizing them to some extent. The mise-en-scene serves to underscore both characters' complicity in the upcoming seduction/rape scene. Alice has been a willing partner in this tryst; she eagerly undresses and dons the costume that Crewe will "paint" her in. By placing both characters in separate halves of the same frame, Hitchcock emphasizes their shared culpability. In *Psycho*, however, although Norman and Marion share the same space, as it were, with only a wall separating them, they don't share the same frame. By having Marion become an object of Norman's lustful gaze, Hitchcock emphasizes their separateness, their otherness. It is true that Marion is guilty of a crime, but she is in no way complicit with Norman in his violation of her privacy, and later of her body. Yet Crewe and Norman are similar in their attempts to appropriate the bodies of their female victims: Crewe, through his painting of Alice, and Norman, through his voyeurism. The undressing of the female character triggers a violent response in both Crewe and Norman, although Norman's response is a psychotic projection of desire onto a disapproving and protective maternal alter ego.

One might ask at this point why sexuality and the female body provoke violence in many of Hitchcock's films. In *Shadow of a Doubt*, Uncle Charlie kills rich widows, and he lures them into his trap by offering himself as a dashing, romantic, sexually attractive male. In *Strangers on a Train*, Bruno kills Miriam after they have been playing a sexually charged cat and mouse game at Leeland Lake. One way to view Miriam's murder is as a rape scene, minus the sex. Because Bruno seems asexual, his pursuit and murder of Miriam appear to be punishment for her free and easy sexuality. In *Rear Window*, Lars Thorwald murders and then dismembers his bed-ridden wife as punishment for her lack of availability as a sexual object. His sexual frustration with his wife, symbolized by their separate framing in adjoining rear windows, results in a murderous rage. In *Vertigo*, Madeline/Judy is killed twice, as it were, mainly as a result of sexual vulnerability and availability, just as Carlotta is punished for her sexuality. The culmination of this disturbing linkage of sexuality and violence comes in *Psycho*, in which Marion's sexuality and eroticism are punished directly on her body. In an essay entitled "Director's Problems," Hitchcock claims that there is a practical reason for such scenes of violence, ". . . violence is good screen material, good screen fare" (Gottlieb, *Hitchcock on Hitchcock* 190). The cinema, of course, is based on movement, and violence does indeed provide movement. Yet there is something disturbing about the linkage between the movement of violence on the screen and the presentation of the female body. Hitchcock once claimed that "Everything is perverted in a different way" (Gottlieb, *Hitchcock Interviews* 51), which Mogg calls "a statement which strikes me as a key to his work" ("Editorial"). That the beauty of the female body would provoke "murderous impulses" is indeed one of the key moral dilemmas of our age. Witness the prevalence of the serial killer in both the real and the cinematic worlds: Ted Bundy and Hannibal Lecter seem to be interchangeable characters in popular culture. It would not be an exaggeration to say that Hitchcock, from *The Lodger* on, had always been fascinated by—obsessed by—men who attack or kill women.

The scene in which Crewe attacks Alice and is killed by her foreshadows the shower scene is *Psycho*, although the scenes look radically different. Yet the similarities reveal that Hitchcock's thematic and stylistic preoccupation span the thirty years that separate the two films. Joel Finler claims ". . . [*Psycho*] appears to bring his career full circle, for there are clear thematic links with his first notable successes in the 1920s such as *The Lodger* and *Blackmail*" (131). The scene that precedes the killing ends with

Crewe roughly running his hands through Alice's hair and then forcing a kiss upon her. Unsettled by Crewe's aggressiveness, Alice retreats behind the screen to prepare to leave the artist's apartment. The killing scene then begins with a medium shot of Crewe. Hitchcock uses symbolic lighting in this first shot, casting shadows on Crewe's face that give him a sinister appearance, very much like the shadows that cover the face of Norman after he has spied on Marion in Cabin 1. Hitchcock's mise-en-scene is similar in both shots. Crewe and Norman are in full frontal position, staring directly out at the audience; both characters' faces are covered with shadows and exhibit consternation and anger. Evidently, both men's gazes on the female body have resulted in anger that will soon turn into violence. Hitchcock handles the killing in *Blackmail* in a circumspect, restrained manner. Crewe's incipient violence is shown by shadows on the wall as he struggles with Alice to get her into his bed. The bed itself is not shown, only the curtain that covers it. The struggle between Crewe and Alice is dramatized through Alice's muffled cries and through the curtain, which billows out, suggesting the violence going on behind it. Hitchcock dollies his camera in to a close-up of a cheese board and knife next to the bed. We see Alice's hand reach out from behind the curtain, grab the knife, and bring it behind the curtain. The struggle continues, and then Crewe's hand, in a reflection of Alice's hand earlier in the shot, thrusts out in a rigid, claw-like position. The audience thus concludes through Hitchcock's mise-en-scene that Alice has been sexually assaulted and that she has killed Crewe in self-defense—all of this information being conveyed by "pure cinema." We then see Alice emerge backwards from behind the curtain, holding up the knife, with a dazed look on her face. Hitchcock lights the shot so that the blade of the knife glows in wicked brilliance.

The parallels to the shower scene are numerous. Both victims, Alice and Marion, are in a state of undress, and both are erotically presented to the audience, the camera literally undressing them. The shadows on the wall will be transformed in the shower scene to the ominous shadow that appears behind the translucent shower curtain. The enclosed space of the curtained bed will become the enclosed space of the shower; the bed curtain will be morphed into the shower curtain. The bread knife, with its rounded edge, will become the sharp-pointed butcher knife of the shower scene. Marion's hand will reach out beyond the shower curtain just as Crewe's hand thrusts out of the curtained bed. There are instructive and provocative differences between the two scenes, though. Alice kills her attacker in self-defense out of the direct gaze of the audience; Norma Bates kills Marion not in self-defense but in defense of her son Norman, and she does it in the direct gaze of a horrified audience. There's no blood on Alice or on the knife; Marion's blood fills the bottom of the tub. After Alice kills Crewe, she backs out of the curtained bed with the knife held in her hand, in an attacking position. Norma Bates approaches the bathtub, pulls the shower curtain aside, and brings the knife directly into the space of the shower.

One wonders whether Hitchcock had *Blackmail* on his mind when he was shooting *Psycho*. Alice and Marion are similar in that they are in relationships but not married. Each transgresses the norms and laws of society: Alice by cheating on her policeman-boyfriend Frank and then later killing Crewe; Marion by having an adulterous relationship with Sam and then later stealing money. Marion and Alice share contrasting fates involving knives: Alice kills a stranger in self-defense and then gets away with murder, thanks to her policeman-boyfriend; a stranger wielding a knife murders Marion as she is preparing to return to Phoenix to redeem herself. In its moral ironies and parallels, *Blackmail* looks ahead to *Psycho*.

Moral ironies continue in *Sabotage* (1936), at the end of which Mrs. Verloc, who has killed her husband, gets away with murder, thanks to her new "protector," Ted, a Scotland Yard detective. *Sabotage* contains a scene that in its montage structure looks forward to the shower scene. Mrs. Verloc has discovered that her husband is a saboteur and that he is responsible for her ten-year-old brother's death. Unlike his mise-en-scene approach in *Blackmail*, in which Hitchcock uses only five shots in three minutes and twenty-five seconds, he utilizes thirty-three shots in almost the same length scene in *Sabotage*. The camera assumes a fourth-wall position, but instead of presenting a contiguous sense of space as he does in *Blackmail*, Hitchcock fragments the space by carving it up into discrete shots. The first twenty-six shots of the scene are photographed from the camera's fourth-wall position. Mr. and Mrs. Verloc are isolated in separate shots, suggesting Mrs. Verloc's alienation from her traitorous and duplicitous husband. The fact that the murder takes place in a domestic setting—at the dinner table, in fact—is in keeping with Hitchcock's statement about keeping murder at home, where it belongs, and with his penchant for linking murder with food or eating. In a tongue-in-cheek article written for *Coronet* magazine during the release of *Psycho*, Hitchcock writes, "May I recommend a meal fit for a killer? Start with an antipasto of one passionate peccadillo and 40,000 greenbacks. The main dish: mayhem, rare. Now you know the menu of my new film-flam—*Psycho*. But as you'll see, much depends on the chef" ("My Recipe for Murder" 49).

The idea of murder is first suggested to Mrs. Verloc in the scene preceding the killing at the dinner table. Verloc makes excuses for her brother Stevie's death and even suggests that he be replaced with a child of their own. Horrified and disgusted, Mrs. Verloc retreats to the movie theater connected to their apartment (appropriately enough, Verloc runs a movie theater as a front for his sabotage—a perverse bit of Hitchcockery), where she involuntarily laughs at a Disney cartoon entitled "Who Killed Cock Robin"—laughs, that is, until she sees the killing of Cock Robin, and Hitchcock shows us a dramatic close-up of Mrs. Verloc's face quickly going from smile to frown. Hitchcock cleverly combines two related ideas in this scene: the first is the killing of Stevie by the bomb that was supposed to be transported by Verloc. The second is the killing of Verloc, an idea planted in Mrs. Verloc's mind, although she is unaware of it at the time. Thus the cartoon links the past and the future. When Mrs. Verloc re-enters the apartment to serve Verloc his dinner, it is indeed his last supper.

Unaware that his wife is seething with anger and revenge, Verloc obtusely says, "Pulled yourself together. That's better." This statement seems to trigger something in Mrs. Verloc, and that something is aggravated by Verloc's vulgar comments about the food, spoken with his mouth full. Hitchcock then cuts to a medium shot of Mrs. Verloc serving the dinner, with knife and fork, and looking to the right of the frame at her husband, who is off-camera. Mrs. Verloc looks down at the knife in her hand, and the camera tilts down. Hitchcock lights the scene so that the knife, just as in *Blackmail*, glows momentarily with reflected light. Mrs. Verloc throws down the knife and fork, perhaps realizing her intentions. Hitchcock alternates close-ups of Mr. and Mrs. Verloc as they both look to Stevie's empty chair. Hitchcock then utilizes the moving camera superbly to dolly in on a close-up of Mrs. Verloc as she slowly realizes what she is about to do. She looks down at the knife, and Hitchcock cuts to a close-up of Verloc now realizing that something is wrong, as he, too, looks at the knife. Then in a surprising shift to Verloc's POV, Hitchcock shows us Mrs. Verloc hesitatingly reach for the knife. With his eyes open in surprise and fear, Verloc stands up and walks around the table, coming closer to the camera, which catches him in a close-up profile. We then switch again to Verloc's POV, this time with a subjective camera moving closer to Mrs. Verloc, who is looking directly out at the audience, now embodied in the squeaking shoes of Verloc, the only noticeable sound.

Shot 27 of this scene is a brilliant subversion of the 180 degree rule; the camera suddenly shifts positions so that the characters' positions are reversed in the frame. In effect, Hitchcock has utilized mise-en-scene and montage to suggest a vortex, the camera literally circling the characters. The genius of this reversal can only be appreciated when one looks carefully at the first twenty-six shots of this scene, in which Hitchcock takes great pains to establish a spatial context for the action. Utilizing fourth-wall position and the 180 degree rule, Hitchcock establishes a patriarchal space, with Verloc on the right side of the mise-en-scene, sitting royally in his chair, waiting for his servant-wife to serve his food. Mrs. Verloc, in her left-side position, establishes the preeminence of the right side of the frame by looking in that direction, toward Verloc, who remains off-camera. When Verloc realizes what his subservient wife may be contemplating, he walks around the table and into tight close-up range, with the camera circling with him. This circular movement facilitates the sudden shift in mise-en-scene. With their positions now reversed, Mrs. Verloc has effectively neutralized the spatial power of Verloc; in fact, she has gained the upper hand. As he tries to reach for the knife, Mrs. Verloc beats him to it, and the camera dollies in to a close-up. Both characters seem to move toward the knife, which is now off-camera. The killing is suggested by the reaction of both characters—Verloc grunting as the knife goes in, his mouth gaping in pain; Mrs. Verloc, crying out in despair. Hitchcock cuts to a close-up of the knife buried in Verloc's stomach with only the handle visible. He cuts to a medium shot of Verloc with his back to us, and of Mrs. Verloc, with her hand on his shoulder, allowing him to drop to the floor. Hitchcock next gives us a close-up of Mrs. Verloc looking down at Verloc; and then, in a POV shot, she looks at the birds that her brother Stevie loved, their chirping now the only sound heard. The last two shots of the scene contrast dramatically. We see a close-up of Mrs. Verloc, who cries out, "Stevie, Stevie," over the body of her dead husband, invoking her brother's name in despair and revenge. For the last shot, Hitchcock positions the camera on the floor, with two sets of feet, one vertical, Mrs. Verloc's, which walk away from the camera suggesting loss, and the other Mr. Verloc's, horizontal, with only the heels visible. What a brilliant way to use mise-en-scene to suggest loss, grief, and death!

The absolute stasis of Mr. Verloc's heels is a potent visualization of death. Fewer than twenty-five years later, Hitchcock will again show death as stasis when Marion's body drops with a sudden, sickening thud across the bathtub wall, her head crushed against the unyielding floor, her feet splayed across the screen, and her eye open with the all-comprehending stare of death. Other foreshadowings of the shower scene in this scene from *Sabotage* include the flashing knife; the montage approach suggesting a vortex of violence; the sense of enclosed space; the revenge killing (Mrs. Verloc kills her husband to avenge the death of her brother; Norman has killed his mother and her lover to avenge his loss of maternal love; Norma kills Marion to avenge the potential loss of her son-lover); and finally, the sudden eruption of terror. Speaking of this furious appearance of terror, Hitchcock says, "Well, that's what life is like. Things happen out of the blue . . . one must never set up a murder. They [*sic*] must happen unexpectedly, as in life" (Bogdanovich, *Who the Devil* 477).

Spellbound (1945) looks forward to the shower scene indirectly; its key scene exhibits narrative, character, and stylistic elements that will reappear in *Psycho*, even though its mise-en-scene structure bears little resemblance to the montage of the shower scene. Occurring about halfway through the film—at approximately the same point as the shower scene—*Spellbound*'s pivotal scene takes place in Dr. Brulov's house, where Dr. Constance Peterson has taken her "patient" (really her lover), Dr. Anthony Edwardes, for psychiatric care. It turns out that Dr. Edwardes is really John Ballantine, a paranoid amnesiac who is suffering from a severe guilt complex over the accidental killing of his brother when both were children and the witnessing of the skiing death of the real Dr. Edwardes.

The narrative and characterological parallels to *Psycho* are manifold. The amnesiac double—Dr. Edwardes and John Ballantine—finds a parallel in Norman Bates, who is both Norma Bates and Norman Bates. Norman is really a paranoid amnesiac, whose guilt over the killing of his mother ("Matricide is probably the most unbearable crime of all—most unbearably to the son who commits it," says the psychiatrist at the end of *Psycho*) results in a radical rupturing of his identity into two opposing but complementary characters. The killing that is the etiology of Norman's amnesia happens when Norman is a teenager; earlier, when he was five, Norman's father had died. These "double" traumas—the loss of a father at a young age and the killing of his mother and her lover in adolescence—thrust Norman into psychosis. Norman is, in effect, a case history of the Oedipus complex. His father dies when he is five, at the age when the Oedipus complex is most intense, according to Freud. The death of the father, we infer, must have plunged Norman into the depths of oedipal guilt: the murderous impulses of the child toward the father seem to have manifested themselves in Norman's mind into the actual death of the father. Unable to resolve the anger and rage at the father, Norman turns with renewed ardor toward the mother, who—in order to protect her young son and satisfy her own need for male sexuality—takes him as a lover. Norman's rage is intensified when Mrs. Bates takes on "another" lover, this relationship precipitating a double homicide. Now split into two identities, Norman shares his body with his mother, Norma, who offers her son the oedipal protection and love that she had originally provided him after the father had died. And Norma offers this protection through the device of the phallic knife, a symbol of the menacing penis that makes the young son fear the stronger, more potent father. In fact, Geoffrey Shurlock, who had become head of the Production Code after Breen's retirement, warned Paramount's Code liaison Luigi Luraschi of the references to incest in Stefano's script. In an inter-office communication dated November 2, 1959, Luraschi informs Hitchcock that it would be impossible to issue a certificate of approval to the film because of the "very pointed description of an incestuous relationship between Norman and his mother" (Special Collections).

One way to look at *Spellbound* is to see it as a psychoanalytical Rorschach Test for *Psycho*. *Spellbound* takes as its theme psychoanalysis. The epilogue to the film states: "Our story deals with psychoanalysis, the method by which modern science treats the emotional problems of the sane." It is significant that *Spellbound* deals with the illnesses of the sane, while *Psycho* presents the illnesses of the insane, and that *Spellbound* ends on a happy note, with the union of Constance and John, while *Psycho* concludes with the destruction of Norman Bates and the ascendance of the maniacal mother.

The scene that crystallizes the themes and style of *Spellbound* is five minutes long and contains twenty-one shots, with an average length of fourteen seconds. This rather long shot length attests to the mise-en-scene structure of the scene. The amnesiac John Ballantine is now without an identity; he knows he is not really Dr. Anthony Edwardes, but he is not really in possession of his true name and past, John Ballantine, perpetrator of fratricide. His purported colleague, Dr. Peterson, now becomes his lover and his analyst. In her protector-healer role she has also become, in effect, his mother. She has taken him to the house of her own analyst and teacher, Dr. Brulov, her mentor and father figure. What Hitchcock constitutes in Dr. Brulov's house is a new family, with the "son" John being protected and healed by his "parents," Constance and Dr. Brulov. With this loving family now formed, Hitchcock presents us with a scene that re-enacts the oedipal triangle in all of its potential violence and terror. This scene is truly subversive and signals Hitchcock's very skeptical and cynical picture of the family structure. Preeminent among the great modernist directors, he saw the passions and desires that become twisted in the dynamics of family relationships, with male and female sexuality at war with paternal and maternal drives and instincts.

The scene begins with a fade-in from blackness to a dark bedroom lit expressionistically with chiaroscuro lighting. The camera is in the fourth-wall position, slightly below eye level. John Ballantine is on the left side of the screen, Constance on the right. The left side position of the paranoid amnesiac looks forward to *Psycho* with its mainly left side placement of Norman. On the right side of the frame is the sleeping figure of Dr. Peterson, bathed in the light from the window. Her position in the right side of the frame indicates her power as lover-mother-healer, the light that spreads over her emphasizing this dominant position. Ballantine's bed lies perpendicular to Constance's; he is literally at her feet. This dark enclosed space is the claustrophobia of the oedipal dynamic: the son-lover sharing the same room—not yet the same bed, as in *Psycho*—with the mother. The pervasive darkness of this room suggests the moral ambiguity of their relationship. The camera dollies in to a medium shot of Ballantine, who sits up in bed, holds his head in his hands, and looks to his left to the off-screen presence of Dr. Peterson; Ballantine's look is of anxiety and guilt. Ballantine gets up from bed, moves to the left of the frame, and reaches inside the bathroom to turn on the light.

For shot 2, Hitchcock positions his camera inside the bathroom, in keeping with the prevailing production standards of 1945. The camera is still in a fourth-wall position, but it has shifted to a somewhat higher angle so that the offending toilet bowl cannot be seen. On the wall opposite from the camera is the bathtub, with the spigots visible. The walls are tiled halfway up with the same kinds of tile we will see in the shower scene. Ballantine drinks a glass of water, his shadow looming large on the wall of the bathtub, Hitchcock graphically reinforcing Ballantine's dual personality. The camera dollies in very slowly, almost imperceptibly, as Ballantine looks at himself in the mirror. Hitchcock avoids the cliché here by not showing us Ballantine's mirror image, reinforcing the mystery of his identity. As the camera reaches close-up range, Ballantine, realizing he needs a shave, reaches for the razor, opens it, and tests its sharpness.

The next ten shots bring us into the mind of Ballantine by combining POV and reaction shots. The first shot is a POV close-up of Ballantine's shaving mug, with its white shaving cream. The brilliant white color sends Ballantine into a panic, as do the four POV shots of the white porcelain sink, chair, marble shelf, and bathtub. Hitchcock's use of white to trigger a violent emotional reaction is an ironic reversal of that color's traditional association with purity and innocence. In *Psycho*, the glowing white bathroom is a prelude to Marion's death. The presence of Ballantine in this white setting also looks forward to the shower scene, but in a reverse way; in the next shot, he staggers from the bathroom, razor in hand, into the dark bedroom. Hitchcock situates the camera in the bedroom, right outside of the bathroom door. Ballantine is totally bathed in darkness, which is emphasized by the glowing backlight of the bathroom. This shot seems to be a reverse image of the shot in the shower scene in which the camera, placed in the shower with Marion, looks out beyond her to capture the ominous, shadowy figure approaching her. The rectangular shape of the door frames Ballantine, and he walks toward the camera, toward us, in a menacing way. In the preceding shot, another POV, Ballantine had looked toward the sleeping Dr. Peterson, and he sees the vertical lines of the chenille bedspread. The graphic representation of Ballantine's paranoia and guilt—the color white and the parallel vertical lines—is a testimony to Hitchcock's awareness of how abstract shapes of the physical environment can become symbolic.

Now, in shot 15, Ballantine looms over the sleeping Dr. Peterson; his upper torso is bathed in darkness as he looks down and to the right side of the frame. Shot 16 is a POV shot of the sleeping Dr. Peterson. The audience is now firmly ensconced in the mind of Ballantine, but they know very little of this character. What they do know, however, is unsettling—that he is a deeply disturbed man, with a razor, hovering over a sleeping woman. This shot is a variation of Hitchcock's suspense formula, with a psychological twist. We know that Hitchcockean suspense is predicated on the parceling out of knowledge diegetically (to the characters) and extra-diegetically (to the audience). The ideal suspense scenario involves having the audience know something crucial that the character doesn't know—the bomb under the table. In *Spellbound*—and later in *Psycho*—Hitchcock forges audience identification with a mysterious character; in addition, Hitchcock makes the audience and the character equally knowledgeable. We feel suspense and anxiety because we don't know who the menacing figure with the razor really is, nor do we know his motivation. The character of Ballantine is equally ignorant. Norman Bates is Ballantine tipped over into the psychotic state. Both have killed family members; both have lover-mother-savior figures; both are ignorant of their true natures and selves.

Shot 17 heightens the anxiety of the audience. Ballantine is presented in a medium low shot; he walks close to Dr. Peterson's bed. In his right hand is the razor held in an open position, its blade subtly shining from the light coming in from the windows. This is a beautifully composed shot, with Ballantine framed on either side by windows bathed in the light of early dawn. These windows are again cataphors. Their diaphanous curtains emit light, but one cannot see clearly through them. Outside, the world tries to shine its light into the dark room. The room, of course, is Ballantine's mind, now dominated by the figure of Dr. Peterson, who becomes a kind of mythic figure who will help lead Ballantine out of the labyrinth of his amnesia and guilt. This shot of Ballantine, in its lighting and camera angle, is similar to the shots of Crewe and Norman before they commence their violent acts against women. All three characters are lit with a chiaroscuro technique, using lighting from below that underscores their dark natures; the camera is below eye level. In *Spellbound*, though, Hitchcock has Ballantine walk past the sleeping Dr. Peterson, much to the relief of the audience.

The last four shots of this scene show bravura technique. If any shots demonstrate what Janet Leigh said about Hitchcock's aesthetic, it is these shots. In discussing with me how Hitchcock directed her in a scene, Leigh recalls that Hitchcock said, ". . . the only requirement I need is that you be where I need you to be for my camera." In shot 18, Hitchcock places his "absolute" camera at the bottom of the stairs. This position is actually a startling and daring shift, for one would expect the camera to be outside the door to the bedroom, because the previous shot had shown Ballantine walking through the door. In earlier shots in this scene, the cut between shots 12 and 13 shows the camera shift position from inside the bathroom to outside the bathroom with the camera positioned in the bedroom, just to the left of the bathroom door. This cut preserves a sense of contiguous space. However, shot 18 disorients the viewer because the camera is not outside the door where one would "expect" it to be; rather, it is at the bottom of the stairs.

The camera placement for shot 18 allows Hitchcock to follow Ballantine walking down the stairs in a seemingly somnambulant state. The camera is positioned at the bottom of the stairs, and it pans slightly to the left to follow the descent of Ballantine. He seems to be following a column of light that is reflected off the stairway wall. The lighting of this shot—in fact of the whole film—has a velvety, rich quality to it. The effect in this scene is stunning, particularly in these last four shots. By placing his camera at the bottom of the stairs, tilting upward, Hitchcock does several things at once without resorting to cutting, thus preserving the mise-en-scene. The first element is the dominating presence of Ballantine, who, because of the low angle, looms over the viewer in a threatening way. The bottom placement of the camera also allows Hitchcock, in one continuous take, to follow the slow, deliberate gait of Ballantine as he seems to float down the stairs in a dreamlike state. In fact, the shot has a pervasive feel of a dream, which is a key element in the psychoanalytical approach to therapy. The placement at the bottom of the stairs also allows Hitchcock to go from a long shot of Ballantine to an extreme close-up of his hand, with glinting razor in firm grasp. Hitchcock accomplishes this startling variation in image size by having Ballantine walk down the stairs, toward the camera, and then walk just in front of it. The light catches the hand and the razor, which suddenly emerge from the darkness at the left side of the frame. This surprising appearance of the menacing razor from the psychologically weighted left side is done subtly. Hitchcock holds the close-up of the razor for at least three beats before cutting to shot 19.

This shot is taken from the same angle as shot 18. But the camera has turned 90 degrees to the right, for a long shot of Dr. Brulov sitting behind his desk. The juxtaposition of razor and Dr. Brulov now adds an additional level of suspense. The object of Ballantine's seemingly murderous quest is not the mother figure of Constance but rather the father figure of Dr. Brulov. In Freud's Oedipus complex, the young boy eventually identifies with his father and resolves his rage and anger at the father by eventually identifying with him. The process of identification involves the young boy's fear of castration by the father, who has more potency than the young boy. The razor in Ballantine's hand thus has an ambiguous psychological meaning. The audience doesn't know it yet, but Ballantine is not a psychotic killer. His somnambulist fugue is the result of the ravages of a guilt complex over the accidental killing of his younger brother. This incident will be revealed only when his ambiguous relationship with Constance and Dr. Brulov is worked out and when Ballantine is able to retrieve the memory of Dr. Edwardes' death.

Shot 19 is an amazing piece of cinematography and a perfect example of pure cinema. Its length of one minute and fifteen seconds makes it the longest shot of the scene and involves a complicated "ballet" of movement. It begins with the camera still at the bottom of the stairs but now focused in a long shot on Dr. Brulov at his desk. Brulov gets up from his desk and walks toward Ballantine. As Brulov gets into medium-shot range, the camera pans left slowly with him as he walks in front of it, now in close-up range. As he passes in front of the camera, the light reflects from his coat, and the camera finishes its pan and settles again on Ballantine's hand clutching the razor. It is as if the light has been reflected off Brulov's coat and transferred to the razor. The movement of Brulov toward the camera increases the anxiety and suspense of the scene: we are not sure what Ballantine intends to do with the glowing razor. Brulov continues past the camera and walks into the depths of the frame. He enters a dark room, turns on the light, and immediately the frame takes on added dimension of depth. The audience's eyes are drawn away from the razor and into the room, where they are enticed into the very center of the frame by planes of light. The mise-en-scene in this part of the shot is amazing. The frame is divided in half. On the left is a close-up of the glowing hand and razor against the velvety black of Ballantine's pants. On the right side of the frame is the rectangular shape of the door, which also frames its own rectangular shape of the table and walls. In the very center of the frame, at its deepest point, is a window decorated with Colonial tie-back curtains. These shapes are in one sense "portals to the past" (using Gavin Elster's phrase from *Vertigo*). These are the doors that must be opened by Brulov and Peterson if they are to "cure" Ballantine and restore his past to him. The window itself is a cataphor for Ballantine's dilemma. The window with its tied-back curtains seems to resemble a theatrical space—better yet, a movie screen. The dilemma for Ballantine—and for us—is that the screen is blank.

Hitchcock holds this shot for at least four beats before Brulov comes back into the purview of the camera. He had "disappeared" into the room and now returns with a glass. He walks toward the camera and past it, in an almost exact reversal of the previous movement. He walks to his desk, and we are now back to the same view that began the scene. But this time, Dr. Brulov's back is turned to Ballantine and to us. He is preparing something for Ballantine to drink. He turns toward us and again walks toward the camera, duplicating his earlier movement. The camera again pans to the left as we see Brulov reach out with a glass of milk, its whiteness corresponding to the brightness of the razor blade, both objects now in the frame. Brulov is handing Ballantine a glass with the same whiteness that has caused Ballantine to panic in the first part of the scene. Shot 20 features a close-up of Ballantine's face, almost perfectly divided in half by the lighting. The left half of his face is in darkness, preserving the left side of the frame for madness; the right side is bathed in soft light. Ballantine's eyes are trance-like as he raises the glass to drink. The last shot of the scene is a startling POV shot seen through the glass as Ballantine raises it to drink. The rim of the glass momentarily blocks the audience's view of Brulov, and the glass itself distorts the image of the psychiatrist. When the glass is raised to a full horizontal level, we see Brulov through a tunnel of glass, and then the whiteness of the milk rises from the bottom of the frame to obliterate Brulov, who is seen also raising a glass to drink. The milk fills the frame, which is transformed into a brilliant white.

This scene is ingenious in its structure and meaning. It begins in blackness, with a slow fade to the dark room of Ballantine's mind. However, it ends in brilliant whiteness, the same color that has caused Ballantine's mysterious panic attacks. The dark-light contrast is also reflected in the close-up of Ballantine's face, divided into halves of darkness and light. Dr. Brulov the threatening father has become Dr. Brulov the healing father. His employment of a literal glass of whiteness will help Ballantine resolve the mysterious conflict of his past. His light side will triumph over his dark half. The last four shots of this scene, with their mise-en-scene structure, have a sense of resolution to them, emphasized by the formal elements of lighting, camera angles, and camera movements.

In analyzing this key scene in *Spellbound*, one can't help being reminded of the shower scene. Instead of the steady mise-en-scene of *Spellbound*'s key scene, with its sense of integral space, the shower scene's staccato editing fragments and explodes the space of the frame, suggesting Norman's splintered mental state. The dark face of the intruder in the shower is Ballantine's dark half overwhelming his light half; the razor, which is never raised to an attacking position, becomes the raised butcher knife. The gentle, calming horizontal movement of the fatherly Brulov as he moves back and forth to help Ballantine becomes the driving, vertical, and diagonal blows of the demented mother, Norma Bates. The soothing white milk with its calming sedative is transformed into the blood of Marion; Ballantine drinks the milk; Marion sheds her blood.

In the final two films that foreshadow the shower scene—*Dial M for Murder* (1954) and *The Wrong Man* (1956)—Hitchcock presents scenes of violence that grow out of marital discord and conflict. *Dial M for Murder* is about "an English marriage gone stale," as McGilligan describes it (468). Margot Wendice has had an affair, and her husband, Tony Wendice, plans to kill her to get her inheritance. There's also an element of sexual jealousy in Tony's plan. If the Wendice apartment were in New York, it would certainly have been one that L.B. Jeffreys would have peered into. Tony Wendice is actually a craftier, more sophisticated Lars Thorwald; he blackmails someone into killing Margot, but the plan backfires when Margot fights off her killer and stabs him to death.

The stabbing scene in *Dial M for Murder* takes place about halfway through the film. Up until this point, Hitchcock's usually fluid camera has been confined to a limited spatial range. Adapted from a stage play, the film has a theatrical feel to it, very much like *Rope*, another film adapted from a play. However, Hitchcock had planned one key scene in the film that would capitalize upon a technical innovation—3-D.

I believe it was the scenes of violence and mayhem that triggered Hitchcock's art-film and experimental impulses. As I have tried to show in these analyses, the human soul and psyche pushed to the extremes of sanity and passion were the creative spurs for Hitchcock. And these creative spurs can be vividly seen in the stabbing of the intruder in *Dial M for Murder*, a scene that Hitchcock hoped would demonstrate his technical virtuosity in the 3-D form. Hitchcock precedes the stabbing scene with a one-minute-long buildup that utilizes six shots to create suspense. He positions his camera outside the Wendice apartment in order to "open" the film up a bit. The audience knows from preceding scenes that the murder of Margot is to take place at 11:00 p.m., when Tony will call Margot to get her to the phone, where she will be strangled by Swann, the intruder, and to establish an alibi for himself. The six shots show Swann walking in shadows toward the Wendice apartment. We also see a shot of Margot asleep in her bed, a close-up of Swann's watch, and a long shot of the corridor outside the Wendice apartment. In these shots, Hitchcock employs mise-en-scene and montage to create suspense, allowing his camera multiple placements to link Margot's fate with Swann's progress toward her apartment. Hitchcock takes full advantage of the aesthetics of cross cutting and parallel editing to suggest two or three actions taking place at the same time but in different places, a feat that the theatrical space has difficulty accommodating.

The killing scene lasts six minutes and forty-two seconds and is composed of fifty-six shots, the majority of which take place in the Wendice apartment. Hitchcock intercuts shots of Tony at his club waiting to make the fateful 11:00 p.m. call that will cue the murderer. Realizing that his watch has stopped, Tony is late in making the call, but Swann has waited just long enough for the call to go through. Hitchcock includes an extreme close-up of Tony's finger dialing the fateful "M" and of the automatic switchboard handling the call. Earlier, Swann had entered the dark apartment and had positioned himself behind the curtain on the left side of the frame, Hitchcock again using that side of the frame for sinister characters. Shot 26 is the pivotal shot in the scene. In the previous shots, Tony awakens Margot and she leaves her brightly lit bedroom, and walks into the dark living room. In shot 26, when she answers the phone, Hitchcock positions the camera right in front of her in a medium shot. In keeping with his suspense formula, Hitchcock has shown the audience the threat—the intruder hiding behind the curtains in the shadow—but of course Margot has not seen the threat. The audience is now in possession of knowledge that creates anxiety and a feeling of helplessness.

Hitchcock's suspense formula relies on audience identification with the character through mise-en-scene and montage, particularly in POV shots. However, the suspense formula is much more complex than it seems at first glance. Not only does Hitchcock use POV shots for the protagonist, but he frequently employs the same technique for the antagonist. This is a bit of Hitchcockery: to have the audience find themselves in the shoes of the killer, whether the killer is Bruno Anthony, Lars Thorwald, Uncle Charlie, Norma Bates, or the intruder, Swann. Hitchcock uses the POV technique to divide the audience against itself and thus to increase its uneasiness. In the shots preceding the stabbing scene, Hitchcock uses two POV shots to put the audience into the character of Swann. When the camera circles Margot in shot 26, it subtly assumes the POV of Swann, Hitchcock accomplishing this subversive move without resorting to a cut. Because we have seen Margot in a medium shot just before the camera begins its movement, we realize just how vulnerable she is, dressed in her filmy nightgown. This shot is reminiscent of *Rear Window*, with Mrs. Thorwald bedridden and dressed in a nightgown. Six years later, Hitchcock would present his most vulnerable character, Marion Crane, naked in a shower. The vulnerability of these characters depends upon a dual identification, with the character herself but also with the stalking killer. Perhaps it was Hitchcock's Catholic upbringing that prompted him to blend in the audience's mind the "innocence" of the victim with the guilt of the perpetrator. We are all amalgams of innocence and guilt, light and dark, unfallen and fallen. This amalgam is trenchantly conveyed at the end of shot 26, when Hitchcock brings his camera to the end of the very slow, circular tracking shot. We are now behind Margot, and she has gone from a medium shot with soft lighting emphasizing her vulnerability to a medium shot of her back, her whole figure in shadow outlined with soft lighting. At the bottom of the screen, we see the tightly pulled scarf rise, and we realize that we are now in the shoes of Swann, ready to strangle Margot.

The next shots show the actual killing. There are sixteen shots in all, beginning with a medium shot of Margot, camera positioned in front of her, with her attacker right behind her, scarf raised. This shot intensifies the audience's sense of suspense by placing both characters in the same frame and thereby multiplying the anxiety of the audience, who have just been put into the shoes of Swann but are now face to face with the victim. The style of the attack shifts from mise-en-scene to montage, in keeping with Hitchcock's practice of following a suspenseful buildup, done in mise-en-scene style, with a scene of terror, done in montage style. Hitchcock speeds up the tempo of the shots and fragments the space by moving his camera from the front to the side as Margot is attacked. Then the camera shifts position several times to show various angles of the struggle, creating the vortex characteristic of Hitchcock's scenes of violence. Several times we see the attacker from Margot's POV when she falls to the floor after she has stabbed her attacker with a pair of scissors. The last shot of the struggle is a shocking close-up, with the camera positioned at the floor, capturing the body of Swann falling on the scissors, his weight forcing them even deeper into his back.

The killing scene in *Dial M for Murder* is the only element of this rather uninspired film to demonstrate Hitchcock's conception of pure cinema. The scene looks forward to the shower scene of *Psycho* in the way it uses suspense and terror to work their power on the psychology of the audience. By dividing viewers against themselves, as it were, Hitchcock generates suspense and creates a sense of helplessness and confusion in the audience. Hitchcock accomplishes this complex process in both the narrative and style of the film. The plot of *Dial M for Murder* features an attractive cad, Tony Wendice, who employs a surrogate killer to dispatch his unfaithful wife. Most of the plot centers upon Tony, who cleverly manipulates the botched murder to make it appear that Margot is the perpetrator. Earlier, Tony has blackmailed Swann, who agrees to murder Margot. Swann stalks her, in a sense, in her own apartment, just as in a different but related manner, Bruno stalks and kills Miriam, Bruno also acting as a surrogate killer for Guy (who, coincidentally, is a tennis player, like Tony Wendice). As I showed earlier in my chapter on mise-en-scene, Bruno becomes a double surrogate—for Guy, but also for the audience, who becomes implicated in murder with him via the mise-en-scene of the film. Thus, when the violence occurs in the film, the audience, having experienced suspense via identification, now experiences terror as killer and victim—both part of the audience's psychology—clash. In the shower scene, when Norma Bates kills Marion Crane, she is acting in a sense as surrogate for Norman. The audience has been brought into Marion's world via the mise-en-scene and montage of the film. Then, in the Bates Motel scene, Hitchcock works his pure cinema magic to shift POV to Norman. The true genius of *Psycho* is that Hitchcock seems to be using the trio of perpetrator, surrogate, and victim of *Dial M for Murder* and *Strangers on a Train*, but is in reality collapsing perpetrator and surrogate into one mysterious figure.

There's a scene in *The Wrong Man* that bears repeated viewings, and this repetition reveals some remarkable anticipations of the structure, themes, and techniques of *Psycho*, particularly the shower scene. Like the other scenes we've examined, this one takes place about halfway into the film, when Rose reveals to Manny the true depths of her descent into madness. Manny has entered Rose's room after his usual late arrival home from work. This scene is a doubling of an earlier scene, at the beginning of the film, before Manny has been accused of a crime. Hitchcock uses this doubling to show just how much Rose has surrendered to paranoid delusions. Even in the earlier scene, though, Rose exhibits a fearfulness and anxiety that seem to be symptoms of a potentially more serious mental problem. The second bedroom scene is 4:30 seconds long and contains forty shots. The camera is in a fourth-wall position for most of the scene. The lighting is expressionistic, with dark, ominous shadows creating a sense of claustrophobia. Large shadows of both Manny and Rose are cast against the walls of the rooms. The characters' faces are lit with harshly contrasting tones of black and white. Hitchcock is using pure cinema to underscore the duality that is at the heart of the film. Manny's dark emanation has been committing crimes that Manny himself has been accused of; Rose's descent into madness has seemed to create a dark dopplegänger. The family is in crisis and is figuratively being torn in two.

The evil that enters the lives of individuals and families in Hitchcock's films sometimes comes in the form of an actual character, like Uncle Charlie or Bruno. However, sometimes evil comes in the form of childhood trauma, as in *Spellbound* and *Psycho*; or evil can enter haphazardly, through mistaken identity, as in *The Wrong Man* and *North by Northwest*. Whatever the etiology of the evil, it manifests itself as a palpable presence in the films, sometimes constructed through the aesthetics of pure cinema.

The Wrong Man—and *Spellbound* before it—prefigures *Psycho* in the portrayal of madness as an enclosed place symbolizing a damaged or deranged mind. In both *The Wrong Man* and *Psycho*, the characters' madness is embedded in the actual set design, lighting, and camera placement of the scene. Rose's claustrophobic bedroom, with its dark, frightening shapes (the characters' shadows) and its oppressive atmosphere, emblemizes her madness. Her statement to Manny about how she feels trapped reminds us of Norman's statements to Marion ("We're all in our private traps") in the dark, foreboding parlor of the motel:

> Don't you see, it doesn't do any good to care. No matter what you do, they've got it fixed so that it goes against you. No matter how innocent you are or how hard you try, they'll find you guilty. Well we're not going to play into their hands anymore. You're not going out . . . we're going to lock the doors and stay in the house. We'll lock them out and keep them out.

Rose demonstrates the depths of her madness in a very brief series of shots that foreshadow the montage technique of the shower scene. Hitchcock has created the stifling, frightening, enclosing space of madness in Rose's bedroom. Now he introduces a sudden, lightning-like explosion of violence as Rose unexpectedly attacks Manny with a hairbrush. The attack takes place in fewer than ten seconds, and it contains ten staccato shots, all taken from different angles, with an odd, almost dreamlike shot of a broken mirror, with Manny's face split in half. One shot pictures Rose with the hairbrush raised in an attacking position.

The way this scene is photographed and edited, I believe, is a key to understanding Hitchcock's intent in the shower scene in *Psycho*. In both films, the sudden, furious, vortex-like outburst of violence is the symbolic manifestation of madness. The knife rending Marion's flesh is very much like the breaking of the mirror in *The Wrong Man*: both actions destroy our sense of the rationalism and order of life. In *The Wrong Man*, it is the rationalist, classical sense that art mirrors life by making it understandable and orderly (hence the cracked mirror), and in *Psycho*, it is the humanistic idea of the sacredness and beauty of the human body.

The Wrong Man—with its stark, expressionistic black-and-white cinematography, its enclosed, claustrophobic spaces, and its portrayal of dark, irrational forces beneath the civilized surfaces of modern life—is a chilling prelude to *Psycho*.

given to author by Terry Williams

Terry Williams, assistant to *Psycho* editor George Tomasini

CHAPTER 10

Terry Williams

Terry Williams has had a long career *as a film editor. His credits include* Family Plot *(1975),* Airport *(1975 and 1977), and many others. Getting to work on* Psycho *brought Terry into the "Hitchcock Family," a group of people Hitchcock worked with over and over again. Like Danny Greene, Terry received no screen credit on* Psycho. *He lives with his wife Merlene in Laguna Hills, California.*

P: What was your first editing job?

T: I finished up a picture for Howard Hawks. I was dealing with the eight-year problem. To become a full-fledged editor you had to work for eight years. And the editor, Stuart Gilmore, had a George Roy Hill picture to do in New York, so he left and then I took over for him and finished the picture. My first editor credit was a Doris Day, Rock Hudson comedy, *Send Me No Flowers*.

P: So, when you got on *Psycho*, where were you in your career?

T: I had been an assistant editor for around five years. I was working as an assistant on *To Kill a Mockingbird* and got taken off that and put on *Psycho* as George Tomasini's assistant.

P: When you were working on *Psycho*, do you remember anything about cutting the shower scene?

T: I do and I don't. For instance, the brouhaha that's going on about Saul Bass. I mean Saul was up in the room maybe a day or two. He came up one time to ask me to look for some stock sky background for the *Psycho* house. As you know, we had those nice blue California days, and so I went to the library and looked up a few cloudy, dark backgrounds and brought them in. I ran them past Bass, and he said, "That's fine. Any one of those will do." So we superimposed them over the house. And, there were a lot of things like that. That was a lot of pictures ago.

P: Were you there on the set? Did you see any of the shooting?

T: No, they pretty much closed the set because of the nudity. That was a big deal in those days.

P: How did you hear about it? Did you just hear that you just couldn't go down on the set?

T: I don't remember.

P: Because Janet Leigh insists that there was no nude woman there. You probably know all about that. You know today if they ran the credits, your name would be in the credits. But I don't think your name is in the credits.

T: No.

P: But everyone who has something to do with the film is now in the credits. I once thought I'd write a book about credits because I think the way credits have evolved over the years is an interesting study of how film has changed. The political and economic structures of the industry are reflected in the credits. While before, you just had a few front credits, beginning credits, now you have the top of the line people and the bottom of the line.

T: You want to do a story? I'll tell you a story. Define producer.

P: I don't know if I can.

T: Nobody knows. Turn on a TV show and you see six, seven producers on the damn thing. And then the associate producers.

P: I've talked with producers when I've brought my film students to Hollywood, and whenever I ask them what exactly a producer does, I usually never could get a consistent or straight answer.

T: I did a number of things with the producers George Schenck and Frank Cardea. Schenck's father was invited, in his golden years, to say something to the Producers Guild. He said, "What the hell have you people done to the producer credit? Who is the producer?"

P: One time my students and I met with one of Spielberg's producers, Gerry Molen, and he said, "The producer is the guy who gets the ship built. And the director is the guy who is the captain of the ship who takes it from here to there, who steers. But the real producer is the one who gets the ship made. Once the ship is made, the director and his crew take it from one place to another." I thought that was a good metaphor for what kind of producer Gerry Molen is. This is a real producer, not some guy who is somebody's agent who maybe put the deal together.

T: I don't think during the whole time I was an assistant we ever had a film that had more than one credited producer. And those producers were, believe me, producers! They were people who just knew this business and came up through the ranks somehow. Hitchcock was the producer on *Psycho*.

P: His goal was to have creative and economic control, and he was able to do that with *Psycho*. He was able to be relatively independent in that film especially because Paramount decided they didn't want to finance the thing when they looked at the script and the story. They said, "This is too controversial; we don't want to be associated with it." So, Hitchcock said, "Okay, I'll put up my own money." This was the smartest move any director ever made! He put up the eight hundred thousand and it grossed domestic $9.2 million. How did you cut the credit sequences?

T: Cutting the credits, you know it is always the last dog hung. You are trying to cut the negative and you've got a release date. Or you have an air date in case of television. And the legal department is out there twiddling their thumbs. One of my duties when I had any time was to bug the legal department and try and get the damn credits done. If you start making prints and a lawyer gets on it and says, "Wait a minute, this guy is main title size and my actor is not, "then we have to go back. That is fine unless you have seventy prints. Then it becomes a big expensive number to do. And now I think it is even more complicated with so many names in the credits. Back then it wasn't quite as complicated because you had front credits and no back credits.

P: I'd like to talk about your working on *Psycho*, the shower scene, when [George] Tomasini was the editor. Did you ever cut a scene without his editorial supervision?

T: Let's clear this up. I did not cut; I was an assistant. Back then you started out as apprentice; then you became an assistant, and eventually—but not always—an editor.

P: Tell me what you did, because I don't know if people understand what an assistant did.

T: First off, one of your major jobs was to put the dailies together, getting everything together for the editor, breaking the film down into small rolls and putting them up in sequential order for him.

P: You had a list of what they shot that you'd match. Do you remember doing anything with the shower scene? Do you remember working with that footage and putting it together in a way that Tomasini wanted it put together? Do you remember what he said to you about it?

T: I normally have a lot of paperwork on a picture, but they were very secretive. They collected all of your scripts. I had to fight to get a script on *Psycho*. I was getting all the process work, and the cars, and I had to arrange all the process plates for all that stuff. I was on well before Tomasini was on the station. And that was when I said, "Where is my script?" I said to Hitchcock's personal assistant, Peggy Robertson, "Tell them I've got to know what I've got and what it's for." Peggy was very secretive and in total control of everything. I think I went to Herbie Coleman, the associate producer, and he said, "Of course. How's he going to work without a script?"

P: Did you ever get a copy of the script? Because Hilton Green still has his copy. He found it in a box, and he didn't ever remember he had it.

T: Oh yeah, I got a copy, but I don't know what happened to it. I do remember getting the script and making notes on what I would need. And when I talked to Peggy Robertson, I told her I thought it was a marvelous script. But she said, "Oh, it's just a filler. It's not a biggy like *North by Northwest*." What did she know? It became Hitchcock's most profitable movie.

P: Who was involved in viewing the dailies? Hitchcock would have been in the dailies. The editor would be there?

T: Yeah.

P: Would you ever be there?

T: Oh, sure.

P: Do you remember looking at the shower scene?

T: I don't remember a lot, but I do remember being a virile young man looking at Janet Leigh and her stand-in thinking, "WOW!"

P: Did the shower scene material look any different than any other scene that had been cut that particular way or shot that way?

T: I had never seen anything like that in a major picture. The nudity, to begin with and, secondly, the stabbing. It was a whole different thing.

P: Did it mystify you as to how it would be put together?

T: No, I thought it would be pretty simple if you had the storyboards. I don't think you could go too far off. I didn't even have to have a script or anything.

P: You knew just how to cut it.

T: Exactly. You have a film sense and you know just how to cut that.

P: What did you edit on?

T: The Moviola, the old green machine. And you know you cut with scissors. Nothing was spliced at the time the cut was made. The cuts were clipped together and put on a shelf. Later, the assistant would hot splice a reel together in the splicing room. A frame would be lost between each cut. You made the hot splice and then took looping ink and painted the frame out. You made a black frame. It wasn't like slapping a scene together with clear tape. Editors would scissor cut the film, put it on the rack, and let it cook for a while. In other words, don't splice it. Then when you run it later, your intentions will show on the screen.

P: Did Hitchcock come into the cutting room?

T: It was hard to get a director to come up and look at a clip on a Moviola. Moreover, the old-time editors like Tomasini didn't want a director to spend any significant amount of time in the cutting room. However, I recall one time, Hitchcock coming to the cutting room to show his wife, Alma, his synchronizer. Alma Hitchcock had been a negative cutter and editor in England. She just thought it was fascinating that we could take a magnetic tape that you couldn't see any striations on, and run it through this machine and hear dialogue. Alma told us about a time that went back to the '20s in London when she was a negative cutter. The director would come up to negative cutting, and then Alma and the director would do a majority of cutting in the negative form. Certainly, things weren't as complex as they are now. But I guess it went on and on. No work print. No machines to help. Just hand pulling the negative. Alma was amazed at some of the "high tech" things that we had.

P: When you were showing dailies, would Hitchcock see the whole scene put together in one sitting? Would he see parts of it? It took seven days to shoot the shower scene. So he would be seeing bits and pieces of stuff that was shot that day. And sometimes they would shoot some bathroom stuff and some other stuff the same day. So I'm wondering if he ever did see just that sequence with Tomasini. Do you remember cutting it in terms of a sequence, or wouldn't you do that?

T: I must admit I don't remember, but I do remember that sequence. My God we had I've forgotten how much coverage. It seems to me we had, like, over seventy shots. They weren't really setups; they said setups but they weren't. They were probably takes. There were an awful lot of shots. There was just a lot of coverage.

P: Hitchcock said there were seventy-eight camera setups. And I think that might have been seventy-eight storyboards that Bass had drawn.

T: That sounds familiar.

P: Did you ever see the storyboards?

T: Oh yeah. I saw them, but I don't remember them at all. It was nothing new to see a storyboard. I am quite sure we didn't have storyboards for the whole film. I now remember a specific number: it seems to me like it was fifty-two cuts and thirty-eight feet.

P: Fifty-two cuts and thirty-eight feet.

T: Flash cutting. We had never seen much of that before. It became the in-thing to do in the 1960s. And one of those cuts ran a long, long way, the pan, the thing that dissolved into the eye. I think I made that a twelve-foot dissolve. The average lap dissolve was four to six feet at most.

P: That is the most brilliant dissolve in any film I've ever seen.

T: It was vivid.

P: Absolutely. Who would have thought to cut from the swirling water going down the drain to the eye? You know you saw that same circular shape in *Vertigo*, in the swirl of the hair, the eyeball in the beginning, then the circling as Scotty goes down the hill following Madeline. That circular shape gets picked up in *Psycho*, the eyeball looking in the Peeping Tom scene and then the swirling water going clockwise and then the frame moves counterclockwise. It's very complicated.

T: Let me tell you a story. I remember sitting with Hitch and Tomasini in the theater. I guess Peggy Robertson was probably there. He had shot the eye and the pull back.

P: Yes.

T: They had blood running down from Marion's mouth. It bubbled somehow and it bubbled right to the lens. We all thought this was pretty gruesome. Hitch looked at George and said, "We can't do that to them, can we, George?"

P: So that ended on the cutting room floor?

T: That was a no sell. But that was pretty wild. Did you ever hear the stories that this was shot in color? A lot of people have said that it was shot in color, and it was too gory. That is bullshit.

P: One critic said that Hitchcock brought in a German camera crew to shoot that scene.

T: He used a TV crew. He had a very fine camera crew.

P: Yeah, Jack Russell. He had done a lot of features.

T: He was a great guy. Oh, he used to aggravate Hitch because he would come into dailies, and we always ran them at lunchtime. Well, Jack was going to have his lunch come hell or high water. So, Jack would get the newspaper in there and read it. And then he'd watch and he would see one or two setups and then he would get up and he would leave. He knew what it was going to look like, but he wanted to make sure the lab did one of them correctly and then they were all going to be right. He would check the overall lighting, and he would see if the timing was correct.

P: Would Hitchcock want him to stay?

T: He never asked him to stay, but it just aggravated him.

P: He was not one to confront people.

T: Well . . . no, he just fired them usually. Speaking of firing, I remember I had a seniority problem with this lifer assistant editor who was also a shop steward. We had all these boxes of reprints, and they needed to be coded. You know you need to get each slate out and match it to a trim that had already been cut and then code it. Well, he kept putting it off and putting it off. And then eventually I had a rack of all these things I had saved, like the shower scene from *Psycho*. I had the whole magillah, and I had some of the funny blows that people make while they are in the midst of the scene. And this son-of-a-bitch assistant chucked the reprints because he didn't want to do the work of coding them.

P: He threw away all the outtakes of the shower scene?

T: Threw them out.

P: What a loss!

T: When you discard film, the junk film is picked up and taken to the lab where they strip the emulsion and remove the valuable silver nitrate.

P: So all that stuff is gone?

T: I could have killed this little bastard. However, all I did was to fire him. Now he is dead, and I shouldn't talk about that.

P: Do you remember what you thought the first time you saw the film put together?

T: This is going to make more money than *North by Northwest.*

P: Did Hitch have a showing for the cast?

T: We had a showing for cast and crew. This is one of the most dramatic screenings I had ever been to. I don't know why, but I was handling the volume control, just in case something went wrong. If you have a theater full of people, you have to crank the gain up because the bodies will absorb the sound. So, I just was there and when Bernard Herrmann's score hit, Jesus, there were grownup people, cast people that had been on the stage when that stuff had been shot, up and screeching.

P: The shower scene happens so fast. You know it is the one that shocks you and sets you up for all the other stuff. When Mother comes out in that bird's-eye shot and stabs Arbogast at the top of the steps, that has been prepared for by the shower scene. It makes everything else possible. Do you remember how you reacted when you first saw it?

T: I probably ran it before anybody. I spliced it. I had a Bell and Howell hot splicer, foot operated. So the minute it was done I ran it through my Moviola, and I said, "God, George, take a look at this!"

P: So, you were probably one of the first to see it.

T: Could well have been. It scared the shit out of me! Bernard Herrmann used fifty-seven strings—no percussion, no woodwinds, no brass, just strings. My God. Scared me at Paramount the first time I heard it, just watching the orchestra.

P: Where you there when they were scoring?

T: I was there for a very short time, until Benny Herrmann threw his baton at one of the fiddle players. I thought it was time to leave. We were over at Paramount where they scored it.

P: Was he temperamental?

T: Oh yeah, but a nice little guy.

P: He threw his baton?

T: George Tomasini and I were there, and George said, "I think we best go over to Nicodel's and have a couple drinks."

P: I'm sure you're aware of the censorship problem the film faced.

T: Let me tell you a little story about that. We were having a screening for Luigi Luraschi, who was the Production Code liaison at Paramount. After he saw the shower scene, he said we had to get rid of the nudity. Hitch said, "That is a tremendous compliment to my directorial skills. There really is no nudity." But Luigi insisted that there was a bare breast in one shot. Remember that the stuff we were showing Luigi had been hot spliced together, and there were many cuts in a very small amount of film. Earlier, I had told Charlie Miller, the projectionist, that if we asked for a rerun of the scene, he not back it up. You can see a lot clearer when you are backing up because there's no sound interrupting your thoughts and you don't have the action of the sequence. So you just look for tits or whatever you are looking for. In addition, half the time it doesn't back up at sound speed; it is going through a little bit slower with no sound, so in a sense it is easier to see little things. So, Luigi wanted us to run that scene again. So I said, "Charlie, would you rewind it and run it again." Of course, he started backing it up. I charged out of there like a bull to stop that goddamn idiot. When I get back down, I said to Luigi, "This thing has so many cuts in it that the machine tears stuff when you are backing it up." Finally, Charlie got the thing rewound and put it back on the machine and ran it again. Luigi said to Hitchcock, "Oh my God, you are right." The scene happens so fast you aren't really sure what the hell you're seeing.

P: So thanks to you, Hitchcock got away with it.

T: What I will tell you, though, is that Hitchcock, after Luigi had passed it to go, had George Tomasini drop a pair of cuts. I don't remember exactly what they were. I think the cuts were of bare breasts, in soft focus. He took these out on his own.

P: I know he took out the overhead shot of Marion Crane slumped across the bathroom wall. It was a clear shot of her buttocks. In his "remake" of *Psycho*, Gus Van Sant inserts that shot in his version of the shower scene. What do you think you learned about cutting working for Tomasini and Hitchcock?

T: I never cut loosely and I cut fast. George was a very fast cutter, and Hitch planned everything out very well. And of course, he didn't provide the editor with a lot of takes. We would have only about a reel and a half on a big day. Tomasini knew what Hitch liked and wanted. Things were storyboarded and planned very carefully in the shooting. I don't mean to say that we "camera-cut," but it was usually obvious what was editorially necessary. I do remember, though, that one day we had about six full reels of dailies. And when I'm syncing the dailies, George comes over and says, "God, the old man got lost." I said, "What do you mean?" He says, "Look at all that film you've got." He meant that Hitch got lost and covered everything. Well, we got into the projection room and he really had covered everything. He made the error of having three people in a pair of two shots so that the middle person would jump screen. In other words, the character would be on the far right and you would cut, and he would jump left. We were running all these dailies and finally it's over and Hitch is totally silent. Then he says, "Well that's all self-explanatory, George." And everybody just laughed out loud.

P: How important has *Psycho* been to your career?

T: It was certainly a great credit to have on my résumé. It's a film that gives you a special distinction. In addition, the opportunity to work on *Psycho* brought me into the Hitchcock "family," a group of people Hitchcock came to know and chose to work with over and over again.

CHAPTER 11

The Culmination of Suspense and Terror

The Shower Scene

Note:

The sad irony of this chapter is that just as I started to write it—having delayed and procrastinated because I knew it was the keystone chapter—Janet Leigh died. I was filled with sorrow as I thought of the passing of an icon and of the thinning ranks of those who actually were in or worked on the film. I knew Janet Leigh both in person and in celluloid. My personal connection went back to June 2002, when I spent the afternoon in her beautiful home—the home where she died on October 3, 2004—talking with her about the shower scene and about working with "Mr. Hitchcock," as she always called him. My research assistant, Jim Dunn, and I had driven up the increasingly narrow, extremely steep road high atop the hills surrounding Benedict Canyon in Beverly Hills to arrive at her home, where we were greeted by her assistant, Kristi Kittendorf, and by her friendly housekeeper. We sat in her living room and talked casually about Psycho, *the film she is most proud of. Her answers to my questions and her occasional digressions were pointed and often feisty. However, she was always polite and gracious, and she even laughed when I asked upon meeting her, "Do I bow down or just shake your hand?" She was clearly somewhat suspicious of scholars and critics who kept returning to the film with new and often eccentric perspectives, including my own. But, if it hadn't been for Janet Leigh agreeing to meet with me, the book as it is now written would not have materialized. Her agreement to an interview led to others; her participation in the book was a kind of imprimatur. I will always be grateful to Janet Leigh.*

My celluloid relationship with Ms. Leigh was quite different, however. I had watched her undressing and dressing; I had seen her, in the midst of a very unhappy relationship, have a tryst in a hot hotel room in Phoenix one Friday afternoon, December 11, at 2:43. I had also seen her steal $40,000, and I had rooted for her, sympathized with her, colluded with her, allied *myself with her. I had taken the plunge with her as she absconded with the money, driving out of Phoenix. To my horror, "we" were spotted by her boss George Lowrey, and "we" were investigated by a suspicious, hostile, and enigmatic highway patrolman. We had driven together in a trade-in secured from California Charlie, and we had sought refuge from the dark and rain in an out-of-the-way motel—The Bates Motel—just fifteen miles from our final destination—Fairvale. I was sixteen when I first saw Janet Leigh die in the shower of Cabin 1 at the Bates Motel. Since that day in 1960, I had seen Janet Leigh as Marion Crane die over and over and over again. In fact, I had never seen one person die so many times. I came to believe that Janet Leigh would never really die, that the reel would always be reversed, and her blood would flow back into her body, her wounds would magically heal, she would put her clothes back on and drive backwards to the beginning of the film and start all over again. The magic of the movies is that I can continue to see Janet Leigh die, but the reality of life is that I will never again sit with her in her living room or run into her at the Polo Lounge.*

It's no exaggeration to say that the shower scene is *the* most analyzed, discussed, and alluded-to scene in film history. Its major images and sounds have become iconic and instantly recognizable. The reasons for the scene's significance are manifold. Technically, the scene is a tour de force; it displays virtuoso montage style. Cinematically, the scene breaks new ground in depicting—and fusing—violence and sexuality in the cinema. Socially, the scene challenges and violates taboos about female nudity, limits of violent behavior, and norms of privacy, hygiene, and excretory function (bathrooms, showers, toilet bowls). Culturally, the scene symbolizes the growing acceptance of explicitness in popular culture—explicitness in language, sexuality, and violence. Intellectually, the scene introduces into public discourse in the most vivid way the sexual theories of Freud and Krafft-Ebing.

The influence of the scene and of the film that contained it is pervasive. First, it provided the *coup de grace* to the already vitiated Production Code, and thus, second, it introduced to the screen (along with other scenes in the film) a much more frank representation of formerly taboo subjects and depictions, such as nudity, bathroom paraphernalia, including the infamous toilet bowl, and, by implication, illicit sex, incest, and necrophilia. Third, as a result of its explicitness, it ushered in a new era of violence in the cinema and concomitantly earned the film the dubious distinction of being the first slasher/horror film. Hitchcock called it "the first shocker I've ever made" (Rebello 199). In fact, the shower scene (and thus the film) became a template for the renaissance of horror films in the late 1970s. Fourth, it helped to create the present exhibition practice of advertising films with set-starting times and with promotional gimmickry. For example, no one was allowed to be seated once the film had begun (enforced by Pinkerton guards), and some theaters stationed ambulances near their entrances for patrons who fainted or suffered trauma because of the film (and we know which scene would cause those reactions!). Finally, the shower scene, and the film that contained it, would help solidify the director as a superstar, as an icon of popular culture, a trend that had been initiated five years earlier with the production of the TV series *Alfred Hitchcock Presents*. It is no coincidence that the camera crew that developed around this series, under the lead of cinematographer Jack Russell, would be used in *Psycho* rather than the Robert Burks team that Hitchcock had used in the other great films from the 1950s. One wonders whether, without the shower scene, *Psycho* would have been named the number one suspense film by the American Film Institute in its year 2000 survey of the one hundred most suspenseful films of all time ("*Psycho* tops!"). An auxiliary note to the promotion of the film is the lengthy trailer-documentary, a delightful introduction to the film structured upon a travelogue/tour of the *Psycho* mansion, led by Hitchcock himself. This promotional piece can be seen as the forerunner of the ubiquitous documentaries that are included in many DVD's.

Naturally, such an important moment in film history has attracted to itself myths, distortions, fabrications, and its own versions of cinematic "urban legends." Hitchcock himself helped to create some of these myths and distortions. For example, he says in one interview, "It's like the bathroom scene in *Psycho*. There it's purely illusionary—the knife never touches the body at any time. It's composed of 78 pieces of film that go through in 45 seconds" (Gottlieb, *Alfred Hitchcock Interviews* 107). In another interview, Hitchcock says the scene lasts "about a minute and a half, that's all" (*Hitchcock on Hitchcock*, 288). In his discussion with Truffaut, Hitchcock claims that he killed off the star "in the first third of the film" (29). As I shall show presently, almost all these details are incorrect.

Comments by members of the cast and crew aggravate additional confusion about the scene. In my interview with Hilton Green, the assistant director of *Psycho*, I asked him whether there is a shot that shows the knife penetrating the flesh. And Green answered, "We never did a thing like that. And that was before the computer things where you could do things like that. It was way before that. We never did a dummy, or never did anything where it penetrated." Janet Leigh claims on *Psycho* that all the shots in the final version of the shower scene were of her, not of the nude stand-in, Marli Renfro (Leigh 75). But Hitchcock says in several different interviews that many of the shower scene shots utilized the nude model. Hitchcock: "I used . . . a naked model who stood in for Janet Leigh. We only showed Miss Leigh's hands, shoulders, and head. All the rest was the stand-in" (Truffaut 277). Perhaps the most famous "myth" about the scene was Saul Bass's assertion that he himself had directed the shower scene, a claim that Hitchcock and almost everyone who worked on the film contested. Two of the most improbable urban legends are that a German crew had shot the shower scene—accounting for its Eisensteinan montage—and that the whole film had been shot in color and that the decision had been made that the blood of the shower scene was too grisly for the audience (Rebello 106).

Some of these conflicting accounts are due to what Rebello calls "the patina of legend." He continues, "As is often the case with classic movie scenes, the precise details of the shooting of the shower sequence have been obscured by time, selective memory, ego, the haze of legend, and controversy" (106). An example of the "haze of legend" is the belief that Hitchcock used cold water in the shower scene to get Janet Leigh in the correct frame of mind. In our interview, Janet Leigh insisted that the water was warm:

P: Going back to that shower scene, I've always heard that to get more shock out of you, they used cold water.

J: That's not true . . . That's the spiel they do on the Universal tour. When they go along and they see the *Psycho* house and they say, "He turned on the cold water!" I was on the tour one day with my children, and I yelled out, "Not true!"

Yet there's also perception itself, which is notoriously subjective. For example, during my interview with Terry Williams, who was George Tomasini's assistant editor, we decided to look at the shower scene so that he could analyze it for me. As my research assistant, Jim Dunn, and I sat in the living room of the Williams' home in Laguna Beach, we watched the shower scene several times with Terry and his wife, Merlene. When we paused the DVD at the shot where the tip of the knife clearly pierces Marion's belly below the navel, both Jim and I said, "See, there it is. It's clear as day." But Terry and Merlene said they weren't sure the knife really was touching the flesh!

Despite the unreliability of individual perception, we do have the film itself. Yet just exactly what is the ur-*Psycho* not such an easy question to answer. Modern technology has now allowed the viewer unprecedented access to the masterworks of the cinema, including *Psycho*. For this study, I viewed the laser disc, a VHS prerecorded version, a VHS version I taped from a broadcast twenty years ago, and finally the Universal DVD version, which includes the original docu-trailer, as well as a valuable documentary on the production of the film. I consulted these different formats because I was convinced that the shower scene was subtly different in the various copies. I had noticed major variations in the extant copies of Eisenstein's famous "Odessa Steps" sequence, from *The Battleship Potemkin*, and I was sure I had seen similar variations in the different versions of the shower scene. In his quirky *A Long Hard Look at Psycho*, Raymond Durgnat claims, "Academic colleagues assure me that in some prints of the film, one shower murder scene shot exposes Marion's breasts" (14). After viewing the various versions several times, I concluded that there were some very minor differences, mainly in the controversial "knife cutting the flesh" shot. We know that Hitchcock insisted that he hadn't created such a shot. He says in an interview, "*Psycho* is probably one of the most cinematic pictures I've ever made. Because there you had montage in the bathtub killing where the whole thing is purely an illusion. No knife ever touched any woman's body in that scene" (Gottlieb, *Hitchcock on Hitchcock* 288). We know that Hitchcock is wrong in this statement. Clearly, there is a brief shot of the knife entering the flesh, although this shot was not in the version I taped from the air. The shot is clearly evident in Richard Anobile's *Alfred Hitchcock's Psycho* in a blow-up of a frame from the shower scene that clearly shows the tip of the knife entering the flesh, with a clearly evident (and chilling) slit of the flesh (101). Now it must be pointed out that this shot is only several frames long and therefore registers upon the viewer's mind in an almost subliminal way, hence, perhaps, accounting for the conflicting perceptions of the scene.

We know that *Psycho* was censored in its various presentations. In fact, while researching the Hitchcock collection at the Margaret Herrick Library of the Academy of Motion Picture Arts and Sciences, I came across a memo dated November 29, 1960, from Paramount Studio's Milt Goldstein confirming a telephone conversation he had with Hitchcock about *Psycho*. In this memo, Goldstein reports the result of his conversation with Hitchcock about the possibilities of foreign countries censoring *Psycho*. Hitchcock, according to Goldstein, left the censoring of the movie up to the discretion of Goldstein's department. Hitchcock insisted, though, that if cuts were made, the impact of the movie must not be compromised. In another Paramount memo, this one dated November 24, 1959, Luigi Luraschi, Paramount's liaison to the Production Code Administration Office, outlines the objections raised by the Code to scripted scenes in the film. Luraschi requests that special care should be taken in the photographing and editing of the stabbing scenes to forestall possible cuts by foreign distributors (Special Collections).

So, the question is, what is the "ur" shower scene? My claim is that it's contained in the 1998 DVD release by Universal Home Video, although the blurb on the box of this DVD perpetuates several of the myths about the scene: "Seventy camera setups for the forty-five seconds of this now famous footage—and not an actual bare breast or plunging knife is to be found in the final cut, just illusion through montage." As I shall point out, there's not much accuracy in this statement or, for that matter, in many of the other statements about details of the scene.

Let's start with the most contradictory pronouncements about the scene: opinions about the length of the scene and the number of shots that comprise it. Watching the Universal DVD, I sat with a timer and notebook, and I used the slow-motion setting for shot tabulation. The actual length of the scene depends upon one's definition of the scene itself. To my thinking, the shower scene does *not* begin with "mother" attacking Marion; rather, the scene begins with Marion tallying up her expenses after she decides to return the money. In her interview with me, Janet Leigh agrees that the scene starts with Marion at the motel desk:

P: I have a theory that the shower scene doesn't begin with you getting into the shower. My belief is that the shower scene begins with you sitting at the desk.

J: Oh, that's the whole sequence . . . the shower sequence starts as she's figuring out at the desk.

Hitchcock's montage scenes of violence depend for their full effect on preliminary mise-en-scene construction that helps shift the film from suspense to terror. For the full effect of the "shocker" that Hitchcock had planned, the audience must be positioned through the mise-en-scene. As Hitchcock states in a *Redbook* interview, "I know . . . [the audience] can all be scared. I play them like an organ. I know exactly when to stop, to relieve them at the right moment . . . ." (Gottlieb, *Hitchcock on Hitchcock* 151). I believe that we should look at the shower scene as beginning with

Marion in her bathrobe sitting at the desk and tabulating her expenses and as ending with the brilliant pan from Marion's eye to the newspaper containing the stolen money and up to the long shot of the Bates house on the hill, from where we hear Norman's cry, "Oh God, Mother . . . blood!, blood!" There's an organic wholeness to the montage and mise-en-scene in this scene. The length of this scene is four minutes, and it's composed of sixty shots, give or take one shot (because there are two shots in the actual bathtub murder that seem like one). However, if we consider the scene as beginning in the bathroom proper, then the scene is initiated with Marion flushing down the torn bits of paper in the toilet bowl. The scene is then three minutes and twenty-six seconds with fifty-four shots. This number is close to Terry Williams' memory of the number of shots: "I now remember a specific number: it seems to me like it was fifty-two cuts and thirty-eight feet." Let's look at the scene in a different way. If the scene begins with Marion stepping into the shower (a high-angle shot of her feet) and ends with her falling across the tub and onto the floor, the scene is then one minute and forty-nine seconds, with forty-nine shots. Let's try it another way, probably the way Hitchcock thought of it. If the scene is the actual murder itself, then it begins with the camera placed inside the bathtub and focusing on Marion with the shower curtain behind her. The camera moves in a bit to catch an ominous, shadowy figure coming through the door and approaching the tub. It would make sense to claim that the scene ends with this same figure leaving the bathroom after the murder. This scene is forty seconds, thirty-four shots.

Even if one argues, as I do, for the four-minute version of the scene, the shot count is no more than sixty, not the seventy or seventy-eight that Durgnat, Hitchcock, Leigh, and others claim for it. Most likely that number was derived from the numbers of camera setups that cinematographer Russell supposedly used for the scene. In his famous interview with Truffaut, Hitchcock states, "It took us seven days to shoot that scene, and there were seventy camera setups for forty-five seconds of footage" (277). Perhaps the inflated shot count comes from the number of storyboards Saul Bass created for the scene. Janet Leigh claims in her book on *Psycho* that Saul Bass's storyboards contained seventy-eight points of view (Wollen 82). However, Bill Krohn points out that there were forty-eight Saul Bass storyboards, from which Hitchcock is supposed to have planned his camera set-ups (225). As for the statements about no knife entering the flesh, I direct viewers to shot 37 (in the four-minute version), in which the tip of the knife enters Marion's flesh just below the navel. As for the claims that the nudity was somehow kept within Production Code rules—Hitchcock claims, ". . . I wanted the bare breast to be conveniently covered." (Gottlieb, *Hitchcock on Hitchcock* 288)—I direct viewers to shots 8 and 51, where the nipples of the nude Marion can be seen, even though they are out of focus and look like dark smudges. As for when the shower scene occurs and when Marion is killed, statements (some from Hitchcock) range from twenty minutes to Hitchcock's statement about killing off the star "in the first third of the film" (*Hitchcock on Hitchcock* 288). Actually the murder of Marion occurs forty-nine minutes into the film, a little under halfway into the one-hour-and-forty-nine-minute film.

Perhaps the most complete accounts of the details of the shower scene are contained in five books. One is Stephen Rebello's comprehensive *Alfred Hitchcock and the Making of Psycho* (1990). Rebello's chapter on the actual shooting of the film contains a subheading entitled "Saul Bass and Screaming in the Shower," which provides as detailed an account of the shower scene as one is likely to find. However, one aspect of Rebello's account is contradicted by my interview with Danny Greene, who claims he created the stabbing sounds of the shower scene by repeatedly thrusting the actual knife into an uncooked side of beef. Rebello cites script supervisor Marshal Schlom, who claims that various types of melons were used to mimic the sound of knife striking flesh (188). Naturally, in this "he said, she said" conflict I tend to believe my origin for the source of the actual sound. Besides, there's a wonderful appropriateness to the story and to its Hitchcockean ending—Danny took the "tenderized" meat home to his wife, who made a wonderful roast out of it. Shades of "Lamb to the Slaughter"! The second book is Bill Krohn's *Hitchcock at Work* (2000), which emphasizes the collaborative nature of Hitchcock's cinema. Krohn adds a substantial insight to the scholarship on *Psycho*. He claims that because Hitchcock wanted to shoot the film fast and economically, he used two—sometimes even four—cameras, a technique used in television shows but not usually in features. This multiple-camera practice had a salutary effect on the film. Krohn states, "To some extent, the use of television techniques to make *Psycho* also contributed to the jazzy rhythm of scenes shot with two cameras . . ." (224). The third book is Richard Anobile's *Alfred Hitchcock's Psycho* (1974), which contains more than fourteen hundred frame enlargements, along with the film's dialogue. Anobile's book is invaluable for Hitchcock scholars who want to study individual frames. However, the frame blowups sometimes are cropped so that the full effect of Hitchcock's mise-en-scene is lost. And there are several places where the dialogue is missing or inaccurate. The fourth book is Janet Leigh's firsthand account of the making of the film. Ms. Leigh's account is very much anecdotal but enjoyable to read. Her introduction to chapter 4, "The Shower," begins: "The bathroom scenes were scheduled to be shot December 17 through December 23, 1959. It's ironic when you think of it: During the day I was in the throes of being stabbed to death, and at night I was wrapping presents from Santa Claus for the children" (65). The virtue of Leigh's book is the first-hand perspective it provides, although it must be pointed out that she perpetuates some of the misconceptions about the scene. The fifth, and most idiosyncratic, is Raymond Durgnat's *A Long Hard Look at Psycho* (2002), which contains the most provocative (and I think eccentric) critical and interpretive look at the shower scene. Durgnat dissects the scene into ". . . six phases (or, since they're so lyrical, let's think of them as 'stanzas' in a poem)" (113). Later, he calls the scene a "bourgeois narrative" and then "a classical five act drama" (119). Durgnat's eccentricity continues as he claims that the shower murder is not a separate film scene, but rather "is one event, but it's two story points" (124). The last book is Robert Kolker's *Alfred Hitchcock's Psycho: A Case Book* (2004), which contains a selection of some of the most provocative and insightful essays on *Psycho*, including Kolker's piece written especially for the casebook.

The first "serious" criticism and appreciation of Hitchcock came from France and, of course, French filmmakers—Truffaut, Godard, Chabrol—all admitted their indebtedness to Hitchcock. In 1955, a major French creative impulse radiated from Henri-Georges Clouzot, whose birth and death dates (1907–1977) closely parallel Hitchcock's (1899–1980). In 1955, Clouzot directed *Diabolique*, a suspense thriller that held the distinction of being "the most frightening and artistic horror picture ever made," according to Danny Peary, who wrote the liner notes for the Criterion DVD (1999). Hitchcock was a great admirer of *Diabolique*. Patrick McGilligan says that in the publicity buildup for the film's release, "Hitchcock had described *Psycho* to the *New York Times* as a story 'in the *Diabolique* genre.' He told Stefano that the French film had influenced his decision to shoot *Psycho* in black and white (like *Diabolique*). Their afternoon meetings were leavened by screenings; and *Diabolique* was shown more than once to Stefano and others on the staff" (583). Danny Peary points out that Hitchcock had borrowed Clouzot's marketing idea of not allowing patrons to enter the theater once the film had begun and also of asking viewers not to divulge the ending. In a humorous reference to the film's title, alternately called *Les Diaboliques (The Devils)*, Clouzot tacks this request after the film's "Fin" title: (translated from the French) "Don't be devils. Don't ruin the interest your friends could take in this film. Don't tell them what you saw. Thank you for them." This is obviously the marketing model for the plea to filmgoers that appeared in some lobbies for *Psycho*'s showings that requested audiences not to divulge the film's ending. Another connection/influence is the source novel for *Diabolique: Celle Qui M'Etait Plus*, written by Pierre Boileau and Thomas Narcejac, who had written the novel *D'entre Les Morts*, the source for Hitchcock's 1958 film *Vertigo* (Peary). Rebello also believes that Hitchcock was always well aware of other black-and-white, low-budget horror films that were making money for Universal-International, American International, and Allied Artists (22).

Psycho and *Diabolique* share many similarities. Rebello claims that Hitchcock was actually in a kind of competition with Clouzot for the suspense crown (20). Peary points out that both films are shot in black and white, and feature a grisly murder, a disposal of a body, a nosy private investigator, plot twists, mordant humor, and sordid sex. In addition, both films blend a kind of tawdry realism with a blatant expressionistic style. This blend can be vividly seen in the most obvious connection between the two films: the famous climax from *Diabolique*, the bathtub scene. Earlier in the film, there is a chilling murder in the bathtub: the brutal Michel Delassalle is drowned by his mistress, Nicole Horner, with the assistance of his wife, Christina. This scene takes place approximately forty-five minutes into the film, very close to the elapsed time before the shower murder in *Psycho*—approximately forty-nine minutes into the film. The murder itself, however, is not presented in a montage style, nor is it particularly noteworthy in technique. Nicole rather matter-of-factly submerges the drugged Michel in the tiny tub of her shabby bathroom. Perhaps the prosaic way that Clouzot handles this scene—mainly through mise-en-scene—adds to its macabre elements.

It is the climax of the film—the second bathtub scene—that has prompted critics to draw parallels between it and the shower murder in *Psycho*. The second bathtub scene comes at the climax of the film, and is, therefore, similar in plot position to *Psycho*'s fruit cellar scene. However, the similarity of setting—bathroom—and of symbolism—water—to the shower scene makes the comparison more telling. The second bathtub scene is a minute-and-a-half in length and is composed of seventeen shots. The scene begins when Christina enters the bathroom and ends with her death, which is verified by Michel, who checks her pulse. The lead-up to this scene is a five-and-a-half-minute scene constructed in mise-en-scene style, shot in a dark, expressionistic manner, with chiaroscuro lighting. The function of the mise-en-scene is to create suspense through lighting, camera angle, and point-of-view shots. Christine is pursuing what appears to be the ghost of her dead husband, Michel. Clouzot shoots the scene to wring from it all of its suspenseful quality, including dark corridors, and high-angle shots of doors slowly opening and of a mysterious man's feet. In addition, Clouzot adds erotic overtones to the film by clothing Christine in a see-through nightgown so that her breasts and nipples are clearly seen. This mixture of eroticism, suspense, and violence was a legacy of the German Expressionist movement in films like *The Cabinet of Dr. Caligari*. Clouzot is also borrowing a page from Hitchcock in this scene by creating suspense through transferring the anxiety of Christine to the mind of the audience through mise-en-scene techniques. The bathtub scene itself, however, does not shift to the same kind of Eisensteinian montage that characterizes the shower scene. Instead, Clouzot maintains a mise-en-scene approach, preferring instead to preserve a realistic sense of space. The audience sees clearly, through Christina's eyes, the grotesque image of Michel rising from the bathtub like a submerged zombie, with bulging white eyeballs. There's no real vortex of violence that characterizes Hitchcock's greatest scenes of terror. The shot length, camera angles, and fourth-wall camera position remain well within classical guidelines, and the 180 degree rule is maintained. These observations are not meant to deny the power of the scene, but only to point out that the bathtub scene in *Diabolique* is indeed horrific, but that it in no way approaches the kind of terror established in *Psycho*, nor does it reach a similar iconic and paradigmatic level.

As I pointed out in chapter two—and as I have endeavored to develop in subsequent chapters—Hitchcock's whole career had been priming him for the challenges of *Psycho*, particularly the shower scene. The disintegration of the studio system and the weakening of the Production Code had put into his hands the power of the producer/director in a cinematic milieu opening itself up to the exigencies and forces of popular culture, with its increasing emphasis on sex and violence. Out of that popular culture had appeared, in 1959, a novel loosely based on the serial killer Ed Gein. Published by Simon and & Schuster as part of their Inner Sanctum Mystery Series, Robert Bloch's *Psycho* was a lurid, grisly piece of pulp fiction, but it captured Hitchcock's interest. His imagination was piqued by one scene in the novel in particular—the killing of Mary in the shower. (Mary would become the model for Marion.) In their interview, Hitchcock answers Truffaut's question about Bloch's novel—"What was it that attracted you to the novel?"—with this: "I think that the thing that appealed to me and made me decide to do the picture was the suddenness of the murder in the shower, coming, as it were, out of the blue. That was about all" (268–269). In his interview with me, Joseph Stefano confirms this: ". . . [Hitchcock] told me one day that he only bought the book because a girl gets murdered in the shower. I don't know whether he's ever said that to anybody else. But that's what he told me."

The passage that caught Hitchcock's attention occurs about a quarter of the way into Bloch's novel. Bloch is quoted in Rebello's book on *Psycho* as claiming about the writing of the novel: "I hit upon a device of ending the chapter by having a shower curtain flung aside" ("Building the Bates Motel" 10). What Bloch writes in the novel is shocking in its bluntness and its finality:

> Mary started to scream and then the curtains parted further and a hand appeared, holding a butcher knife. It was the knife that, a moment later, cut off her scream.
>
> And her head. (39).

Knowing Hitchcock's stylistic and thematic preoccupations helps one to understand why this passage struck a resonant chord in him. First, there's the situation of a naked woman in the shower, with all of its visual potential for exploiting the weakening Production Code. Then, of course, there's the knife, which, as I've shown above, had been a favorite Hitchcock motif since *Blackmail*. The suddenness of the attack on the helpless girl also must have appealed to Hitchcock because many of his victims are women and because the attack contained the potential for a montage presentation of a vortex of violence. Then there's the killing itself, a horrible crime, a beheading, one that must have appealed to Hitchcock's very British fascination with gruesome crimes. In a 1963 interview with Oriana Fallaci, Hitchcock says, "I don't get such a kick out of anything as much as out of imagining a crime. When I'm writing a story and I come to the crime, I think happily: now wouldn't it be nice to have him die like this? And then, even more happily I think: at this point people will start yelling . . . it must be because I'm English. The English use a lot of imagination with their crimes. They have the most amusing crimes in the world" (Gottlieb, *Alfred Hitchcock Interviews* 56). And finally, there's the subversion of Hitchcock's usual pattern of male versus female violence. In *Psycho*, Hitchcock presents a scene of violence in which a female attacks another female—or so it seems to the audience at the end of the scene. In addition, the attacker, although of mysterious identity at the time of the attack, seems to be the mother of the gentle, boyish Norman Bates. This character presentation is certainly unique in Hitchcock's oeuvre, and it certainly was shocking and perverse to the audience of 1960, who didn't regularly see women killing other women.

One can trace the evolution of the shower scene from the Bloch novel to its cinematic manifestation in the shower scene of *Psycho*. The shower scene has the same brutality and finality of the Bloch passage. The thirty-three words that comprise this shocking passage translate almost perfectly into the thirty-four shots that make up the actual murder itself (from the appearance of mother to her departure from the bathroom). What's interesting about the film adaptation is that the essentials of Bloch's novels are preserved in the scene: the shower, the shower curtain, the naked victim, the attacker, the knife, the enclosed space, and the grisly murder. The connection can be traced from the Bloch passage quoted above to the description of the shower murder contained in Joseph Stefano's first draft of the screenplay dated October 19, 1959.

28. INT. MARY IN SHOWER,
And we see the shadow of a woman fall across the shower curtain. Mary's back is turned to the curtain. The white brightness of the bathroom is almost blinding. Suddenly we see the hand reach up, grasp the shower curtain, rip it aside.

Cut to:

29: MARY—ECU,
As she turns in response to the feel and sound of the shower curtain being torn aside. A look of pure horror erupts in her face. A low terrible groan begins to rise up out of her throat. A hand comes into shot. The hand holds an enormous bread knife. The flint of the blade shatters the screen to an almost total silver blankness.

30: THE SLASHING,
An impression of a knife slashing, as if tearing at the very screen, ripping the film. Over it the brief gulps of screaming. And then silence. And then the dreadful thing as Mary's body falls in the tub.

31: REVERSE ANGLE,

The blank whiteness, the blur of the shower water, the hand pulling the shower curtain back. We catch one flicker of a glimpse of the murderer. A woman, her face contorted with madness, her head wild with hair, as if she were wearing a fright-wig. And then we see only the curtain, closed across the tub, and hear the rush of the shower water. Above the shower-bar we see the bathroom door open again and after a moment we hear the sound of the front door slamming.

Cut to:

32. THE DEAD BODY,

Lying half in, half out of the tub, the head tumbled over touching the floor, the hair wet, one eye wide open as if popped, one arm lying limp and wet along the tile floor. Coming down the side of the tub, running thick and dark along the porcelain, we see many small threads of blood. CAMERA MOVES away from the body, travels slowly across the bathroom, past the toilet, out into the bedroom. (Krohn 224–225).

Hitchcock employed graphic designer Saul Bass to create a series of storyboards that would capture in images what Stefano had described in words. The resultant editing style was accomplished in the vein of Eisensteinan montage. Hitchcock's visual interpretation of Stefano's words results in the creation of the most vivid and disturbing vortex of violence that he had ever created. The extreme staccato editing removes the film from a realistic space to an almost purely abstract space of terror—a revolutionary cinematic space that would have long- term consequences for cinema but also for society.

How Hitchcock accomplishes this feat is the subject of the following analysis of the shower scene. In my analysis, I should like to view the shower scene as a discrete three-act structure.

Act I: Marion's *Mea Culpa*

Act II: The Revenge of Mother

Act III: The Descent of Marion: The Ascent of Norman/Norma

Act I: Marion's *Mea Culpa*

The fifteen shots that comprise the first act of the shower scene allow Hitchcock to use the geography of the screen to create a realistic space and place. This first part of the scene has a mise-en-scene structure; the fifteen shots take up 1:22 seconds, with an average shot length of almost six seconds. Hitchcock is carefully preparing his audience for the shock of the shower murder. Part of his preparation is to create a visual transition to the shower scene through the last shot of the motel scene. In this shot, Hitchcock shows a long shot of Norman sitting at the kitchen table; the enclosing vertical lines of the tall and narrow doorway frame him. Norman sits at the table in profile, facing the right side of the screen as he nonchalantly plays with the sugar container with his left hand. The next shot shows a medium shot of Marion, sitting at the motel desk, also in profile and also facing the right side of the screen writing something down with her right hand. Vertical lines, too, frame her—the mirror to her left and the window to her right. What better way to convey the connection between these two characters, whose fates have become inextricably intertwined? Both are in traps, suggested by the vertical composition; both are struggling to free themselves from these traps, Norman by "defying" his mother's warnings about Marion, and Marion by defying society's mores and laws; both have unleashed forces over which they have little control.

In this first shot of the shower scene, Hitchcock takes great pains to position his camera to anchor the audience to a specific milieu—Cabin 1 of the Bates Motel. We have seen this space earlier during the Bates Motel scene, when Norman brought Marion's luggage into the cabin. In that shot, Hitchcock positioned his camera as the fourth wall, its exact location opposite the entrance to the bathroom and above the bed, which can be seen at the bottom of the screen. There are windows at each end of the room: the window that Norman opens to let air into the room is at the left side of the screen. In the middle of the wall opposite the camera is a standing mirror reflecting the flowered wallpaper on the wall where the camera is positioned. To the extreme right of the frame is the door to Cabin 1. Next to the door is the second window of the room, with shirred café curtains, the exact duplicate of the other window. In the next shot of this scene, Hitchcock positions his camera as the fourth wall, but this time he chooses the wall that contains the door to the cabin and the window next to it. From this position, Hitchcock can show Marion searching for a hiding place for the money she has stolen. In this shot, we see a small part of the wall where the camera had been positioned earlier, its flowered wallpaper a stark contrast to the flat gray of other walls. We had learned earlier in the Peeping Tom scene why the wallpaper decorates this part of the room: its wall shares a wall with the parlor of the Bates Motel so that the hole that Norman peeps through is disguised by the floral pattern of the wall paper.

When Wallace Stevens says, "Reality is an activity of the most august imagination," he could be referring to Hitchcock's mise-en-scene. In film after film, Hitchcock meticulously crafts his spaces and places to position his camera in the most imaginative way to advance the narrative, to develop his characters, and to create a sense of real space and time. Hitchcock realized the importance of space and place to his conception of pure cinema. In the 1972 American Film Institute interview, Hitchcock answers a question about the placement of the camera: "Well, I think mainly it is a matter of the interest in the composition. I have a horror of what I call the passport photograph: shooting straight in. It's dull, it's not interesting, and a slight variation on that is not so much the desire to get anything in the way of sharp angles, low or high or what have you, but merely to avoid this standard level shot" (Gottlieb, *Alfred Hitchcock Interviews* 95). In the analyses of the films that pave the way for the shower scene, I have shown how he constructs space and place, whether the large monument of *Saboteur*, the merry-go-round of *Strangers on a Train*, or the enclosed space of Rose Balestrero's bedroom. In each case, the principles of the classical style, with its reliance on realistic spaces and places, guide Hitchcock. However, there are other spaces and places in Hitchcock's world, and these are the spaces of terror, and the interior spaces of dreams, madness, and evil. Sometimes these spaces and places are mutations of the "real world" of the film, such as when the dining room of the Verloc apartment is transformed into a place of murder, or when Rose Balestrero's bedroom suddenly becomes an evocation of her deranged mental state, or when L.B. Jeffrey's apartment symbolizes his entrapment and his collusion with the malevolent Lars Thorwald. At other times, though, Hitchcock's spaces and places are purely in the realm of dream, such as Scotty's nightmare that plunges him into madness in *Vertigo* or John Ballantine's dream in *Spellbound* that is a key to his paranoid state. These spaces and places are partly constructions of mise-en-scene, but they are also created by montage, by the fragmentation and explosion of the world created by mise-en-scene. These scenes are designed to bring the audience and the characters face-to-face with the anarchic forces of evil and destruction—with terror, pure and simple.

The shower scene in *Psycho* is the culmination of Hitchcock's creation of space and place in the construction of mise-en-scene and montage. In the fifteen shots of the first act of the shower scene, Hitchcock returns us to Cabin 1 of the Bates Motel. As Marion is sitting at the desk of Cabin 1, we see to her right the window of the room and to her left the standing mirror. Both of these are familiar cataphors. Marion faces the window as she is writing; it represents a possible escape from her trap if she can just return the money. The mirror to her left is her past; it reflects her dopplegänger in the person of the thief Marie Samuels. Not in the shot but looming in the audience's imagination is the shower, for Marion is sitting at her desk in her bathrobe, under which is her desirable body that Hitchcock has given us very brief glimpses of in the motel scene.

Hitchcock's mise-en-scene frequently underscores the dramatic anticipation contained in individual shots. In effect, there's a dramatic "carry-over" from shot to shot, and this "carry-over" provides aesthetic weight to a given shot. For example, the shot of Marion at her desk contains within it not only cataphors and visual composition, but also the various narrative threads that have been developed in earlier shots and scenes. We know at this point in the film that Norman's character is now connected to Marion's character, but we don't know to what extent. In earlier scenes, we had seen Marion in various stages of undress. This shot of her at the desk, though, contains in it the possibility of seeing Marion naked, and thus we would be aligned with Norman, who had seen her earlier as she prepared for her shower. We know that Marion is now only fifteen miles from her destination—Fairvale, Sam's hometown—and we wonder if she will reach that destination, for we remember that no one seems to stay at the Bates Motel ("twelve vacancies"), that Norman's mother is somehow a threatening presence (". . . tell her she'll not be appeasing her ugly appetite with my food or my son! Or do I have to tell her . . ."), and that she had mentioned to Norman in the parlor scene her intention of returning to Phoenix to extricate herself from her own trap. The dramatic carry-over in these opening shots is reinforced by Bernard Herrmann's score, which presents a reprise of the motif used in the hotel scene that opens the film. In the first act of the shower scene, Marion is again in a rented room, but this time she'll be sharing the room with Norma Bates rather than Sam Loomis.

At this point, the audience's identification with and sympathy for Marion seems to be at its highest point. This identification is reinforced by the second shot of the scene, which is an extreme close-up, from

Figure 10. The shower scene begins with this shot of Marion figuring her "debt."

Marion's POV, of her writing down figures on a small notebook placed over a bankbook bearing the name "Bank of Phoenix." On the notebook page, Marion is subtracting $700 from $40,000, and the audience realizes the significance of this brief shot, which is also weighted with narrative importance, this time looking not only backward in time to the theft itself and her purchase of the used car but also forward in time to the possible return of the money and the restitution of the $700 from her personal bank account. This is an extremely important shot, for it shows us a dimension of Marion we had seen only fleetingly in the opening scene—her moral imagination and her sense of guilt, which have now seemed to assert themselves in a positive direction.

Shot 3 returns to the same camera position as shot 1, but shot 3 contains an important plot point for the second half of the film. Marion tears out the sheet of paper that she had been using to figure her "moral" debt, rips it up, and then looks for a safe place to dispose of it. She looks down and to her right, but thinks better of it, and then turns her back to us and looks over her left shoulder, to something off-camera. As she gets up from her chair, the camera follows her by panning to the left, where it shows her entering the bathroom door, the torn paper still in her hand. As she passes the mirror, we see her reflection, reinforcing the double motif that Hitchcock has been developing in the first half of the film. At the entrance to the bathroom, Marion also walks past the picture of the bird placed on the wall outside the bathroom. If the mirror presents us with Marion's dopplegänger, then the bird is definitely a reminder of Norman, whose taxidermist's art is focused solely on birds. In shot 4, Marion reaches down to throw away the torn paper, choosing a disposal method that will cover her trail, so to speak, but that will also hold a clue to her disappearance when Marion's sister Lila finds one piece of the torn paper later in the film. At this point, Herrmann's music fades out, putting the emphasis on the visuals of the bathroom.

For the next four shots—5 through 8—Hitchcock has positioned the camera in the bathroom itself, but unlike in *Spellbound*, with its discrete camera positioning, Hitchcock's placement is direct and bold: shot 5 is a startling high-angle close-up of the toilet bowl, the camera positioned right next to Marion so that we see her hand reach into the bowl to dispose of the torn paper. This is a disquieting shot for the audience of 1960, whose sensibilities had been protected by the Production Code and by prevailing standards within the studio system of modesty both in bathroom hygiene and in sex. To make the shot even more unsettling, Hitchcock presents the audience with a slightly discolored toilet seat, in keeping with the general run-down appearance of the Bates Motel. The camera is now clearly in a forbidden and taboo space, but the camera is not positioned behind a wall, viewing the proceedings through a peephole; rather it is in the bathroom itself, looking directly into a toilet bowl and watching (and hearing) it being flushed by Marion. Hitchcock had finally been able to show a toilet on screen, a depiction that McGilligan attributes to Hitchcock's "toilet fixation." The brief glimpse of the swirling water with

Universal Pictures/Photofest

Figure 11. Hitchcock challenges taboos in the first image of a toilet in American cinema.

the white pieces of paper floating on it must have been an unpleasant—and shocking—reminder of where our "waste" goes. This shot is also a vivid foreshadowing of the bathtub drain, which also disposes of Marion's blood after she has been attacked by Norma Bates, and of the swamp that swallows Norman's victims.

Shot 6 continues the taboo-shattering and introduces elements of claustrophobia and intimacy. Hitchcock places his camera behind Marion, at an eye-level angle so that we see the shower behind and to her left. She reaches down to close the lid of the toilet and then moves to the right. The camera subtly pans to follow her as she closes the door and moves to a close-up position. We are now in the tiny bathroom with Marion. She has closed the door and moved closer to us. Marion is in what anthropologist Edward T. Hall calls the "intimate" space. It would perhaps be helpful here to recall Hitchcock's words to Peter Bogdanovich in his invaluable interview with the great filmmaker in 1963. "If I'm looking at acting or looking at a scene . . . I am looking at a screen. . . . In other words, I do not follow the geography of a set. I follow the geography of the screen" (4). In these shots of the shower scene, Hitchcock places us in intimate proximity with Marion Crane. Earlier, we were in Cabin 1 with her; now we are in the bathroom, with the door closed. Shot 6 continues with Marion again turning her back to us as she moves left to right, the camera panning, toward the shower. With her back fully turned toward us, Marion removes her robe, and we see her bare back from the bottom of her shoulder blades up. We now see the genius of Hitchcock in utilizing the geography of the screen and the size of the image. In the cinematic world of 1960, the only place Hitchcock *could* position his camera was behind Marion Crane: full frontal nudity would be totally unacceptable—and perhaps even illegal. However, showing us Marion's bare back in such close proximity creates a sexual intimacy that was daring for the time. In effect, Marion's back is a synecdoche for her nude body. Shot 7, taken from a high angle, continues the synecdoche by showing Marion's bare legs as she steps out of her robe and then her slippers and into the tub, the camera panning and tilting up to just the top of her knees. This shot is in keeping with the classical and studio style of suggesting full nudity through a shot of bare legs.

However, shot 8 ups the ante, so to speak, by showing a nude Marion, but not a clearly visible nude Marion. Coming between the camera lens and Marion is the translucent shower curtain, which provides just enough visual "cover" to keep the audience (and the censors!) guessing as to what they had just seen. Adding to the uncertainty is the brief length of the

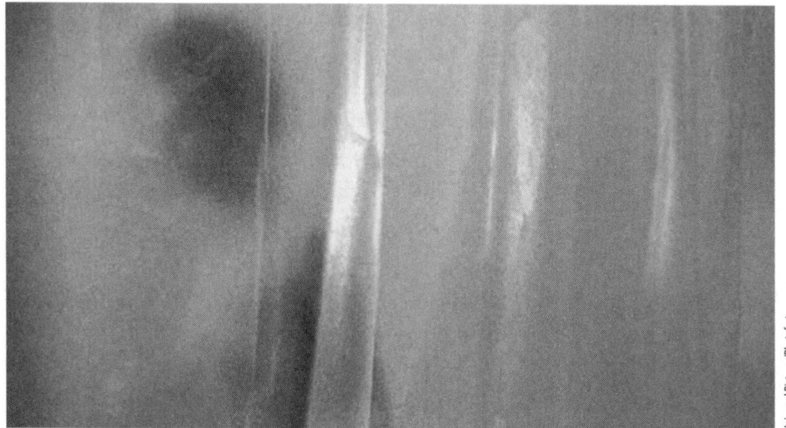

Universal Pictures/Photofest

Figure 12. The translucent shower curtain allows Hitchcock to present nudity, but also to "screen" it.

shot, no more than a second long. Clearly, Hitchcock has shifted audience focus here; he is not creating this shot for the "traditional" audience of the 1960s—the adults; rather, he is constructing these subsequent shots for a newer group of viewers—the youth audience. To Truffaut's statement about this new audience for *Psycho*—". . . it occurred to me that *Psycho* was oriented toward a new generation of filmgoers. There were many things in that picture that you'd never dare in your earlier films"—Hitchcock answers, "Absolutely" (268).

The very brief nude shot of Marion contained in shot 8 would be part of the censorship problems the film faced. In his interview with me, Terry Williams, editor George Tomasini's assistant, remembers screening the shower scene for Luigi Luraschi, the Production Code liaison for Paramount Pictures, the film's distributor. Williams says that Luraschi complained to Hitchcock that Marion's bare breasts were visible in several shots. Williams recalls Hitchcock's reply, "That is a tremendous compliment to my directorial skills. There really is no nudity." Shot 8 would certainly have been one such shot: however, the shot's very brief length and the translucent shower curtain helped to mute the explicitness of the shot. After a second showing, Luraschi agreed with Hitchcock that the "offending shots" were more suggestive than explicit, a tribute to Hitchcock's artistry rather than an example of a Code violation. Hitchcock's protestation aside, shot 8 and subsequent shots do usher in a new explicitness in the depiction of the female body.

For the last seven shots of this fifteen-shot Act I, Hitchcock does something daring: he places the camera (and us, the audience) in the shower with Marion. Hitchcock's strategy of terrorizing the audience is now clearly unfolding. He begins the shower scene in Cabin 1; then he continues the scene in the bathroom, with the door closed; now he has positioned the camera in the shower itself. It is as if we have stepped into the shower with Marion. The spaces become more and more confining. Is Hitchcock putting the viewer into the very same jail cell that he mentions over and over again in interview after interview? In such close proximity to a naked woman, we feel hemmed in on all sides. Hitchcock emphasizes this sense of entrapment by the whiteness of the shower walls and the shower curtain. Rebello points out that Hitchcock "insisted upon dazzling white plastic tiles, gleaming fixtures . . ." (119). With the camera placed at just about eye level in shot 9, its purview seems to lack anchors that would ground and center it: there is no set decoration—no pictures, furniture, windows—only a blank whiteness punctuated by the horizontal and vertical lines created by the tile squares. At the very top of the frame is the showerhead.

What's even more disconcerting is that the camera is directly in front of Marion, just as it was in parts of the car scene. We are no more than fifteen or eighteen inches away from the naked Marion, whom we now see from the front. We are in the most intimate of spaces. This direct, frontal presentation of a nude protagonist is the most daring presentation of the female body in the history of American cinema up until 1960. Other aspects of popular culture had paved the way for this display, such as the launching of *Playboy* magazine in 1953, and the 1953 publication of Alfred Kinsey's explosive and controversial *Sexual Behavior in the Human Female*. In 1957, the notorious serial killer Ed Gein, the model for Norman Bates, was arrested, and the media delighted in exploiting the grisly and horrific crimes he had committed against women ("Pop History of the Fifties").

The frontal close-up of Marion in shot 9, and in the subsequent six shots, also presented censorship challenges for Hitchcock. In the introduction to his invaluable book on *Psycho*, which contains hundreds of frame enlargements, Richard Anobile claims that Hitchcock

> was forced to censor the shower scene. Even today, the bottom of the screen is masked to prevent a glimpse of Janet Leigh's breasts. For this book, I had hoped to present an uncensored version, if, in fact, one existed. But Universal Pictures, the current owner of the film, had

> only a masked version available for its use. William Hornbeck, head of Universal's editorial department, did his best to track down the original negative of the films but it seems to have been lost in the transfer from Paramount. (6).

Richard Franklin, director of *Psycho II*, says this about the masking: "Until very recently it was common for us to expose a full 35mm negative and then mask to 1.85, either on the internegative, or just leave it to the projectionist. . . . But either way, it's likely there was other material which included Janet's cups on the full negative and that such material would have been masked in the interneg, even if the entire print was not." In addition, Eric Carlson claims that the film did have the masking when it was shown on TV in the 1970s.

The last seven shots of the prelude to the shower murder allow Hitchcock to cement firmly the connection between Marion and the audience. By placing us in her intimate space face-to-face with her, Hitchcock has put us in the same boat as Marion; further, he has positioned us so that we confront a naked Marion, the most vulnerable character in Hitchcock's oeuvre. In his interview with me, Joseph Stefano says about Marion in the shower, "But the truth is, there's something about the total helplessness of this woman." That something, of course, is that we are in the same confined space as the helpless Marion. Hitchcock reinforces this connection in shot 10, which is a POV close-up of the showerhead; the water seems to be coming down right on us. Shot 11 returns to the same position as shot 9, but then the next three shots are taken from a different camera placement. Hitchcock shifts his camera to the right so that it is in the position of the shower curtain. We see Marion in profile; the camera captures a medium shot, with Marion's arm "conveniently" blocking any view of her breasts. Behind Marion is the wide, white expanse of the tiled shower wall, with the bright glow of a reflected light seen in the upper left-hand corner of the wall. In shot 12, and in the other showering shots, Marion's face breaks into a smile as the cleansing water washes over her. Janet Leigh told me of her mindset when she played this scene, ". . . you're really cleansing your soul as well as the travel dirt." Marion's face does indeed look ecstatic in this shot, and in the next shot, number 13, which is an almost exact duplicate of number 12, but the tone of the shot darkens somewhat. Gone is the light in the upper left-hand corner; the tiles don't seem to glow. In fact, the whole frame has a gray, somewhat grainy texture. Is this brief shot a textural key to things to come? The showering water is coming down from the upper left-hand corner of the screen, and it is pouring down diagonally onto Marion's body. She has her back turned to the direction of the shower, and her arms are raised, first near her throat, and then up to a diagonal position in direct contrast to the direction of the shower. These conflicting diagonal lines add tension to these supposedly soul-cleansing shots. Whether they realize it or not, Hitchcock's audience is being subtly prepared for the onslaught of the knife in Norma's hand, which strikes down in a diagonal position. Shot 14 is another shot of the shower head, but it is not shown from Marion's POV but is rather seen from the same position as the previous two shots—from the fourth-wall position of the shower curtain. The last shot of this "preparation" for the shower murder again shifts camera position, but this time it is located on the wall opposite from the shower curtain so that the flow of the shower is opposite to the previous shot—from the top right side of the screen downward.

We know from our earlier analysis that this fluid, circular camera maneuvering is part of Hitchcock's strategy to initiate a vortex of violence. The mise-en-scene approach of the fifteen shots of Act I has been to slowly disengage the viewer from a realistic sense of space and place, and of time. One way this is accomplished is to cut the viewer off from familiar settings and cataphors, such as windows, doorways, and mirrors, etc. Hitchcock accomplishes this severing from realistic space and place by relentlessly and methodically enclosing the viewers in smaller and smaller spaces, cutting them off from the outside world by the shower curtain and subjecting them to claustrophobic stress. By shot 15, the audience is sufficiently disoriented for Hitchcock to begin the assault on Marion—which is also the assault on the viewers' sensibilities. Shot 15 is dark and gray in tone. We see Marion in profile, with her head back and mouth open. Behind her is the shower curtain, now prominently featured; it takes up over three-fourths of the background. Its translucency gives the frame an abstract, sinister appearance. The brilliantly white tiles have now been replaced by a cheerless gray expanse, much like the sky before an approaching thunderstorm.

Act II: The Revenge of Mother

The actual shower murder itself begins with Norma opening the door to the bathroom and approaching the shower, this action viewed through the translucent shower curtain. The scene ends with Norma leaving the bathroom. This segment is forty harrowing seconds long and contains thirty-four shots. Terry Williams, Tomasini's assistant editor and the man who first put the scene together, calls the style "flash cutting." He continues, "We had never seen much of that before. It became the in-thing to do in the 1960s."

The shower scene begins with a shot similar to the last shot of Act I, but with a major difference. The camera is in approximately the same position, opposite the shower curtain, but Marion is framed off-center, to the right of the screen. This off-center position is a visual echo of shots from the Bates Motel scene, during which Norma and Marion are shot off-center, leaving a large part of the screen blank. The water continues to cascade from the top right of the screen. The curtain, though, seems to take up the complete rear of the screen, behind Marion. The overall gray tones of the scene are slightly modified by a light that seems to emanate from the top of the screen, behind the shower curtain, providing a silhouetting of Marion, with the shower water glowing on her shoulders. The space that Hitchcock creates in this shot seems divorced from the previous spaces of the film, almost all of which seemed anchored to specific places—the hotel room, Marion's apartment, the Lowery real estate office, the car, California Charlie's used-car lot, even Norman's parlor. This first shot of Act II shows Marion turning to her left, toward the shower, and raising her head to get the full effect of the water on her face. At the same time, she raises her hands to her throat and then presses them together, as if in prayer (a reinforcement of her new moral awareness?). Marion then turns to her right, toward the camera, and she puts her hands behind her neck and closes her eyes. Just as Marion fully faces the audience, we see out of the corner of our eye a movement behind the shower curtain—a movement so subtle and inconspicuous that it registers almost unconsciously on our mind.

This dividing of the screen into right and left halves we have seen before in *Blackmail*: the artist Crewe on the left side of the screen; Alice undressing on the right. In the shower scene, Hitchcock again divides the screen in half, this time through the crease of the shower curtain, which is in the middle of the frame. Hitchcock also uses image size and camera focus to create dramatic tension. Marion is in clear focus and in a close-up shot. The movement in the left side of the frame is in soft focus and in a long shot. In addition, the movement comes from the left side of the screen, the side reserved for Norman. The subtle, surreptitious movement seems almost to register on our reptilian, primitive brain that detects threatening movement from the side that our forward-placed eyes have trouble detecting. This is directional movement that stands our hairs on end. It is the kind of movement and direction that horror film directors rely on, reserving the sides of the screen, particularly the left side, for threats to the characters.

The camera dollies in, seemingly drawn to the approaching form seen through the shower curtain. This part of the shot creates anxiety in the audience because the dolly-in is matched with a movement toward the camera. But the approaching "thing" is unrecognizable because of the obscuring translucency of the shower curtain. The length of this first shot of the second act increases the audience's tension: sixteen seconds. The movement behind the curtain begins three seconds into the shot, so the audience has about twelve or thirteen seconds to try to figure out what is happening. Hitchcock is using his "tried and true" suspense technique of crossing the diegetic barrier by providing the audience knowledge that the character does not have. Just as in *Dial M for Murder*, the character has her back turned to the danger; the difference, though, is that in *Dial M for Murder*, the audience has seen Swann and knows of his plan to kill Margot. Hence, the audience is "in league," in a sense, with him. However, in *Psycho*, the audience is aware only of the approaching menace; they are not sure what it is. Thirteen seconds into this first shot, Marion disappears from the right side of the screen as the camera dollies in. At this point appears the silhouette of a large, very dark figure shown from the shoulders up. To the right of the figure is the dim glow of the bathroom fixture. Screening the figure from the audience is the shower curtain, its folds and the water droplets from the shower obscuring our view.

Universal Pictures/Photofest

Figure 13. Hitchcock's suspense in action: give the audience knowledge that the character doesn't have.

Watching this dark apparition approach the shower, one is reminded of the scene in *Rear Window*, when Lars Thorwald opens L.B. Jeffreys' door and appears as a large, dark figure of menace, or the scene in *Strangers on a Train*, when the dark silhouette of Bruno suddenly appears in front of Miriam and us and begins to strangle her. These dark figures are our own dark selves, our evil emanations that embody our murderous, destructive impulses. When Bruno strangles Miriam, we remember Guy twice telling Anne Morton that he'd like to break Miriam's neck. In *Rear Window*, as Lars approaches L.B. Jeffreys, we remember Jeff's fascination with and his obsessive interest in Thorwald's crime. In Hitchcock's imaginative world, we are all like the good neighbors Joe Newton and Herb Hawkins in *Shadow of a Doubt*, who are obsessed with crime and with the best method of killing one another. All of the time, of course, residing in the very house of the Newton family, is the consummate killer, Uncle Charlie. Is Hitchcock saying that we all harbor in our houses—in ourselves—our own Uncle Charlie—or our own Norma Bates?

When the dark apparition finally reaches the shower curtain, it casts a dark shadow over itself, like a dark stain on its face. And then in one sudden, stunning movement, the figure thrusts aside the shower curtain with its left arm, the curtain slicing across the screen, from left to right. What the curtain reveals is a frightening, dark figure, with its right arm raised and with a huge knife held in attack position, its blade diagonally pointing down from the top left of the screen, the dark point reminding us of the birds' beaks in the parlor of the Bates Motel. To the right of the figure is the light fixture of the bathroom seen in soft focus, providing the back lighting that helps to obscure the face. This is the appearance of the mother, Norma Bates. Her appearance is accompanied by what is perhaps the most recognizable cue in film music history: the shrieking strings that eerily mix with the sound of the shower curtain rings and of Marion's frightening scream.

Hitchcock chooses to present this character dramatically; that is, she makes her appearance as if she is a character in a play or on a movie screen back when movie theaters had curtains that parted to reveal a screen, as in 1960. The character's slow approach to the shower and then her sudden move into prominence show Hitchcock's genius in using lighting, camera movement, and character movement to create suspense and fear. What is truly striking about this part of shot 1 is that Norma makes her dramatic appearance to the audience before she makes her appearance to Marion. In other words, the dark figure with the wicked knife is a threat to us; the

Universal Pictures/Photofest

Figure 14. The dark, menacing figure with upraised knife seems to attack the audience as well as Marion.

raised knife is pointing at us. It takes the next shot for the audience to realize that Marion is not yet aware of the threat, for her back is still turned. Thus, it is we who are the first recipients of the revenge of mother.

Perhaps in no other film has Hitchcock so identified the audience with the victim. At first glance, the dramatic introduction of Norma Bates seems to be a POV shot—until we remember that the last time we saw Marion, just a few seconds earlier, her back was turned to the shower curtain. When she disappears from the frame, it is as if we are now alone in the shower with the ominous figure approaching. But we, unlike Marion, can see the threat, so when the curtain is pulled aside, it is like the climax to a musical movement—a cymbal clash. At this point in the film, the audience is both knowledgeable and ignorant. It knows of an approaching menace, but it doesn't realize what that menace is. The identity of this dark figure, although no longer obscured by the shower curtain, is still a mystery. The actual attack on Marion, considering its importance in film history, is amazingly brief, only forty seconds. The thirty-four shots that comprise this brief segment are staccato in effect. The shots dazzle and, shock—even paralyze—the audience. It is as if the flashbulb of a 1960s camera had all of a sudden turned into a strobe-light. In the thirty-four shots of the actual attack, Hitchcock seems to be calling on the full arsenal of Eisensteinian montage techniques. As the chart below shows, Hitchcock uses the elements of mise-en-scene—type of shot, camera position, camera angle, camera movement, lighting and focus, POV, and subject (what the camera sees)—and he combines (Eisenstein would say "constructs") the various shots that contain these elements through montage to create a space of pure terror.

The most obvious and powerful Eisensteinian technique used in the attack is metric montage. If one were to turn down the volume and just observe the metric rhythm, one would see a regularity of beat—a relentless pounding that matches the increased heartbeat of the audience. In fact, if one were to estimate that the average or typical heartbeat of an audience member was eighty beats a minute, then the heart would beat seventy-five seconds a minute. If one were to divide the thirty-four shots into the twenty-four-second length of the attack, one would discover that the average length of the shots is seventy-two seconds. It seems that Hitchcock has discovered the basic physiology of fear and has utilized it in the "pure cinema" of the attack. Then, if one were to watch the attack again, but this time with Bernard Herrmann's score, one would see how the relentless rhythm of the music intensifies the metric montage.

Shot #	Shot Type	Camera Position	Camera Angle	Camera Movement	Focus	POV	Subject
1	CU	I	Eye	Dolly in	Sh	En	Marion, but then Norma
2	CU shoulder	0	Eye (Below)	S	So	En	Marion, shoulder shot
3	CU tight	0	Eye (Below)	S	B	En	Marion's head and open mouth
4	CU Ex	0	Eye (Below)	S	So	En	Marion's screaming mouth
5	CU	I	Low	S	Sh	En	Norma in shadow, arm raised, first blow
6	CU	0	Eye (Above)	S	So	En	Marion turning, hands up, to fend off blow
7	CU	I	Eye (Above)	S	Sh	M	Norma, closer, second blow
8	CU	0	Low	S	B	En	Marion, waist level, arm
9	MS	A	Bird's Eye	S	B	En	Marion grasping Norma's wrist to fend off
10	CU tight	0	Eye (Below)	S	B	N	Marion's face turning side to side

Table continued

Shot #	Shot Type	Camera Position	Camera Angle	Camera Movement	Focus	POV	Subject
11	MS	A/I	Bird's Eye	S	B	En	Knife coming in from left, Marion fending off
12	CU	0	Eye (Below)	Slight	B	N	Marion's head, mouth open, moving sideways
13	MS	A/I	Bird's Eye	S	B	En	Knife blade from left
14	CU	I	Eye (Below)	S	So	M	Norma's head in darkness
15	CU	0	Eye (Below)	S	B	N	Marion moving from left of screen to right
16	CU	I	Eye (Below)	S	So	N	Norma in close-up, bright light behind her
17	CU Ex	0	Eye (Below)	S	B	N	Marion twists head to left
18	CU Ex	I	Eye (Below)	S	B	N	Norma with knife slicing down
19	CU Ex	0	Eye (Below)	S	B	N	Marion moving back and forth, hand in front of face
20	CU Ex	I	Eye (Below)	S	B	N	Norma's hand holding knife now appears clear
21	CU Ex	0	Eye (Below)	S	B	N	Marion's face contorted, almost unrecognizable
22	CU Ex	I	Eye (Below)	S	B but then Sh	N	Norma's hand holding knife becomes clear for an instant
23	CU Ex	0	Waist level tilt down	Sh	En		Marion's stomach, knife tip goes in
24	CU Ex	0	Eye (Below)	S	B	N	Marion's face moves to right of screen and off camera
25	MS	I	Low	S	So	N	Top of shower rod, knife comes down from right
26	MS	0	Waist	S	B	En	Marion's back, raises arm to block blade
27	CU	0	Eye (Below)	S	So	N	Marion turning her back to camera

Table continued

Shot #	Shot Type	Camera Position	Camera Angle	Camera Movement	Focus	POV	Subject
28	CU	O	H	S	Sh	En	Marion's legs from knees down, blood in tub
29	CU Ex	O	Eye	S	B	N	Marion turning her back
30	CU	O	Eye	S	Sh	N	Marion turning back, knife comes down
31	CU	O	H	S	Sh	En	Marion's legs from thigh down
32	CU	O	Eye	S	B	N	Marion's hand, with fingers spread
33	CU	O	Eye	S	B	N	Marion's head from behind, right arm up
34	LS	I	Eye (Below)	S	Sh	E	Norma leaves

LEGEND: CU (close-up); CU Ex (extreme close up); MS (medium shot); LS (long shot); I (inside shower); O (outside shower); A (above shower); AI (above and inside shower), Sh (sharp); So (soft); B (blurry); En (Enunciator); N (Norma); M (Marion); S (static).

Rhythmic montage involves patterns of movement and thus includes type of shot, camera position, movement, POV, and subject. The first two columns of the chart show the variation in shot type and camera position. Shots 2, 3, and 4 are all of Marion; the camera is positioned outside the shower, next to Norma; the three shots go from a close-up of Marion from the shoulder up, to a tight close-up of Marion screaming, to an extreme close-up of Marion's gaping mouth, with water dripping from it. This three-shot assemblage reminds one of the stunning three-shot sequence in Eisenstein's *The Battleship Potemkin*, during which the attack of the Cossacks is signaled by three successive shots of a woman's head snapping back in terror. The remainder of the shots in the shower scene attack vary from extreme close-ups to medium shots, with the camera positioned outside (eighteen shots), inside (nine), and above (three) the shower. This vortex also leads to the creation of a purely abstract space of terror.

The total effect of this variation in camera placement is to create a powerful vortex that engulfs both Marion and the audience in a swirl of violence. An additional element of rhythmic montage is movement within the frame. Norma delivers nine vicious blows, with her hand moving vertically

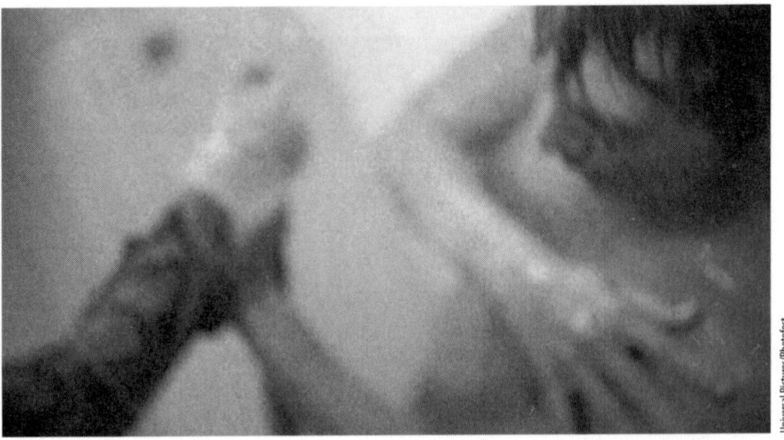

Universal Pictures/Photofest

Figure 15. Sex and violence are historically yoked in the shower scene.

and sometimes diagonally from the top of the screen down. Marion's movement, on the other hand, is horizontal: her head turns from right to left as she tries to ward off the blows. In addition, near the end of the attack, Marion turns her body away from the direction of the knife blows. She moves across the camera from her left and presents her back to the attacker. Hitchcock also includes two high-angle shots of Marion's legs and feet turning and buckling as she weakens from the knife blows. The rhythm of Herrmann's score, which works in unison with the plunging blade, matches the diagonal movement of the knife.

In order to intensify the vortex of violence, Hitchcock varies camera angles and also camera focus to try to capture the extremely violent action on film. Hitchcock claims to have shot the scene in slow motion: "I had the camera slow and the girl moving slowly so that I could measure out the movements and the covering of the awkward parts of the body, the arm movement gesture and so forth" (Rebello 111). The vortex happens so quickly that it is sometimes difficult to determine whose POV the camera represents. Clearly, though, there are three POVs that alternate: the enunciator's, Marion's, and Norma's. These POV shots, in the case of Marion and Norma, are connected to the camera position and angle: Norma's POV shots are from outside the shower; Marion's, from inside. The three bird's-eye shots are from the enunciator's point of view, as is the controversial knife-entering-the-flesh shot, number 23. This close-up shot is taken from a camera position slightly below the navel of Marion, and the shot clearly—but briefly—shows the tip of the knife entering the flesh. It is the only shot to show the penetration of the knife, and it is as chilling a shot as any Hitchcock ever made. What makes the shot even more controversial than the explicit violence is its erotic overtones. If bare breasts were taboo in the milieu of the late 1950s, then bare female bellies, especially bellies that show an expanse of flesh below the navel, were even more so. Hitchcock was able to get away with such a daring shot because it was part of the flash cutting of the scene.

The scene's power, over and above its technical brilliance, owes much to the disturbing linkage of sexuality and violence. Kolker's essay, "The Form, Structure, and Influence of *Psycho*," claims that the shower murder ". . . speaks to the assaultive power that makes up the politics of rape" (242). I agree with Kolker up to a point. We must remember that the knife may indeed be a symbol of the phallus, but that it is *not* a phallus. The killing of Marion is a sexual act only secondarily. The sexuality is in the representation of the female body.

In Hitchcock's *Frenzy* (1972), the brutal murder of Brenda by the serial killer Bob Rusk takes place after he rapes her but can't achieve satisfaction. The murder is the result of the rape. In *Psycho*, though, the murder of Marion is only tangentially related to the sexual desires of Norman. His lustful peering at Marion has triggered the jealous rage of the mother, and it is she who kills Marion. The method by which Hitchcock shoots and edits the shower scene, however, makes it very difficult to determine who the attacker really is. Only at the end of the twenty-four seconds—or

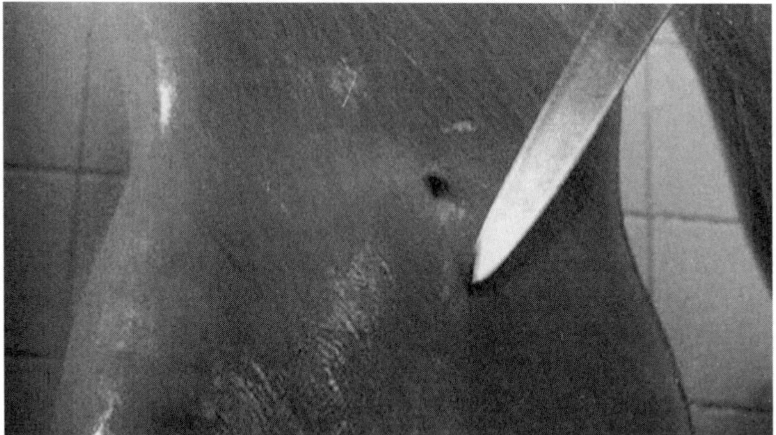

Figure 16. The controversial "knife-entering-the-flesh" shot is almost subliminally presented.

perhaps halfway through—do we realize that it is indeed a woman who is doing the stabbing.

In many ways, the vicious attack on Marion is actually an attack on the female body and on its potential for arousing sexual desires in the male. Norma kills Marion because she has aroused Norman; in the same way, Hitchcock constructs his shower scene so that it is an attack on female sexuality itself. The knife penetration in shot 23, coming so close to the sexual organs of Marion, seems to be a punishment for Marion's erotic appeal to men.

These POVs in the shower murder present the same method of camera position that we saw in the carousel scene from *Strangers on a Train*, with its three camera views: outside the carousel, on the carousel, and under the carousel. In addition, the fluid and flexible camera placement of the shower scene adds another dimension to the creation of the vortex of violence and the space of terror. The camera seems everywhere: in the shower, outside the shower, above the shower. The camera's angles, too, vary from slightly below eye level, to above eye level, to high angle, to bird's eye, to low, and to waist and back. This camera method has the effect of fragmenting the body of Marion, of "cutting it up"; in this way, the form of the film reflects—even creates—the content. An additional effect of the alternation in camera position and angle is to create disorientation in the viewer, because the attack is viewed from the position of the victim, the attacker, and the witness—enunciator.

Act III: The Descent of Marion: The Ascent of Norman/Norma

The last act of the shower scene is two minutes long and contains eleven shots, with an average length of eleven seconds. After the furious vortex of Act II, Hitchcock returns to a more leisurely montage pace in order to release the tension built up in the audience. If Hitchcock plays his audience like an organ, then in this last act he reduces the tempo and volume of his playing somewhat. Linda Williams claims, "Anyone who has gone to the movies in the last twenty years cannot help but notice how entrenched this rollercoaster sensibility of repeated tension and release, assault and escape has become." She also says about the audience reaction to the murder, "From the very first screenings, audience reaction, in the form of gasps, screams, yells, even running up and down the aisles, was unprecedented" (15).

The shower murder of Act II is perhaps the greatest example in all of cinema of the universal power of visual images. Hitchcock says to Truffaut about the power of the murder montage:

> My main satisfaction is that the film had an effect on the audiences, and I consider that very important. I don't care about the subject matter; I don't care about the acting; but I do care about the pieces of film and the photography and the sound track and all of the technical ingredients that made the audience scream. I feel it's tremendously satisfying for us to be able to use the cinematic art to achieve something of a mass emotion. And with *Psycho* we most definitely achieved this. It wasn't a message that stirred the audiences, nor was it a great performance or their enjoyment of the novel. They were aroused by pure film. (Kolker 20).

In the "pure film" of Act III, the first shot is a tight close-up of Marion's hand, fingers outspread, trying to grip the slippery wall of the shower. The hand slides down to the bottom of the frame as the fingers flex and bend in agony. This downward movement becomes the predominant direction of Act III as Marion literally falls to her death. The second shot continues this movement. This medium shot of Marion shows her turning her body toward the camera and then sliding down the shower wall with a dazed look on her face, as the camera tilts down to follow her descent. For this shot, Hitchcock puts Marion to the far right of the frame, leaving a large expanse of the shower wall on the left side of the frame. This peripheral

Universal Pictures/Photofest

Figure 17. Marion "descends" into death: the third act of the shower scene.

positioning of Marion is a visual echo of earlier shots from the Bates Motel scene, during which both Norman and Marion are "trapped" in peripheral positions of the frame. This positioning, coupled with Marion's descent, tends to prefigure her approaching death and her disappearance from the narrative. At the end of this rather long shot (eighteen seconds), the camera tracks back slowly, as Marion reaches the bottom of the wall. She reaches out her hand, extends it into the emptiness of the left side of the frame, as if reaching toward us, the audience, for help. But, alas, we can do nothing, having been "assaulted" as she has, and now sitting in our seats, gasping, crying, screaming, trying to look away, but unable not to look, both shocked by the violence but fascinated by the eroticism of Marion's naked body. Bernard Herrmann's score intensifies the audience's shock with its bass chords, which eventually give way to the eerie flow of the shower, the last sound that Marion will hear.

Shot 3 of this last act of the shower scene is a disorienting extreme close-up of Marion's hand grasping the shower curtain. Hitchcock has chosen a long lens for this shot in order to keep the foreground in sharp focus but the background very blurry. The camera's angle is now at the same level as Marion; its position is just outside the shower, on the other side of the curtain. Hitchcock has chosen a lens with a short focal distance to keep Marion's body in very soft focus, but not soft enough to prevent us from seeing the outlines of Marion's breasts and the contrasting darkness of her nipples. Shot 4 continues the disorientation by its camera placement:

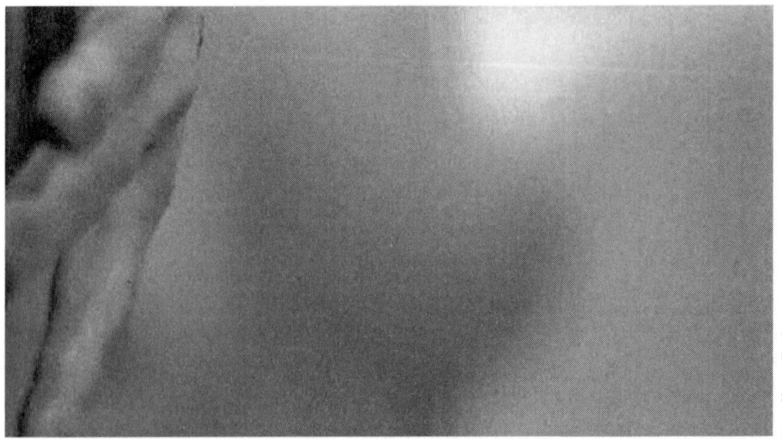

Universal Pictures/Photofest

Figure 18. Hitchcock challenges the Production Code by exposing bare breasts.

a bird's-eye shot of Marion in the tub. We see that she has fallen to her knees and that she has grasped the shower curtain for balance. The shower curtain rod cuts diagonally across the frame, dividing it roughly into two irregularly shaped rectangles. On the left side is Marion on her knees in the tub. Her right hand is grasping the shower curtain, the rings of which extend halfway up the rod's length. Streaking across the top of Marion's head is the shower water moving parallel to the bar's diagonal thrust. On the right side of the frame, we see the bathroom floor, tiled in the same pattern as the wall. At the top right of the frame, we see Marion's bathrobe on top of the toilet. Because this shot is less than a second in length, it registers very quickly, almost as if it were a still painting or photograph. If one were to freeze this brief shot and study its compositions, one would be convinced that he were looking at an abstract painting, for its formal composition is striking.

Shot 5 is a close-up of the shower curtain seen from a low angle, presumably Marion's; the curtain becomes taut, and then it suddenly pulls away from its hooks, which snap and then spin around the rod. At this point, it would be helpful to remember Neil Hurley's claim that Hitchcock's two primary fears are space and height (10). They are both vividly presented in this scene. The enclosed space of the shower has effectively precluded Marion's escape: there is literally nowhere to go but down to death. In his interview with me, Joseph Stefano says about these shots:

> What's happening on screen is a terrible feeling. First of all, the thing that got me is that if I were going to be attacked and murdered, the shower's about the last place I would want that happening because I would be naked and trapped in a compartment. How do you defend yourself? . . . You just start thinking about your body, what's happening. I think that before I would think that I was dying or I was going to be killed, I would think about how scarred I was going to be.

The height anxiety is presented indirectly. Marion's grasping of the shower curtain can be seen as a variation of the ubiquitous dangling scenes in many of Hitchcock's films, as widely separated in time and storyline as *The Lodger* (1926), *Young and Innocent* (1937), *Saboteur* (1942), *Shadow of a Doubt* (1943), *Strangers on a Train* (1951), *Rear Window* (1953), *To Catch a Thief* (1954), *Vertigo* (1957), and *North by Northwest* (1959). Hanging on for dear life, Marion is reaching out for help and support but finds only a cheap motel shower curtain that pulls away easily from its moorings, like life itself.

We know from many interviews with Hitchcock and his associates that the shower scene was indeed altered to conform to studio system policies and to the Production Code. We also know, however, that Hitchcock was able to get away with some very daring shots. Terry Williams, George Tomasini's assistant, claims that Hitchcock dropped at least two shots from the shower scene, although it is not clear just what these shots are. One deleted shot, however, can be verified, and this is the bird's-eye shot of Marion as she falls across the bathtub wall, having failed to find support in the shower curtain. Joseph Stefano says about this shot in his interview with me:

> The thing that used to break my heart about it was a final shot that Hitchcock couldn't put in the movie, because he knew the censors would not allow it. It's a high overhead shot of Marion, lying over the tub, and that shot prevented any sexual thought. All I could think was, "All that youth, all that beauty. All down the drain." It made me think of all the girls I ever liked and how easy it is for men to kill women.

This shot was just too daring for the cinematic and social milieu of the late '50s and early '60s. However, during my research, I discovered a still of this deleted shot, and I've included it in the photo section of this book. It was just not possible to show the bare buttocks of a character on the screen, so this shot had to go. Clearly, the figure in the shot is not Janet Leigh but rather her nude stand-in, Marli Renfro. As Joseph Stefano says, the shot is both shocking and heart-breaking, a perfect visual symbol of Marion's life and death.

In the present age of cinematic cornucopia with multiple-disc releases of films featuring director's cuts, outtakes, and variable endings, etc., it is important to remember how profligate some studios were with film negatives and with deleted scenes. Two famous examples come to mind: the "lost" footage of Orson Welles' mangled masterpiece *The Magnificent Ambersons* (1942) and of Erich Von Stroheim's *Greed* (1925). Hitchcock was careful *not* to shoot too much coverage and not to print multiple takes. However, the shower scene was an "experiment" in Eisensteinian montage; Hitchcock shot more than his usual footage. During my interview with Terry Williams, I was shocked to discover that Terry's assistant had thrown out all the outtakes from the shower scene. Considering the seminal position of the shower scene in film history, the disposal of the shower scene outtakes has to be one of the great losses in cinema history.

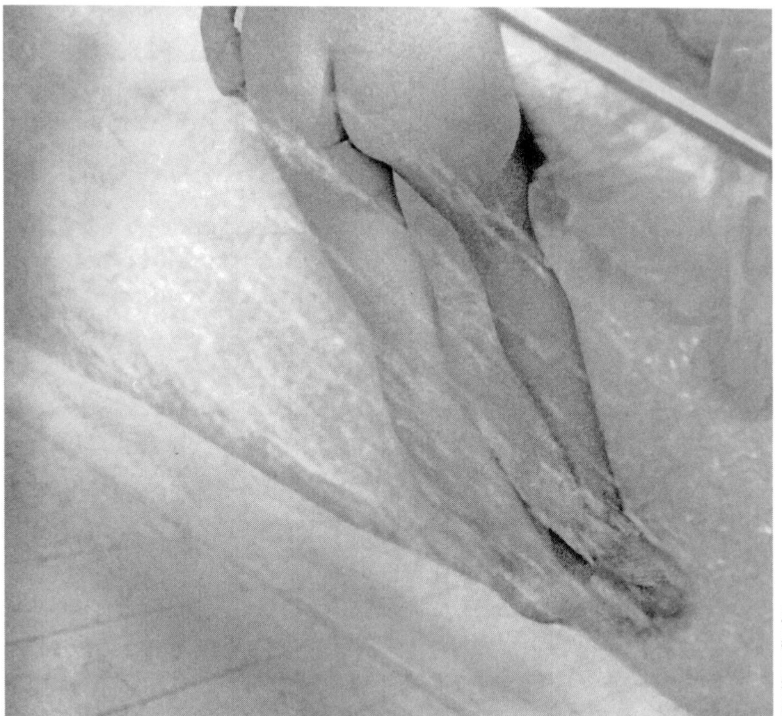

Universal Pictures/Photofest

Figure 19. Nude figure slumped across tub wall—a rare still from an outtake of the shower scene, revealing the bare buttocks of stand-in Marli Renfro.

In shot 6, Hitchcock creates one of his signature cinematic techniques: he positions his camera on the floor just outside the tub wall. We see Marion fall across the tub wall, bringing the shower curtain with her. Her head slams the bathroom floor with a sickening thud, and her arm falls across her face, blocking our view. This is a disorienting shot; it places the audience in the same position as the victim at the same time as it completes the downward movement that characterizes the third act of the shower scene. The audience is now on the floor of the bathroom with Marion. Putting us on the same level as Marion allows Hitchcock to make a parallel between the physical assault on Marion and the cinematic assault on the audience.

Shot 7 is a transitional shot; it prepares the audience for what is perhaps the most creative—but shocking and startling—shot pairing in cinematic history, the dissolve from drain to eye. Shot 7 is a repeat of shot 10 from the first act of the shower scene: a low-angle, POV shot of the showerhead, but this time not from Marion's POV since she is slumped across the bathtub wall, but rather from the enunciator's POV. The sense of loss that this brief shot generates is powerful. As we look at the showerhead, we realize what is at the bottom of the tub. Hitchcock uses the water as a transition to the next shot, shot 8, a high-angle shot of the bathtub floor, with Marion's splayed feet extending the full horizontal length of the frame. This is a heartbreaking shot, but it's shocking as well because seeping out from beneath the feet, just above the ankles, is a dark stream that the audience recognizes as blood. This chilling symbol of Marion's life ebbing away becomes the focal point of Hitchcock's camera, which pans to the left to follow the mixture of blood and water as it flows toward the drain.

Robert Kolker says that great art is "formally complete and contextually open" (206). Kolker explains that the "closed form opens up the picture (or the piece of music) and allows it to keep communicating with us at emotional and intellectual levels often so profound that we either experience more at each viewing or hearing or we take pleasure in having the original experience over and over again" (206–207). In making his claim that *Psycho* is great art, he discusses "the dark power of its images" (207). Certainly the mixture of blood and water is one of the film's darkly powerful images. The contextual openness of this image is patently obvious: the "sacrifice" of Marion by the jealous mother Norma invites one to see the shower scene as a subversion of religious imagery: the admixture of blood and water, the two potent fluids of Christian ritual, leads Marion not to redemption and salvation, but rather to death and nothingness. The archetypal mother Norma does not bring life but rather death. All of the elements of birth are presented in the shower scene: water, the origin of life; blood, the essential fluid; nakedness, our original condition; the knife, the instrument to cut the umbilical cord. These appear in conjunction with Marion's attempt to redeem herself, to save herself from crime and punishment. Yet in *Psycho*'s "bleak vision," as Kolker calls it, there is no chance for redemption. The imagery of the shower scene is not birth but death.

In shot 8, as the camera continues to pan left to trace the flow of blood and water, it comes to rest on the shower drain. The camera then dollies in to an extreme close-up of the drain, the center of which is a gaping black hole. Swirling counter clockwise around this hole and emptying into it is the blood and water mixture. Then, in one of the most stunning dissolves in cinema history, the black hole of the drain metamorphoses into the eye of Marion for shot 9. This is probably Hitchcock's most contextually open shot: it literally begs for interpretation and reveals more of its meaning with each viewing.

The dissolve to an extreme close-up of Marion's eye in shot 9 is accomplished graphically through a continuity of shapes—the round drain and the oval eye—but a discontinuity of directions—the counter clockwise flow of water down the drain and the circular clockwise movement of the camera. This dissolve is Hitchcock's visual representation of the vortex of violence, which in his films always leads to death and destruction. The camera dollies back to reveal the grotesque effect of the vortex of violence—Marion's face crushed against the unyielding tile of the bathroom floor. What a chilling visualization of the fragility of human flesh when it comes into contact with the hard, unyielding reality of physical mass! Human flesh has no chance when it comes into contact with a cold tiled surface or with the terrible hardness of a knife blade. Shot 10, a close-up of the showerhead, interrupts the dollying out of the camera, and, according to many commentators, was inserted to cover up a glitch in the production process: Marion (Janet Leigh) undercuts the static representation of her death by inadvertently swallowing. Supposedly, Alma Hitchcock, Alfred's sometimes collaborator and trusted critic, noticed the movement during a screening, and so an insert of the showerhead was spliced in to cover the glitch.

Shot 11 is a continuation of the dollying out, but the camera suddenly tilts up and pans right, leaving Marion out of the frame. In terms of standard studio narrative practices and the Hollywood style, this is a stunning camera move, for it effectively removes the protagonist and the star from the storyline. Joseph Stefano talked about this narrative "problem" in his interview with me: "After the shower scene, we've lost the person we were with, that we identified with, that we cared about. Remember, we didn't want that cop to arrest her. We wanted her to get away with the money. . . . Then suddenly she's dead. . . . And so I said to Hitch, 'At that time, the movie is over unless we get the audience to care about Norman.'" Shot 11 is therefore a narrative transition. It's length—at thirty-four seconds, the longest single shot in the scene—allows Hitchcock to make the narrative shift from Marion to Norman. Hitchcock accomplishes this through a brilliant and complicated series of camera moves—tilting, panning, and dollying—that take the audience away from Marion, out of the bathroom, and into the motel room. The camera dollies in on the hidden MacGuffin, the $40,000 folded up into a newspaper, holds on that image for two beats, and then tilts up to the window through which we see the ominous house on the hill, with glowing, roiling clouds behind it, and we hear Norman say, "Mother, Oh God, Mother! Blood! Blood!" In the light emanating from the door of the house, we see the tiny figure of Norman run out the front door and start down toward the motel.

Thus ends the shower scene and the first act of the film. I prefer to see *Psycho* as a two-act film rather than the a standard three-act structure-film. The film's form is more akin, I believe, to the two-act structure of the television series, *Alfred Hitchcock Presents*. If one views the film's form in this way, then one can see the shower scene as a structural device that allows the story to shift narrative gears and move away from Marion and toward Norman. In effect, the film starts over again, in a grotesque kind of looping, with Norman and the dead Marion in the motel room, just like Sam and the alive Marion in *their* hotel room. Norman is like Sam in the debt he owes to his dead father; Sam's alimony to his wife finds a parallel in Norman's payment to his mother of his own life. In effect, Norman gives life to his mother, just as she gave life to him. At the end of the shower scene, Marion has descended to death, but Norman and, by extension, Norma have ascended to narrative power by becoming the twin protagonists of Act II.

CHAPTER 12

Homage

Always make the audience suffer as much as possible.

—ALFRED HITCHCOCK

In his essay that concludes *A Casebook on Psycho* (2004), author/editor Robert Kolker discusses the paradox of *Psycho*. It is "a film so grim and dark . . . a film that takes . . . [the audience] down the drain and out from the swamp." Yet, at the same time, it is a film "we keep wanting to look [at] again to experience the pleasure of it, the pleasure of fear, and the ways in which that pleasure is created" (206). In effect, the audience covers their eyes while at the same time peaking through their fingers. The part of the film that epitomizes this paradoxical reaction is the shower scene.

Cyndy Hendershot provides insight into the paradoxical response that the shower scene evokes. In analyzing the Cold War horror film, she incorporates the theories of French essayist and philosopher Georges Bataille, who discusses the interplay of taboo and transgression. Bataille believes, according to Hendershot, that the transgressive act is caused by the power of the taboo itself. Georges Bataille maintains that in the case of sexual transgression, ". . . the object of the prohibition was first marked out for coveting by the prohibition itself: if the prohibition was essentially of a sexual nature it must have drawn attention to the sexual value of the object (or rather, its erotic value)." According to Hendershot, Bataille believes that the emotions of horror and fear "inspire the act of transgression." Hendershot says, "It is the experience of terror that allows the transgression to accrue value." Bataille also states, "The taboo gives the transgression a value it would not possess outside of its relationship to the taboo. . . . The limits imposed by the taboo make the transgressive act one that is appealing . . ." (2).

I believe that Bataille's theories can help us understand the cultural power that the shower scene exerts. From the 1930s through the 1950s, both the Production Code and the studio system had created a potent environment of taboos. But, as Hendershot claims, "As taboos are emphasized more and more in 1950s America, the allure of transgression was heightened" (1). By 1959, the taboo dam was about to burst, and the shower scene in *Psycho* was the precipitating force. The twin taboos of sex and violence, and the fear and terror they evoked, had created an irresistible desire for transgression. The shower scene was the result. Not only did Hitchcock give Marion a secret erotic and adulterous life, but he presented her erotically. Moreover, in Norman, Hitchcock creates a character with an overpowering drive to violence, but Hitchcock suggests that the etiology of the violence lies in incest and necrophilia, probably the most powerful of taboos even today.

The fact that audiences are both attracted to and repelled by the sex and violence on the screen helps to explain why they keep returning to the scene and to the film. It is a testament to the cultural power of taboos that the scene continues to have this transgressive allure, even though the society that the film was made for has been dramatically transformed in the last fifty years. Undoubtedly, the shower scene also has nostalgic appeal. In its various transformations as homage and sometimes as satire, there is a recognition that the shock value of the scene has lessened somewhat. However, both sex and violence, although much more explicitly presented today, still have taboo power. And the film has not lost its shocking effect. In fact, in a nonscientific critics' poll conducted by *Total Film* magazine in 2004, the shower scene in *Psycho* was voted the "best movie death" of all time ("*Psycho* shower scene tops poll" 1).

An additional explanation for the scene's grip on the audience, past and present, is its anomalous position in Hitchcock's oeuvre. The scene's explicit violence and its nudity were not part of Hitchcock's suspense formula. In fact, the scene contradicted, somewhat, Hitchcock's own claim that "Fear is a feeling that people like to feel when they are certain of being in safety" (Perry 2). However, as Bill Krohn points out in discussing Stefano's screenplay, ". . . instead of descriptions of the knife entering the body, the script offers a series of image and metaphors which make the sequence an attack on the spectator's vision, on the screen where the scene is being projected, and on the film itself" (225). Stefano's script describes the murder in this way:

29: MARY—ECU,

. . . a hand comes into shot. The hand holds an enormous bread knife. The flint of the blade shatters the screen to an almost total silver blankness.

30: THE SLASHING,

An impression of a knife flashing, as if tearing at the very screen, ripping the film. Over it the brief gulps of screaming. And then silence.

Dennis Perry claims that in the shower scene, Hitchcock had subverted his own idea of fear in the midst of safety that was the touchstone of his previous films. Perry calls this idea of feeling fear while experiencing safety "the paradox of the sublime" (4).

Clearly, the response of audiences to *Psycho* goes beyond the paradox of the sublime. The fear that the audience feels while watching the shower scene is the result of powerful taboos, and so the transgression of these taboos becomes the act of viewing itself. The goal of such cinema is to create a feeling of terror in the audience.

The complex audience response to the shower scene is the key to understanding why it has taken on a life of its own, over and above the film that contains it. How else would one explain the fact that the scene appears in advertisements, in sitcoms, in late-night comedy shows, in comic books, in single-camera dramatic television shows, and in films. It's as if the scene has become its own *raison d'etre*. The shower curtain and the knife have become as recognizable—maybe more so—as the skull and grave from the grave diggers' scene in *Hamlet*. The complex, contradictory responses of the audiences to the shower scenes help to explain its position as *the* iconic scene in all of film history. I realize that this is quite a sweeping claim, but I believe it can be supported by the various manifestations of the shower scene in almost all aspects of popular culture.

One night, as I was taking a break from writing this book, I decided to watch television. During a commercial interruption, I was startled to see a woman preparing to enter the shower. I saw the woman turn her back and remove her robe, revealing a bare back. I then saw a high-angle shot of the woman's legs as she stepped into the shower. The translucent shower curtain closed. Then shots of the shower rod clips and the showerhead appeared. The woman looked down, and I heard the familiar strings of the *Psycho* score. An off-screen voice said, "It's spider season." I realized

I was not only watching the shower scene from *Psycho* but also seeing an ad for Terminix. All of a sudden, I felt that I was on a busman's holiday: I just couldn't escape the shower scene. Only two weeks before, my wife and I had taken our nephews Ian and Zach to see the Pixar film *Finding Nemo*. Near the end of the film, the Australian dentist's daughter, Darla, a real terror, appears in the doorway to the accompaniment of the strings from the shower scene. Just that brief aural cue alone is enough to alert the audience to her danger. For a Christmas present this year, I received a DVD of *Looney Tunes Back in Action: The Movie*, which features a hilarious send-up of the shower scene, with Bugs Bunny standing in for Marion and screaming obstreperously in the shower. There's even an in-joke featuring a hand squirting chocolate syrup in the water of the tub!

It seems that *Psycho* and the shower scene have become firmly entrenched in the infrastructure of popular culture. Examples of the scene's influence abound. The film has made several appearances in *The Simpsons*, the most notable of which occurs in the episode entitled "Itchy and Scratchy and Marge," which was aired on December 20, 1990. In this episode, Homer's daughter Maggie attacks him with a large mallet. The scene is presented in the style of the shower scene, complete with Eisensteinian montage and the familiar strings of Bernard Herrmann's score. In Steven Spielberg's television series *Amazing Stories*, an episode that aired on October 13, 1986, entitled "Welcome to My Nightmare," features a teenager named Harry who is obsessed with horror films and who would rather watch movies than live his own life. After wishing that his life were more like the certainty of a movie, he becomes trapped in the film *Psycho* and is attacked in the shower scene by Norma Bates. Fortunately, he realizes his error and is saved at the last minute as the bottom of the bathtub drops away (Kerzoncuf, email). Universal Studios has created a marketing phenomenon out of *Psycho* and the shower scene. On the tour at Universal Studios, Florida, one can see a demonstration of how the scene was shot and also buy *Psycho* hats, T-shirts, ashtrays—even a shower curtain imprinted with the outline of a female figure. In 1992, Innovation Comics came out with a three-volume comic book series on *Psycho*. Volume 2 features the shower scene in a twenty-seven-panel layout with very realistic looking drawings, which were done with the cooperation of Janet Leigh. The shower scene has also entered the domain of toys and memorabilia. When I interviewed Danny Greene, the supervising sound editor for *Psycho*, he gave me a *Psycho* memento that I have brought to several conferences where I talk about *Psycho*—a large plastic replica of the shower scene knife, complete with sound effects: a button in the handle triggers the slashing strings of the Herrmann score. I believe Hitchcock would have been amused. These and other reflections of *Psycho* and the shower scene in shows as diverse as *Law and Order*, *Murder She Wrote*, and *Saturday Night Live* are a testimony to the cultural staying power of the scene. There's even an Australian band called The Shower Scene from *Psycho* (Mogg, email).

There are other indications of the cultural ubiquity of the shower scene. One is the Internet. When I first conceived of this project, I got 18,000 hits when I typed "shower scene+Psycho" in Google. Today, I typed in the same words, and I got 26,400! The shower scene is growing on the Web. Sites include everything from "official" Alfred Hitchcock pages to "edit your own shower scene" activities. One site features ten stills from the shower scene showing the disputed "knife entering the flesh" shot. Other sites perpetuate many of the "myths" about the scene, including the cold water in the shower, the number of shots in the actual shower murder, etc. Even in the art world, the shower scene and the film that contains it have been the subjects of several exhibitions. In 1992, *Psycho* had its own art exhibit, curated by Christian Leigh, who also edited the very handsomely printed exhibit catalogue. In addition, New York's Museum of Modern Art, in 1999, featured a multi-media kiosk to celebrate the centenary of Hitchcock's birth. One exhibit was extremely popular: a "shot-by-shot deconstruction of *Psycho*'s shower scene," accompanied by recorded commentaries from Hitchcock interviews (Robischon). The Museum of Modern Art at Oxford put up an exhibit entitled "Notorious: Alfred Hitchcock and Contemporary Art," which showcased Douglas Gordon's *Psycho* (Romney). Hitchcock's one-hour-and-forty-nine-minute film is extended to twenty-four hours, making the shower scene last almost fifty-three minutes!

Kolker claims, "The commercial, critical, and later, scholarly success of *Psycho*, the fact that it was a catalyst for a whole series of 'slasher' films that have now gone on for so long that they are consciously made as parodies and its formal methods and its darkness, have made it tempting to imitate" (249). This imitation has sometimes been in the form of satire, as in Mel Brooks' *High Anxiety* (1977), when Brooks, playing Dr. Richard Harpo Thorndyke, is attacked in the shower by a loony bellhop (Barry Levinson) wielding a rolled up newspaper as a weapon. Instead of blood, the ink from the newsprint goes down the shower drain. The 1970s initiated a series of revisionary takes on classic film genres, such as the Western (*Blazing Saddles*, 1974; *Little Big Man*, 1970) and film noir (*The Long Goodbye*, 1973; *Chinatown*, 1974). In a sense, the 1970s was America's great "film decade," during which scholars, critics, and audiences were rediscovering and re-evaluating Hollywood's film legacy. Film classes burgeoned in the academy, and critics under the influence of Andrew Sarris and the auteur theory were rewriting film history. In effect, Hitchcock films became part of the revision and re-evaluation that took place in the scholarly and cinematic world of the 1970s. It is no coincidence that Hitchcock's career effectively came to an end in 1975, with the release of *Family Plot*, a film with very little violence, at the same time that the effect of the changing attitudes toward taboos and transgression and toward the American film canon was starting to take place. In 1980, the year that Hitchcock died, a Hitchcock admirer and emulator made a film that became emblematic of the shifting attitude toward the taboos of sex and violence: Brian DePalma's *Dressed to Kill* is a suspense thriller patterned on *Psycho* and contains a clear homage to the shower scene. Just as in *Psycho*, the "heroine," Kate Miller (Angie Dickinson), is killed off relatively early in the film, but she is killed in an explicit razor slashing on an elevator. All the ingredients of the shower scene are there: the enclosed space, the "tainted woman" (she is having an affair, like Marion), the mysterious female attacker, and the glowing, wicked blade. What is different though is the explicit violence and the gore. Kate is slashed across the wrist, the face, and the neck; the attacker cuts her down the middle, starting at her neck and traveling downward. This grotesque scene is shot in color, with blood gushing from all the wounds. Kate even reaches her hand out for help, just as Marion does. Earlier in the film, we had seen Kate taking a shower; through the glass we can see a full frontal shot showing breasts, nipples, and pubic hair. Kate even masturbates as she looks at her husband shaving. It seems as if DePalma is using the shower and the elevator to show just how much things had changed in the America of the 1980s.

Whether as satire or homage, the shower scene has become a cultural index or marker. Its ubiquity testifies to the fascination audiences have with the changing nature of taboos and with the varying levels of transgression a society can tolerate or allow. These levels are clearly evident in the sequels, the prequel, and the remake of *Psycho*. Richard Franklin, director of *Psycho II* (1983), presents a revision of the original *Psycho*, with Norman discovering his "real mother," Emma Spool, at the end of the film and then killing her again and giving her his voice and life. The film begins with the shower scene from the original *Psycho*. I asked Richard Franklin why he had decided to begin with this iconic scene. He stated:

> I took the view that all that was necessary for a viewer seeing *Psycho II* (whether or not they'd seen the original) was to know Norman Bates killed women while in drag. This is set up via a combination of this prologue and the courtroom scene.
>
> Hitchcock's story essentially ends (at the beginning of Bloch's novel) with the death of Marion. The rest is simply a detective story after the fact sustained by the mystery of the banshee in the old dark house. I felt we could begin our story with the aftermath (twenty-two years later) of this death. Obviously, the shower scene also gets the film off to a strong start and allowed audiences pre DVD and before the film was available on tape, to see its best scene as it looked on its first release. . . .
>
> Jerry Goldsmith rerecorded the shower murder cue, for copyright reasons, and we remixed from the original sound elements. The scene is still surprisingly strong with only the sound effects.

In *Psycho II,* Franklin edits the shower scene from the original *Psycho.* Gone is the famous dissolve from the drain to Marion's eye, most likely because this long dissolve keeps the focus on Marion, but Franklin's film is about Norman. In fact, all the subsequent *Psycho* films focus on Norman, ironically restoring the emphasis of the Bloch novel that was the impetus for the series. Block's *Psycho* begins with Norman, not Marion. What Franklin adds to the film, however, is emblematic of the changes in American culture in the twenty-three years separating the two films. The world of 1960 was culturally light years from the world of 1983. The intervening years had witnessed the assassinations of John Kennedy, Robert Kennedy, and Martin Luther King Jr.; the civil rights movement; the Vietnam War and protests; the growth of the youth culture; the generation gap; the increase in crime; the burgeoning of rock music and rock culture; and the increasing tolerance for transgressing the taboos of sex and violence in almost all aspects of popular culture.

In *Psycho*, there are two murders; in *Psycho II*, that number is trebled, and the murders are more grotesque and shocking than Marion's killing. The ubiquitous butcher knife is plunged graphically into flesh, and the red blood pours out. Lila Crane, Marion's sister, the character reprised by Vera Miles, is killed in a shocking way. The butcher knife is plunged down into her open, screaming mouth and out her neck. Emma Spool, Norma Bates's sister and, it turns out, Norman's real mother, is killed by a shovel wielded by Norman, who viciously slams the tool down on her head, and she falls to the floor, twitching and shaking. Edward Gross, writing in the magazine *Cinefantastique*, says of *Psycho II*:

> Writer Tom Holland responded to charges leveled by some at the film, that instead of emulating Hitchcock, *Psycho II* wallowed in the excesses of the currently popular slasher genre. "I didn't want to do a slasher film," said Holland. "At the same time, as you can tell from parts of the film, there was a feeling from the studio that there should be enough shock moments to satisfy the slice-and-dice crowd out there. Given today's market, I couldn't really disagree with them a lot. If you think about it, it was *Psycho* that opened up that whole genre."

Psycho III and *Psycho IV* push the envelope even further. In *Psycho III*, directed by Anthony Perkins, five murders occur, and all are bloody, including one that takes place on a toilet seat as a young woman is urinating; she has her throat cut. There is no fancy editing to disguise the violence, only special effects that allow the viewer to see the knife slash her throat and blood spurt out. It's sobering to think that a 1960s audience was shocked by a brief shot of a toilet seat, while a 1983 audience gets to see not only the toilet seat, but someone using it and then getting murdered in the act! Also included in *Psycho III* are male and female nudity and explicit sex. There's even a suicide scene in a bathtub full of bloody water. In addition, the woman attempting to commit suicide, hallucinating from loss of blood, looks up from her bloody bath and mistakes Norma Bates, knife in hand, for the Virgin Mary!

Psycho IV is a prequel and therefore exposes the incestuous connection between Norma and Norman that is the etiology of his madness. A young Norma, grieving her husband's death, takes the teenage Norman to bed with her but castigates him when he gets an erection. She alternately teases and punishes him, causing sexual confusion. She dresses him up in female clothes and taunts him. Then she takes a lover, and they both abuse and humiliate Norman. In revenge, he poisons both of them, but keeps his mother's corpse out of unbearable guilt over his matricide. In his mother's outfit, he commits gruesome crimes, killing two young women, both murders presented explicitly and graphically.

Although *Psycho III* is bloodier and more gruesome than *Psycho IV*, the latter film is more daring in its presentation of taboos and transgression. In the original *Psycho*, the administrators of the Production Code condemned Stefano's script because of its veiled references to incest.

Although *Psycho IV* contains no shower scene, the scene's imprint—its fingerprints—are all over the film. *Psycho* opened the taboo floodgates, and we are still reeling from the effects.

The grip that *Psycho* still holds on contemporary filmmakers was evident in 1998, when Gus Van Sant directed a remake of *Psycho*, billed as a shot-by-shot replication of the film. Van Sant, fresh from the success of *Good Will Hunting* (1997), was able to convince Universal Studios to let him remake the Hitchcock classic. Editor Amy Duddleston had the daunting task of editing the shower scene. I asked her if she and Van Sant thought of the shower scene as the set piece of the film. She replied, "Yes, definitely. We got all the shots as they are in the original. We cut it the exact way it was cut originally. But there was something not quite right with it." In response, Van Sant lengthened the scene slightly and added some shots. In chapter 11, I claim that the shower scene is four minutes long and contains sixty shots. Van Sant's version is four minutes and seventeen seconds and contains seventy-one shots. The additional shots are of two types. The first is material that Van Sant adds to give the scene his own stamp (e.g., two shots of clouds and one shot of Marion's pupil dilating as she is dying). The second type is made up of shots that are additions to ones Hitchcock used in the original. Van Sant adds two shots of Marion's feet wading in the bloody water of the tub. These added shots are in keeping with the more explicit presentation of violence in the film. In addition, Van Sant "restores" the controversial shot that Hitchcock had to remove over Joseph Stefano's objections: the bird's-eye shot of Marion slumped across the tub, buttocks exposed, and legs slightly spread. This, indeed, is the most powerful shot of Van Sant's scene. One wonders how a 1960 audience would have reacted to such a shot. Van Sant also lengthens the vertiginous camera move as the drain dissolves into Marion's eye. Another alteration happened serendipitiously. Because of a synching problem, Herrmann's music comes in a beat or two late when Norma pulls open the shower curtain. In viewing the first dub, Van Sant and Duddleston realized the problem but liked the result. In our interview, Duddleston said to me, "That was a beautiful mistake. It was a happy mistake." Because most of the audience knows the scene, the tardy arrival of the music is oddly effective.

Will the shower scene continue to hold its position in the culture of twenty-first-century America? I think so. As long as we have taboos about sex and violence, we will continue to experience desires to transgress these taboos. If we do consider 1960 as a turning point, we might also come to view the shower scene as the fulcrum for the lever of cultural change.

CHAPTER 13

The First Time

> I vividly remember a Saturday matinee in 1960 when two girlfriends and I spent much of the screening with our eyes shut listening to the music and to the audience's screams as we tried to guess when we might venture to look again at the screen whose terrors were unaccountably thrilling.
>
> —LINDA WILLIAMS

Fred Simon, Documentary Filmmaker

I had never before seen anything even remotely that scary. It's only with the wisdom of hindsight, and having seen the film since then, that I realize that the horror of the scene took place not on film (for the stabbing was not explicit anyway, right?) but rather in how my imagination filled in the blanks of what I didn't see. With his typical genius, Hitchcock had *me* create a scene far worse than anything he could have shown.

I guess it's been forty-one or forty-two years since I saw *Psycho*. The fact that I have any memory of that first viewing at all is a huge statement about the film.

I saw it on a summer evening, at the Allen Theatre, one of the grandes dames of theaters of downtown Cleveland. My friend Jay and I took the train (the "rapid") downtown at dusk. As fourteen-year-olds, going downtown alone at night with no adult supervision was very unusual, and very exciting. It may well have been a "first"; and I know we were feeling very grown up, very independent. I remember walking up Euclid Avenue, Cleveland's main drag, and entering the theater as the summer dusk was fading into darkness. We bought our tickets and made our way up to the balcony. Strangely though, my clearest memory is not of the film itself, but the hour or two after it ended.

Leaving the theater, we of course were shaken. We went back down onto Euclid Avenue. It was only 9:00 or 9:30, and the street was undoubtedly fairly well lit and probably reasonably trafficked. To me though, it was full out dark, and it had become a terrifying place, very different than it was two hours earlier.

We had to walk several long blocks back to the train (rapid transit) that would take us home to the suburbs. Every shadow was menacing, every person a demon. The landscape had changed. Each darkened doorway a threat.

I remember, in particular, the double doorway of Bond's Clothes on the corner of 9th Street and Euclid Avenue. In the display windows, male mannequins stood in suits, their snap-brim hats shadowing their faces. They drove me across to the other side of Euclid. Jay followed. Although I felt pretty much frozen, I kept moving only because not moving would have been scarier. We were certainly no longer grownups.

I had no idea what Jay was feeling, because we didn't talk. Not a word. Neither of us. Not all the way down Euclid, not onto the train. Not all the way home. I think we were afraid of the uncool terror we would reveal if we spoke.

Although "freaked out" was a phrase still five years into the future (it was only 1960), it describes perfectly what I was feeling.

Epilogue

Jay and I weren't friends for very long. I heard that he grew up to become a dentist, but that might have happened anyway.

• • •

Wes Craven, Director, *Nightmare on Elm Street, Scream*

I didn't see *Psycho* when it first came out. I was a Baptist in a conservative church that forbid moviegoing. I remember my mother talking about the movie to a neighbor woman (it was the buzz of the town). Years later, when I was on my own and becoming a movie devotee, I caught the movie in an art house theater in New York.

By the time I got to the shower scene in *Psycho*, of course, I was already fully convinced that I was watching the work of a master craftsman that was unpredictable, wickedly wry, and capable of anything. Still, nothing quite prepares the viewer, not years of references to it, not having watched other scenes of bloodshed, not having tried to imagine it a hundred times in the past. It's simply overwhelming, and the first time that I realized one of the great truths to making frightening movies: that the first monster the audience must fear, and must fear beyond anything else in the story, is the filmmaker himself.

Hitchcock's sophistication, humor, carefully storyboarded shots, all give the sense that you're watching a finely constructed watch move through its cycles. But then there's this scene—and the watch shatters, the humor vanishes, and one is left in utter isolation with the victim—realizing this is not a civilized movie, after all—it is primal, savage, and heading straight for the jugular of your most deeply hidden fears. A sense of disorientation sets in—as it does when once-in-a-lifetime things occur—then terror—then the wish to run—then the horror when you realize you're paralyzed—unable to move, unable to look away.

You're never the same again. Like getting off the most shattering roller-coaster imaginable. Dizzy, shaky, giddy, and laughing. Glad to be alive.

I guess that's why it's a classic, no?

• • •

Carolyn Harrison, English Professor

I was at the Jersey shore, probably in August. My aunt and uncle treated me to the movie: "Your money's no good tonight, Carolyn." The movie house was built on stilts out into the bay, so the front third of the theater was suspended over lapping water! There had been lots of talk about the movie, although I doubt I knew any details (Hitchcock keeping secrets). *Psycho* was a revelation, much like *The Graduate* in my mind: groundbreaking, a beginning, a foretelling of cultural film expression for the future. Hugely frightening. I believe that I watched most of the movie from between my fingers. The screaming music contributed to the suspense and horror. I felt exhausted when the movie was over. And all the time the waves lapped against the foundation!

• • •

Horace Fleming, Classical Music Radio Host

I decided to take another look at the film after many years and found that the first half held up, for me, with an almost undiminished intensity. Wow! What a tale! It interests me, too, that we were both the same age when the film was released. There is no question that the shower scene is the culmination of Hitchcock's masterpiece, and, as cinematic *art*, may yet prove prophetic. Hitchcock, who loved women, was fearless in his vision of their exploitation. I had forgotten how beautiful Leigh was, is.

Incidentally, Perkins went to Rollins College in Winter Park, FL, where I lived and went to school in the early '60s. I saw the film there when it was first released.

Psycho is a film about Eros, Mars, and the destabilizing force of Aphrodite, who, some say, "was born from the foam that gathered about the severed parts of the emasculated Uranus."

The screenplay was written by Joseph Stefano in the late '50s, and American sexuality was very deep in the closet. It's not a stretch, if memory serves, to say that most Americans were still living in a nineteenth-century world where the naked ankle could signal loose morals." What Hitchcock's black-and-white nightmare of brutality and lust did was unmask the erotic nature of control, the hidden bedrock of male fantasy, which played well to the curiosity of a culture given to the burgeoning titillation of the undeveloped adolescent male libido. The film was released in 1960, when I was sixteen.

More than ever, sex is the prime mover in our world of sell and be sold, especially when you add violence, and especially when that violence is directed against the eternal object of unfulfilled, adolescent fantasy: *woman*. What Hitchcock did in *Psycho* was to marry the two: violence and sex. It becomes apparent that after the murder, sex falls away as a prime mover in the plot, replaced by horror at the unraveling insanity of the epicene monster Norman Bates, played brilliantly by Anthony Perkins in the defining role of his career. After the shower scene, there is virtually nothing erotic in the film; Eros has given way to Mars.

• • •

John Baxter, Author, *A Pound of Paper*, *Stanley Kubrick*, *Woody Allen*

Some countries chronically lag behind the zeitgeist. While it may have been 1960 in the rest of the world, when *Psycho* arrived in my native country of Australia, World War II had yet to be fought, and the British Empire still ruled.

The Prince Edward in Sydney was a cinema palace in the grand style, with chandeliers, marble halls, and a mighty Wurlitzer organ wedged into a grotto in one wall of the auditorium, where a beaming peroxide blonde played "Lady of Spain" and other favorites before every screening. Amid this threadbare opulence, the advertising for *Psycho*, and particularly the life-sized cardboard standee of Hitchcock, pointing to watch and warning that nobody would be admitted after the first few minutes, made an incongruous juxtaposition. (Years later, when the TV series *Ironside* had a bungalow adjacent to Hitchcock's at Universal, Raymond Burr, its star, placed one of these effigies in his toilet, where it could be clearly seen from next door. An assistant explained, "Mr. Burr is tired of hearing about 'Raymond Burr in Alfred Hitchcock's *Rear Window*.' Now he can see Alfred Hitchcock in Raymond Burr's rear window.")

On islands like Australia, where the points of entry are few and easily monitored, censorship flourishes out of simple geography; it's easy to do, so it *is* done. The government assessed every incoming film, purged it of nudity and violence, and occasionally banned it entirely. Some cuts, particularly to sex scenes, showed the niggling precision of those physicists who assay cigarette ash and compute the weight of the smoke. A couple of frames trimmed from *Darling* ensured we didn't catch a subliminal flash of Julie Christie's nipple as she fell forward onto a bed, and *Butterfield 8*, while retaining Elizabeth Taylor's confession to Eddie Fisher that she'd been molested as a child, omitted her subsequent admission that she *enjoyed* it.

Since any adult story demands some reference to sex, flashes of sensuality did survive. Violence and horror, however, had no such redeeming merit. *King Kong*, *Dracula*, and *Frankenstein* had been long suppressed, and even mild efforts like *The Creature from the Black Lagoon* existed only in truncated versions. As for crime and gangster movies, the slightest sign of blood was looked on as an incitement to homicide and riot.

Psycho, and particularly the shower sequence, attracted speculation long before its local release. Rumors suggested that the censors had cut part of it, or perhaps the whole scene. We later found that Hitchcock visited Sydney at the furor's height, and, using the same flattery and misdirection he'd employed with the Production Code in America, convinced them to leave it intact.

Not knowing this, most of Sydney's film community was in the Prince Edward on opening day, craned toward the screen, alert for that tell-tale blip that indicated a cut. Before long, however, we'd forgotten what we were there for.

The heavy-breasted Janet Leigh of the opening hotel room sequence, for instance. We'd seen her ample curves in movie costume, but never in a *deshabille* so domestic; never so . . . well, undressed. It was like walking in on your sister in the bathroom. Then there was the monochrome photography. Traditionally, black and white signaled either art-house seriousness or low-budget exploitation. Into which category did *Psycho* fall? Even for those of us who, French/English dictionaries in hand, had puzzled out some of the essays in *Cahiers du Cinema*, and who already possessed an inkling that there might be more to Hitch than the amiable joker of *Alfred Hitchcock Presents*, were startled by the confidence, even arrogance, with which he annexed what we'd later call the Slasher Movie in the name of Art.

For most Australians, the concept of the "art film" began and ended in continental Europe with the literary adaptations of Claude Autant-Lara and the melodramas of Marcel Carne. We were astonished when the enigmatic cycle cop of *Psycho*, employed as a symbol of menace, tipped a knowing wink to Cocteau's *Orphée*. Bernard Herrmann's music confused us further. That Herrmann went to compose for Hitchcock after doing *Citizen Kane* seemed to us simply more evidence of the way serious composers, even in the European cinema—look at Malcolm Arnold and Georges Auric—were forced to labor in the movie factory. For proof that Herrmann and Hitchcock had sold out, we needed to look no further than the failure of *Vertigo* two years before, dismissed as the cheesiest kind of psychic thriller, a slightly upmarket competitor to William Castle's half-witted *The Tingler* and *House on Haunted Hill.*

Now, however, as the *wheep-wheeping* and *thrum-thrumming* of Herrmann's strings dragged us behind the shower curtain and into nightmare, we could feel the suspicion roused by the black-shaded cop harden into a certainty. *Psycho* was more than just another thriller and Hitchcock no simple entertainer.

Among Australia's rugged plant species is a thorn called the bindi. A tiny tetrahedron of iron-hard wood, each corner armed with a needle-sharp spine, it lodges itself so securely in the sole of a sneaker as to be unextractable, even with pliers. *Psycho*, and the shower scene, had that effect. One could not get them out of one's mind. At each step, the spike insistently aggravated the initial wound.

Once the film magazines published frame-by-frame breakdown of the shower scene, we had the material for analyzing its effect, if not the tools for doing so. Understanding the impact of these images demanded wider cultural horizons and a more precise critical vocabulary. By the time Sam Fuller's *Shock Corridor* was banned outright by the censors three years later, and *The Naked Kiss* the following year hacked off its opening sequence of a hairless whore attacking the pimp who'd shaved her bald, we had the rudiments of both. Clearly we were in the presence of something fresh; a more aggressive art cinema, rooted not in the literature of Europe but in the America of the paperback, the comic book and the tabloid. Still trash, but now the Higher Trash, informed by a new and lively aesthetic.

In an environment charged with accumulated resentment, one cultural event can serve as a lightning rod. In Australia, critics were soon placing the censors under sustained attack, and preaching the rehabilitation of whole genres once considered beneath artistic consideration. Within a few years, film festivals were exempted from censorship, then members-only cinemas, until the whole cinema scene in Australia was liberalized. By widening the definitions, *Psycho* and the shower scene began it all.

• • •

Franklin Lewis, Attorney (retired)

I first saw the movie *Psycho* in the summer of 1960 at the Hippodrome Theater in downtown Cleveland. First-run movies were only shown downtown at that time. I went with my best friend, Phil Gould, the second of my three best friends named Phil. We were both big movie fans and especially Hitchcock fans. We had loved films like *Rear Window* and *Vertigo* and were ready for, what we thought, would be another typical Hitchcock movie: many twists and turns and much entertainment. We didn't expect what we got. Things went along smoothly until the shower scene. While Anthony Perkins was doing the job on Janet Leigh, Phil looked at me and said, "Franklin, you're completely white!" I answered, "If I am, then you're the same color." My heart felt like it was going to jump out of my chest for the rest of the movie. I felt some relief when the film ended and also thought what an eerie masterpiece it was.

• • •

Don Heiser, Attorney, (retired)

When someone mentions *Psycho*, I have an overriding and immediate feeling of sweat and fear. At such times, most of the details of the movie and the scene don't readily come to mind, but there is a cloudy aura of anticipation, gloom, darkness, and death.

I saw the film at one of the theaters in the Heights area (could have been at the Cedar Lee, the Heights, the Fairmount, the Center-Mayfield, or the Shaker) during the late summer or early fall of 1960—the period between graduation from college and the beginning of law school. I went on a Friday night with a group of guys that usually went to a movie, out for a hamburger, and cruising on Friday nights.

It was really eerie when Anthony Perkins, dressed as a woman, went to the motel. However, I didn't think anything bad would happen to Janet Leigh because she was so beautiful, so innocent looking. I am ordinarily not taken by surprise by events in movies. I usually can predict what is going to happen. Nevertheless, on that night, I was sitting on the edge of my seat with my arms upright from my knees and my head resting in my cupped hands. When the knifing occurred, I was completely unprepared as to what was occurring. I bolted upright. I was terrified. I had never before, and never since, witnessed a movie scene as surprising and shocking.

For a split second, and only a split second, the audience was quiet. Then there was an eruption of shrill screams, held breaths released, and "Oh my Gods." The screams were not like those in *Halloween* and similar movies, where you expected to be scared (and would be disappointed if you were not), but screams of terrified shock, fear, surprise, and uncertainty as to whether you saw what you thought you saw or were only imagining it. When the show emptied out, people were wandering around with eyes wide open, still unbelieving what they saw and still saying saying, "Oh my God."

I am starting to shake just writing this letter.

• • •

David Freeman, Author, *The Last Days of Alfred Hitchcock, It's All True*

Memory plays tricks and makes new meaning, so at this distance I can't be certain of what actually happened, though there are vivid images in my mind some forty-five years later of seeing *Psycho* on its first release. It was in the outer suburbs of Cleveland and I was in high school. Word of how shocking this movie was had reached Willoughby North High School in advance of the local opening. That may not seem notable in today's world of incessant publicity. Things were quieter in the 1950s. I was aware of Hitchcock and had seen other of his movies. Most vivid were *The Lady Vanishes* and *The 39 Steps*, pictures that were linked in the public's mind and that often turned up as a double bill in what were then called art houses. But those pictures were set in a distant Britain—where I had not yet been—and in the 1930s, which to me might have been the nineteenth century. I had seen them several times. That too requires an explanation. There were no videotapes and certainly no DVDs. Movies that played in art houses weren't often seen on TV. To have seen anything more than once was unusual.

Psycho, I knew, was set in the American Southwest. I hadn't been there either, but it was more recognizable than 1930s Britain. I had to sneak around a bit to see it. My parents hadn't explicitly told me not to go, though I knew they wouldn't approve. I no longer recall the lie I told, but off I went in the company of another young miscreant to a theater in the neighboring town of Mentor to see what all the fuss was about.

The picture opens, famously, with a glimpse through a hotel window at Janet Leigh in her underwear. That sort of thing was usually limited to European movies. I was quite taken with it and thought at first that those shots were what all the fuss was about. The movie soon settled down and so did I. I can't recall my feelings until the scene preceding the shower sequence—the conversation between Leigh and Tony Perkins that is a prelude to the murder. I was hoping she would do the right thing and return the stolen money. I could feel that possibility forming in her head. Perkins—Norman Bates forever—was the cause of her better self emerging and yet he gave me the creeps. It was unsettling. After their talk, as Norman watched through his secret peephole as she undressed, I watched her too—hoping, I'm sure, for another glimpse of flesh. I was aware that this made me little better than creepy Norman, but I was young and the prospect of nudity had my attention. Then mom comes in with her knife. The visceral shock of it shook me. My pal clutched my arm and everyone at the Mentor Theatre—many of them teenagers like myself who had probably lied to someone about where they were—screamed in an unholy mix of fear and guilt. The terror in that old theater was palpable, like a physical object—a giant stone, perhaps, that had descended on us all.

I can't say why, but after I screamed I glanced around (already a nascent journalist, I suppose) and saw people holding onto one another. Some were trembling and one young woman I recognized from school was in tears. I don't recall anyone running out of the theater. I certainly wasn't going anywhere. The past can often seem naïve to the present. After all, we know what came next. *Psycho* was about to usher in generations of slasher movies. None quite so well done and few as frightening, but they've been coming at us ever since.

Since that long ago time, I've seen *Psycho* on several occasions, once with Hitchcock himself. I told him some of my memories I've recounted here. He was interested in my adolescent linking of those shots of Janet Leigh with the prospect of more nudity. He had contemplated, or so he claimed, playing those opening shots of Leigh topless. He said the censors wouldn't permit it. He didn't think the scene as written would have played if he had used a "model" in place of Leigh. It meant he wasn't satisfied with those early scenes. He didn't speculate about any changes to the shower scene. He had spent a week shooting it and thirty-odd years preparing for it. He got it right and he knew it.

• • •

Ted Valvoda, College Professor

It was a special date. My future wife, Mary Alice, and I were going to see a movie at one of the first-run, ornate movie theaters in downtown Cleveland. The movie, we had heard, was spooky, and I especially enjoyed spooky. After all, I had grown up spending Saturday nights and Sunday matinees thrilling to *Frankenstein*, *Dracula*, *The Wolfman*, and *The Mummy*. I thought *Psycho* would be something like those goose-bump-inducing flicks.

The movie began, and it wasn't anything like those monster fests I was used to. Here was a lady who stole some money and was on the lam, checking into a rundown motel in the midst of nowhere. What's so scary about this, I thought. Then she got ready to take a shower. Hmm. This could be more interesting. She turned the shower on, and she proceeded to shower in a rapid series of film cuts. Then a shadowy figure loomed up behind the shower curtain, pulled the curtain back, and the screen cut to an upraised arm wielding a large knife. The music shrieked—*eeh, eeh, eeh! aseeh*—as the intruder repeatedly slashed Janet Leigh. I was breathless, and Mary Alice was almost in my lap, gripping me in fright.

It was all over so fast, we had to sit there and try to process it. What had just happened? Who did that? Why? There was no relaxing for the rest of the picture. Hitchcock had seized and was holding our full attention.

At the end, just for good measure, Hitchcock hit us again with the first sight of mummified momma and the identity of the killer. We were stunned. We had never seen anything like this before.

As we filed out of the theater when the film was over, I still remember vividly, that, although we were surrounded by a large crowd of other moviegoers, *no one was talking!* The silence was eerie. I have never attended any other movie in my life that has had such an emotional impact on an entire audience.

• • •

Alain Kerzoncuf, Physician (retired), Hitchcock Scholar

Answering your question is not so easy. I mean we all have remembrance of the first time we saw *Psycho*, but can we separate the shower scene from the other parts of the movie? (Arbogast on the stairs, "mom" on her chair, cop at the car window, etc.) So I'm going to give you the details I remember, even if it's not exactly what you're looking for.

It was on October 1960, in a Champs Elysées cinema named "Monte Carlo," mid afternoon. Not the rush hour. Rated 18: since I was twenty (but I looked very young), the girl at the box office asked for my ID. Anyways, I was aware, after reading some newspapers and cinema journals, of the shower scene mainly, but not of the ending. I must admit I did not actually immediately realize that this scene was a "chef d'oeuvre." We are talking of "the first time," aren't we? But I clearly remember the "cellar scene" for one simple reason: the screams from the girls in the audience (I have to add that, this time, I was watching the film alone, that is without any friend). One more point: I don't recall having been scared so much. You see, I was in first year at medical school, spending the morning at the hospital and the afternoon dissecting dead bodies, and, even very young, no more influenced by the image of death. Hard to imagine, I agree, but true. Clouzot's *Les Diaboliques* had been an important and repeated subject of conversation when I was sixteen, in your equivalent of high school. Everyone was aware of the story about "the eyes"! In 1999, at the "Cinémathèque Francaise" retrospective, I had the opportunity to watch *Psycho* again on the big screen. What impressed me was the fact that young people in the audience, who apparently were seeing the film for the very first time, couldn't help demonstrate during the same "cellar scene," thirty-nine years later . . ! It still works!

• • •

Amy Skerry, Therapist

I remember seeing *Psycho* with my then boyfriend, Johnny B. He had great excitement in anticipating this very frightening first-of-its-kind movie. Being squeamish, I was very nervous about what I might see. The movie was amazing and shocking. My greatest shock was that I said "yes" when Johnny asked at the end of the movie, "Wanna sit through it again?" When the movie was over the second time, Johnny turned toward me, made a toothless skull face, and of course I screamed. Showering has not been the same since.

• • •

Carol E. Fynn, English Teacher

Seeing *Psycho* was one of the most intense experiences I have never had. Yes, I am one of the few who has never seen the horrific assault in the shower because my mother wouldn't let me. Yet, dozens of friends so delighted in describing the carnage to me that I had to double-check the lock on the bathroom door anyway. The cold prickle climbed up my neck in honor of my intrepid friends who had a legitimate right to the terror.

Seeing the movie had become a rite of passage, a red badge of courage, and I hadn't even bought a ticket. Like any unfaced fear, it grew to phobic proportions until, in my thirties, I still leaned on the lame excuse that "my mom wouldn't let me." No matter how stunning the shower scene was, it can't compare to amorphous nightmares I've created of the experience I've never had.

• • •

Marilyn H., English Teacher

I was in high school, and I was on a date with the first chair of the trumpet section of our band. Bedford, Ohio, took its high school marching band seriously back then; our band director had played the giant sousaphone and had the honor of dotting the "i" in the script "Ohio." I was one of two feature twirlers in the majorette line, and my guy was a tall, thin, beautiful Italian boy who lived to blow his horn.

We went on movie dates in those days: the boy picked me up, paid my way, and took me to Manners where we got curb service from car hops who set up little flat trays on the driver's side of the window ledge. I always ordered French fried mushrooms; it was my only food indiscretion since I monitored every swallow.

The shower scene in *Psycho* reassured me that I was right not wanting to see this film. It didn't scare me because of the latent sexuality or suddenness of the attack on a vulnerable person. It scared me, scarred me, filled me with despair, because I lost hope of being rescued from my own victimization. I wasn't going to physically die like the older blonde girl in the movie. No, outraged citizenry would insist that outraged cops find my victimizer and bring him to swift, controlled-fury justice.

My fear was not being stabbed in the shower behind a clear, plastic curtain. My fear was being fingered again in my bed under the covers by the daddy-sized molester who came in the quiet of the night since I was two years old, whispering, "Be quiet or I'll smack you." How still I lay, how stunned I was, just like the girl in the shower, stabbed over and over. Each wound pulled her further into herself for self-protection; I knew that. I watched her eyes during that film, and I can't get the screaming violin "music" out of my head since. I wanted to see the steps of dying by violation.

But the scene ended and then my own horror film took over, and there was no music, only silence. And the girl in the movie lost blood; the bad guy ran away but would be pursued and caught. The world would punish him without flinching. I'd always thought I could get daddy in trouble if I told the cops what he was doing. I wasn't sure if they'd agree he was wrong; that's what kept me quiet. But I figured it must be if he came at night, and scared me with his threats. Then I hoped it was wrong for him to touch me just because I didn't want it. Now I knew nobody was going to save me from my little nightmare, compared to the big things cops have to investigate. My hope was lost. I retreated into myself, wounded, not even dead.

• • •

Nathan Phillips, Film Buff

I am not certain that you will be interested in the *Psycho* reaction of someone who first saw the movie over three decades after it wrapped production, but nevertheless I couldn't resist offering something.

I think this perspective is important because everyone born after a certain point and tuned in remotely to any kind of pop culture grew up with the shower scene. Every edit, every cut (pun intended), every note of music, every scream, and every sound effect is practically subconsciously implanted in us early in life. How many films have a scene like that? There's no moment like it.

I'm writing you mostly because this reaction always mystified me. Despite being intensely fond of *Vertigo* and *Lifeboat* and *Alfred Hitchcock Presents*, I couldn't imagine that the scene as described to me could have so much significance.

I finally figured out when I at last originally saw *Psycho*. I'm afraid I can't recall the year but it would have been at some point in the mid-'90s and I would have been somewhere between twelve and fourteen. Knowing full well that Janet Leigh would be gone before the film was halfway finished, I still found myself consumed by her journey, her errors in judgment, her moral dilemma, and her maddening struggles with guilt, police, and salesmen. By the time I got to the scene at the car lot, with the cop standing across the street, I forgot this was the famous shower movie, the Bates Motel movie, one of the movies everyone's seen and everyone knows back to front.

I was seduced by Anthony Perkins' character when he appeared. People often speak of the suave charm in Hitchcock's villains, but Norman Bates is the only one who caught me off guard entirely. He's almost a little boy. "Twelve cabins, twelve vacancies." You can't imagine that he's a murderer. You refuse to believe it. And keep in mind, this is *Psycho*—no one sees *Psycho* today without knowing who Norman is and what he's going to do. I had seen images from the film all my life and yet the movie's spell was cast and I believed the guy was just a victim. My mind was not on showers. It was on Leigh and the way she saw herself in Perkins, the way she understands him and wants to escape his fate. As he says, "We're all in our private trap."

Then along comes The Scene. It rips through you and the rest of the movie. It destroys your impressions and wrecks everything you've learned thus far in an instant of pandemonium. It is terrifying, orgasmic, hilarious, senseless, unexpected, and inevitable. You sit down to watch *Psycho* for the first time and you know it's coming; you sit down to watch it the twentieth time and you know it's coming, but you still don't expect it. It isn't even "somehow this time it won't happen"; it's "it simply won't happen."

I think what's special about the scene—and what shook me about it—doesn't actually lie within it. The editing is brilliant. The music is even more so, and the execution on every front is flawless. But look at it on its own and I don't think it amounts to much. It's technically brilliant, but emotionally it has no resonance. It is because of the morality play before it, unfolding almost like an episode of Hitchcock's TV show, that it carries its remarkable weight. It is a testament to the delicacy of craft that goes into making a film, certainly to Hitchcock's virtuosity with just that. I think it's the subtlety of *Psycho* that gives the shower sequence its hot-knife-through-butter effect . . . and as good as the remainder of the movie is, you're still recovering from that one massive loss when you leave.

Hitch's films are full of these iconic sequences. They were clearly designed to be iconic—whether death-defying fights on the Statue of Liberty and Mt. Rushmore or chases through the British Museum—and they still seem fresh to me, but I think this portion of *Psycho* holds something unique because of its interior conflict. You love it and you dread it, and no matter what you think, you're still not ready. Because I first saw *Psycho* with the baggage of all my prior knowledge about it already securely upstairs, and it had of course built three decades worth of a reputation, I think it says a great deal that I was completely taken aback by this single jolt of power. I cannot begin to imagine the sensation of witnessing this stunt in a theater in 1960, but I do know that it left me reeling alone in my room eons later. I don't think that's a small achievement.

• • •

Terry Meehan, Film Teacher

After the shower scene (at the Vine Theater in Willoughby, I think), this is what I thought:

"Oh, that was a masterpiece of editing and scoring. In about forty-five seconds, Hitchcock has turned the audience's expectations on its ear and changed filmmaking forever."

Yeah, right.

Here is what I really thought:

"Fight her off! You can't die!" (I had a terrible fifteen-year-old's crush on her.) "She can't be dead! But I saw all those knife stabs go in! Wait! Her eyes are still open! She's not dead!" It was several minutes before I finally accepted the fact that she was no longer to be in the movie.

• • •

Don Gray, Projectionist

New films always seemed to open on Sunday afternoons, at least long ago in the Kentucky town of Hopkinsville. Such was the case with *Psycho*. As a teenager interested in projectors, I had borrowed the Simplex manuals from the projectionist at the Princess theater. I returned them when I went to the theater for the first showing of *Psycho*. The house was full of hundreds of Hitchcock fans. The projectionist told me that not only was the truck late in delivering the print, but one of his projector's changeover mechanisms wasn't working. He asked if I would help him change over the reels manually. This meant that I had to stare at the upper right-hand corner of the screen for the cue marks to let me know when to close the lamp dowser. One of the set of marks happened to be at the scene where Martin Balsam starts his deadly climb up the *Psycho* house stairs. I could hear the audience's screams, but couldn't risk taking my eyes off that tiny corner. It was some time afterwards before I finally saw the scary moment that I had missed that afternoon.

On the subject of the *Psycho* house, I was taking a back lot tour of Universal Studios a couple of years after the filming, and saw the exterior building used for the film. This was long before trams and a shark named Bruce. You rode a Greyline bus through the streets, and, maybe, came upon an actual shoot in progress. It seems that the house wasn't full size, but my memory isn't quite what it used to be. I need to dust off my snapshots of that California trip to see if I took a picture of that famous structure.

• • •

Diana Tinkley, Assistant to Gerry Molen (retired)

When my best friend, Margaret Clothier, and I first heard about *Psycho*, we were very eager to see it. However, we were only sixteen years old and the movie was rated "X" (in England), which meant we had to be eighteen or over to attend. We decided we just had to see the movie, secretly. While Margaret's parents were out, we went through her big sister's make-up and clothes. After applying lavish make-up and "sophisticated" type clothing, we went to the Ritz, Muswell Hill in North London for the evening performance. We fooled the cashier at the Cinema and took our two-shilling seats at the back of the stalls. After seeing the second feature, news and documentary, we were ready, albeit a little scared, for the feature presentation. When the shower scene appeared we were terrified; we clung to each other and screamed, but we watched the whole thing. People around us must have been screaming too and probably running out of the theater, but we were so involved in our own sense of fear and anxiety and we didn't notice. After we calmed down, we watched the rest of the movie on the edge of our seats, too terrified to watch any more. When we finally emerged from the Cinema, all our make-up was gone from our faces; Margaret's sister clothes were a mess, and all we could think of was getting back to the safety of our homes. We never did tell our parents or Margaret's big sister!

By the way, like many people I am sure, whenever I take a shower, that scene still comes back to mind, especially if I am alone in a motel room.

• • •

Jules Ryckebusch, College Professor

I, too, saw *Psycho* in 1960; it was at the Victory Theatre in Holyoke. I was twenty and Sandy had just informed me that she was pregnant (with Jules). We might have gone together, but then again it might have been the little girl next door. I was sexually active at the time and clearly remember Janet Leigh's breasts. They were fantastic and encased in a bra I think was designed by Uplift and the Marquis de Sade. Those were the days when sex was a quiet topic but tits were supposed to look like bullets. Anyway, thinking back to that time and movie I am still impressed by how Hitchcock so brilliantly avoided our possibly anticipating such a scene by distractions and strange hints. The shower scene in *Psycho* bowls us over because Hitchcock has set up the pins so well we can't see it coming.

Almost all movies that highlight moments of intense horror lead us up to the scenes by scary foreshadowings. Hannibal Lecter comes with an advance biography. We know what he can do and hold onto our chairs waiting to see him do it, or at least the results of it. The Elm Street genre of horror film simply stuns us when the jack jumps out of the box. There is even the sympathetic horror movie; the two most famous, I assume, are *Frankenstein* and *King Kong*. While the central horrific figures are certainly scary and very grotesque, we find ourselves on their side as they are pursued by humans driven by fear, ignorance, and the basic elements of prejudice. But there is nothing in the early stages of *Psycho* that even hints at the possibility that we are soon going to meet the craziest killer in the history of the cinema. No doubt Hitchcock insisted on only a beginning-to-end viewing of this film for that very reason. He has to set us up, quite literally. To walk in on the shower scene might be disconcerting, even scary, but the reaction for most people would probably be, "What the hell is going on here?" You wouldn't have met pleasant, kind, and perhaps slightly kinky Norman while thinking about the $40,000, sexy Janet Leigh and the stalker cop in the dark shades. You simply wouldn't have been prepared for the fabulous madness of the moment. The buildup has somehow stripped us naked and left us alone for Norman's visit. Still, the event itself is a masterpiece of orchestration.

When we meet Norman, we are greeted by a very nice, accommodating, and apparently shy young man. Yet we still don't suspect Norman for what he is. His peephole into the guest's room strikes us as something naughty, but little more. In fact, many in the audience were probably quite anxious to become fellow voyeurs. We already had a taste of Janet Leigh's sexy body in the opening scene. She is the focus, not Norman. Especially as she undresses for her last shower. Eyes are important. They symbolize perception, and we see Norman's through the peephole and his victim's after death. All of this is going on as we begin to ask ourselves if we believe what we are seeing. We are looking at the blood flowing in circles as it goes down the shower drain; earlier, we had seen a note being flushed down the toilet. We are also watching the very efficient and matter of fact process of cleaning up after a brutal stabbing. Part of the horror in this scene lies in the routine, practical behavior of Norman Bates. He is eerily disinterested and quite efficient. Just as the note is flushed into eternity, so too is her new car as it sinks down and into the perfect swamp. As insane as it is, Norman has just committed a perfect crime. We are horrified and impressed.

We have all seen far more brutal and bloody scenes in movies. Rape, massacre, dismemberment, explosions, rivers of blood—all fall into the dime-a-dozen category. However, we are rarely so drawn into a scene of psychotic mayhem that we feel a part of it. Hitchcock, in this famous scene, has indeed pulled us into his special matrix.

• • •

Chris Lambert, Contributing Author, *Superman at 50*

I'm probably the only person on the face of the earth who can truly say that upon my first viewing of the 1960 Hitchcock classic, I was bored. That's right. I don't mean let down by the surprise ending or disappointed by the stark look that the director had devised for the film. I mean out and out bored. But then again, I was only six years old.

Now before anybody starts screaming, "What in the world is a parent taking a six-year-old to see a movie like *Psycho* for?" I first have to clear up a point or two. My dad and I both had a fanatic passion (although mine, due to my age, was still in its rudimentary stages) for movies. Secondly, there were plenty of old black-and-white movies on all the time when I was a kid. They used to be listed in the *T.V. Guide* as "suspense/melodrama," so I was used to seeing some blood and killing in my movies. And in hindsight, take away the famous shower scene (get ready for some controversy here) and you have no more, and no scarier than an average, well-done melodrama of the late '50s/early '60s.

Lastly, my dad would help me in my appreciation of film by pointing out camera angles, how stunts and special effects were managed, and different actors and actresses from different types of movies. "Now Chris, that guy on the left is Bob Steele; he used to be a big cowboy star," to which I would reply, "Hey dad, I saw an old movie today and Whit Bissell got all the way up to fourth in the credits." So to make a long story longer, my folks thought I might be ready for such a movie. Besides, I had already been taken to the theater to see *Journey to the Center of the Earth*, as well as Hammer's, *Horror of Dracula*, so I wasn't fazed about the hoopla I had read in the papers surrounding this movie.

So it was under these guidelines that I sat in the back seat of my parents' blue Ford at the Euclid Avenue outdoor theater and began watching the future classic from between my mom's and dad's shoulders. But I quickly lost interest and began playing quietly by myself, lying flat along the long, single cushion that formed the backseat of the cars in those days.

But just as I could bear the boredom no longer, I heard “that sound.” You know, that single, screeching violin note, played over and over. I quickly propped my head up between my parents and saw a woman being stabbed to death. I remember thinking to myself, “Come on, try and duck or something! That old lady’s going to kill you.” But she couldn’t hear my thoughts and moments later she stared out at me, her eyes wide open. I thought that was cool, that she died without closing her eyes. In the cowboy movies, that’s how I usually knew someone was finally dead. They closed their eyes and slumped forward. But strangely enough, except for that scene and the car getting shoved in the quicksand, the movie made no impression on me whatsoever.

Flash forward sixteen years, and I’m now taking film directing classes at Cleveland State University. I see that *Psycho* is being shown at the Mayfield Cinema, a once great movie theater, now a revival house for old and foreign films. I wanted to see the movie in a new light, a more mature perspective. I was not a Tony Perkins fan, although I enjoyed him in *Fear Strikes Out* and *The Tin Star*. But I wanted to see how this role, as I had read, ruined Perkin’s career.

In the opening scene, between Janet Leigh and John Gavin, I knew for its time, this movie featured an adult theme, an affair between two people in a motel, the woman stealing money to set up the couple’s future love nest. And yes, as a twenty-year-old, I could see that Perkins was so convincing that the role might have dogged the rest of his career.

And then there was the eye shot. I now saw it differently. I marveled at the tilting camera of the director and how long Janet Leigh had to keep her eyelids open to get that shot. When I was six, I thought it was cool. Now at twenty, it haunted me more than any other shot in the film, maybe in Hitchcock’s career. That single eye looked out at me, holding so much planning, such guilt and finally such redemption from within the structure of the movie’s plot and the character’s motivation.

In my favorite scenes of all time, I’ll never forget that eye. It was the same one I originally saw when perched on my knees, peeking out from the back seat, the movie screen perfectly framed by the shadows of my parents’ heads.

• • •

Nandor Bokor, Physics Professor

The first time I saw *Psycho* was during a Hitchcock season on Hungarian television in 1983 or 1984. I was around fourteen or fifteen, an adolescent, deeply religious (Catholic), sensitive, very impressionable. I watched it in our dark living room with my mother and my elder sister, in dead silence. (My father was asleep.) That Hitchcock season was my first experience with Hitchcock, and that was what made me a lifelong Hitchcock fan. I loved all the previous films shown in the series. I was impressed and awed by their complexity, their visual beauty, their dramatic ideas. I liked to think that I was able to concentrate on the camera work, on the clever directorial ideas, on the way Hitchcock manipulates the viewers (everyone except me!), without letting myself get carried away by the plot. This is not what happened when I watched *Psycho*. Ironically, it was not the shower scene that made the biggest impression, but this was the Hungarian television's fault. They used to have a Sunday program back then, in which they tried to direct the viewers' attention to coming attractions of the next week, and the way they did it was to show scenes from programs of the next week. In this particular Sunday program, *Psycho* was also advertised (except for a brief and scandalous showing in an art cinema in the 1960s that only lasted about a week, the censors had never let it be shown in Hungary before). Incredibly, the scene they picked to show in this program was the shower scene, which of course destroyed the surprise element completely when we watched the film itself. Moreover, taken and shown out of context, it seemed simply a cinematic tour-de-force and didn't have any emotional impact on me, since I had absolutely no idea who the girl was. Consequently, when we watched the film itself, Janet Leigh's murder didn't come as a shock to me, and as I remember, I could watch the scene as I do today: merely enjoying the cinematic beauty of it. (If I remember correctly, that week's TV magazine also mentioned the shower scene, weakening any chance of surprise even further.) On the other hand, I expected that nothing really terrible was going to happen after that (since the shower scene was to be *the* terrible event in the film), so the killing of Arbogast was probably the biggest shock I have ever experienced when watching any film. I remember being at a complete loss, since he was so self-assured, so calm; I relied on him so much for solving Marion's murder. I could almost say I went into a panic, and simply did not see any way out. This had been a shocking murder story so far, but if the detective himself can be killed, who knows what is going to happen at any time from now on?

So I think that that is the scene that left me the biggest impression in my life (more so than any other scene in any movie every since). It wasn't the shower scene from *Psycho*, but it was nevertheless a scene from *Psycho*. I was utterly bewildered, completely helpless, and all I can remember about the rest of that evening was after the film was over, I tried to behave very bravely. I pretended that I didn't really like the film, that I was angry with Hitchcock for the final shot of Mrs. Bates' head (for relying on "such a cheap effect"), etc., when in fact I was simply scared to death.

• • •

Sally Joranko, College Professor

In 1960 my husband and I had just joined the world of adults: college was over, he had a job, and we were first-time parents. In our set of young marrieds, it was cool to see films (as opposed to movies), and *Psycho* was a film—supposedly a psychological study, not a mere horror movie. We and the other couple who wanted to see it were also intrigued by the no-latecomers-admitted policy.

We maintained our cool until the shower scene. My husband and the other couple gasped. I was instantly reduced by those screeching violins to the child who had been sent with a dime to Saturday matinees with my younger sister. We loved musicals and anything with Elizabeth Taylor, but our favorites were *The Mummy* and *Abbott and Costello Meet*, alternatively, *The Wolf Man*, *Frankenstein*, and the dreaded *Dracula*. When the dark vampire "came out" as himself, my sister and I clutched each other and shrank down so we could see the horror only through the gap between the seats ahead of us. Somehow the terror was manageable in narrow glimpses rather than the full screen.

That's what I did when I saw the dark figure of Anthony Perkins in drag, his arm cocked to strike with the knife, as Janet Leigh would have seen it. So much for my cool.

• • •

Enrique Senra, Electrical Engineer (retired)

I remember being in the Gran Teatro in Huelva, Spain, necking with my girlfriend and occasionally watching the movie.

I knew that soon I would get to see Janet Leigh naked (or so I thought). As the silhouette appeared in the shower scene, my girlfriend and I stopped necking and became totally absorbed in the scene. I was filled with both lust and fear. When Janet Leigh screamed, my girlfriend clung to me in terror, and I felt both anguish for what was happening to Janet Leigh and also disappointment in having my dream of seeing her naked go down the drain with her blood. As the scene ended, I tried to hide from my girlfriend the awful fear I was feeling. I could hear gasps from the audience and then only silence.

• • •

Sally Carr, College Professor (retired)

I first saw *Psycho* the summer of '59 or '60 (whenever it came out). I spent that summer as a graduate counselor at the University of Michigan Fresh Air Camp for Emotionally Disturbed Boys. (Imagine that logo on a T-shirt!) We only had a day and a half off each week from our duties, and we had all heard about this new movie where you had to be there at the beginning—no late entries! This sounded like a fun thing for us to do before serious partying began, so a van-load of counselors and staff went into Ann Arbor to the State Theatre. As it happened, we took over the balcony of the theater and were amazed at the children we saw there: they minded their parents, didn't fight or swear—it was a reality check! There *were* "good" kids out there.

After the lights went down, we settled back prepared to be entertained, secure in our graduate students' "coolness." What a shock! As the stabbing music shrieked, so did we; our coolness evaporated. I remember holding on to the two people sitting next to me—we all sported black and blue marks for days afterward. Our whole group was twisting and turning in our seats as we tried not to watch and tried not to miss anything at the same time. I don't remember the sounds we made, but I remember the silence after the shower scene was over. People were gasping for breath and leaning against each other for support.

We left the theater in a daze, and it took a few beers at the Old German before we actually got around to talking about the movie. What with that shower scene, and the bathtub scene from *Diabolique* it was hard to keep clean that summer.

• • •

Lydia Distefano Thiel, College Professor

I don't know where I was when I first saw *Psycho*. But I do know *how* I was. Let me back up a bit to something that happened before *Psycho* was even created as a film. It was the late fifties, and I was an adolescent living in Johnstown, Pennsylvania. There I frequented movie theaters on occasion, the Majestic, the Embassy, the State, the Lyric, and the Dale Theater. At the Dale Theater on one summer night, I sat amidst others and watched Janet Leigh and Tony Curtis in *Houdini*. I remember vividly my awe as I looked and listened. There they were—Tony Curtis as "the Great Houdini" and Janet Leigh as his wife and assistant, Bess. I loved the name "Bess" and the beautiful face that came with it. It was their first film together, and, to me, they were both magnificent. I had seen their faces on fan magazines, of course, and like adolescents, I let myself be caught up in the images of movie stars that Hollywood circulated on the covers of these magazines. And in that theater those covers came alive.

So where was I when *Psycho* first hit town? I cannot remember in which locale Hitchcock first unleashed his horrific tale for me. I was in my twenties when I first saw the film. I no longer read fan magazines. The marriage between Leigh and Curtis was crumbling or had already crumbled. I was not so easily awestruck anymore. Then there she was again, the lovely Bess. No. No. It wasn't Bess. It was someone named Marion Crane, a worried Marion Crane, who takes a trip and wanders into the Bates Motel. Why is it all so ominous? Why does Anthony Perkins seem so twisted? What's wrong with the music? Then and there the terror begins. I cringed, and I gasped. "Bess" meets with a violent end—in a bloodbath in a bathtub! She was gone. I wondered about the tragic set of circumstances that could transport this beauty from her place beside the harmless Houdini to her place beside the evil Norman. I was forced to let go of Bess and to surrender to the merciless power of the cinema.

• • •

Don Cook, Therapist

I don't recall exactly how old I was but I do remember being younger than many of the other people in the audience. I was thrilled every Sunday when my siblings and I headed off to the Stillwell Theatre in Bedford, Ohio. This was a reward bestowed upon us by my parents on a weekly basis. I later figured it was a convenient way for my parents to get rid of the five of us for a short reprieve. Nonetheless, I was very excited. I loved "scary" films and knew we were about to view a film that had been widely talked about. As I pondered the film recently, I vaguely remember that I was slightly bored and a little disappointed in the beginning of the film. Thinking to myself, "What was all the fuss about?" Then the shower scene started and I was a little shocked that a naked woman was taking a shower. Of course nothing was really revealed but at that age . . . everything is a possible kick. I was sitting between my oldest and second oldest sister and I was holding the popcorn. I remember the build-up of the music and maybe feeling a little uneasy, but the theater was dead silent. The next thing I knew the shower curtain was flung back, and my sister along with a few other people in the audience let out a scream. I was petrified! The jerking music, the darkness of the woman's face horrified me. I felt that I was pressing back into my seat as if I was on a rollercoaster and we were taking the first hill. I crushed the popcorn between my knees and gripped the chair arms so tight I'm sure my knuckles were white. The film proceeded and ended. I was better prepared for other scenes as they unfolded and thoroughly enjoyed the film. I do remember my sisters making fun of me because of the look on my face during that scene and feeling a little plucked because it was very apparent to me they had the same reaction as I did.

• • •

Eric Carlson, Film Buff

No other movie in my whole life proved so damn hard to see as *Psycho*, and so haunting (indeed, terrifying) in my mind during those years that I could not see it. Seeing *Psycho* was a multi-year chase, with plenty of suspense and twists.

Psycho first came out in the summer of 1960. I was too young to see it. I do remember that summer, and I remember a few movies (of interest to a child) that came out then: Disney's *Pollyanna*, *The Time Machine* with Rod Taylor, and William Castle's latest shock offering *13 Ghosts*, the scary trailer of which sent me diving to the floor of the family car at the drive-in. *13 Ghosts* was the movie that kept me awake in the summer of *Psycho*. I have no memory of *Psycho* from that summer at all.

Psycho entered my consciousness in March of 1965. Paramount rereleased it. I saw the ad in the newspaper, with Leigh in bra, the tag line "*Psycho* and the Shower-Bath Scene Are Back!" (note the specificity: "Shower-Bath"), and that great big, terrifyingly slashed word: *PSYCHO*. A word I couldn't even pronounce. As I've noted before, a kind of "buzz" arose with the *Psycho* rerelease. Enough neighborhood kids and parents started talking about it that I learned this was the most horrifying movie ever made, and in it, a man dressed up like his mother and stabbed a lady in a motel shower one hundred times. (I never got to experience the twist ending.) He also chopped off her head (some kids mixed up Bloch's book with the movie.)

I can't say that I thought about *Psycho* all the time from then on, but whenever reminders turned up, I sure did. I would see the word *Psycho* on marquees as a second feature to movies like *Mirage*, for instance, and a quick chill would set in. The motel, the house, the shower—all frightening beyond words in my young mind.

Summer of 1965: I saw the *Psycho* trailer in a musty old theater. (It was a coming second feature.) Terrifying.

Summer of 1966: I saw the CBS TV network commercial with mother pulling back the curtain, knife in hand. Terrifying. (CBS canceled the showing.)

November 1967: First showing on Los Angeles television, KABC-TV, Channel 7. The black-and-bilious-green billboards were all over Los Angeles, and they were terrifying, especially at night: the creepy old house with Perkins in Frankenstein-shadow standing next to it; Perkins with one hand over his mouth and the other outstretched. And those scary slashed letters, huge in the night skies over my head: *PSYCHO*.

I wasn't allowed to watch that late Saturday night broadcast, but many classmates were. And I got one of them to tell me all about the movie, start to finish, on Monday.

That's when I found out about Arbogast for the first time. I remember the conversation:

Me: "So you saw *Psycho*?"

Friend: "Yes. I wish I didn't. The scariest movie I ever saw. Those murders were horrible!"

Me: "Wait. Did you say, "murders"? Just the lady in the shower gets killed, right?"

Friend: "No, no. The detective, too."

Me: "What detective?"

Friend: "In the house. On the stairs. And it's *worse* than the shower."

I'd been walking around with only the shower murder in my mind for nearly three years. Now I had this other shock image to contend with. And the other kid, either from overactive memory or to fool me, made Arbogast's murder sound far more awful than it really was.

February of 1968: KABC-TV runs *Psycho* again for a second "Sweeps month" ratings killing, again on a late Saturday night. My parents go out for the evening. I manage to stay up until *Psycho* comes on. I watch it. The hotel scene starts. I'm excited. Then, a commercial, with a quick clip of what's coming: Norman running down from the house. It looks creepy. I'm more excited. I sit through the cop stop, the car lot scene. Marion starts driving in the rain and—my parents come home, turn off the TV, send me to bed. For several years, all I'll have as a memory of *Psycho* is the first twenty-five minutes. And I never got to the Bates Motel.

Fall, 1968: I'm in a mall bookstore with my family. On display, a new book: *Hitchcock/Truffaut*. I'm flipping through it, looking at pictures, when it hits me: There will be pictures from the forbidden *Psycho* in here!

I flip toward the back of the book. Bing! Janet Leigh and Gavin on the bed, Leigh in that great bra. The shower scene, which, actually, looks rather abstract and hard to follow—and not particularly scary. But then I flipped to the page with Arbogast's murder. And that *was* scary.

You see, my friend had described the scene as a horrible slaughter, and here was a photo to set my mind reeling: Martin Balsam, mouth agape, eyes wide open, blood pouring down his brow and cheek. Pure terror on his face. And this gruesome image was "locked in" for me to look at, as opposed to the quick glimpse offered in the movie itself.

In that year, at that age, this was truly the most horrible thing I'd ever seen in my life. The hair stood up on the back of my neck. I felt weak. I closed the *Hitchcock/Truffaut* book quickly, went home, and had about five nights of sleeping with the lights on.

(And that, dear reader, is where my fascination with Arbogast undoubtedly began. The most powerful image of my young life led me to fixate on the nuances of writing, acting, characterization, and filmmaking that led up to that image.)

1969: *Psycho* hits the theaters again. "See the version TV dared not show." But Universal, which now owns the film, means the canceled CBS showing. My friends assure me that the local 1967–1968 showings were uncut, the murders and Ma's face shown in all their glory.

I can't convince my parents to take me to see this *Psycho* rerelease. We drive past a drive-in one night, and I manage to see a brief glimpse, in the night sky beyond the trees outside the drive-in, of Arbogast in the foyer. Chilling.

The TV season 1969–1970 passes with no *Psycho* showings anywhere. It leaves my mind. My family moves hundreds of miles north of Los Angeles, to the California Central Valley. *Psycho* country.

Early in the 1970–1971 TV season, I'm flipping through the *TV Guide*, looking for movies to watch. When I see it: *Psycho*. Sunday night. Out of San Francisco. Far away.

Depending on the weather, we can get San Francisco stations with grainy static. I get clearance to watch the film. (I'm so old now, my parents figure it won't scare me, anyway. Thanks.) I wait for Sunday night. I turn on our TV. *Psycho* comes on. This is my first time, sort of.

The reception is poor. Snow, and static, and a picture that only "holds still" for about two minutes at a time. I get as far as Marion driving in the rain. That's where I had to turn it off in 1968.

But wait, there it is: the Bates Motel. Marion is in new, unknown territory. And so am I. I saw all of *Psycho* that night in October of 1970, but not really. I kept having to pound the TV with my fist, adjust the antenna. I could barely see the murder scenes, or Mother's face. I could barely hear anything. Sometimes the screen dissolved into snow for minutes on end. When the film ended, I was disappointed. I hadn't really seen *Psycho*.

A few months later, in February of 1971, I was again flipping through the *TV Guide*, looking for movies. And I saw: *Psycho*, Friday night. My local channel was showing it. (Evidently, Universal released a thriller package to various local stations during that 1970–71 season: *The Birds*, *Mirage*, and *Charade* were also shown both out of San Francisco and later in the town where I lived.)

My schedule was clear. A friend was recruited to watch with me. The night came. The signal, being local, was crystal clear, and I finally saw *Psycho*. Start to finish, uncut. There were commercials, but I was used to that. *Psycho* didn't really scare me that night. I remember holding my breath involuntarily as Marion got in the shower and Arbogast climbed the stairs, but the actual murders were rather disappointingly quick and nongraphic, given what I'd been told over the years. The mothers in the fruit cellar were impressive, but not terribly frightening when I knew the twist. Still, the movie impressed me, and haunted me in a whole new way. The imagined movie in my head of over six years' gestation was suddenly replaced by the real movie, and it was, indeed, an entirely different movie (much more visually elegant, for one thing.)

My childhood adventure with *Psycho* ended that night in 1971. The horrifying "mental movie" was gone, and with it, several years of being frightened by my own fantasy of it. But I would now begin my adventure in truly seeing and understanding *Psycho*. I would catch it about once a year on TV, or [at] college/revival showings. I found that it *could* scare me, in memory in the late night after I watched it, or if I was outside my home at night after a recent viewing. (Norman's skull-grin was a spooky memory.) It had residual power.

In 1972, I bought a new album of Herrmann's Hitchcock themes, and I could listen to the *Psycho* score to my heart's content, jittery opening theme, screeching violins, "three notes of madness," and all.

In 1974, I bought Richard Anobile's frame-by-frame blow-up book of *Psycho*, and I could study the scenes, shots, and speeches of *Psycho* to my heart's content. (No, I never listened to the album while reading the book.)

In 1979, I attended that full-house college screening where everybody screamed and it was 1960 again.

In 1982, I made my first tape of *Psycho* off of TV. And I've never been without the movie to view—once a year, at my leisure—again.

To me personally, the funniest thing is that there isn't conclusively a "first time I saw *Psycho*." There are these three choices:

1. February 1968, when I saw it only as far as Marion driving in the rain hearing voices.
2. October 1970, through a snow-and-static fuzz out of San Francisco.
3. February 1971, clear as a bell, but not as a "virgin."

Or maybe, the first time was when that kid told me the whole movie, start to finish, on recess periods and at lunch, and I constructed that horrific version in my head.

The first time I saw *Psycho*? I have no idea.

• • •

Charles W. Mealy, School Superintendent (retired)

I saw the film *Psycho* in the fall of 1960. At the time I was a sophomore at Kent State University, Kent, Ohio.

Several friends and I walked to downtown Kent, to the only theater in town, to see the film. We were vaguely aware that there was supposed to be a scary scene in this movie, unlike other scary scenes. We all enjoyed Alfred Hitchcock's films.

When the shower scene occurred, it seemed as though everyone in the theater screamed, jumped, and grabbed one another. It was a truly shocking and unforgettable scene that left people gasping and panting.

Following the viewing of this film, I remember people sneaking into the shower room in the dormitory and yanking the shower curtains back on some poor unsuspecting soul who was showering and yelling at him. The poor soul in the shower would scream, much to the delight of the prankster. Taking a shower was never the same after seeing *Psycho*.

• • •

Carol Mealy, School Teacher (retired)

I first saw the film *Psycho* on the campus of Bowling Green State University, Bowling Green, Ohio, during my sophomore year. At the time, I lived in William's Hall, a particularly old and creaky-sounding dormitory. I roomed with two other girls, both of whom happened to be my sorority sisters. Since this was not a large dormitory, the shower rooms were small. Many times, only one or two girls would be using them at once. All the more scary for the shower curtain to be pulled aside and a "friend" to scare the living daylights out of you. I remember no long warm showers, as the goal was to shower as quickly as possible and get out of that room. I can still feel my heart beat with fear when I recall those times.

• • •

Gloria M. Gartner, College Professor

I don't actually remember my first time seeing the shower scene. In a recent viewing, however, I remember being filled with fear as I heard the music, and knew the scene was coming. Surprisingly, when I actually saw the scene again, it was much less frightening than I had remembered or anticipated. It seemed much milder than what we see in the movies today.

• • •

Judith Doerr, College Administrator

I did not see it when it originally came out—perhaps because it was rated "B" by the Legion of Decency. By the time I did see it, I already knew about the shower scene and about the ending, so—while it still had the power to engage me—it could not have the impact or make the impression that it must have made to those who attended the film without knowing these things.

• • •

Bill Johnston, Computer Engineer (retired)

In the early 1960s, I was midway through my lengthy—and unintentionally extended—six-year college career, attending the University of Cincinnati's chemical engineering school. As it was a cooperative education school, we would attend seven weeks of fire-hose classes, then work at a paying job—followed by a vacation, for usually about nine or ten weeks. At the time I went to see *Psycho*, I was in the midst of a seven-week classroom term. I had not really heard much about the movie other than it was scary; certainly I had heard nothing about the shower scene. One of my friends in the fraternity house where I lived suggested we go see the movie. It was showing in downtown Cincinnati. I distinctly remember the shower scene, and almost nothing else about the movie. I was already in a state of heightened alert and holding my breath from the build-up, when the scene began. My friend, known for his rational approach to all issues, jumped and unexpectedly grabbed my arm, scaring the *daylights* out of me! Never really being a big fan of horror movies or the like, and totally not expecting such a strong reaction from my normally rational companion, this made an even greater impression on me. I also remember feeling relieved that it was over and done with, and that I no longer had to worry about what happened to Janet Leigh (of whom I had been a secret admirer all through my adolescence).

I rarely remember much about stories I have heard, movies I have seen, or jokes I have heard. But I have never forgotten that shower scene.

• • •

Bill Krohn, Author, *Hitchcock at Work*

I saw *Psycho* in Santa Fe. I had already read the book (I still have the Fawcett paperback with Marion screaming on the cover, which for some reason was published before the film's release), so it held no surprises for me. I suppose I was scared during the shower scene, but I was mainly hoping to catch a glimpse of Janet Leigh nude, and I came away feeling that I more or less had. However, despite Leigh's insistence in her book that she wasn't doubled much, the production reports, as summarized in my book on Hitchcock, show that my adolescent lust was largely misdirected that day.

The film remains my favorite Hitchcock, ever since I showed it to my then-wife, Veronique, a French girl who had never seen it. Having always known that Norman was Mother, it was vicarious fun to watch it with someone who still didn't, after all these years. Then she invited her friend Giselle over to show it to her, and couldn't keep herself from giving the game away as she indulged in her favorite pastime of commenting on the film she was showing. When Marion overheard Mother cussing out Norman through the window, Vero grabbed Giselle by the shoulder and informed her: "That's the voice of the so-called mother!"

• • •

Stephania Byrd, College Professor

I was eleven when I first saw *Psycho*. It was about a week before my twelfth birthday. My mother and my eight-year-old sister and I had gone to the drive-in to see it. My mother was a big Hitchcock fan; my dad did not care for scary movies. The sun was setting and the movie began—I remember feeling like the film grew darker as night fell. When Janet Leigh got in the shower, it was pitch black outside the car.

My sister was in the back leaning over the front seat to eat popcorn from the bag we had brought from home. I was drinking Nehi soda—Rock "n" Rye—iced from a bucket in the front seat near my feet. As the music reached its crescendo, the stabbing began and I squirted soda out of my nose. My mother tried to warn us, but the violence was swift. My sister shrieked and hid on the floor of the backseat, and my mother told us that she would never take us to see another thriller if we were going to embarrass her like this.

• • •

Dave Thomas, Attorney and Filmmaker

I remember quite well my first viewing of *Psycho*. I was a junior at Miami University in Oxford, Ohio. *Psycho* was a film scheduled for an undergraduate film course.

The time of the screening was mid-day, in November, just prior to Thanksgiving break. As I was staying on campus for the holiday, I was in no particular hurry that afternoon. As I calmly walked to the screening, I watched as everyone else clamored about against the whipping winter winds in a hustle to get out of the small college town.

The screening was scheduled to take place in an auditorium on campus. As I nonchalantly made my way, I happened to meet a very attractive blonde co-ed from California. She was a senior, and also staying on campus for Thanksgiving. I got her number. I also met her later, but that's another story . . .

Back to the screening. I entered the sparsely crowded auditorium and selected my seat in the middle of nobody. I did take one last look around me prior to the clacking of the projector. I wanted to see who was there with me. And then, it started.

From the first shots and sounds, I was transported into horror. Even now, fifteen years later, I get goose bumps thinking about sitting there and watching the movie.

The film, obviously, began on a nice sunny California-type day. Very nice. Yet, not so nice.

By the time the film ended and I walked outside with Bernard's violins screeching in my ears and Norman in my head, I was beautifully scarred.

What a masterpiece! If I wasn't around for the original theatrical release, this was a great substitute. Time had dulled the original notorious and well-known plot lines, and the subsequent mass of horror films to follow had blurred any connections to the original by the time I saw *Psycho*. I went into my screening fresh, unsuspecting, just as Mr. Hitchcock would have preferred.

• • •

Bram Hamovitch, College Professor

I never had the opportunity to see *Psycho* and would like to explain why this is the case. When the movie was released in 1960, I was an eleven-year-old child living in the province of Quebec. At that time, children under the age of sixteen were not permitted to go to movie theaters, with the exception of Saturday-morning children's specials. I believe that this government regulation reflected the need for civil lawmakers to accede to the Catholic Church in areas that relate to public morality. Thus, stores and bars were not open on Sundays and drive-in movie theaters ("passion pits") were not permitted in the province. I am glad to report that the power of the church over civil authorities has waned considerably since those days.

• • •

Patrick McGilligan, Author, *Alfred Hitchcock: A Life in Darkness and Light*

I'd be happy to participate in your chapter, except for the fact that I don't have the slightest recollection as to when I first saw *Psycho*. I missed the original showings, because I was only nine-years-old and not going to movies. I must have seen it in college, but don't recall how or when. I know this is unusual—when I went around on my book tour, answering questions from audiences, I could see that people recall their first experience with *Psycho* the way people also remember where they were when they heard that JFK had been assassinated. Thinking about it, one's memory of seeing *Psycho* for the first time is really generational.

• • •

WORKS CITED

Allen, Richard. "Hitchcock After Bellour." *Hitchcock Annual.* 2002–03: 117–147.

American Film Institute. "Psycho Tops AFI's List of the 100 Most Thrilling American Films," 4 Jan. 2004: 1–4. Accessed at: <*http://www/afi.com/tv/thrills.asp*>.

Anobile, Richard, ed. *Alfred Hitchcock's Psycho*. New York: Avon Books, Darien House, Inc., 1974.

Auiler, Dan. *Vertigo: The Making of a Hitchcock Classic*. New York: St. Martin's Griffin, 1998.

Bellour, Raymond. *The Analysis of Film.* Edited by Constance Penley. Bloomington, IN: Indiana University Press, 2000.

Belton, John. *American Cinema/American Culture*. New York: McGraw-Hill, 1994.

Bloch, Robert. "Building the Bates Motel." In *The Fine Art of Murder*. Edited by Ed Gorman et al. New York: Carroll Graf Publishers, Inc. 1993.

Bloch, Robert. *Psycho*. New York: Simon and & Schuster, 1959.

Bogdanovich, Peter. *The Cinema of Alfred Hitchcock*. New York: The Museum of Modern Art Film Library, 1963.

Bogdanovich, Peter. *Who the Devil Made It: Conversations with Legendary Film Directors.* New York: Ballantine Books, 1997.

Bouzereau, Laurent. *The Alfred Hitchcock Quote Book*. New York: Citadel Press Book, 1993.

Carlson, Eric. Email message to author. 4 January, 2005.

Cohen, Paula Marantz. "James, Hitchcock and the Fate of Character." In *Alfred Hitchcock: Centenary Essays*. Edited by Richard Allen and S. Ishii-Gonzales, 16–27. London: British Film Institute Publishing, 1999.

Coleridge, S.T. *Biographia Literaria*. Edited by J. Shawcross. Oxford: The Clarendon Press, 1907.

Crawford, Larry. "Subsegmenting the Filmic Text: The Bakersfield Car Lot Scene in Psycho." *Enclitic*, vol 5.2/6.1:1982. 35–43.

Doherty, Thomas. *Pre-Code Hollywood.* New York: Columbia University Press, 1999.

Douchet, Jean. "Hitch and His Audience." In *Alfred Hitchcock's Psycho: A Casebook.* Edited by Robert Kolker, 62–73. New York: Oxford University Press, 2004.

Durgnat, Raymond. *Films and Feelings*. Cambridge, MA: The MIT Press, 1967.

Durgnat, Raymond. *A Long Hard Look at Psycho*. London: British Film Institute, 2002.

Elliott, Deborah. "The 180 Degree Rule." *Words of Art*. Accessed at: <*http://www.ouc.bc.ca/fina/glossary/0_list/180degreerule.html*>.

Feinstein, John. *The Punch: One Night, Two Lives, and the Fight that That Changed Basketball Forever*. Boston: Little, Brown and Company, 2002.

Finler, Joel W. *Alfred Hitchcock: The Hollywood Years*. London: B.T. Batsford Ltd., 1992.

Franklin, Richard. Email message to author. 18 February, 2004.

Freeman, David. *The Last Days of Alfred Hitchcock: A Memoir Featuring the Screenplay of "Alfred Hitchcock's The Short Night."* Woodstock, New York: The Overlook Press, 1999.

Giannetti, Louis. *Understanding Movies*. 10th ed. Upper Saddle River, NJ: Pearson Prentice Hall, 2005.

Gibbs, John. *Mise-en-Scene: Film Style and Interpretation*. London: Wallflower, 2002.

Gladwell, Malcolm. *The Tipping Point: How Little Things Can Make a Big Difference*. New York: Little, Brown and Company, 2000.

Gomery, Douglas. "Hollywood as Industry." In *American Cinema and Hollywood: Critical Approaches*. Edited by John Hill and Pamela Church Gibson. New York: Oxford University Press, 2000.

Gottlieb, Sidney, ed. *Alfred Hitchcock Interviews*. Jackson: University Press of Mississippi, 2003.

Gottlieb, Sidney. "Early Hitchcock." In *Framing Hitchcock: Selected Essays from the Hitchcock Annual*. Edited by Sidney Gottlieb and Christopher Brookhouse. Detroit, MI: Wayne State University Press, 2002.

Gottlieb, Sidney, ed. *Hitchcock on Hitchcock: Selected Writings and Interviews*. Berkeley, CA: University of California Press, 1995.

Gottlieb, Sidney and Christopher Brookhouse, eds. *Framing Hitchcock: Selected Essays from the Hitchcock Annual*. Detroit, MI: Wayne State University Press, 2002.

Gross, Edward. "Psycho II." *Cinefantastique*, March 1986: 31+.

Hendershot, Cyndy. "The Cold War Horror Film: Taboo and Transgression in *The Bad Seed*, *The Fly*, and *Psycho*." *Journal of Popular Film and Television* 29:(Spring 2001): 20–31. Accessed at: *<http://proquest.umi.com/pqdlink?>*.

Hitchcock, Alfred. "My Recipe for Murder." *Coronet* 48:(5):49–61.

Hitch: The Genius of Alfred Hitchcock: Alfred the Auteur. Dir. Tim Kirby. Princeton, NJ: Films for the Humanities and Sciences, 2003.

Hurley, James Stephens, III. *After the Panopticon: Surveillance, Scopophilia, and the Subject of the Gaze*. Dissertation. University of Virginia, 1997. Ann Arbor: UMI, 1997. Att: 9738875.

Hurley, Neil P. *Soul in Suspense: Hitchcock's Fright and Delight*. Metuchen, NJ: The Scarecrow Press, 1993.

The Illustrated Hitchcock. Dir. John Musili. Kent, CT: Creative Arts Television, 1997.

Inside Hitchcock. Dir. Richard Schickel. Oak Forest, IL: Maljack Productions, Inc., 1985.

Kapsis, Robert. *Hitchcock: The Making of a Reputation*. Chicago: University Press, 1992.

Kendrick, Walter. "'Psycho' Babble," *The Village Voice* 35: (32): 91–92.

Kerzoncuf, Alain. Email message to author. 30 March 2004.

Knight, Deborah and George McKnight. "Suspense and Its Master." In *Alfred Hitchcock: Centenary Essays*. Edited by Richard Allen and S. Ishii-Gonzales, 107–121. London: British Film Institute, 1999.

Kolker, Robert, ed. *Alfred Hitchcock's Psycho: A Casebook*. New York: Oxford University Press, 2004.

Konigsberg, Ira. *The Complete Film Dictionary*. 2nd ed. New York: Penguin Reference, 1997.

Krohn, Bill, *Hitchcock at Work*. London: Phaidon, 2000.

Kuhn, Annette. "History of the Cinema." In *The Cinema Book*. Edited by Pam Cook. New York: Pantheon Books, 1985.

Leff, Leonard J. and Jerold L. Simmons. *The Dame in the Kimono: Hollywood, Censorship, and the Production Code*. 2nd ed. Lexington, KY: University of Kentucky Press, 2001.

Leigh, Christion. *Psycho/Curated by Christian Leigh*. New York: The Kinsttall, 1992.

Leigh, Janet, with Christopher Nickens. *Psycho: Behind the Scenes of the Classic Thriller*. New York: Harmony Books, 1995.

Leitch, Thomas M. *Find the Director and Other Hitchcock Games*. Athens, GA: University of Georgia Press, 1991.

"Lissajous Figure." A Dictionary of Psychology. Oxford Reference Online. 14 March 2005. Accessed at: *<http://www.oxfordreference.com/views/ENTRY.html>*.

Luraschi, Luigi. "Inter-Office Communication: Mr. Hitchcock, Re: *Psycho*." 24 November 1959. Special Collections. The Margaret Herrick Library. Fairbanks Center for Motion Picture Study. Academy of Motion Picture Arts and Sciences, Los Angeles.

Macdonald, Dwight. "Eisenstein, Pudovkin and Others." In *The Emergence of Film Art*. edited by Lewis Jacobs. New York: Hopkinson and Blake, 1969.

"The Making of *Psycho*." Dir. Laurent Bouzereau. *Psycho*. Dir. Alfred Hitchcock. Universal Home Video DVD, 1998.

McFarland, Thomas. *Coleridge and the Pantheist Tradition*. Oxford: Clarendon Press, 1969.

McGilligan, Patrick. *Alfred Hitchcock: A Life in Darkness and Light*. New York: Regan Books, HarperCollins, 2003.

McGowan, John. "Post Modernism." Accessed at: *<http://www.press.jhu.edu/books/hopkins_guide-to-literary-theory/postmodernism.html>*.

Modleski, Tania. *The Women Who Knew Too Much: Hitchcock and Feminist Theory*. New York: Routledge, 1988.

Mogg, Ken et al. *The Alfred Hitchcock Story*. London: Titan Books, 1999.

Mogg, Ken. "Editorial." In *The MacGuffin: Journal of the Film/Alfred Hitchcock Special Interest Group*. 27 December 2000: 1.

Mogg, Ken. Email message to author. 10 March 2005.

Monaco, Paul. *The Sixties: 1960–1969. History of the American Cinema*. Vol. 8. General Editor: Charles Harpole. New York: Charles Scribner's Sons, 2001.

Naremore, James. "Hitchcock and Humor." *Strategies* 14(1), 2001:13–25.

Peary, Danny. Henri-Georges Clouzot's *Diabolique*. Criteron DVD, 1999.

Perry, Dennis. *Hitchcock and Poe: The Legacy of Delight and Terror*. Lanham, MD: The Scarecrow Press, 2003.

"Pop History of the Fifties." Accessed at: *<http://www.fiftiesweb.com/pop/pop-history.html>*.

Psycho: Dir. Alfred Hitchcock. Universal House Video DVD, 1998.

Psycho: Dir. Alfred Hitchcock. *Alfred Hitchcock's Psycho*. Wheeling, WV: Innovation Comics, 1992.

"Psycho Shower Scene Tops Poll." *The London Free Press Today*. 21 May 2004. Accessed at: *<http://www.canoe.ca/newsstand/LondonFreePress/Today/2004/05/>*.

Randall, Richard S. "Censorship: from *The Miracle* to *Deep Throat*." In *The American Film Industry*. Edited by Tino Balio. (rev. ed.), 510–536. Madison, WI: University of Wisconsin Press, 1985.

Rebello, Stephen. *Alfred Hitchcock and the Making of Psycho*. New York: St. Martin's Griffin, 1990.

Rebello Stephen. "Alfred Hitchcock Goes Psycho!" *American Film*. April 1990. 38–43; 48.

Ringler, Stephen M.A. *Dictionary of Cinema Quotations from Filmmakers & Critics: Over 3400 Anxioms, Criticisms, Opinions and Witticism from 100 Years of the Cinema*. Jefferson, NC: McFarland & Company, Inc., 2000.

Robischon, Noah. "Psycho, Circus." *Entertainment Weekly*. 21 May 1999: 85.

Romney, Jonathan. "A Hitch in Time." *New Statesman*, 19 July 1999: 35–36. 27 July 2003.

Ryall Tom. *Alfred Hitchcock and the British Cinema*. London: Athlone, 1996.

"Saul Bass . . ." Interview with Bass. *Cinefantistique*. 16.

Schickel, Richard. "We're Living in a Hitchcock World All Right." *New York Times Magazine*. 29 September 1972. Section 6.

Schneider, Steven. "Manufacturing Horror in Hitchcock's *Psycho*." *CineAction* 50 (Oct. 1999): 70–75.

Sklar, Robert. *Movie-Made America: A Cultural History of American Movies*. New York: Vintage Books, 1976.

Sloan, Jane. *Alfred Hitchcock: A Filmography and Bibliography*. Berkeley, CA: University of California Press, 1995.

Smith, Susan. *Hitchcock: Suspense, Humor and Tone*. London: British Film Institute, 2000.

"Sometimes You Feel Like a Nut . . . Sometimes You Don't." [James R. Thompson] February 6, 2003. Accessed at: *<http://www-scf.usc.edu/rjrthomps/paper.html>*.

Special Collections: Hitchcock. Margaret Herrick Library, Fairbanks Center for Motion Picture Study. Academy of Motion Pictures Arts and Sciences, Los Angeles, CA.

Spinelli, Ralph. Email message to author. 26 November 2002.

Spoto, Donald. *The Dark Side of Genius*. New York: DaCapo Press, 1999.

Sterritt, David. *The Films of Alfred Hitchcock*. Cambridge: University Press, 1993.

Stevens, Wallace. *Opus Posthumous*. New York: Alfred A. Knopf, 1957.

Thomas, Deborah. "On Being Norman: Performance and Inner Life in Hitchcock's Psycho." *Cineaction* 44:(1997): 66–72.

Thomson, David. *Overexposures: The Crisis in American Filmmaking*. New York: William. Morrow and Company, Inc., 1981.

Toles, George. "'If Thine Offend Thee . . .': *Psycho*, and the Art of Infection." In *Alfred Hitchcock: Centenary Essays*. Edited by Richard Allen and S. Ishii-Gonzales, 159–174. London: British Film Institute Publishing, 1999.

Truffaut, Francois. *Hitchcock*. (Rev. Ed.). New York: Simon & Schuster, 1984.
Turim, Maureen. *Flashbacks in Film: Memory & History*. New York: Routledge, 1989.
Weis, Elisabeth. *Alfred Hitchcock's Aural Style, Dissertation*. Arbor: UMI. Columbia, 1978.
Vest, James M. *Hitchcock and France: The Forging of an Auteur*. Westport, CT: Praeger, 2003.
Wells, Amanda Sheahan. *Psycho*. London: Longman, 2001.
Williams, Linda. "Learning to Scream." *Sight and Sound* 4(:12) (Dec. 1994): 14–17. OCLCWEB. 31 May 2002.
Williams, Tony, "'Special Effects' in the Cutting Room." In *Underground USA: Filmmaking Beyond the Hollywood Canon*. Edited by Xavier Mendik and Steven Jay Schneider, 51–62. New York: Wallflower Press, 2002.
Wollen, Peter. "Rope: Three Hypotheses." In *Alfred Hitchcock: Centenary Essays*. Edited by Richard Allen and S. Ishii-Gonzales. London: BFI Publishing 1999.
Wood, Robin. *Hitchcock's Films*. New York: Castle Books, 1965.
Wood, Robin. *Hitchcock's Films Revisited*. New York: Columbia University Press, 1989.

Index

A

Academy Awards, 67
Alfred Hitchcock (Douchet), 45
Alfred Hitchcock (McGilligan), 47
Alfred Hitchcock and the Making of Psycho (Rebello), 226
Alfred Hitchcock Presents, 5, 29, 36, 41–43, 128, 136, 177
  "Breakdown," 105
  camera crew, 86
  "Lamb to the Slaughter," 36, 90, 99, 183
  "Revenge," 42–43, 104
Alfred Hitchcock's Psycho (Anobile), 223, 226, 295
Alfred Hitchcock's Psycho (Kolker), 47, 227
Amazing Stories, 264
American Film Institute, 135
The Analysis of Film (Bellour), 82
And God Created Woman, 44
Angels in the Outfield, 23–24
Anobile, Richard, 223, 226, 240–41, 297
antitrust cases, 40, 43
Arnold, Malcolm, 275
art exhibits, 265
audience narratives, 270–301
audience psychology, 9–10, 63, 151, 163, 199, 224
Auric, Georges, 275
Australia, 273–76
Autant-Lara, Claude, 275
"auteur" label and auteur theory, 31, 45, 47, 75, 266

B

baby boomer generation, 36, 37, 40
Balaban, Barney, 37
Bass, Saul, 17, 66, 80, 123, 161, 163, 210, 222, 225
Bataille, Georges, 261–62
bathrooms, 92, 94, 109, 198–200, 237–59 passim. *See also* bathtubs; toilets
bathtubs, 228, 229, 268, 291
The Battleship Potemkin, 32, 223, 249
Baxter, John, 273–76
beheading. *See* decapitation
Bellour, Raymond, 46, 82, 84
Belton, John, 7–8
birds, 109, 110, 115–20 passim, 195, 236–37
The Birds, 45
Birth of a Nation, 32
Bitter Rice, 44
black-and-white films, 77, 208, 228
black humor, 9, 31, 90, 111, 114
The Black Orchid, 51, 52
The Blackguard, 30, 74
Blackmail, 30, 32, 105, 189–94 passim, 230, 243
Bloch, Robert, 8, 16, 37, 40, 51, 118, 125, 176, 229–31 passim, 293
blood, 159, 203, 215, 238, 266–69 passim, 286, 295
Bogdanovich, Peter, 46
bras, 6, 119, 175, 176, 285, 295
  ad for *Psycho* and, 293
  color symbolism of, 93, 164, 168
  of moleskin, 56
  in *Rear Window*, 39

Breen, Joseph, 6, 31
British Film Institute, 47. See also *Sight and Sound*
Bugs Bunny, 264
Burks, Robert, 131, 158, 160, 221
Burr, Raymond, 274

C

The Cabinet of Dr. Caligari, 74, 229
Cahiers du Cinema, 31, 45, 75, 139, 274
camera work. *See* cinematography
Cannes Film Festival, 46
Carlson, Eric, 241, 293–96
Carne, Marcel, 275
Castle, William, 275, 293
"cataphors," 86–88 passim, 99, 100, 106, 107, 121, 142, 146, 160, 200, 202
Catholic Church, 35, 45, 119, 205, 301
Catholics, 6, 38, 44, 289
censorship, 6, 8, 13, 60, 125, 223–24, 239, 240
  Australia, 274, 276
  Hungary, 289
Chabrol, Claude, 45, 227
children
  as film viewers, 287, 299–300
  Hitchcock and, 131
  in films, 34, 156
  molestation victims, 281–82
Christianity, 45, 82, 161, 258
cinematography, 76–121 passim, 195
  camera angles, 77, 118, 145, 147, 155, 158–59, 175, 200, 201, 206, 229
  in shower scene, 234, 238, 247–52 passim, 257
  close-ups, 194, 243
  dissolves, 93, 102, 145, 167, 215, 257, 259
  dollies, 198, 244, 259
  establishing shots, 80
  fade-ins, 99
  long shots, 93, 145, 147, 152, 163, 167, 243, 254
  panning shots, 80, 87, 94, 95, 113, 145, 147, 200, 202, 215, 259
  tracking shots, 80, 94, 114, 120, 147, 205, 254
  See also dailies; framing; lighting; point of view
Citizen Kane, 47–48, 275
Clatworthy, Robert, 86
claustrophobia, 104–6 passim, 198, 242
Clouzot, Henri-Georges, 227–29, 280
Cocteau, Jean, 275
Coleman, Herbie, 213
color film: wrongly said to have been used for *Psycho*, 215
Columbia University, 46
comic books, 263, 264
Covolo, John, 33
Craven, Wes, 271–72
Crawford, Larry, 82
credits. *See* film credits
Currier, Dick, 180
Curtis, Tony, 291–92

D

Dahl, Roald, 90
dailies, 212, 213, 218
dangling scenes, 255
The Dark Side of Genius (Spoto), 46
Darling, 274
Davy, Alan, 132
decapitation, 40, 125, 230, 293
D'entre Les Mortes (Boileau and Narcejac), 228
DePalma, Brian, 266
Diabolique, 227–29, 280, 291
Diabolique: Celle Qui M'Etait Plus (Boileau and Narcejac), 228
Dial H for Hitchcock, 54
Dial M for Murder, 23, 31, 146, 189, 203–7, 244
"dirty jokes," 94
doors, 86, 109, 113, 121, 199, 202
double features, 3, 31
doubles and doubling, 35, 93–96 passim, 106, 174, 177, 196

double meanings, 114–15
in *I Confess*, 77
in shower scene, 235, 236
in *Spellbound*, 196
in *Strangers on a Train*, 34, 35
mirrors and, 87, *101*, 107, *111*, 169
montage and, 147, 148
of locations, 153
of mise-en-scène, 121
of scenes, 207
See also stand-ins
Douchet, Jean, 45, 138, 157
Dressed to Kill, 266
Duddleston, Amy, 269
Durgnat, Raymond, 223, 227

E

editing. *See* film editing
edtors. *See* film editors
Eisenstein, Sergei, 141, 157
montage and, 7, 11, 138, 153, 160, 246–47
in *The Battleship Potemkin*, 32, 147, 223, 249
Elliot, Debbie, 150–51
evil, 161, 297, 234
The Exorcist, 66
Eyemo cameras, 26
eye-line match shots, 62, 87, 141, 142, 149, 150
eyes, 118–20 passim, 127, 229, 259, 286, 288

F

family, 41, 90. *See also* marriage; parent and child
Family Plot, 134, 266
Famous Players-Lasky, 30, 75, 140, 142
fear and fears, 261
of heights, 151, 255
Hitchcock on, 9, 148,
Hitchcock's own, 99, 105, 151, 255
Feinstein, John, xv
film credits, 79, 80, 84, 163, 211, 212
film editing, 7, 11, 147, 152–54 passim, 200, 208, 212, 213
cross-cutting, 204
parallel editing, 204
splicing, 213, 214, 217
staccato editing, 11, 162, 203, 208, 232
tempo, 160
See also jump cuts; montage
film editors, 181, *209*, 210–18, 269
film studies, 45–47 passim
Finding Nemo, 264
Finler, Joel, 191
Fleming, Horace, 272–73
Foley, James, 2
food, 114, 194
foreshadowing, 82, 147, 286
framing, 82, 87, 92, 102, 109–20 passim, 174, 198–205 passim
in *Rear Window*, 191
shower scene, 233, 243, 249, 253–55 passim
Franklin, Richard, 129, 139, 241, 267
Freeman, David, 277–78
French film critics, 45, 131
French filmmakers, 45, 227
Frenzy, 104, 251
Friedkin, William, 66
Fuller, Sam, 275

G

Gainsborough Pictures, 74
Gavin, John, 57
Gein, Ed, 229, 240
General Electric Theater, 128, 129
German Expressionism, 30, 74–75, 77, 229
Germany, 30, 73, 140
Gibbs, John, 73
Gladwell, Malcolm, xv
Godard, Jean-Luc, 227
Goldstein, Milt, 223–24
Gomery, Douglas, 40
Gone with the Wind (film), 29
Gordon, Douglas, 265

Gottlieb, Sidney, 76
Green, Hilton, 28, *122*, 123–37, 213, 221–22
Greene, Danny, *178*, 226, 264
  interview, 179–87
Griffith, D. W., 7, 32
guilt, 119, 171, 198, 201, 236

H

handheld cameras, 26
hands, 156–57, 202
Harrison, Carolyn, 272
Harrison, Joan, 184–85
Hayes, John Michael, 12–13, 40, 54
Hays Code. *See* Production Code
Hays, Will, 6
Heche, Anne, 23, 58, 130, 183
Hendershot, Cyndy, 261
Henley Telegraph, 140
Herrmann, Bernard, 85, 182, 235, 237, 250, 254, 264
  cast and crew reaction to his *Psycho* score, 216
  Citizen Kane and, 275
  credits music, 79
  Joseph Stefano on, 59
  montage and, 247
  Psycho remake score, 269
  record album, 297
  shower scene instrumentation, 217
  Vertigo score, 161
High Anxiety, 265
Hitchcock (Chabrol and Rohmer), 45
Hitchcock (Truffaut), 45
Hitchcock, Alfred, 20, 30–49, *50*
  audience psychology and, 9–10, 63, 151, 163, 199, 224
  bibliography, 47, 226–27
  cameos, 88
  children and, 131
  critical reputation, 44–48
  Diabolique and, 227–29 passim
  early life and work, 30–32 passim, 73–75, 140
  fame, 67
  fears, 99, 151, 255
  Hilton Green on, 123–37 passim
  Horace Fleming on, 272, 273
  Janet Leigh on, 16–17, 21
  Joe Stefano and, 2, 51–70 passim
  mise-en-scène and, 73–121
  montage and, 9, 138–77
  "myths and distortions of," 221
  Nandor Bokor on, 289, 290
  no-late-admissions policy and, 4, 227
  on distinction between suspense and terror, 148–49
  ownership of films, 36–37
  Production Code and, 6–7
  "pure cinema" and, 73, 75, 78, 139, 148, 207
  violent films preceding *Psycho*, 189–208
  Wes Craven on, 271–72
  See also *Alfred Hitchcock Presents*

—films:
The Birds, 45
The Blackguard, 30, 74
Blackmail, 30, 32. 105, 189–94 passim, 230, 243
Dial M for Murder, 23, 31, 146, 189, 203–7, 244
Family Plot, 134, 266
Frenzy, 104, 251
I Confess, 7, 38, 39, 76, 79, 87, 91, 93
The Lady Vanishes, 149, 277
Lifeboat, 31
The Lodger, 151, 191
The Man Who Knew Too Much, 66, 91, 149
Marnie, 31, 96, 102, 159
Mirage, 293, 296
Mr. and Mrs. Smith, 91
The Mountain Eagle, 30, 74
North by Northwest, 37, 87, 91, 151, 172, 207, 213
Notorious, 31, 79, 83, 100
The Pleasure Garden, 30, 74

Rear Window, 13, 36–40 passim, 76, 87, 91, 97, 106–7, 119, 121, 142–48, 151, 158–60 passim, 175, 191, 245
Rope, 31, 33, 76, 79, 87, 144, 146, 204
Sabotage, 105, 189, 193–96
Saboteur, 149–53, 157, 160, 172
The Secret Agent, 75, 149
Shadow of a Doubt, 31, 35, 76, 79, 87, 90, 109, 145–53 passim, 157–61 passim, 172, 191, 245
The Short Night, 134
Spellbound, 31, 104, 189, 196–203, 207, 208, 234
Strangers on a Train, 7, 34–35, 89, 91, 93, 105, 109, 147, 148, 153–61 passim, 191, 245, 252
The 39 Steps, 75, 149, 277
To Catch a Thief, 87, 151
The Trouble with Harry, 31
Vertigo, 19, 33, 47–48, 70, 97, 100, 104–5, 151, 153, 161–62, 172, 191, 228, 234
The Wrong Man, 31, 35, 91, 109, 189, 203, 207, 208
Hitchcock, Alma, 54, 55, 127, 131, 136, 214, 259
Hitchcock and Poe (Perry), 140
Hitchcock Annual, 47
Hitchcock at Work (Krohn), 139, 226
Hitchcock's Films (Wood), 45
Holland, Tom, 268
homosexuality, 64
horror films, 228, 274, 279
Houdini, 291–92
humor, 34. *See also* black humor
Hungary, 288–89
Hurley, Joseph, 86
Hurley, Neil, 151, 255

I

I Confess, 7, 38, 39, 76, 79, 87, 91, 93
imagination, 23–29 passim, 57
incest, 90, 112, 262, 268
Innovation Comics, 264
internal monologues, 171
Intolerance, 32
irony, 43, 101, 109, 193

J

Jackson, Jack, 182, 183
jump cuts, 11

K

Kael, Pauline, 48
Kammerspielfilm. See *The Last Laugh*
Kapsis, Robert, 5, 47
Kerzoncuf, Alain, 279–80
key grips, 126
keys, 108
kissing, 83, 163
Knight, Deborah, 86
knives, 11, 19, 56, 122, 124, 125, 189–96 passim, 208, 221–25 passim, *251*
as phallus symbols, 251
description in script, 132
in Bloch's novel, 230
replica with shower scene score, 265
Kolker, Robert, 47, 227, 251, 258, 261, 265
Krohn, Bill, 139, 225, 226, 262

L

The Lady Vanishes, 149, 277
Lambert, Chris, 287
Landis, John, 130
Lang, Fritz, 30
The Last Laugh, 74, 75
Leff, Leonard, 44
left-handedness, 111
Leigh, Christian, 265
Leigh, Janet, 2–3, 8, 12, *15*, 126, 274
as Marion Crane, 5–6, 18, 21–22
fictional autobiography, 84–85
as sex object, 278, 285, 290, 299
death, 219–20
interview, 16–29

in *Houdini*, 291
on Hitchcock, 16–29 passim, 77
Psycho remake and, 23, 25, 66
Psycho: Behind the Scenes of the Classic Thriller, 227
stand-in, 124, 164, 176, 222, 256, 257
Leitch, Thomas, 77
Lifeboat, 31
lighting, 92, 97–108 passim, 113–120 passim, 173, 198–208 passim
in *Blackmail*, 192
in *Diabolique*, 229
in *Rear Window*, 158–59
in *Sabotage*, 194
in shower scene, 241–45 passim
Jack Russell and, 216
Lloyd, Frank, 134
Lloyd, Norman, 184
The Lodger, 151, 191
London, England, 32
London Film Society, 33, 141
A Long Hard Look at 'Psycho' (Durgnat), 223, 227
Looney Tunes Back in Action, 264
Lord, Daniel, 38
Luraschi, Luigi, 217, 218, 224, 239

M

MCA, 51, 129, 180, 181
MGM, 179, 180
MacGuffin, 47
MacGuffins, 166
The Man Who Knew Too Much, 66, 91, 149
Manson, Charles, 13–14
Marion Crane (film character), 9–12 passim, 81–121, 164–76 passim, 190, 193
Ann Heche as, 23, 58, 130, 183
Janet Leigh as, 5–6, 18, 21–22
fictional autobiography, 84–85
shower scene, 235–60 passim
marketing, 4, 31, 227, 228, 264
Marnie, 31, 96, 102, 159
marriage, 89–98 passim, 102, 170, 203
masking of screen, 240–41
masturbation, 64, 266
McGilligan, Patrick, 30, 31, 45, 78, 88, 203, 227, 237
McGowan, John, xvi
McKnight, George, 86
Milo, George, 86
Milton, John, 161
Mirage, 293, 296
mirrors, 87–88, 95, 100, *101*, 107, 110, *111*, 169
in shower scene, 233, 235
in *The Wrong Man*, 104, 208
mise-en-scène, 33, 73–121, 138–53 passim, 159–69 passim, 173, 177, 203–7, 224–29 passim, 233–35 passim
in *Rope*, 31, 144
in *Sabotage*, 195
Mise-en-scène (Gibbs), 73
Mr. and Mrs. Smith, 91
Modleski, Tania, 46, 164
Mogg, Ken, 36–37, 141, 191
Molen, Gerry, 211
moleskin, 27, 56
Monaco, Paul, xvii, 11, 31, 32
montage, 9, 29, 33, 138–77, 208, 224
Eisenstein and, 7, 32
in *Sabotage*, 193, 196
in shower scene, 246–49 passim, 253
in *The Wrong Man*, 208
See also eye-line match shots
The Moon is Blue, 44
Moore, Julianne, 64, 66
morality, 37–38, 81, 119, 158, 164, 301
mother and son, 35–36, 85, 91
Motion Picture Producers and Distributors Association (MPPDA), 6. *See also* Production Code
The Mountain Eagle, 30, 74
Moviola editing machines, 213, 214
Mulvey, Laura, 46, 164
murder: of Sharon Tate, 13–14
Murnau, F. W., 30, 74, 75

Museum of Modern Art, 46, 67, 265
Museum of Modern Art, Oxford, 265
music. *See* score

N

The Naked Kiss, 275
Naremore, James, 43
narrative, 8–9, 140
necrophilia, 262
Nichols, Bill, 46
no-late-admissions policy, 4, 221, 290
"Norma Bates," 85, 90–91, 94, 107, 110–17 passim, 192–93, 203, 207
  shower scene and, 242–52 passim
Norman Bates (film character), 8, 82–86 passim, 91–121 passim, 173–77 passim, 190
  audience and, 282–83, 286, 292, 299
  compared to *Spellbound* character, 199–200
  dual personality of, 35, 196–97
  Joseph Stefano on, 63–64
  in remake, 66
  in sequels and prequel, 267–68
  in shower scene, 235–38, 260
  See also Peeping Tom scene
North by Northwest, 37, 87, 91, 151, 172, 207, 213
Notorious, 31, 79, 83, 100
nudity, 11, 186–87, 226, 238–41 passim, 254, 257
  below the navel, 251
  censorship and, 274
  closed set and, 211
  Hilton Green on, 124, 129
  Hitchcock and, 226, 278
  implied, 120
  in *Dressed to Kill*, 266
  in remake of *Psycho*, 23, 269
  in *Psycho II*, 129
  Janet Leigh on, 27, 29
  Joseph Stefano on, 56–57
  Production Code and, 28, 31, 164, 176, 217–18, 226
  Terry Williams on, 211, 213

O

Oedipus complex, 35, 36, 85, 106, 116, 177, 196–201 passim
  in Bloch novel, 51
  in *Strangers on a Train*, 148
Orphée, 275
Ortega y Gasset, José, 176
Osbourne, Ozzy, 1, 13
The Outer Limits, 51, 53, 58
outtakes, 133, 216, 256

P

paintings, 88–89, 118
Paramount Pictures, 30–32 passim, 36–37, 61, 128, 212, 223–24
parent and child, 81, 85, 94, 197–98, 281–82. *See also* mother and son
Peary, Danny, 227
Pechter, William, 5
Peeping Tom scene, 8–10 passim, 28, 118–20, 215, 234
The Perfect Murder, 23
Perkins, Anthony, 25, 64
  as director of *Psycho III*, 268
  as Norman Bates, 6, 176, 273
    stand-in, 187
Perkins, Osgood Robert, II, 25
Perry, Dennis, 140, 263
Playhouse *90*, 51
The Pleasure Garden, 30, 74
plot, 33
Poe, Edgar Allan, 104, 140
point of view (POV), 9, 84, 87, 100, 106–13 passim, 141–44 passim, 165–76 passim, 207
  enunciator's, 97, 106, 121, 143–44, 166, 176
    in shower scene, 247–52 passim, 258
  in *Dial M for Murder*, 206
  in *Rear Window*, 39, 106–7, 143–44, 159
  in *Saboteur*, 150, 151

in *Shadow of a Doubt*, 152
in shower scene, 247–50 passim, 257–58
in *Spellbound*, 198–99
police, 90, 99, 102, 145, 153–56 passim, 170, 171, 275
polls, 47–48, 262
popular culture: shower scene in, 263–65
Positif, 45
postmodernism, xvi–xvii
prequel. See *Psycho* (Van Sant film)
Price, Frank, 134
priests, 38, 39
producers, 211–12
Production Code, 6–7, 22–32 passim, 36–44 passim, 188, 262
mise-en-scène and, 144
on morality, 158
Psycho and, 11, 22, 32, 256
bedroom and bathroom settings and, 94, 186, 237
incest and, 268
irony and, 119
Joseph Stefano on, 60–61
nudity and, 164, 176, 239
opening sequence and, 27–28
semi-nudity and, 168
stabbing scenes and, 224
projectionists, 284
prostitution, 96
Psycho (Bloch novel), 40, 125, 229–31 passim, 293
Janet Leigh on, 16
Joseph Stefano and, 8, 51, 118, 176
rights purchase, 37
Psycho (Van Sant film), 23, 25, 58, 64–66, 130, 183, 185, 218, 269
Psycho II, 26, 123, 129, 266–68
Psycho III, 123, 129, 268
Psycho IV, 26, 51, 113, 123, 129, 268–69
Psycho: Behind the Scenes of the Classic Thriller (Leigh), 227
psychoanalysis, 31, 52–54
publicity, 4–5, 59
Pudovkin, V. I., 141, 147, 168
The Punch (Feinstein), xv

Q

Quigley, Martin, 38

R

radio, 41
Randall, Richard, 43
rape, 42, 63, 104, 251
razors, 201–3 passim
Rear Window, 13, 36–40 passim, 76–81 passim, 158–60 passim, 245
dangling scene in, 151
ending of, 89
lighting in 158–59
montage and, 142–48 passim
POV in, 97, 106–7, 171–72, 175
sex and violence in, 191
voyeurism in, 119
windows, in 87, 121, 160
Rebello, Stephen, 18, 37, 176, 183, 222, 226, 240
rectangles, 109, 121, 199, 202
redemption, 116, 118, 149, 258, 288
remake of *Psycho*. See *Psycho* (Van Sant film)
Renfro, Marli, 124, 176, 222, 256, 257
Republic Studios, 128
revenge, 42–43, 196
Revue Productions, 128, 129, 180
The Rite of Spring (Stravinsky), 11
Robertson, Peggy, 132, 213
Rohmer, Eric, 45
Roman Catholic Church. *See* Catholic Church
Rope, 31, 33, 76, 79, 87, 144, 146, 204
Rothman, William, 46
Russell, Jack, 81, 86, 111, 113, 117, 126, 128, 132, 215–16, 221
Ryall, Tom, 46, 141

S

Sabotage, 105, 189, 193–96
Saboteur, 149–53 passim, 157, 160, 172
satire, 265
Schlom, Marshal, 226
score, 85, 235, 247, 250, 254, 263–65 passim
- audience response, 272, 275, 281, 288–93 passim, 300
- credits and, 79
- Joseph Stefano on, 59
- *See also* strings

The Secret Agent, 75, 149
Selznick, David O., 10, 30, 33, 139, 141
sequels. See *Psycho II*; *Psycho III*; *Psycho IV*
sexuality, 5–6, 31, 115, 119, 120, 273
- censorship and, 274
- implied, 29, 39, 81
- in *Psycho IV*, 268
- in *Rear Window*, 39, 40
- in television, 43
- in *Vertigo*, 104
- marriage and, 96
- Production Code and, 144
- as taboo, 262
- violence and, 191, 273

Shadow of a Doubt, 31, 35, 145–53 passim, 157–61 passim, 245
- black comedy in, 90
- California setting, 172
- camera as voyeur in, 76
- charming psychopath in, 109
- opening mise-en-scène, 79
- sex and violence in, 191
- windows in, 87

Shamley Productions, 128
Shock Corridor, 275
The Short Night, 134
Sight and Sound, 19, 47
silent films, 30, 32, 47, 171, 189
Simmons, Jerold L., 44
Simon, Fred, 270–71
The Simpsons, 264
Sloan, Jane, 46
Socialist Realism, 7, 30, 138–41 passim
Soul in Suspense (Hurley), 151
sound, 32–33, 182–86 passim, 189, 245. *See also* score
sound editors, 179
Soviet Socialist Realism. *See* Socialist Realism
space, 146, 151, 172, 173, 192, 195, 196, 203, 234
- shower scene and, 240–43 passim
- *See also* claustrophobia

Spellbound, 31, 104, 189, 196–203, 207, 208, 234
Spielberg, Stephen, 24, 264
Spinelli, Ralph, 3–6 passim, 11–12
Spoto, Donald, 32, 34, 46–47, 54, 77, 136
staircase scene, 125–26, 284, 289–90, 294, 295
stand-ins, 124, 129, 164, 176, 187, 222, 256
Statue of Liberty, 150, 157
Stefano, Joseph, *xviii*, 1–3 passim, 12–14 passim, 28, *50*
- first draft of *Psycho* screenplay, 231–32
- interview, 51–72
- Norman Bates and, 35, 176
- on Marion Crane, 169
- on Norman Bates, 8

Stevens, Wallace, 234
storyboards, 17, 66, 123, 139, 214–15, 218, 225, 232
Strangers on a Train, 7, 34–35, 91, 109, 153–61 passim, 245, 252
- "enunciator" camera in, 93
- marriage in, 89
- opening montage, 147–48
- overeating in, 105
- sexuality in, 191

strangulation, 40
Stravinsky, Igor, 11
strings, 11, 81, 217, 245, 263–65 passim, 275. *See also* violins

studio system, 30, 36, 38, 40, 43, 188, 262

T

taboos, 31, 94, 106, 109, 115, 120, 261–69 passim
Tamiroff, Akim, 26
Tate, Sharon: murder of, 13–14
taxidermy, 115–16, 175
television, 5, 31, 36, 41, 181–82, 226, 264, 265
commercials, 263
Hungary, 288–89
theft, 96, 100, *101*, 166, 236
13 Ghosts, 293
The 39 Steps, 75, 149, 277
3-D, 204
The Tingler, 275
The Tipping Point (Gladwell), xv
To Catch a Thief, 87, 151
toilets, 11, 28, 29, 31, 60–61, 125, 186, 237, *237*–38, 268
absence of, 198
Tomasini, George, 209, 211–18 passim
Total Film, 262
Touch of Evil, 16, 26
triangulation, 118, 155–56, 169
The Trouble with Harry, 31
Truffaut, François, 45, 169, 227, 239
24 Hour Psycho, 265
Two Bits, 2

U

underwear, 110. *See also* bras
Universal Studios, 37, 129, 130, 181, 240–41, 264
Universum Film Aktiengesellschaft (Ufa), 30, 74
urination, 29

V

Van Sant, Gus, 23, 25, 58, 64–66, 130, 183, 185, 218, 269
Vaughn, Vince, 65
vengeance. *See* revenge
Vertigo, 69, 104–5, 151
camera placement and movement in, 97, 100
doubling of locations in, 153
nightmare in, 234
sex and violence in, 191
Sight and Sound ranking, 19, 47–48
source novel, 228
vortex-like shapes in, 161–62
western setting of, 172
violence in films, 57, 144, 157–60 passim, 175, 188–91 passim
violins: audience response, 281, 288, 290, 300
VistaVision, 31, 32
voyeurism, 7, 76–81 passim, 101, 102, 116–20 passim, 175, 186
audience and, 9, 102, 286
in *Rear Window,* 38, 76–81 passim, 142, 175

W

Wasserman, Lew, 36–37, 135
Welles, Orson, 26, 48, 86, 137, 256
Weltner, George, 37
westerns, 172
wide-screen films, 31, 32
Wiene, Robert, 74
Williams, Linda, xvi, 252, 270
Williams, Terry, *209*, 210–18, 222, 239, 242–43, 256
Williams, Tony, 33
windows, 86–87, 99, 106, 109, 118, 121, 142, 160, 191, 202
in shower scene, 233, 235
Within Screaming Distance, 2
Wollen, Peter, 141
Wood, Robin, 32, 46
The Wrong Man, 31, 35, 91, 109, 189, 203, 207, 208
Wulff, Hans J., 86
Wyler, William, 128
Wynn, Keenan, 136–37

Y

Young and Innocent, 149, 151
youth audience, 5, 13, 239